William Faulkner

Daniel J. Singal

The FRED W. MORRISON *Series in Southern Studies*

The University of North Carolina Press

Chapel Hill and London

William Faulkner

The Making of a
Modernist

© 1997 The University of North Carolina Press
All rights reserved
Manufactured in the United States of America
The paper in this book meets the guidelines for
permanence and durability of the Committee on
Production Guidelines for Book Longevity of the
Council on Library Resources.
Library of Congress Cataloging-in-Publication Data
Singal, Daniel Joseph, 1944–
William Faulkner: the making of a modernist /
Daniel J. Singal.
p.   cm. — (Fred W. Morrison series in Southern studies)
Includes bibliographical references (p.   ) and index.
ISBN 0-8078-2355-4 (cloth: alk. paper)
ISBN 0-8078-4831-x (pbk.: alk. paper)
1. Faulkner, William, 1897–1962 — Criticism and
interpretation. 2. Modernism (Literature) — Southern States.
I. Title. II. Series.
PS3511.A86Z9686   1997
813'.52 — dc21   96-51459
CIP

03   02   01   00   99   7   6   5   4   3

For my father,

LAURENCE M. SINGAL,

and in memory of my mother,

ROSE C. SINGAL

CONTENTS

ILLUSTRATIONS

ACKNOWLEDGMENTS

In Faulkner, the past never ceases to exist but continues to live into the present. Just so, the many invaluable gestures of help and encouragement that I have received on this project over nearly four decades from teachers, friends, colleagues, editors, and family live on in the pages of this book. Some of them may not recall how important their contribution really was, but I remember well and would like to take this opportunity to thank them.

My introduction to Faulkner came under the aegis of Frank J. Smith Jr., an extraordinary English teacher who had not only the good sense to have his eleventh-grade students read both the complete version of "The Bear" and *Intruder in the Dust* but the pedagogic skill to make them entranced with such a difficult author. I also owe a great deal to Donald Fleming for enticing me into the field of American intellectual history and for taking seriously the ideas of a college freshman on Faulkner, even when they conflicted with his own. William Leuchtenberg, displaying the generosity for which he has become legendary, allowed me to write a master's essay on the Snopes trilogy under his direction in a seminar that was ostensibly focused on the New Deal. Although he is a political historian by training and predilection, I invariably found his observations about Faulkner astute and valuable.

Certain individuals provided crucial support at key moments. Matthew Hodgson, the director of the University of North Carolina Press at the time I began writing this book, was a source of constant encouragement and insight. It was he who suggested that I attempt to synthesize the existing scholarly literature on Faulkner, and it proved to be excellent advice. His successor at the Press, Kate Douglas Torrey, grasped what this project was about as soon as she inherited it. The many hours I devoted to carrying out her recommendations for revision testify to my respect for her editorial judgment. Also essential to this enterprise was the friendship and wisdom I have received over the years from Jack Wilson, who for more than a quarter century has served as my example of how the historian's life should be lived.

A number of other friends have given this book skillful readings while in manuscript. David Hollinger read it twice, going far beyond the call of duty. His judicious critique has improved everything, from broad-scale concepts to minor matters of language. Karen Halttunen likewise went through the text with a trained eye, making suggestions that were so good that I used virtually every one of them. This book also benefited greatly from the comments of Donald Kartiganer, as well as from his exquisite, pathbreaking scholarship on Faulkner. In addition, my postmodernist colleague Lee Quinby was kind enough to read a sizable portion of the manuscript and to supply much helpful counsel. She has rescued me, I hope, from several infelicities, even though I do persist in my retrograde historian's mistake of believing that authors have intentions worth studying.

No one reading this book could fail to realize my immense debt to the Faulkner scholars who have preceded me. It would be impossible to overstate what I have learned from their published work, even when I felt compelled to take issue with their findings. I am likewise indebted to my fellow members of the Southern Intellectual History Circle, a group that has met for nearly a decade now under the organizing genius of Michael O'Brien and that has supplied me not only with general intellectual sustenance but with many worthwhile perspectives on the nature of southern thought and culture.

This book would not have been possible without the financial support provided by the John Simon Guggenheim Foundation, as well as the George A. and Eliza Gardner Howard Foundation. I was also the beneficiary of a generous leave policy at Hobart and William Smith Colleges that, along with the Guggenheim and Howard awards, gave me those vital blocks of unencumbered time required for this sort of writing. I would particularly like to thank Dean Sheila K. Bennett for all her good humor and understanding, as well as my colleagues in the Department of History, especially my fellow Americanists James L. Crouthamel, Carol V. R. George, Robert A. Huff, and Clifton Hood. I am also grateful to Carroll W. Brewster, former president of Hobart and William Smith, and his late wife, Mary, for a very special gift relating to Faulkner that has been truly inspiring.

I have been aided again and again by the remarkable staff at the

Hobart and William Smith library, most notably by Joseph J. Chmura III, Michael R. Hunter, Charlotte Hegyi, and Paul W. Crumlish. H. Wesley Perkins of the sociology department at Hobart and William Smith helped me to understand the effects of alcohol on the brain, as did Dr. Andrew Stern and Dr. David Goldblatt, who shared their expert knowledge of neurology with me. Two other friends, Charles W. Eagles of the University of Mississippi and Richard Latner of Tulane University, were kind enough to take on research assignments regarding Faulkner in their localities, providing me with information and materials that were not available in the frozen North.

Both Robert W. Hamblin, director of the Center for Faulkner Studies at Southeast Missouri State University, and Lisa K. Speer of the John Davis Williams Library at the University of Mississippi displayed exemplary patience in helping me to locate and decide upon suitable photographs to use as illustrations. It was likewise a pleasure to work with the many talented people at the University of North Carolina Press who became involved with this project, including Grace Buonocore, a most meticulous, skillful, and forbearing copyeditor; Rich Hendel, who designed this book with his customary unerring eye for detail; the aggressive and imaginative marketing staff led by Kathleen Ketterman; and Pamela Upton, who deftly orchestrated the process of production.

Mention should also be made of the many students enrolled in the seminar that I have offered on Faulkner since the mid-1980s. Much of the time they have taught me rather than vice versa. That was especially true of Evie Krasnow, Carolyn Jerose, Laura Stewart, Roger Schwartz, Jim Kuhnert, Katrina Redmond, Eren Celeboglu, Lauren Carpenter, Erin Donnelly, Elena Boneski, Brett Taylor, and Maureen Cahill.

My daughters, Hannah and Rachel, grew up with this book. They were simply wonderful, gracefully accepting their father's obsession with a writer whose work they could not begin to fathom for most of that time (though they have now become avid readers of Faulkner themselves) and doing everything possible to keep up my spirits when the writing was not going well. Even more incredible was the support and forbearance of my wife, Sarah. Always loving, encouraging, and cheerful, even when she had had her fill of Faulkner (her support ended in the vicinity of chapter 6, she would say in jest), she was also a first-rate editor, spotting problems of interpretation and expression on page after page.

Although my parents were not immediately involved with the writing of this book, it nonetheless belongs to them. It is hard to think of two people who have been more devoted to their children, giving them every opportunity to develop their talents and taking pride in every accomplishment. Many instances of kindness and colleagueship and affection have helped to bring this book into existence, but their contribution has been the most important of all.

William Faulkner

INTRODUCTION

One thing alone can be said with assurance about William Faulkner: modern scholarship has not neglected him. Evidence of flush times in Faulkner criticism can be found everywhere—one recent Faulkner bibliography contains almost six hundred pages of entries, Faulkner conferences are held with increasing frequency, and the flood of doctoral dissertations continues unabated. "In the past few years," claims Arthur F. Kinney, "critical work on Faulkner has exceeded that of any other author in English save Shakespeare." All this attention would surely have amused Faulkner himself, who went through most of his career virtually ignored by academic writers. At present, though, we may be reaching the point of surfeit. Why, then, another book on Faulkner?[1]

Curiously, amid all that has been published on Faulkner, one subject remains largely unexplored—the structure and nature of his thought. To the extent that critics have dealt with the content of his mind, they have usually thrown up their hands in despair, unable to detect any thread of intellectual consistency. "I mean this quite literally," an exasperated Walter J. Slatoff announces, "both the form and meanings of his works are governed much less by any controlling ideas, or themes, or dramatic or aesthetic considerations than by a succession of temperamental impulses and responses." Joseph Gold likewise finds that Faulkner's beliefs "defy analysis." Such has been the general verdict of Faulkner scholarship until recently. It has depicted Faulkner as an untutored denizen of the backwoods—the "country man" or "farmer" that he constantly proclaimed himself—whose thinking did not really go beyond conventional pieties such as courage, pride, and honor and whose sheer genius enabled him to produce great literature devoid of any acquaintance with the cultural currents of his time. Faulkner for his part did everything he could to foster this conception. "I'm not even an educated man," he once protested in an interview. "I didn't like school and I quit about the sixth grade. So

I don't know anything about rational and logical processes of thought at all." As if taking him at his word, literary scholars by and large have been unwilling to attribute "ideas" to Faulkner, and intellectual historians have almost invariably steered clear of him.[2]

Faulkner, however, was anything but a literary bumpkin, and this book insists that we can learn much about his art by relating it to the cultural and intellectual discourse of his era—and much about that era by coming to terms with his art. This does not mean attempting to locate a stable body of ideas that supposedly suffused and governed the entirety of his work. Rather, it entails adopting a dynamic approach, viewing him as a writer caught in the midst of a momentous transition between two major historical cultures—the Victorian one into which he had been born in late-nineteenth-century Mississippi, and the Modernist one he discovered and absorbed through his extensive readings. His earliest work clearly reflects late Victorian and post-Victorian modes of thought, while by the midpoint of his career he had become in most respects a twentieth-century Modernist. This journey from one sensibility to the other was neither swift nor easy; many highly cherished values had to be discarded along the way, to be replaced by others with which he would never be entirely comfortable. In fact, I argue, it is this very conflict of cultures within him, never entirely resolved even late in his life, that provides the crucial key to making sense of Faulkner.

Perhaps no other major American writer had to struggle as hard as William Faulkner did to become a Modernist. Raised in rural Mississippi, where, as Michel Gresset puts it, "the spirit of the nineteenth century ran unchecked well into the twentieth," he received what can only be called a thorough immersion in the Victorian ethos. All through his formative childhood years this all-encompassing culture held virtually exclusive sway over him. Drilled into him by his mother, perhaps the most influential figure in his life, Victorian moralism was reinforced wherever he turned in his remote southern community until it had become a basic, ineradicable component of his being.[3]

The Victorian culture that Faulkner inherited can in turn be traced back to the rapidly expanding urban bourgeoisie at the onset of industrialization in early-nineteenth-century England and America. In retrospect, it is not hard to see what made those early Victorians so enthusiastic about their new culture. Not only did it value thrift, diligence, and persis-

tence—attributes crucial to success in a burgeoning capitalist economy—
but it held out the vision of a world largely free from sin and discord,
reflecting their immense optimism about the progress that the industrial
order would bring. To them, Victorianism seemed distinctly uplifting, a
set of values that offered moral certainty, spiritual balm, and the hope that
the world might at last rid itself of the barbaric baggage remaining from
humankind's dark, preindustrial past. Nearly a century later, when Faulkner was coming of age, this same culture would be regarded by many as
fossilized and deeply oppressive, but in its day it was the light that gleamed
in the eyes of millions on both sides of the Atlantic, a chief source of
strength in their effort to initiate what they believed would be a far better
stage in human history.[4]

At the core of this evolving belief system stood a distinctive set of
values and assumptions that shaped the way Victorians perceived their
world. These included a belief in a predictable universe presided over by a
benevolent God and governed by immutable natural laws, a corresponding conviction that humankind was capable of arriving at a unified and
fixed set of truths about all aspects of life, and an insistence on preserving absolute moral standards based on a radical dichotomy between that
which was deemed "human" and that regarded as "animal." It was this
moral dichotomy above all that constituted the deepest guiding principle
of the Victorian outlook. On the "human" or "civilized" side of the dividing line fell everything that served to lift humans above the beasts—
education, refinement, manners, the arts, religion, and such domesticated
emotions as loyalty and family love. The "animal" or "savage" realm, by
contrast, contained those instincts and passions that constantly threatened self-control and therefore had to be repressed at all cost. Foremost
among those threats was, of course, sexuality, which proper Victorians
conceived of as a hidden geyser of animality existing within everyone and
capable of erupting with little or no warning at the slightest stimulus. All
erotic temptations were accordingly supposed to be rooted out and all passions kept under the tightest possible control; "the aura of secrecy and the
stigma of shame compromised their lovemaking even in marriage," notes
Stephen Kern. A glorious future of material abundance and technological
advance was possible, Victorians were convinced, but only if the animal
component in human nature was effectively suppressed.[5]

Equally important was the way this moral dichotomy fostered a tendency to view the world in binary terms. "There is a value in possibilities," Masao Miyoshi observes, "but the Victorians too often saw them

in rigid pairs—all or nothing, white or black." Sharp distinctions were made in every aspect of existence: Victorians characterized societies as either civilized or savage, drew a firm line between what they considered superior and inferior classes, and divided races unambiguously into black and white. They likewise insisted on placing the sexes in "separate spheres" reflecting what Rosalind Rosenberg describes as "the Victorian faith in sexual polarity," which deemed women "by nature emotional and passive" and men "rational and assertive." All of these dichotomies, it was believed, were permanently rooted in biology and in the general laws of nature. The "right" way, the moral way, was to keep the boundaries fixed and clear.[6]

Put in slightly different terms, what the Victorians aspired to was a radical standard of innocence and purity. They were engaged in an attempt to banish from their lives, so far as they could, all traces of evil and corruption and to create a brave new world suffused, in Matthew Arnold's words, with "harmonious perfection." Nineteenth-century thinkers, writes Donald H. Meyer, "longed for a universe that was not just intelligible, reassuring, and morally challenging, but symphonic as well." The great paradox, of course, was that, in seeking that harmony, the Victorians depended on the moral dichotomy, with its inherent divisiveness. But the paradox is resolved when one realizes that the Victorians used that dichotomy precisely to erect a barrier between themselves and any person or thing that might prove disharmonious. That explains their insistence, at least in public, on a constant attitude of moral optimism, focusing on that which was "lovely, admirable, and hopeful," as well as their moral conception of aesthetics, in which art was to emphasize the beautiful and inspiring. It also accounts for their predilection for hero worship, through which the values of purity and goodness were enshrined in individual personalities. To be sure, actual behavior during the nineteenth century often diverged significantly from these high standards. In the sexual realm in particular, Victorian couples tended to observe their culture's strictures in the breach, with varying degrees of guilt. But the point is that, for the Victorian middle class, innocence remained a powerful and almost universal cultural ideal. Even when conduct deviated from it, the ideal continued to be venerated.[7]

To be sure, a full account of Victorian culture would pay close attention to the persistent layer of doubt and uncertainty that could frequently be found beneath the surface of moral optimism. As Meyer puts it, "The later Victorians were perhaps the last generation among English-speaking intellectuals able to believe that man was capable of understanding his universe, just as they were the first generation collectively to suspect that he never would." Among the highly educated especially, there was often a vast discrepancy between the public pose and the inner reality of foreboding that caused many Victorians to attempt to avoid introspection. "I'll look within no more," Robert Browning declared, though it was a pledge he could not keep. But these subtleties, although essential for an understanding of Victorian culture as it existed in England and mainstream America, are far less relevant to the American South. The version of Victorianism that Faulkner encountered while growing up was certainly not riddled with morbid introspection; what he knew initially of Browning and Tennyson concerned their poetry and public selves, not their private anxieties. For intellectually inclined southerners, Victorian thought meant typically the "sweetness and light" of Matthew Arnold, who boasted how "the command to *resist the devil*, to *overcome the wicked one*" had become "such a pressing force and reality" to his generation. "And we have had our reward," he observed, "not only in the great worldly prosperity which our obedience to this command has brought us, but also, and far more, in great inward peace and satisfaction."[8]

That bracing message was bound to appeal to educated southerners in the post-Reconstruction era as they struggled to regain both economic and cultural parity with the North. Amid the poverty and turmoil that had followed military defeat, they longed for the "worldly prosperity" and "great inward peace and satisfaction" that Victorian "prophets" like Arnold seemed to promise. At the same time, the ideal of innocence spoke directly to the deep guilt many of them felt about the South's role in bringing about secession. Victorianism also had the advantage of being an international culture that was then setting the standards toward which all educated and upwardly mobile people in the "civilized" world appeared to aspire. No wonder that middle-class southern families such as the Falkners who had managed to regain their financial footing began adopting proper manners, steeping themselves in nineteenth-century British literature, and furnishing their homes in the approved Victorian style in order to cement their claims to respectability.[9]

As was the case wherever it took root, Victorian culture in the South rapidly meshed with the society's residual culture and became adapted to local needs. By 1880 this process led to the emergence of the "New South Creed," a set of beliefs advocating a shift away from the region's traditional reliance on plantation agriculture toward a future based on industry, commerce, and urbanization. New South "prophets" such as Henry W. Grady, the dynamic editor of the *Atlanta Constitution*, sounded much like their British counterparts fifty years earlier in urging that southerners put aside their leisurely ways in favor of a new commitment to enterprise and efficiency. Grady and his associates also preached a fervent gospel of national reconciliation to bind up the wounds of civil war and maintain the southward flow of northern capital, along with an insistence that southerners, because of their long experience with such matters, be allowed to handle their racial problems by themselves.[10]

Ironically, New South thinkers coupled their commitment to modernization with a strong element of nostalgia in the form of an unyielding determination to preserve that vital centerpiece of Old South culture and regional identity, the Cavalier myth. Indeed, this mythology, with its vision of the South as the last remaining home of aristocracy in America, blended perfectly with the Victorian cult of gentility. Just as the rising businessman in England or the North felt the need to acquire the persona of the gentleman, New South promoters and entrepreneurs took upon themselves the mantle of the antebellum planter. In this fashion, they could justify to themselves and their society their acquisitive behavior and, at the same time, assert their identity as southerners.[11]

Such was the function that the Cavalier mythology had performed for the planter class in antebellum times. Though it appeared initially in seventeenth-century Virginia, the myth did not really begin to flourish until the 1830s, when thousands of ambitious and sharp-dealing men, often from lowly origins, flocked to the newly opened lands of the Deep South and made swift fortunes raising cotton. Fearful of the raw and unstable state of their communities, and of the precariousness of their freshly acquired status as planters, these "Cotton Snobs" sought comfort in the belief that theirs was a relatively fixed social order presided over by a class of refined gentlemen whose perfect self-control set an example for all to follow. In most instances, this was not a matter of deliberate pretension but of a nearly automatic response to a deeply felt psychological need. "So innocent was the thing," W. J. Cash tells us, "that quite often it was done without putting away the memory of the artisans, the *petit bourgeois*, the coon-hunting pioneers, who were their actual fathers."[12]

Thus arose the identity that southerners would employ to define their distinctiveness well into the twentieth century and to compensate for what they secretly believed were the defects of their society. If the region was in fact impoverished, ravaged by war, plagued by illiteracy and racial conflict, and ruled all too often by corrupt demagogues or self-made New South promoters, southerners could take refuge in their image of the South as an aristocratic society organized in quasi-feudal fashion and blessed with remarkable stability and cohesion. "The Southern gentleman," claimed one writer as recently as 1957, "is tolerant, kindly, broadminded, non-puritan, moderate, hospitable, and courteous. . . . A totally integrated personality, he is also supremely gregarious and sees himself as rightly into an organic familial and social order that has a sense of purpose and continuity." Such a man might exhibit a hot temper, but only when provoked by a direct affront to his honor. Above all, he did not seek to advance his own interests or gratify his ambition but to benefit his community and region. His counterpart, the southern lady, was—according to the mythology—equally a paragon of moral innocence and selflessness whose prime concern was upholding the canon of sexual purity. These roles were not, it should be stressed, mere window dressing. "The relishing . . . of the idea of men as chivalrous knights and women as castellated ladies was not merely coincidental, nor was it frivolous," Joel Williamson assures us. "On the contrary it was immanent and deadly serious." [13]

In this fashion, the Cavalier ideal came to embody the essence of Victorian culture in the South and to dominate the imaginations of most southerners at the time Faulkner was growing up. Accordingly, the southern writers of Faulkner's generation would each need to make a separate peace with this powerful symbol of their nineteenth-century legacy. Only then could they be free to embrace the culture of their own times.

"On or about December 1910," declared Virginia Woolf, "human character changed." Historians tracing the origins of Modernist culture have quarreled with Woolf's exact choice of date, but they have increasingly come to agree that sometime around the turn of the century the intelligentsia in Europe and America began to experience a profound shift in sensibility that would lead to an explosion of creativity in the arts, transform moral values, and in time reshape the conduct of life throughout Western society. Modernism, Peter Gay reports, "utterly changed painting, sculpture, and music; the dance, the novel, and the drama; architecture, poetry, and thought. And its ventures into unknown territory percolated from the rarefied regions of high culture to general ways of thinking, feeling, and seeing." [14]

Despite the heightened attention now being paid to Modernism, its definition remains elusive. Perhaps the most prevalent view until recently did not see it as a full-scale historical culture at all but rather equated it with the beliefs and lifestyle of the artistic avant-garde at the turn of the twentieth century. Used in this sense, the term usually connotes radical experimentation in artistic style, a deliberate cultivation of the perverse and decadent, and the flaunting of outrageous behavior designed to shock the bourgeoisie. The entire movement, according to this definition, was composed of a small number of highly talented poets and painters based in the bohemian quarters of certain large cities, most notably Paris, New York, Vienna, and Berlin, culminating in the work of such "canonical" masters as Picasso, Pound, and Joyce. Others, like Irving Howe and Lionel Trilling, allow Modernism slightly more range by depicting it as an "adversary culture" originating in bohemia but later adopted more generally by twentieth-century intellectuals in their estrangement from mass society. In either case, Modernist thought emerges as essentially negative and rebellious in character and as far too amorphous ever to be pinned down with precision.[15]

However, a growing number of writers would contend that those identifying Modernism with bohemia have confused the tip for the whole iceberg by focusing on the more visible and spectacular manifestations of the culture while missing its underlying structure. As they see it, far from being anarchic, Modernist thought represents an attempt to restore a sense of order to human experience under the often chaotic conditions of contemporary existence. Not just the plaything of the avant-garde, it has assumed a commanding position in literature, music, painting, architecture, philosophy, and virtually every other realm of artistic or intellectual endeavor. Moreover, Modernism, in this formulation, has cast its influence well beyond the intellectual elite to encompass much of contemporary middle-class Western society, manifesting itself in such diverse contexts as suburban housing, television advertising, and popular music. In short, as Ricardo Quinones puts it, Modernism "has acquired such extensive and pervasive cultural force that it may be said to characterize an epoch. . . . As romanticism dominated the nineteenth century, Modernism has come to dominate the twentieth."[16]

To be sure, Modernism was never a monolith. On the contrary, the evolving culture was to find expression in a multitude of shapes and voices, created and re-created by individuals who adapted its core beliefs to their specific circumstances and needs. It is readily possible, to take a few examples, to distinguish a late Modernism (or, more exactly, several late Modernisms) that came into existence by the 1950s from the early Modernism prevalent in the first decades of the century, or the Modernist sensibility characteristic of New York City from that of the Midwest. Likewise, Modernism has looked quite different within the domain of the social sciences than, say, within the humanities or mass media. One must always take this broad variance into account in any attempt to understand Modernism. Nonetheless, it is possible, by going back to the early 1920s and consulting the works of the culture's leading progenitors, such as Freud or Joyce, to find what might plausibly be called its quintessential version—one in which its key ideas and values were most fully elaborated and articulated. It was this more or less "pure" strain of Modernism that William Faulkner would encounter at the start of his career and work hard to assimilate, attempting (as he wrote of one autobiographical protagonist who becomes a Modernist artist) "to permeate himself with becoming one in it." Accordingly, that strain of Modernism must be our focus here.[17]

The first signs of that culture appeared in Europe during the mid- to late nineteenth century, as various artists, philosophers, and psychologists, chafing under the burden of what they viewed as Victorian repression, began to seek out new forms of experience. Most conspicuous at the outset were the French symbolist poets and impressionist painters, both of whom would have a significant influence on Faulkner. Moving beyond the stable and seemingly objective world of Victorian positivism, the two movements began to explore the far murkier and less predictable operations of human perception and consciousness. At the same time, parallel developments were taking place in more formal fields of thought. Writers as diverse as Bergson, Nietzsche, and William James agreed that experience should be understood as a continuous flow of sensations and recollections—what James termed "the stream of consciousness"—and that this raw sensory flux was as close as human beings could ever come to knowing reality. Abstract concepts, along with all the other products of rationality that the Victorians had valued so highly, were seen as inherently faulty precisely because they represented an attempt to stop the experiential flow and remove knowledge from its proper dynamic context. As James insisted, "When we conceptualize we cut and fix, and exclude anything but what we have fixed, whereas in the real concrete sensible flux of life experiences compenetrate each other." His writings, accordingly, suggested an obligation to loosen restraints, open oneself to the world, and perfect one's ability to experience experience—exactly what the Victorians most feared.[18]

As Modernism continued to develop during the twentieth century, what its various manifestations had in common was a determination not only for expanding the range of consciousness but for fusing together disparate elements of experience into new and original "wholes." Put simply, its fundamental aim has been to reconnect all that the Victorian moral dichotomy tore asunder—to integrate once more the human and the animal, the civilized and the savage—in order to combat the allegedly dishonest conception of existence that the Victorians had introduced. Far from being an aimless descent into irrationality, Malcolm Bradbury and James McFarlane insist, Modernism involves "the interpenetration, the reconciliation, the coalescence, the fusion—of reason and unreason, intellect and emotion, subjective and objective." McFarlane, in fact, identifies three stages in the development of the culture: a first stage of early rebellion that emphasized "the breaking up . . . of those meticulously constructed 'systems' and 'types' and 'absolutes'" that the Victorians had assiduously created; a second stage marked by "a re-structuring of parts, a re-relating of the fragmented concepts"; and a final stage characterized by "a dissolving, a blending, a merging of things previously held to be forever mutually exclusive." Thus, he concludes, "the defining thing in the Modernist mode is not so much that things fall *apart* but that they fall *together*"; the true end result of Modernism "is not disintegration but (as it were) super-integration."[19]

This insight explains so much that had puzzled previous writers on Modernism. It allows one to make sense, for example, of the strategy employed by Modernist painters from the cubists onward of placing all planes and perspectives on the canvas *simultaneously*, so that the viewer could not select individual facets of the painting for attention but would have to experience it as a fused whole. The same passion for integration accounts for the predilection of twentieth-century thinkers and writers for such devices as paradox (which joins seeming opposites) and ambivalence (the fusing of contradictory emotions, such as love and hate). One also finds this modality at work in the practice of cinematic montage, with its juxtaposition of diverse events and experiences; in the resort to multiple overlapping harmonies and rhythms in contemporary music, especially jazz (which also blends the primitivism of its African origins with modern sophistication); and in the attempt to break down boundaries between stage and audience in twentieth-century theater.[20]

The most deep rooted effort at integration, however, concerns the Modernist attempt to reconstruct human nature. If the Victorians sought to place a firm barrier between the "higher" mental functions, such as rational thought and spirituality, and those "lower" instincts and passions that Freud would in time ascribe to the "id," Modernists strove to unite these two levels of the psyche. Thus where the Victorians held "sincerity" to be their most prized character trait, with its injunction that a person's conscious self remain honest and consistent, Modernists have demanded "authenticity," which requires a blending, as far as is possible, of the conscious and unconscious strata of the mind, so that the self presented to the world approaches the "true" self in every respect. Above all, that means forswearing conventional and stereotyped models of personal identity in favor of an identity that is continuously being fashioned out of the ongoing lessons of one's own experience. This, as Lionel Trilling observes, represents a far "more strenuous" standard than did the code of sincerity and necessitates precisely the sort of intense self-knowledge that the Victorians sought to avoid—hence the resort to stream-of-consciousness technique in Modernist novels in order to capture what D. H. Lawrence called the "real, vital, potential self" as opposed to "the old stable ego" of nineteenth-century literary characters.[21]

Yet it is just at this point that a massive paradox arises, for with the universe characterized by incessant change, the goals of perfect integration and authenticity always remain elusive. Though we must constantly seek to coalesce the varied fragments of our existence, Modernists have believed, we must also be aware that we will never succeed. In fact, complete integration would not be desirable, for that would mean stasis. Only within the sheltered realm of the mind—in self-contained intellectual systems such as mathematics and logic, or in imaginary settings conjured up for the purposes of art—can we approach true integration. Otherwise, all that pertains to nature and life must be construed dynamically, as continuous process. The only lasting closure, in Modernist terms, comes with death.

This paradoxical quest for and avoidance of integration accounts for the special role of art within Modernist culture. Precisely because it represents a realm where that quest can be pursued with relative safety through surrogate experience, art has become a medium for radical experimentation in new ways of amplifying perception, organizing the psyche, and extending the culture. Art's mission, as Susan Sontag observes, has become one of "making forays into and taking up positions on the frontiers of consciousness (often very dangerous to the artist as a person) and reporting back what's there." What especially suits art for this task is its reliance on the devices of symbolism, metaphor, and myth—all of which have the ability to connect things from different realms of experience that cannot be readily joined through logic. Art in this way can bridge the rational and the emotional, the objective and subjective—breaking apart conventional beliefs and rejoining the resulting fragments in a manner that creates relationships not suspected before. In short, where the Victorians saw art as didactic in purpose—as a vehicle for communicating and illustrating preordained moral truths—to Modernists it has become the principal vehicle for exploring and fashioning meaning in a world where meaning must constantly be re-created. This, indeed, would prove one of the new culture's foremost attractions to Faulkner as he struggled to make sense of his region's troubled plight in the midst of a twentieth-century world undergoing rapid transformation.[22]

Thus the Modernist worldview has taken shape. It begins with the premise of an unpredictable universe where nothing is ever stable and where human beings accordingly must be satisfied with knowledge that is partial and transient at best. Nor is it possible in this situation to devise a fixed system of morality; moral values must remain in flux, shifting continuously in response to changing historical circumstances. To create those values and garner whatever knowledge is available, individuals must subject themselves to the trials of experience. Above all they must not attempt to shield themselves behind illusions or gentility, as so many were said to have done during the nineteenth century. Rather, the Modernist ethos insists on confronting the ugly, the sordid, and the terrible, for that is where the most important lessons are to be found. In stark contrast to Victorianism, Modernism—in its ideal form—eschews innocence and demands instead a full, candid apprehension of "reality," no matter how painful that might be. Such was the vision of existence that William Faulkner would discover as a young man and seek to make his own.

Given their attributes, it seems evident that the two major cultures that came to coexist within Faulkner were bound to conflict, not only in their modes of perception and belief but in their respective approaches to structuring the psyche. There is, after all, no such thing as a generic human persona that remains the same in all times and places. On the contrary, Warren Susman informs us, the self is to a large extent historically determined, with each cultural era producing its own characteristic "modal" self as individuals construct their identities from the norms and prototypes that happen to be in circulation at the moment they come of age. "As cultures change," he adds, "so do the modal types of persons who are their bearers." To be sure, the process is anything but simple—many idiosyncratic factors relating to family circumstances and the vagaries of personal experience come into play. The modal self, accordingly, should be thought of as an ideal type that is only approximated, never exactly replicated. Nonetheless, the almost ubiquitous human inclination to adapt to one's social environment tends to ensure that the adult self will reflect the reigning culture in most cases.[23] *

*Recent advances in neuroscience suggest that the link between culture and self is not only psychological in nature but physiological. When we speak of a "self," practitioners of that field remind us, we are in fact referring ultimately to a mass of soft tissue within the brain through which runs a myriad of electrical channels and connections. And what determines the structure of those crucial circuits, aside from genetic endowment, is the individual's ongoing interaction with his or her cultural and social environment, especially during the initial decades of life.

The process by which this occurs has come to be known as "neural Darwinism." We are born, reports Gerald M. Edelman, with a vast surplus of brain cells that first organize themselves into groups and then enter into a fierce competition for survival. In essence, those neuronal groups receiving stimulation from the environment are able to expand and join with other groups into networks, whereas those not stimulated (well over a majority of the original cells) atrophy and die. It is a relentless winnowing, but by the time it has ended, around age twenty, the remaining cells have formed highly efficient circuits that, in effect, are custom-made to perform all the mental functions required by the social setting in which the individual exists. Through an extraordinary instance of the Darwinian principle of adaptation, our brains become matched to our world.

In this fashion, the self that is biologically created comes to a considerable extent to reflect the influences and imperatives of the surrounding culture. "To those of us in the field," writes Marian Diamond, another leading neurobiologist, "there is absolutely no doubt that culture changes brains." The findings of Dr. Tadanobu Tsunoda of the Medical and Dental University of Tokyo illustrate how powerful that shaping process can be. For those raised within Japanese culture, he discovered, the area of the brain governing emotional perception and sexual function is located in the left cerebral hemisphere (normally associated with logic and calculation), whereas for Occidentals it can almost invariably be found in the right hemisphere. This "switching," with all of its consequences for the expression and evaluation of emotion, appears to be due entirely to cultural and linguistic factors and, once established, becomes virtually permanent: "A Japanese child raised as an American until the age of nine will henceforth perceive his emotions like a non-Japanese, predominantly in the right hemisphere, after his return to Japan."

It should quickly be added that most neuroscientists do not view this link between self and environment in reductionist terms. On the contrary, they repeatedly stress (often with a sense of awe) how dynamic and creative the human brain can be in

One can hence speak of a characteristic Victorian modal self, existing in the mid- to late nineteenth century, that echoed the Victorians' vision of their ideal world: solid, unified, and stable. Their firm assumption held that character was (or, at least, ought to be) defined largely by social role, which in turn was normally fixed by heredity, upbringing, and vocation. That meant that, once an individual had matured, any noticeable shift in character was to be viewed with suspicion. The objective for the Victorian middle class, accordingly, was first to ascertain one's true self and then to remain faithful to it. The last thing a person wanted was to have his or her character appear plastic or multiform (an especially important consideration if the individual was in reality a self-made recruit to the middle class). Rather, the self presented to the world should be consistent, even monolithic, in every possible respect.[24]

By the end of the century, however, new ideas about selfhood started to emerge. According to the "empiricist" school of psychology that became highly influential at this time, the self was not a distinct, immutable entity that could be pinpointed inside the mind of each individual but rather, in Judith Ryan's words, "a bundle of sensory impressions precariously grouped together and constantly threatened with possible dissolution." In place of the "substantial, consistent self" of the Victorian era, the "fluid, unbounded self" associated with Modernism was coming into being. This was, of course, a daunting proposition for those raised on Victorian precepts, and almost from the start there were efforts to temper it. The self might in fact be evanescent, argued William James, a leading empiricist, but in practice we tend to *feel* that we are solid and continuous beings, and since that illusion proves comforting, it should be permitted. A few decades later, Freud went much further in restoring a modicum of coherence to the psyche and in setting the terms by which selfhood would

---

its ability to use existing circuitry in new ways. What differentiates the brain of the human species from those of other animals, it would seem, is precisely the way it can send signals to itself, rather than depending on those originating in the external environment, allowing it a significant degree of control over its own development. Even so, the research also clearly indicates that the cerebral structures formed during a person's childhood have great tenacity. This suggests that, once a given culture becomes embedded within the architecture and operations of a person's brain, its characteristic modes of thinking and feeling cannot easily be dislodged.

See Edelman, *Bright Air, Brilliant Fire*, 238–40, 81–94; Marian Diamond, quoted in Healy, *Endangered Minds*, 49; Greenough, Black, and Wallace, "Experience and Brain Development," 555–67; Tadanobu Tsunoda, "Hemispheric Dominance in Japan and the West," in Klivington, *Science of Mind*, 54–55.

be understood in the Modernist era when he assigned the ego the task of organizing the assorted fragments of identity acquired over the years into a more or less consolidated persona. As Freud and his successors described it, however, that process never reached closure. In the twentieth century, the reigning model of the self would be based, as Ronald Bush puts it, on "a state of continuous becoming."[25]

All his life Faulkner would struggle to reconcile these two divergent approaches to selfhood—the Victorian urge toward unity and stability he had inherited as a child of the southern rural gentry, and the Modernist drive for multiplicity and change that he absorbed very early in his career as a self-identifying member of the international artistic avant-garde. Indeed, by the time he reached maturity, both had become so deeply embedded in his being that neither could effectively be suppressed or jettisoned. The tactic he ultimately arrived at for coping with this dilemma, most likely without being consciously aware that he was employing it, was that of "compartmentalization," in which, as Roy F. Baumeister explains, "one confines the potentially conflicting components to separate spheres of one's life." Put simply, there would be two William Faulkners.[26]

In fact, self-division of this sort is not unusual among literary artists, existing as such individuals do partly in reality and partly within their own imagination. "I think that a writer is a perfect case of split personality," Faulkner once remarked, doubtless drawing on his own experience. "He is one thing when he is a writer and he is something else while he is a denizen of the world." The syndrome can reach the point, clinicians tell us, where it closely mimics schizophrenia, with the writer cultivating a private "inner self" that, like the true schizophrenic's, is kept rigorously hidden from public view except in his or her work. The Irish poet William Butler Yeats, to take one instance, maintained what he called his "objective self," embodying the codes and rituals of his daily existence, and a subjective "antithetical self" that found expression in his inner consciousness and art. In some cases the two selves can become so distinct that they receive different names. One thinks of Charles Dodgson, the meek, retiring mathematician who could indulge his extraordinary gift for fantasy only through adopting the persona and pen name of Lewis Carroll, or Samuel L. Clemens, a thoroughly divided man who simultaneously installed himself as a member of the bourgeois establishment while pillorying its pretensions through the frontier perspective of his alter ego, Mark Twain. Awkward though such devices might be on occasion, the writers in question have been unable to function without them.[27]

William Faulkner may not have adopted a separate name for his literary self, but he was profoundly self-divided, as those who knew him well reported again and again. To understand him, his wife once insisted, one had to begin with the fact that he was "so definitely dual," to the point where there were "two Bills." In his youth, he experimented with an extensive repertoire of trial identities, ranging from the battle-scarred First World War aviator to the bona fide southern aristocrat to the bohemian writer and small-town derelict. By the late 1920s, however, a pattern of two central selves—old-fashioned country gentleman and contemporary writer—became reasonably well established. On occasion these two Faulkners would appear in startling juxtaposition. "You might see him riding a horse some day, all liveried up as they say—had on the dress like a colonel," notes an old friend. "Then he'd come out . . . with long whiskers and look like a hippie." More typically, though, each self retained a favored realm where it held sway. The extensive divide between his dual incarnations even came to astonish Faulkner himself. "I wonder," he wrote a close acquaintance in the early 1950s, "if you have ever had that thought about the work and the country man whom you know as Bill Faulkner—what little connection there seems to be between them."[28]

In the words of Michel Gresset, the Modernist Faulkner, with his "malleable or bending self," was "formed through the act of writing and through nothing else." He was not often sighted in normal life, though he did surface periodically in places like New York, Paris, and Hollywood in the company of congenial friends (in New York his favorites included the futurist architect Buckminster Fuller and the avant-garde puppeteers Jim and Cora Baird). Rather, this Faulkner existed primarily within the isolated confines of his work space. "Withdrawing into a small room or study (the one at Rowan Oak would be deliberately plain, almost bare, recalling nothing so much as a monk's cell), taking the symbolic doorknob with him, he entered a world completely his own," David Minter tells us. There he was free to summon up the most lurid and perilous materials from his unconscious, exploring territory that his Modernist self sought to make its own. Often he would resort to a trancelike state to sustain this self, writing at a "white hot" pace and consuming a fair quantity of alcohol as he worked (though rarely allowing himself to become actually inebriated while writing). Even though his ostensible subject matter remained the South, this was primarily a cosmopolitan William Faulkner whose first loyalty went to his reading audience of all times and places.[29]

The other Faulkner was the one encountered in Oxford, whose actions remained based on nineteenth-century values and who increasingly made his peace with the traditions of his native town. This Faulkner would find it necessary to buy and restore a large antebellum home, as well as a working plantation, take ritual walks to the town square dressed like a country squire, and display a fondness, as one neighbor put it, "for tweeds, pipes, and riding to the hounds." Perhaps most striking is the way the author of *Sanctuary*, who dealt more explicitly with sexuality than almost any other American writer of his day, maintained a high standard of Victorian prudery in his everyday public behavior. Repeatedly we are told by those who knew him in Oxford of how Faulkner would take offense at profane language and walk away at the first sign of off-color humor (though he would delight in telling "gamy" tales while in Hollywood and readily employed obscenities in his professional correspondence). "If someone started telling dirty stories, he was gone," a close friend and hunting companion notes. "He would leave and he wouldn't come back until you got through with the story." Nor would he discuss literary topics with his fellow townspeople under any condition, going so far as to refuse to allow the person who helped him wrap and mail his manuscripts to see their titles, and to respond with stony silence when his personal physician made the error of inquiring about a book he happened to find Faulkner reading. Likewise, when the wife of his old friend and mentor, Phil Stone, tried to engage him in conversation about an author she knew he admired, Faulkner, she reports, "did not just fail to reply; his silence was like a mallet on my head." [30]

To a considerable extent, the story of the main part of Faulkner's career centers on his continual effort to juggle these two identities, altering and repositioning them to meet his ever changing needs as a novelist and resident of rural Mississippi. In this process of incessant psychic fine-tuning, neither identity would achieve complete dominance. While his Modernist self was in fairly firm control by the start of the 1930s whenever he sat down to work, the Victorian self remained present, ready to block or censor its Modernist counterpart if the latter became too bold. Likewise, the Modernist Faulkner would intermittently appear on the streets of Oxford, dressed in bohemian attire and lost in a dreamworld. In effect, throughout this period of his life his identity, taken as a whole, came to encompass both of his selves set in tension against each other, engaged in negotiating an endless series of temporary arrangements and truces, with the Modernist Faulkner tending to gain strength year by year. That pattern would continue until the early 1940s, when for various reasons the momentum would shift toward the traditionalist Faulkner, ushering in a new and far less productive stage in his writing.

In light of this intricate structure of selfhood that Faulkner evolved, it should be no surprise that identity would take its place as a major subject—perhaps *the* major subject—of his fiction. To the extent that he believed it possible to assign the blame for his region's tragic plight to one key causal factor, it would be what he came to regard as the inauthentic, myth-laden model of identity handed down to succeeding generations of southerners by the antebellum planter class. That faulty identity, he felt, could be held directly responsible for the catastrophe of the Civil War, as well as the South's subsequent descent into virulent racism and poverty. As a consequence, he would devote the greater part of his efforts as a Modernist writer both to savaging the mythic Cavalier and to searching for an ideal twentieth-century southern identity with which to replace it. That search would give rise to a series of characters who would in some manner bring together within their selves attributes of culture, race, and gender that traditional southern society had tried to separate. In their willingness to undergo immense suffering as the price for violating fundamental taboos, these exemplary figures were meant to stand as no less than contemporary invocations of Christ, redemptive models that Faulkner was offering to light a better path to the future for the South in particular but also the wider world.

What seems utterly astonishing, in retrospect, is that so many of these Modernist Christ figures that Faulkner put forth would turn out to be either black or female—astonishing because this son of turn-of-the-century Mississippi had unthinkingly absorbed all the prevailing modes of racist and sexist thinking from his environment that one might expect. "You can't tell me these niggers [in the North] are as happy and contented as ours are," he wrote his parents from New Haven soon after World War I; "all this freedom does is to make them miserable." Within a decade, though, his perspective would change diametrically. Reexamining race through Modernist eyes, he would arrive at the revolutionary insight that the "nigger" persona did not arise from biological traits but instead represented an identity that southern whites had imposed on blacks in order to demean and subjugate them. Following that insight as far as it would take him despite stiff internal resistance from his traditionalist self, Faulkner would arrive at Joe Christmas, the protagonist of *Light in August*, who comes not only to accept but to proudly embrace the "nigger" identity with which he is saddled even though his skin color (and, most likely, his ancestry) fully qualifies him as white. It is hard to imagine anything more subversive in the 1930s South than a multiracial Christ, yet that is what Christmas becomes when he is, in effect, crucified for insisting on integrating his dual selves, being white and black at the same time. As we will find, though, Faulkner could mount this devastating attack on racial stereotypes only by keeping his own dual selves by and large compartmentalized. In daily life he would continue to relate to blacks on his accustomed basis of paternalistic superiority and freely employ the term *nigger*.[31]

The same pattern appears in his treatment of women. To the end of his days the nineteenth-century attitudes toward sex and gender that he had internalized as a child would remain to encumber him, rendering problematic his relationships with his wife and many of the other women with whom he interacted as an adult. Like so many men of his era, he would both idealize women as paragons of sexual purity and simultaneously resent them for the moral standard they seemed to enforce on him. One of the primary reasons he was drawn to Modernist culture in the first place, one suspects, is the promise it held of delivering him from that repressive standard, allowing him to revise significantly his view of women. Aware through his readings in Modernist texts that the self was always constructed through experience, not predetermined by genetics, he began to explore gender in the same way he had race. He would commence with what might be called an unveiling of the southern lady, revealing her to be a person with the normal range of human passions and sexual drives behind her facade of absolute purity, and then proceed to create a number of female characters who broke decisively not only with the "belle" identity but with Victorian mores in general. Such a daring move, however, was bound to upset his internal psychic balance. If his Modernist self deeply admired these liberated women, the Victorian part of him required that the narratives in which they appeared duly punish them for their sins, either through death or some form of mutilation.

That punishment notwithstanding, two of these figures would come closer to his vision of Christ-like perfection than any other characters in his fiction. Charlotte Rittenmeyer of *The Wild Palms* and Linda Snopes of *The Mansion* each undergo a terrible travail following their revolt against conventional gender roles, but we are to understand that their suffering, like that of Joe Christmas, occurs because they embody a superior model of identity for which their society is not yet prepared. Living self-consciously by Modernist values (and just as self-consciously rejecting the nineteenth-century moral dichotomy in all its manifestations), they each attain androgyny, fusing into a provisional whole those identity elements that Faulkner considered the finest attributes of maleness and femininity. As Faulkner portrays them, these two women can assume virtually any role normally reserved for a man, while still retaining that special capacity for intuiting the feelings of others and attending to the needs of the weak and downtrodden that, for him, distinguished members of the opposite sex.

As it happens, this portrait of heroic androgyny has led some critics to designate Faulkner an incipient feminist, just as the ordeals to which he subjects Charlotte and Linda, along with earlier women characters, have convinced others to see him as a hopeless misogynist. Although both labels carry a measure of truth, they fall decisively short of capturing the full reality of William Faulkner. Only an interpretation that takes into account the tensions arising from his conflicting selves can do that. On gender, as with everything else, his position in his best fiction was that of a Modernist engaged in a continuous rear-guard action against a significant part of his own psyche.

Perhaps no other major American writer would struggle as hard as Faulkner did to become a Modernist, fighting to overcome the claims of family and region. His career would be spent gathering up the fragments of myth and culture that had been bequeathed to him in order to recast them into a workable identity that could withstand the new conditions of twentieth-century life and perhaps offer the possibility of heroic action. As with all Modernist quests, his struggle would fall short of success, but out of it would also come his greatest art.

CHAPTER 1

Progenitor

The First William Falkner

Anyone intent on coming to terms with William Faulkner must begin with one question: How could a country boy with little formal education from a small town in northern Mississippi, perhaps the most culturally backward area in the nation at the time, produce *The Sound and the Fury*—one of the great masterpieces of Modernist literature? The question becomes even more intriguing when one recalls that Faulkner was raised in staid Victorian propriety by a culturally ambitious mother and that his family ties, on the paternal side at least, ran directly to the old planter class and its Cavalier mentality. To be sure, there were other American Modernist writers of Faulkner's generation who hailed from the provinces—Hemingway and Fitzgerald come immediately to mind—but they generally spent four years at an East Coast university and soon afterward transported themselves to centers of artistic innovation such as Paris in order to soak up additional influences and gain badly needed support. Faulkner, however, stayed at home for the most part, in a community that took virtually no interest in his work, and carried a far heavier load of nineteenth-century cultural baggage than most of his American literary contemporaries. Yet the fact remains that none of them was to equal his achievement in the twentieth-century novel. Clearly, the answers to this puzzle are not self-evident; to find them we must take careful stock of the forces responsible for producing Faulkner's complex sensibility and for setting him on his difficult passage toward Modernism.

Perhaps most important among those determining influences on Faulkner was his family. Its founding figure, Colonel William Clark Falkner, the great-grandfather after whom the future novelist would be named, had been a leading lawyer in the Mississippi town of Ripley, a military hero during the Civil War, the founder and principal owner of a thriving local railroad, and the author of a commercially successful work of fiction. At the same time, the Old Colonel, as he was called, had killed two men during a feud early in his life, was voted out of his command by his own soldiers, appears to have made a small fortune selling contraband behind enemy lines during the latter part of the war, built his railroad in part through shady transactions and the use of convict labor, and was eventually gunned down on the main street of Ripley by an embittered former business partner. His son, John Wesley Thompson Falkner, was less violent, though still controversial. President of the First National Bank of Oxford, Mississippi, a state legislator and respected lawyer, he ultimately lost control of the bank and was known for bouts of heavy drinking and reckless driving, including one joy-riding incident in which he threw a brick through the bank's window. "It was my Buick, my brick, and my bank," he later explained. One finds, in short, a family justly proud of its achievements but also widely perceived as arrogant, pretentious, and impulsive. For a sensitive boy with literary ambitions, sorting out the ambiguous legacy of being a Falkner would be no simple matter.[1]

At the core of that legacy stood the Old Colonel himself. "While Bill built no railroads and took part in no duels," his brother observes, "I always felt that he more or less unconsciously patterned his life after the Old Colonel's." Asked as a child about his goal in life, Faulkner would answer that he wished to become: "A writer, like my great-grandfather." And when a publisher in 1924 requested a brief autobiographical sketch, his response began with the fact that he was the "great-grandson of Col. W. C. Falkner, C.S.A., author of 'The White Rose of Memphis,' 'Rapid Ramblings in Europe,' etc.," as if *everyone* knew who that famous author was. Surely it is also significant that Faulkner hung a large portrait of this illustrious ancestor above the mantel in his home and later took special pains to ensure that the Old Colonel's monument in the Ripley, Mississippi, cemetery—a life-sized statue atop a fourteen-foot pedestal that the Colonel had commissioned himself—was kept clean and in good repair.[2]

What seemed to fascinate Faulkner most was the aura of mystery and paradox surrounding the first William Falkner—the way his saga had be-

The oversized statue of Colonel William C. Falkner that stands above his gravesite in Ripley, Mississippi. In Flags in the Dust *his great-grandson would describe the monument in some detail, noting especially how the head "was lifted a little" in a "gesture of haughty pride." (Courtesy Brodsky Collection, Center for Faulkner Studies, Southeast Missouri State University)*

come enshrouded by legend, bestowing on him a kind of mythical status and perpetuating the controversies that had plagued him through life. "People at Ripley talk of him as if he were still alive, up in the hills some place, and might come in at any time," Faulkner told Robert Cantwell. "It's a strange thing; there are lots of people who knew him well, and yet no two of them remember him alike or describe him the same way. One will say he was [very short] like me, and another will swear he was six feet tall." Men who served with the Old Colonel in the war would gather every year well into the twentieth century to recollect his gallantry, embellishing the tales a little more each time. His old enemies, meanwhile, were just as persistent, refusing to walk on the same side of the street as a Falkner descendant.[3]

Although even his modern biographer finds it difficult to penetrate the mysteries at times, the general contours of the Colonel's strange career can be limned out. The story is hardly a typical one, but it does capture, in its mix of violence and acquired gentility, ruthlessness and benevolence, most of the salient tendencies of nineteenth-century southern society and culture—which may be why it has proved so susceptible to mythologizing. It begins with his birth in the Tennessee mountains in 1825, his frontier boyhood in Missouri, and his decision somewhere around age sixteen to leave home penniless and seek out a long-lost uncle in Mississippi. Arriving in Ripley in the early 1840s, he soon made a name for himself by helping a sheriff's posse corner a murderer and by publishing, on the day the culprit was executed, a sensational pamphlet containing a narrative of the man's life. Falkner also started to practice law in his uncle's office and to acquire the real estate that would in time make him one of the largest landowners in the county.[4]

It did not take long, however, before what Donald Duclos refers to as a "pattern of violence, ambition, daring, and even arrogance" in Falkner's behavior made itself manifest. One can detect it, for instance, in his suspect record of service in the Mexican War. Exactly how he landed in trouble is unclear: one account has him leaving camp against orders in pursuit of a young Mexican woman whose companions defended her by shooting him in the hand and foot, another has him foolishly riding into an ambush in territory his commander had set off limits. As he later confessed in a poem he wrote about the war:

> Full well I know the feeling of lead —
> I have never fought, but freely bled,

> Mexican soil hath drank my gore,
> But I disgrace, instead of glory, bore.

However, Falkner did not allow his penitence to stand in the way of his practical ambition. Although he had spent only one month in the war zone and rapidly recovered from his wounds (though losing three fingers of his left hand), he would afterward inform the world without embarrassment of how he "served twelve months in the Mexican War," leave a clear impression that he had done so heroically, and insist successfully that the federal government pay him a full pension as a disabled veteran.[5]

A few years later he landed in far deeper trouble. A close friend named Robert Hindman, under the apparently mistaken belief that Falkner had blackballed his attempt to join a temperance organization, accosted Falkner with a gun in May 1849. Three times the pistol misfired at point-blank range, but by then Falkner had reached for his knife and stabbed Hindman to death. Despite his easy acquittal on grounds of self-defense, the incident, as so often happened on the frontier, led to a simmering feud with the Hindman clan and its allies. In February 1851, the feud suddenly heated up when Falkner, for reasons now unknown, dispatched with his pistol one Erasmus V. Morris, a Hindman supporter. Despite the fact that nearly the whole left side of Morris's head had been blown away, Falkner once more claimed self-defense. This time, though, community opinion seems to have been heavily weighed against him—the grand jury indictment speaks presumptively of Falkner "not having the fear of God before his eyes but being moved and seduced by the instigation of the devil." His second acquittal, due largely to the skill of his lawyers, provoked a widespread outrage and redoubled the anger of the Hindman camp.[6]

Was Falkner, as he would always protest, an innocent victim of a simple misunderstanding here? Perhaps, but it is striking how quickly and fervently so many of his fellow townsmen turned against him, to the point where he found it necessary to leave Mississippi for extended periods of time. "I have been persecuted and hunted down like a savage wild beast," Falkner wrote shortly after the Morris trial, "and at every corner, instead of friendship sweet, I find deadly foes, ready to take advantage when they find me unarmed." According to the Hindmans, however, finding him unarmed was a highly unlikely prospect—Robert's aggrieved father avers to "the known character of Falkner for violence—His Bowie Knife & pistols are constantly about his person." Whatever the actual facts of the case, the affray continued until 1857, when Colonel Matthew Galloway, the editor of the *Memphis Appeal*, managed somehow to reconcile the two parties and prevent what would otherwise have been a murderous duel between Falkner and Thomas Hindman Jr. The feud ended, but the image it had generated of Falkner as bloody, unscrupulous, and impulsive hovered about him literally until his dying day.[7]

Whether he was unscrupulous or not, one senses that Falkner, with his love of combat and glory, was precisely the sort of man for whom wars were invented and that he thus almost welcomed the outbreak of hostilities in 1861. Quickly springing into action, he was elected colonel of the Second Mississippi Infantry and led it with unusual gallantry at the First Battle of Manassas. Twice the horse he was riding was shot out from under him, but just as often he remounted another and resumed leading the charge against enemy lines. Wearing a black feather ostentatiously in his cap, he was dubbed by an admiring General P. G. T. Beauregard the "Knight of the Black Plume," a sobriquet that became part of his war legend.[8]

However, as so often happened with Falkner, this initial success quickly turned sour. By the spring of 1862 his troops, tired of his excessive drill and formality and perhaps fearful that his daring in combat would needlessly cost them their lives, chose a new commanding officer. When the Confederate government refused his request for a commission, Falkner returned home to organize his own irregular unit of Partisan Rangers that operated mainly in the area around Ripley. The band enjoyed some minor successes stealing horses and supplies, but when Falkner launched an ill-advised raid against far more numerous Federal forces at Rienzi, his men were ignominiously routed (a disgrace compounded when he chose to abandon them, fleeing by himself in order to save his skin). A similar outcome at the Battle of Hernando in April 1863 finished his military career on a note of anything but glory. His activities for the next two years remain strangely unknown, but there seem to be strong grounds for the widely held suspicion that he was running contraband past the Confederate blockade around Memphis and selling it at great profit to the Yankee troops who held the city. One thing is clear: by the war's end, the Colonel had become fabulously wealthy, even though his home and all of his properties had been destroyed in the fighting.[9]

It was that status as one of the two richest men in Tippah County, coupled with the legends (as opposed to the realities) of his military record, that allowed the Colonel to upgrade his local reputation in the postwar era and emerge, as Duclos puts it, "the great leader of reconstruction and progress in the entire northern section of Mississippi." Like other Redeemers throughout the South, Falkner promoted reconciliation with the North, engaged in frequent acts of public benevolence at home, maintained close ties with Wall Street, and generally espoused the New South Creed. Once Reconstruction ended in 1877, his main project became the building of a railroad linking Ripley to the Gulf of Mexico and to points north. Through a series of complicated financial deals that at times apparently bordered on illegality and through the brutal exploitation of convict labor, the Ship Island, Ripley, and Kentucky Railroad had grown to a thriving enterprise by the mid-1880s, and the Colonel dreamed of extending the line all the way to Chicago. His mounting wealth and pretensions were reflected in his 1883 decision to expand his home from a simple, one-story structure into what Duclos calls "one of the great [architectural] oddities of the area"—a three-story Italian villa "with balconies, gables, iron grillwork, and even portholes on all four sides."[10]

Though all of these activities took place very much in public view with a fair degree of community acclaim, there appears to have been one aspect of the Old Colonel's life at this time that was far more private and surely did not enhance his stature in Ripley. As Joel Williamson has discovered, strong evidence indicates that Falkner, beginning just before the war, maintained a black "shadow family" within his household, consisting of a light-skinned mulatto mistress named Emeline and, in all likelihood, at least two daughters he had fathered by her. This situation, of course, immediately conjures up the conventional image of the wealthy planter sexually exploiting his helpless female slave, but existing records point to a very different sort of relationship. If anything, Falkner seems to have been more closely tied emotionally to Emeline than to his white wife, who would eventually leave him and move to Memphis. It also appears, if the information handed down through Emeline's descendants can be believed, that he not only sent the older daughter (named Fannie Forrest Falkner after his favorite sister and favorite Confederate general) to a nearby black college but visited her there often, bringing bouquets of flowers. However this behavior might be judged by later-twentieth-century standards, there can be no question that it violated fundamental racial norms in the Colonel's own day, yet, strong minded as ever, he resolutely persisted in it. Whether his great-grandson ever knew about this alternate branch of the family remains entirely a matter of conjecture.[11]

Far more certain is the fact that, by the 1880s, a much more serious threat had loomed up for Falkner in his festering feud with Richard J.

Thurmond, a partner in the railroad who sold his shares to Falkner in 1886 when they could no longer get along. Tension between the two mounted as the Colonel continued to promote himself as a community benefactor while reviling Thurmond as a coldhearted capitalist. In William Faulkner's estimate, the Colonel, with his arrogance, "probably drove [Thurmond] to desperation—insulted him, spread stories about him, laughed at him." The outcome was almost inevitable. On November 5, 1889, the day Falkner was elected to the state legislature by an overwhelming margin, Thurmond approached his unarmed rival on the street and shot him fatally in the mouth. In part owing to Thurmond's ability to buy influence with the jury, and in part because of the powerful undercurrent of animosity against Falkner still present in the community, the murderer was soon after acquitted.[12]

These dramatic events in his great-grandfather's life assuredly fascinated William Faulkner, as the fictional exploits of characters such as John Sartoris, Thomas Sutpen, and Carothers McCaslin amply attest, but what appears to have intrigued him even more was the Old Colonel's literary career. Being like his great-grandfather, after all, meant being a writer. Altogether Falkner produced five books—three novels, an epic poem on the Mexican War, and an account of his travels in Europe. Most were issued by vanity presses and enjoyed limited sales, but one, *The White Rose of Memphis*, initially serialized in a Ripley newspaper but published as a book in 1881, sold 160,000 copies and remained in print until the late 1920s. As Cantwell notes, its success was due not only to its adherence to the literary formulas of the period but also to Falkner's considerable talents as an author, especially his flair for characterization and his ability to interweave complex plots.[13]

Most striking, though, is the sensibility these works reveal. However violent and conflict-ridden his life may have been, however mercurial his temperament, when setting pen to paper the Colonel was intent on presenting himself as the epitome of gentlemanly refinement and self-control. What one finds, in other words, especially in his later books, is a perfect specimen of the Victorian mentality in the South, complete with New South boosterism, moral dualism, and an emphasis on gentility. Colonel Falkner might not have begun life as a proper Victorian, but he most definitely wished to appear as one by the end. His writings, as a consequence, provide unusual insight into the way the southern variant of that culture took shape and functioned and also into how it would in time manifest itself to members of William Faulkner's generation.

Falkner's first published work, *The Siege of Monterey*, was composed in 1851 in the Cincinnati hotel room where he took refuge following his second acquittal for murder. An epic, as its author tells us, of "love, war, blood-lust and glory," it is clearly the product of an exuberant but troubled twenty-six-year-old writing partly to excuse and explain his recent misbehavior and partly for the pure pleasure of expressing himself:

> I hope this has not made us foes,
>   But if you don't like it, just go to the devil.
> I like very well to scribble poetry and prose,
>   And I am fond of fun, frolic and revel.
> I acknowledge I am at times very unruly,
>   But when I do wrong I regret it truly.

The poem is filled with standard nineteenth-century poetic conventions, reflecting especially the influence of Byron—including heroic battle scenes and the usual tearful separations and reunions of star-crossed lovers. Where it differs from the genre is in its frequent references to sexuality, as in one long passage reporting the author's visit to a striptease show the previous night:

> I saw,—sure enough, it don't matter what,
> I paid my money and begrudge it not;
> At any rate I saw the heavenly sight,
> And I intend to see it again to-night.

There are also repeated allusions to the female anatomy, described variously as a "harbor" or "heaven" or as a "garden" containing "ambrosial food for man's delight" and "grazing sweet." Although always indirect, such erotic imagery goes well beyond what the era generally thought permissible and suggests a young man barely able to restrain his surging impulses and enthusiasms. The bits and pieces of high "Culture" that he had absorbed were not yet sufficient to cloak his hill-country upbringing, resulting in a peculiar cultural style perhaps best described as "frontier Victorianism."[14]

Thirty years later, we meet a different William Falkner in *The White Rose of Memphis*—one who had ostensibly dropped the last vestiges of his frontier self and acquired all the polish and worldliness of a London literary lion. Though set in Memphis during the 1870s "to save time," the story, he tells us, could as easily have taken place in any large, civilized city. Throughout the book the author is obviously striving (too obviously at times) to demonstrate how social life in the post-Reconstruction South is as prosperous, sophisticated, and refined as that found anywhere and how he, the author, is an excellent judge of such matters. Thus the opening scene—a masquerade ball aboard the *White Rose*, a Mississippi riverboat docked in Memphis—in which "fantastic costumes, sparkling jewels, white, blue and red plumes [to emphasize the region's newfound patriotism], rustling silk, shining satin, soft velvet, sparkling diamonds, high-heeled boots, splendid music, the popping of champagne bottles, the hum of many voices, the merry laughter, the brisk and graceful movement of charming women, were all contributing to the dazzling show." Thus we are also carefully informed of how, at a typical Memphis dinner party, "the flow of wit increased until every guest began to participate in it. Politics and religion—finance and agriculture—science and art—music and history, were all largely discussed." [15]

Equally striking is the language—both that used by the narrator and that placed in the characters' mouths. The denizens of Falkner's fictional world are forever baring their burning brows "to the falling dew" or moistening graves with their tears. And their conversations, even at moments of intense emotion, sound like a strained imitation of what the author thinks would transpire in an elegant British salon:

> "That document conveys the best news, my darling, that I have heard since you told me you would be mine."
> "To what part of it do you refer?"
> "That wherein she says she is going to spend the winter with you. It will be a great consolation for me to know, when I am so far from you, that you will have a sweet friend for a companion. I was thinking of the long, dreary winter days and nights [in Memphis?!] that you would be compelled to pass through alone, but now how could you be lonely with such a lovely little cricket as Viola?"
> "I dare say she will prove a great comfort to me, yet she cannot fill the aching void that will be caused by your absence."

Doubtless Falkner was to some extent following literary convention here. As he understood it, this was the way people were supposed to talk in novels. But one also detects an effort to leave the impression that such a "high" style of speech came naturally to the educated classes in his part of the South and that the author himself was steeped in genteel perfection. [16]

As one might expect, the main source of values throughout is the Victorian moral dichotomy. The characters accordingly are either heroic and pure, or cowardly and villainous. Representing the first category is Edward Demar, the chief protagonist, whose "gentle disposition" and "even temper" render him "the very soul of honor, the paragon of men, the embodiment of truth, and a stranger to deception." Standing beside him in the circle of nobility is his wife-to-be, the "angelic" Lottie Wallingford, "a radiant model of perfection." Further candidates for sainthood include Lottie's "heroic" brother Harry and his fiancée, Viola Bramford, another "model of perfection" and "little angel." Arrayed against these forces of light are numerous villains, most notably that vile ruffian and confidence man Benjamin Bowles, "whose features exhibited unmistakable signs of dissipation and brutality" even in his youth and who grew up to become proprietor of a Memphis "gambling hell." In the description of a police detective, Bowles "is extravagant beyond measure, loves wine and women, keeps four fast trotters at Burton's, bets high at the gaming table, and occasionally dines his friends extravagantly." Nothing could be worse.[17]

The question inevitably raised by this cautionary tale of innocence triumphing over evil concerns the glaring discrepancy between the author's actual life and his literary sensibility. How could a man who had led such a bloody and "extravagant" career himself, who literally left a trail of corpses behind him, write such a genteel text? We know that the Colonel had strong sexual drives that he indulged frequently, as in the adventure that cost him three of his fingers in Mexico, yet there is not the slightest hint of sexuality in *The White Rose of Memphis*. Likewise Falkner's was so clearly a typical nineteenth-century American success story—a poor boy rising through his own strength, talent, and energy to become the town's leading citizen—yet one finds no trace of personal striving or ambition in this novel. On the contrary, the chief characters either miraculously inherit great wealth or, in the case of Bowles, acquire it by illicit means. And, finally, though it is a fact that the Colonel seemed almost to crave violence and excitement through most of his life, no less than three times—and in almost identical language—he has his characters declaim against "the barbarous practice of dueling," declaring solemnly that "it is prohibited by the laws of the land, and positively contrary to God's holy ordinances."[18]

The discrepancy between reality and fiction becomes even more striking in light of the autobiographical elements Falkner has inserted in the story. It is more than just coincidence, for example, that Demar and the two Wallingford children, orphaned in their early adolescence, trek on foot from their hill-country home to find a long-lost uncle in Memphis, that Demar is later unjustly accused of murder, and that he is challenged to a duel that a certain "Colonel Calloway" works to prevent. Beyond doubt Falkner was dipping again and again into his own experience, yet the resulting novel seems anything but experiential or authentic by twentieth-century standards. Instead of the swashbuckling and at times tragic saga one might expect, we find what a reviewer for the *Memphis Sunday Appeal* in 1881 accurately characterized as "a beautiful story, charmingly told, and haloed with an atmosphere of purity and sweetness." How can this be explained?[19]

The answer, one suspects, lies in the Colonel's attempt to use the medium of literature to help cement his own self-made identity as a Victorian gentleman. What we find in *The White Rose of Memphis* is *not* pure fantasy or an unabashed indulgence in mythmaking but rather an attempt by the author to reshape his psyche and his world in terms of a cultural standard to which he fervently aspires. Falkner *wants* to become the even-tempered and polished Demar, who wins the angelic Lottie for his bride and whose obvious sincerity inspires trust and confidence in all who know him. In creating Demar and employing him as a narrator, he is in effect fashioning for himself a plausible Victorian persona that he can use to help convince himself—and his readers—that he has at last shed his frontier roughness and become what he most hopes to be. In this connection, it is highly revealing that Falkner, in assigning Demar a costume for the shipboard masquerade, drapes his alter ego not as Ivanhoe or an English king but as Ingomar, "the noble Barbarian Chief," whom the pure and lovely Parthenia had "subdued and tamed," leading him "with the rosy chain of love from the barbarian camp to the walks of civilization, converting a heartless savage into a fond and gentle lover."[20]

To underscore Demar's inherent virtue, Falkner provides a contrasting figure in Harry Wallingford—an essentially "good" person who initially lacks the requisite self-control. As Lottie laments, Harry may be "a dear, noble-hearted brother, but he never has put the curb on his temper—in fact, he never has tried to control his passions; and . . . no one can be happy who can't manage his passions." Wallingford's emotions flare up often, but never more flagrantly than when he mistakenly suspects Demar of cheating on Lottie. "Crazy with passion," he accuses his steadfast friend of stabbing him in the back and challenges Demar to a duel—exactly as Robert Hindman had done with William Falkner. Falkner sees to it, however, that the outcome in fiction is more in keeping with Victorian standards than was the case in real life, for Harry eventually comes to understand his sins and prostrates himself on the ground, begging God for help. The concluding pages of the novel disclose that this once "proud, passionate man of ungovernable temper" has turned into a gentle and eloquent preacher, converting hundreds to religion in the cities he visits. The moral lesson is transparent and the effective rewriting of history accomplished.[21]

Along with this emphasis on gentlemanly self-control, Falkner's chief preoccupation in this book centers on the problem of ascertaining true identity. Almost every episode entails some form of disguise, deception, or false accusation; almost every dramatic crisis hinges on whether those individuals whose selves are sincere and pure can triumph over those whose personalities are in some way counterfeit. The novel's key moments come when actual identities are revealed—when the mask of a scoundrel is stripped off, or when the innocence of a sincere person is affirmed. The clearest instance of this occurs at the conclusion of the prolonged masquerade ball aboard the *White Rose* that Falkner employs as a device for framing his narrative. Enchanted by the opportunity to dress up as royalty and aristocracy, the passengers decide to keep their disguises on while "Ingomar" tells his tale, but they are forced to end these "innocent amusements" when the demonic Ben Bowles sneaks into their midst, decked out appropriately as Napoleon, and begins literally to pick their pockets. In the novel's climactic scene, the masks finally come off, and the real identities—of gentleman and confidence man, respectively—are made manifest.[22]

The other major instance of false identity in the book involves Viola Bramford, who is accused of poisoning her little brother to avoid sharing her parents' estate with him. Despite her outward appearance of sweetness and beauty, evidence begins to pile up suggesting that Viola had all along been the secret mistress of Ben Bowles, visiting him often at night and exchanging notes with him to plan the murder. "Could it be," asks Demar, "that she who looked like the very embodiment of purity was the horrible thing that I blush to think of?" Or as the lawyer Hogjaw puts it, "It is horrible to think that such a beautiful creature could be so cruel! It will make me suspect everyone!" Her essential innocence, however, is dramatically reaffirmed at her trial when it becomes clear that it had been Viola's wicked stepmother who had perpetrated the dastardly deed in the hope of securing the Bramford family fortune and who had disguised herself by borrowing Viola's dress for her liaisons with Bowles. In this manner, true identities are again discovered—Viola's virtue shines forth more brightly than ever, while the stepmother, overcome with remorse, ends her own life, though not before leaving behind a full confession blaming her downfall on her pernicious "love of display."[23]

The outcome serves to underscore a primary assumption of the culture Falkner was trying to assimilate. The Victorians believed—or at least wanted to believe—that each person's character was essentially fixed and that outward appearance and behavior were sure signs of it. Since beauty, truth, and innocence all proceeded from the same source, one should be able to tell at a glance who was pure and who was not. The trouble, of course, was that those who were impure, either out of weakness or sheer viciousness, kept hiding their actual selves, creating a situation in which one needed to "suspect everyone" to an extent. But, as *The White Rose of Memphis* recurrently shows, Victorians had no doubt that those falsifying their appearances would in time betray themselves. Beauty and gentleness, if genuine, would always correspond to inner worth, while ugliness, slovenliness, and rudeness would just as surely signify evil. When one encountered a man whose "offensive scent of mean whiskey and tobacco pervaded the atmosphere for ten feet in every direction from his filthy body," as does Demar, one could safely presume him a sadistic "ruffian."[24]

The social implications here are both obvious and powerful. As Karen Halttunen has skillfully demonstrated, the reason nineteenth-century middle-class Americans developed this obsession with sincerity and its outward signification is that they lived in such a comparatively fluid social situation. Fortunes were rising and falling at a rate previously unknown, with the result that status often became uncertain, and individuals were forced to create new selves to match their new circumstances. In this situation in which all seemed to be changing, it is little wonder that people put such a premium on consistency and trustworthiness. Especially if they had recently risen from rags to riches themselves, it was supremely comforting, and often a psychological necessity, for them to believe that status and moral worth would always coincide, that both ultimately reflected inborn character—and that their newly acquired genteel stature was thus thoroughly deserved. Just below the surface in such persons it was usually possible to find, in Halttunen's words, "the secret conviction that, like the jackdaw in Aesop's fable, they were simply strutting around in borrowed peacock's feathers." No one, of course, illustrates these tendencies better than that classic self-made man of the South, Colonel William C. Falkner.[25]

That is why in Falkner's fiction, and in Victorian society generally, people considered sincere and therefore "good" were those who stayed in their "rightful" social places, while those deemed insincere were usually guilty of pretending to a higher status than was properly theirs. A "confidence man" like Bowles was feared so much precisely because he symbolized the dangers of excessive ambition and temptation that so many Americans of that day were experiencing as they looked out upon their social order. Accordingly, it was essential for them to believe that such dangerous overreaching would always be visible in the form of inappropriate behavior or bad taste, no matter what efforts the person took to hide it. Though Bowles dresses in a style that is "fashionable, faultless, and eminently exquisite," the careful observer still "could see an indescribable something" indicating "that Satan had sealed him as his own property." Perhaps it was the large and flashy diamond pin that Bowles wore, or "the gaudy rings on his fingers," or his "very glossy" and "richly perfumed" hair. One might be equally inclined to suspect the bona fides of Miss Jemima Tadpoddle, a minor villain in the story, who, among other things, "had as much paint on her face as a Commanche chief would have used in three months while on the war-path." [26]*

The world of Falkner's fiction is prototypically Victorian (and thus differs from that of his great-grandson) in one other crucial respect: it is controlled by a benevolent deity who ensures that all stories have a happy and moral ending. "The hand of a kind Providence seems to have guided our destinies," declares Harry Wallingford in the concluding chapter, summing up with understatement a major theme of the book. Throughout the text, references appear to a "mysterious influence" that bolsters the resolve of Falkner's heroes, warns them of troubles ahead, and sees to it that they are in the right place at the right time. The same providential spirit makes certain that villains are fully punished, that those of pure character

---

*One fascinating exception to the rule that all must remain within their initial social stations is the detective Zip Dabbs, whose occupation requires him to be able to transcend class lines in a flash in order to mingle with and spy on the evildoers at the bottom of society. "I have seen him spading in a garden, in an old red flannel shirt, the hottest day of the summer season," a friend tells Demar, "and at night, dressed with exquisite taste, making the most melodious music on the piano." But for Dabbs, switching identities is done professionally and almost clinically, rather than as a result of social pretension on his own part—he has "reduced the art of disguising to a perfect science." One senses that Falkner himself deeply coveted this skill. The practice of moving effortlessly from an old flannel shirt to "exquisite" gentlemanly attire could also be found, of course, in his great-grandson, who, as a Modernist, sought deliberately to transcend the notion of a fixed identity. See Falkner, *White Rose of Memphis*, 158, 160.

and high status reap well-deserved rewards of boundless prosperity, and that the worthy poor get their modicum of charity. At times the characters speak explicitly of a just and caring God; more often they and Falkner attribute events to a kindly "spirit" or "influence" or "fate." But in either case no doubt exists that the underlying pattern in human history is always discernibly moral.[27]

In keeping with this Victorian worldview, Falkner also assumes that the "soul" plays the dominant role in human psychology. Far from being the mere figure of speech that it would become in the twentieth century, the soul for Falkner represents nothing less than the center of a person's being—a spark of the divine that is capable of outliving the body and can "commune" directly with another's soul if two individuals are in love. In consequence, souls fly freely through this novel, including one dramatic scene when Lottie's comes to visit Edward and Harry on a train as they are rushing to her bedside when she is gravely ill. Falkner is in fact so intent on maintaining his spiritualist beliefs in the face of mounting attacks on them from naturalistic science that he has Edward write Lottie a brief disquisition on the subject while pursuing his medical studies in Philadelphia:

> Scientists assert that the brain is the dome of thought; but if it is so, I must say that the dome of thought is a very insignificant dome. No, it is the soul that dwells in the head, sitting back on its throne, that directs and moves everything. It is not dependent on this little lump of fat [i.e., the brain] for its existence, nor is it in any manner indebted to it for the thoughts that man produces. The soul sits on a throne in a man's head, and issues orders, like a king from his earthly throne; all parts of the body are moved by orders from the soul; just as great armies are moved by orders of the king. When the body falls into decay, the soul steps out uninjured and reports to its Creator for duty. Who made this incomprehensible thing called a soul? God.

Nothing, one suspects, could ever make William Falkner give up this intensely held belief in a fundamental dichotomy between body and soul, between the physical and spiritual realms.[28]

If the Colonel was determined to present himself as a man steeped in Victorian pieties, he was equally resolved in this novel to avoid any mention of the recent war in which he had so actively participated, save for a few short speeches in the standard New South mode concerning the need to forget politics and get on with the business of reunion. There was also a minor subplot, so typical of the literature of this period, in which the daughter of a northern carpetbagger is won over by a gallant southern Ivanhoe. "I [have] given my hand and heart to a (so called) rebel," she announces, "and I mean to show him that a Yankee heart can and will love him; and I wish all the people of the North and South loved each other as well as I love Ralleigh; what a great and glorious nation would ours be!" But other than these stock devices of the reconciliation novel, Falkner stayed notably clear of the intersectional conflict. Though the action takes place in Memphis during the late 1860s and 1870s, there is no mention whatever of Reconstruction.[29]

That would change dramatically in his next book. *The Little Brick Church*, a novel published in 1882 in the hope of building on the success of *The White Rose of Memphis*, follows the same sentimental romance formula as its predecessor, providing, in its author's description, "a plain, unvarnished tale with love for its foundation, truth for its walls, courage, virtue, honor and fidelity for its general finish." However, perhaps because his reputation had become reasonably well established, Falkner now felt free to vent, at least indirectly, some of his real attitudes toward the North. Using a venerable New York gentleman as his narrator and mouthpiece, he pins the chief blame for poisoning relations between the sections on northern slave traders during the colonial era who supposedly waxed rich by importing large numbers of Africans into the United States and selling them to unsuspecting southerners. "Consequently," Falkner's Yankee obligingly confesses, "we are more guilty than our brethren of the South." Southern planters, he explains, would always "treat their negroes with the tenderest humanity," while the typical northern trader would beat and starve his chattels for the pure pleasure of it. The great mystery, Falkner has his spokesman conclude, is how a just and moral Providence allowed the evil North to get away with it: "God permitted the people of Massachusetts to burn innocent women at the stake, and yet He did not kill them . . . He let them live and prosper. That State is one of the more wealthy and prosperous in the Union, yet we know that more bloody crimes have been committed on her soil than any other. God's great purpose has been accomplished."[30]

Why, Falkner seems to be asking, even pleading, did God not forgive the South its sins instead of visiting such terrible destruction on it? Despite his constant New South–style calls for harmony, the tone here is one of barely restrained anger toward and envy of his former enemy—mixed with deep-seated guilt about his own region's role and a sense of utter perplexity about the intentions of the Supreme Being that he conceived of as guiding human affairs. These were precisely the emotions, arising out of their Civil War experience, that southern writers of Falkner's generation sought with all their strength to suppress, but which their successors would inevitably need to face in making sense of their past.

The Colonel's final literary endeavor consisted of a series of travel letters sent to his hometown newspaper from Europe in 1883 and later published as a book. The trip itself was designed to capitalize on his new genteel persona—he had hoped to organize a touring party and serve as its guide to Old World culture, but in the end only two maiden schoolteachers were waiting in New York to embark with him and his daughter Effie. What they received, if *Rapid Ramblings in Europe* is any indication, was a quick-paced and highly moralistic introduction to the wonders of European civilization. Falkner took special pains to register his outrage over the sexual explicitness of so many of the artworks he saw (the statues in the Louvre required "a cart-load of fig-leaves") and at the "inhuman barbarity" of rulers such as Henry VIII and Bloody Queen Mary. His greatest scorn, however, was directed at the French medieval philosopher Peter Abelard for his seduction of young Héloïse.* "At the mature age of forty," Falkner explains, "when men of virtue and integrity are supposed to be able to subdue and control their evil passions, [Abelard] . . . did, like a savage wolf, destroy an innocent lamb." In this fashion, the Colonel was attempting to convince his readers—and, most important, himself—that no matter what had occurred in his flamboyant earlier years, *he* was now a gentleman in full command of *his* evil passions.[31]

But it was too late: in just a few more years he lay dying in the street, his mouth ripped apart by a bullet of vengeance, leaving to his great-grandson the awesome task of determining just who Colonel William Clark Falkner had really been and what meaning lay concealed in the piece of history he so dramatically came to symbolize.

*In his comments on Abelard, Falkner may have been mimicking Mark Twain's tongue-in-cheek description of the philosopher as "a dastardly seducer" and "unprincipled humbug" in *The Innocents Abroad*—the book on which *Rapid Ramblings* was modeled. If so, Falkner, in his own remarkable innocence, completely missed Twain's intended parody of American bourgeois moralism. See Twain, *Innocents Abroad*, 198, 193–94.

CHAPTER 2

Poplars and Peacocks, Nymphs and Fauns

The second William Falkner entered the world on September 25, 1897, in New Albany, Mississippi, a small town some fifteen miles south of Ripley where his father had recently taken up duties as passenger agent for the family railroad. Less than two years later, Murry Falkner became auditor and treasurer of the line, and the Falkners moved up to Ripley, but the arrangement did not last long. Claiming that he needed to put business considerations before all else, J. W. T. Falkner, who had inherited ownership of the Gulf and Chicago from the Old Colonel, sold it to a larger railroad in 1902 and effectively deprived his son of the one job Murry would ever find fulfilling. By all accounts, the effect on Murry's personality was devastating, leading him to retreat into passivity and depression for the rest of his life. That same year, almost exactly on William's fifth birthday, the family made its final move to the university town of Oxford. It was there, with his grandfather solidly established as a lawyer and politician and his father soon regarded as a ne'er-do-well, that the future novelist grew up.[1]

His early childhood was happy and normal for the most part, though marred by growing tension between his dissimilar parents. A large, handsome, and muscular man, Murry also tended to be inarticulate and emotionally withdrawn. After losing the railroad, and with it his dreams, he sought refuge in outdoor activities such as hunting and camping and in the livery stable he owned for a time. His pleasures came from training his horses and dogs and from the rough comradeship, heavy drinking, and profanity he shared with his hunting companions. To Maud Butler Falkner, however, nothing could have appealed less than such masculine crudity. A tough-minded, austere woman, as tiny and delicate in her build as her husband was tall and robust, she was determined to make her home a model of Victorian refinement and to prevent her four sons from acquiring their father's frontier manners and lack of ambition. Just before she died, she asked William to assure her that she would not have to see her husband in heaven, explaining, "I never did like him." William for his part appears to have tried hard to avoid taking sides in the conflict, though his small build and artistic temperament almost inevitably led him to identify more with his mother. He did, however, share his father's love of the outdoors, and if their relationship was distant and difficult at times, it was not notably hostile.[2]

Although he attended the Oxford public schools through the tenth grade, most of his education took place outside its walls. Later in life, when asked his advice on the best preparation for becoming a writer, Faulkner would invariably reply: "Read, read read. Read everything—trash, classics, good and bad, and see how they do it. Just like a carpenter who works as an apprentice and studies the master. Read! You'll absorb it. Then write." In his case that regime of omnivorous reading began under the tutelage of his mother and maternal grandmother, who introduced him to classic children's literature, including Grimm's fairy tales, *Robinson Crusoe*, Stevenson's *Treasure Island*, *Uncle Remus*, and in time the novels of Dickens and Cooper. Both women were also talented amateur painters who taught him to draw and endowed him with an enthusiasm for the visual arts that would play a larger role in his literary development than has often been appreciated. By the fifth or sixth grade William began exploring his grandfather's library, discovering Dumas, Scott, and the other nineteenth-century romantics. At home, meanwhile, he was happily devouring Kipling, Twain, Poe, Voltaire, Conrad, Balzac, Shakespeare, and, by the eighth grade, his particular favorite, Melville's *Moby Dick*. "It's one of the best books ever written," he reportedly told one of his brothers at the time.[3]

It was also during this period of early adolescence that a distinct personality change began to occur. Where previously he had been an attentive, if quiet, child in school, he now increasingly drifted off into his own dreamworld or played hooky. He would often be found sitting motionless in front of the courthouse or in his father's livery stable listening to older men of the town swap tales and memories. According to innumerable accounts, he seemed to be observing everything, though invariably he said nothing. As time went on, Faulkner developed these traits into a virtual art form in which he would remain silent, seemingly oblivious and perfectly still no matter what the distraction for hours at a time. "He rarely moves," an astonished visitor would later remark. "Everything about the way he holds himself is stately and sedate, composed and motionless—almost to an inhuman extent." People in Oxford, of course, did not see this behavior as impressive; rather, they concluded from it that young Billy was exhibiting the same shiftlessness they associated with his father.[4]

What they failed to realize—and what Faulkner likely was not yet aware of himself—was that this constant drinking in of sights, sounds, and experiences was as vital a part of his education as his reading. The stories and gossip fast accumulating in his head represented a veritable oral history of his community and, by extension, his region. An acquaintance from those early years recalls how he would stop before Faulkner on the square and wave a hand "up and down in front of his eyes, with never a sign of recognition or anger, or anything else." Years afterward the friend came to understand exactly what Faulkner had been doing: "The bootleggers, the moonshiners, the half-beaten-to-death wives and the half-starved children born without benefit of clergy or resulting from incestuous passion were all around the square. There, Bill would stand from early morning until dark, looking them over, so as to file them away in his mind against the day when they would be needed." That treasure trove of literary material was supplemented by the black folklore acquired in the cabin of Callie Barr, his black mammy, and the accounts of Confederate heroism he heard from his paternal grandfather. The elder Falkner, who had taken on the full trappings of the traditional southern gentleman, delighted especially in regaling his young visitor with the military exploits of the Old Colonel, even permitting the boy to handle relics that the great man had left behind. Thus everywhere he went, in every niche of his society, William Faulkner looked and listened and learned.[5]

Although these were valuable years for Faulkner, they were also difficult ones. As he continued to withdraw from the community and act strangely, other adolescents predictably began to taunt him. The fact that he was so short—only five feet, five inches when full grown—and immature in appearance did not help. Nor did the canvas vest that his mother insisted on strapping him into for two years so that he would learn, as Minter puts it, "to walk as his great-grandfather was said to have walked, with his head high and his back rod-straight." That posture, along with his tendency to ape his grandfather's penchant for fancy and formal clothes, soon led to the pejorative nickname of "Count." Faulkner responded in turn with still more aloofness and, as he got older, with the defense mechanism unfortunately bequeathed to him by his male forebears—heavy drinking. Although he managed to maintain some of his older friendships, the only person who seemed fully to understand him, aside from his mother, was his childhood playmate and adolescent sweetheart, Estelle Oldham. Petite, lively, intelligent, and attractive, she shared his appreciation of things artistic, though she also enjoyed the conventional social whirl. But even this relationship was clouded: her parents, who ranked among the more prosperous families in Oxford, were determined that their daughter would marry someone of wealth and stature. Faulkner's own mounting sense of inferiority likewise began to come between them, to the point where he would stand alone and silent at dances while other boys competed for Estelle. Her departure for college in 1913 only added to his isolation.[6]

The following year, however, a new and highly influential companion entered Faulkner's life. Though Philip Avery Stone was destined to fulfill his family's expectations by becoming a lawyer, one senses that his interests and temperament were far better suited to a professor of English. Four years older than Faulkner, he had returned from his senior year at Yale in 1914 steeped in literary studies and with a library that ranged from ancient classics to the latest Modernist masters. Firmly persuaded of his young friend's talent and eager to assume the role of literary mentor, Stone proceeded to loan Faulkner books, encourage him to write poetry, and convey to him the essence of a Yale education. Their conversations over the following decade would cover not only literature but philosophy, history, and politics as well. As it happened, Stone took special pride in his knowledge of the Civil War and saw to it that his protégé read extensively in the primary and secondary accounts of that era. He was also fascinated by the recent rise of "redneck" politicians in Mississippi—a development that, as a self-identified aristocrat, he strongly opposed—and made sure that Faulkner kept his eye on this and other ways in which southern society was starting to change. Through these perpetual discussions with Stone, Faulkner rapidly began to extend, deepen, and better comprehend that store of observations he had long been gathering. Beyond that, receiving such support from someone who could fathom and appreciate him at a time when few others did must have seemed a gift from heaven.[7]

Estelle Oldham in 1913, at the time that she and William Faulkner were constant adolescent companions. (Courtesy Mississippi Collection, John Davis Williams Library, University of Mississippi)

Stone's most crucial contribution to Faulkner's development was surely the sweeping introduction he provided to Modernist culture. Through Stone's guidance, Faulkner encountered the major poets of the late nineteenth and early twentieth centuries, beginning with the French symbolists and continuing through Swinburne, Housman, the imagists, Yeats, Aiken, Pound, and Eliot. Stone's holdings included not only the published work of these writers but also a wide variety of "little magazines," such as *Poetry*, the *Little Review*, the *Egoist*, and the *Dial*, filled with the most recent experimental verse. Thus it was that the young William Faulkner, who up to that time had spent his whole existence in Oxford and its environs, was able to read T. S. Eliot's "The Love Song of J. Alfred Prufrock" when it first appeared in *Poetry* in 1915. Though his own taste ran strongly to verse, and more often to Victorian than to contemporary writing, Stone encouraged his pupil to savor the novels of Hardy, Tolstoy, Dostoyevski, Dreiser, and Anderson, among others, as well as excerpts from James Joyce's *Ulysses* published in the *Little Review* between 1918 and 1920. He also loaned and sometimes gave Faulkner treatises on aesthetics, criticism, philosophy, and psychology—Henri Bergson's *Creative Evolution*, Stone reports, "seemed to interest him" especially, along with such influential works of the postwar era as Ludwig Lewisohn's *A Modern Book of Criticisms*, Elie Faure's *History of Art*, and James Harvey Robinson's *The Mind in the Making*. In sum, the future creator of Yoknapatawpha may not have read every important post-Victorian and early Modernist work in print during his youth, but, thanks to Stone and to his own lifelong habit of voracious book buying that began at this time, he had probably read as much as any other writer of his generation, and possibly more. How he would assimilate the cosmopolitan imperatives of this new culture to the rural southern world he inhabited remained to be seen.[8]

His first efforts to transcend that familiar world were not auspicious. Following his romantic inclinations and deep-seated desire to match the swashbuckling exploits of his namesake, Faulkner tried to enlist as a pilot as soon as the United States entered the First World War, but he found himself rejected because of his weight and height. The blow was doubly cruel because it came in the wake of Estelle Oldham's engagement to another man. Though she offered to elope with him, Faulkner insisted on having her family's consent first. Perhaps he sensed that he was simply not ready for marriage, or perhaps his intuition was sending him prescient danger signals that having Estelle as a wife would prove far different from having her as a childhood sweetheart. Whatever the case, he chose to stand by while her new husband carried her off to Hawaii. By April 1918, when the wedding took place, Faulkner was in New Haven living with Phil Stone, who had returned to Yale for a law degree. There he perfected his British manners and accent for an attempt to join the Royal Air Force in Canada, even going to the extent of inventing a false British lineage for himself and inserting a *u* in his surname (presumably because he believed it would make it look more British).* If he could not have Estelle, he told himself, he could at least gain glory fighting with a branch of the elite RAF. Once again, however, luck was not on his side: though accepted into a pilot training program in Toronto, Faulkner never saw action and most likely did not even fly a plane. As he later wrote of a young cadet in *Soldiers' Pay*, "they had stopped the war on him." After nine months away, Faulkner returned to Oxford in December 1918, defeated in all his high ambitions.[9]

Appearances, however, were soon employed to compensate for a disappointing reality. Dressed in an expensive new RAF officer's uniform that he was not actually entitled to wear, Faulkner stepped off the train with a swagger stick and a limp. For years he would tell stories of how he had crashed his plane—either behind Allied lines in France, or into a hangar on a joy ride during his training—and of how he had to wear a silver plate in his skull as a result. The accounts varied with his audience and mood. An all too credulous Sherwood Anderson, for example, would describe Faulkner in a 1924 sketch as "a cripple" with a "slight limp" and a "look of pain that occasionally drifted across his face." Although initially rejected for war service because of his size, Anderson noted, relying on what Faulkner had told him, "after he got in he turned out to be a first rate

---

*Much confusion exists about the timing and significance of this change in the spelling of his surname. In his biography of Faulkner, for instance, Frederick R. Karl at one point deems the change "of great significance," since "it was Faulkner's way of moving outside history and establishing himself without the weight of any immediate historical past." Later in his text, however, after observing how Faulkner went back and forth for several years on whether or not to include the *u* (which in turn accounts for the difficulty scholars have had in pinpointing the date of the change), Karl concludes: "For Faulkner, the name change had been slight, and since it was slight, we cannot judge how meaningful it was for him to shift." In fact, Karl may ironically be correct twice. Back in 1918, when the *u* first made its appearance, it probably did not indicate any noteworthy transformation in Faulkner's conception of himself, but by the mid-1920s, when he started using it consistently, it almost certainly served within his mind as a means of both denoting his new identity as a prose author and separating himself by just the right amount from the Old Colonel and his family's past—allowing him, one might say, to be a Falkner but also to be Faulkner. See Karl, *William Faulkner*, 18, 146.

flyer, serving all through the war with a British flying squadron" until he "got into a crash and fell." Despite having two legs broken ("one of them in three places") and a badly injured head, Faulkner, according to Anderson's report, bravely eschewed medical treatment. " 'When I got better,' " he quotes Faulkner as saying, " 'I faked, said the nerves of my leg didn't hurt, said the nerves up in my face didn't hurt. It was a lie of course. The nerves of my leg and of my face have never quit hurting. I guess maybe, if I had told the truth, they might have fixed me up all right.' " The most remarkable thing about this persona of the wounded pilot is that Faulkner seems at times to have fully believed in it himself.[10]

Indeed, that persona was only one of many that he periodically tried on during the next several years as he entered what appears to have been a classic "identity crisis." As children grow up, Erik H. Erikson tells us, they automatically identify with "part aspects" of people whom they admire or come into contact with, especially their parents, other role models, and ideal figures they seek to emulate. To a certain extent these various identity fragments will fit together easily and complement each other; to a certain extent they are bound to clash. The task that besets young adults is precisely one of selecting the most meaningful fragments and coalescing them into a "workable identity" that will provide a sense of "inner sameness and continuity" throughout adult life. For those raised in stable traditional cultures, this process can be relatively easy: "ready-made" identities, so to speak, are always at hand. But in a fast-changing environment like that of the early twentieth century, and especially for an individual like Faulkner with ties to more than one culture, the complications may become serious — leading either to the eventual creation of a new personal identity or to a disabling state of "identity confusion" in which the individual never finally ascertains just who he or she is.[11]

For Faulkner, the immediate postwar era was marked precisely by this sort of uncertainty. Assuming a variety of roles, he was capable of presenting himself to the world as anything at any time. Now he was the heroic aviator in a sharply pressed blue uniform and British-style clipped moustache, strutting about Oxford with his nose in the air. Now he was the shiftless son of a once prominent family carousing in the streets with the town drunk. Now he was the sociable 1920s college student, neatly dressed, actively involved with his fraternity, contributing to the student newspaper and yearbook, and avidly playing golf in his spare time. Now he was the sartorial Falkner, taking dandyism to excess and earning from his fellow students the still more disdainful title "Count No-Count." And,

Faulkner in his "Count No-Count" persona, posing with the members of the American Expeditionary Force Club at the University of Mississippi in the early 1920s. The cigarette holder and sideways glance (while everyone else in the group looks at the camera) bespeak his effort to be different. (Courtesy Mississippi Collection, John Davis Williams Library, University of Mississippi)

finally, now he was the bohemian artist, unshaven, in the shabbiest clothes, often barefoot, wandering about the town or countryside oblivious to his surroundings. Enrolled as a special student at the University of Mississippi for a year, he took a genuine interest in his French literature courses, ignored the others, and skipped all examinations. He would regularly attend proms and formal dances, though always alone, save for the bottle of corn whiskey he proceeded to consume. It was also at this time, Blotner notes, that he commenced a pattern of "alternation between home and away" in which he "would indulge his taste for roaming and then return to his base," sojourning in Memphis, in New Orleans, or on the Mississippi Gulf Coast but coming back to Oxford. Altogether it was for Faulkner a period of searching, experimenting, and exploring, of deciding which possibilities he would need to pursue and which he would have to foreclose.[12]

The same held true in his art. Faulkner had started writing poetry seriously in 1914 about the time he met Phil Stone; now, after his return from Canada, he embarked on a course of imitating the techniques and imagery of other poets — trying on, as it were, literary role models in an attempt to fashion his own artistic identity. Scholars have uncovered a host of such "echoes" and borrowings in Faulkner's verse, primarily from fin de siècle figures like Swinburne and Housman but also with particular frequency from T. S. Eliot. At times Faulkner would simply translate the work of one of the French symbolists, adding to it his own embellishments. On other occasions he would seek to replicate the world-weary tone of Swinburne, or expand on a particular trope from Keats, or even appropriate whole lines, as in this patent reworking of Eliot's "Prufrock":

> Let us go then; you and I, while evening grows
> And a delicate violet thins the rose
> That stains the sky;

One thing is true of all these experiments: eclectic though they may be, the poems avoid all reference to Faulkner's own familiar world, language, and fund of experience. "Instead of the blue hills of North Mississippi," Cleanth Brooks points out, "there are wolds, leas, and downs. On these downs grow heath and gorse and may. The cottages have thatched roofs." In short, the frame of reference was still very much British and Victorian. It was as if Faulkner, like the Old Colonel before him, assumed that local materials could not qualify as "literary."[13]

The dominant sensibility in this verse is likewise late Victorian to post-Victorian. The early Modernist poets he had read in *Poetry* and the

Little Review may have intrigued him, but what served his needs best at this time was the gentle probing against the boundaries of Victorian restraint carried on by the late-nineteenth-century symbolists and decadents. Writers such as Verlaine, Swinburne, and Wilde had managed to explore sexuality and other forbidden emotions while still keeping them at arm's length through indirection and allusion. Their chief device for doing so had been the use of figures from classical mythology, especially fauns, nymphs, and satyrs, who were by definition part human and part animal and whose playful antics in a sylvan landscape retained a sense of innocence that would not have been the case had full-fledged human beings been involved. For these artists, Ilse Dusoir Lind explains, "the faun expressed delicacy and grace combined with an erotic freedom, a spontaneity of sexual feeling, which Victorian mores did not allow." Moreover, the eroticism in their work was always carefully sublimated—it stood not for sexual passion per se but for some higher aesthetic purpose, some transcendent form of beauty far beyond mortal experience. In this way, fin de siècle writers could gain a measure of liberation without threatening the nineteenth-century moral values to which they still adhered.[14]

This sensibility can readily be seen in Faulkner's major poetic work, *The Marble Faun*, written in the spring of 1919 but not published until 1924. Its title figure, an ornamental statue of a faun in a formal garden, is awakened to a desire for "wild ecstasy" by the coming of spring but at the same time is unable, as H. Edward Richardson puts it, to escape his marble bonds and "know the animality of life." The faun may dream of finding an ideal woman, but it remains wholly unclear whether he really *wants* to become a sensual being or whether he in fact prefers to experience life solely through his imagination. Sexuality itself he perceives as an "unclean heated thing," enticing but also highly repulsive. In the end, the faun finds consolation in his immortality and cool, peaceful silence:

> Why cannot we always be
> Left steeped in this immensity
> Of softly stirring peaceful gray
> That follows on the dying day?

Clearly the faun's dilemma represents a projection of Faulkner's own, with the marble bonds symbolizing the Victorian repression that he both did and did not wish to overcome. Minter's description of the faun holds as well for the young poet who could so often be found motionless as a statue: "Sentenced to sitting and peering, to brooding and yearning, . . .

[the faun] is sad beyond measure, not only for things dreamed and missed, but also because he cannot understand the forces that constrain him." [15]

Thus commenced the first skirmish in the lifelong battle that was to take place within Faulkner's psyche. A part of him would always want to give vent to his own intense passions and to pursue the insights about human nature he had discovered in his reading, grappling directly with the moral questions posed by the animal component of the human personality. Another part of him, at first the more powerful because it was associated with his mother and other early childhood influences, was determined to block such explorations and preserve the nineteenth-century cultural ideals of purity and innocence. The early poetry, then, can best be seen as a series of tentative forays into forbidden territory armed with symbolist techniques but with his Victorian moral compass still firmly in hand. What was drawing him ever so hesitantly into that terra incognita, in time leading to his embrace of Modernist culture, was precisely the desire to escape that repression—to stop being a marble faun.[16]

Most notable among those forays are the poems in which Faulkner gingerly experimented with the subtle methods devised by the symbolists for conveying sensuality. In "A Poplar," for example, the slim tree, quivering in a slight breeze, is meant to suggest a nymph or dryad alive with sexual expectation:

> You are a young girl
> Trembling in the throes of ecstatic modesty
> A white objective girl
> Whose clothing has been forcibly taken away from her.

In many respects the key words in this passage are "white" and "objective," with their connotations of purity, distancing, and emotional neutrality. Likewise the oxymoron "ecstatic modesty" helps to preserve the necessary veneer of innocence (as, in a different way, does the modifier "forcibly")—while at the same time paradoxically rendering the erotic element more tantalizing. What does not appear in any form is true passion or emotion, with all the moral complication it might raise. Rather, the poem remains on a level that is allusive, stylized, and therefore, from Faulkner's vantage point, safe.[17]

Even more stylized, and also more explicitly sexual, is the verse play *Marionettes*, written in the fall of 1920 for a student drama group with which Faulkner was associated at Ole Miss, though never actually performed. Its plot is minimal and predominantly static: the curtain opens on the drunken harlequin Pierrot asleep at a small table on one side of a formal garden, complete with pool and fountain, two symmetrical poplar trees, a marble colonnade, a peacock, and a cold white moon above. Pierrot, a common figure in Faulkner's verse, was, as Judith L. Sensibar notes, "the darling of the Symbolists and early Modernists," representing for them a symbol of art, dissolution, and sensuality as safely removed from reality as was the more classical faun. The sleeping Pierrot dreams that the youthful virgin Marietta enters the garden wearing a white robe. Her outward movements are as controlled and mannered as the garden itself, while inside she is burning with repressed desire. His songs—or rather, those of his "Shade"—entrance her with "moon madness," allowing him first to seduce and then to abandon her. The dream—and play—concludes with Marietta, no longer dressed in white and wearing long jade fingernails, returning to an autumnal garden to stare narcissistically at her reflection in the pool, meditating on how she, too, will soon age and die.[18]

Accompanying the text in the six copies that Faulkner handcrafted was a series of pen-and-ink drawings that, according to Faulkner's friend Ben Wasson, caused many in the community to view the work as "salacious." Done in the style of Aubrey Beardsley, whose famous illustrations of Oscar Wilde's *Salome* were widely regarded as the epitome of English decadence, they included one full-page study of Marietta seated between two peacocks with both breasts exposed that could not help but cause a stir in Oxford—a reaction Faulkner doubtless both anticipated and relished. Even so, the fact remains that the eroticism in *Marionettes* does not exhibit the outright lasciviousness and morbidity found in that of the decadents but rather seems extraordinarily subtle and tame. Faulkner's figures "were chaste and often austere," Blotner notes, "very different from Beardsley's combinations of the sinister and beautiful."[19]

Sexuality in and of itself was not Faulkner's chief concern. Rather, as Gary Lee Stonum astutely points out, it was employed here primarily as "a metaphor for something beyond itself"—for an ecstasy and passion beyond human flesh, partaking of a timeless beauty transcending all earthly experience. In keeping with the symbolist tradition, the purpose of *Marionettes*—and of most of Faulkner's other verse as well—was to enable the reader to escape mundane reality and enter a dreamlike poetic landscape where such absolute beauty might be found. To be sure, that spiritual ideal could never be apprehended directly; it could be known only through an aching sense of its absence, by the symbolic hints one found in the setting or the graceful actions of the poetic characters—though as time went on it would increasingly find embodiment in the image (never the reality) of a young girl or nymph seen from afar and pursued in vain, as in prose sketches such as "Nympholepsy." The aim of such exercises was not to plumb the depths of experience or make the reader aware of the endless complexities of reality, as would be the case in genuine twentieth-century Modernism. Rather, this "visionary aesthetic," as Stonum calls it, was based on the fin de siècle assumption that art was far superior to experience, existing primarily to put us in contact, however momentarily, with a "higher" realm that could elevate and inspire.[20]

This quest for a transcendent ideal posed one insurmountable difficulty, however. Since the quest could, by definition, have no resolution, not even a proximate one, each poetic work necessarily reached the same basic impasse. Faulkner, Stonum explains, came again and again to the point where "the absent ideal" was found to be unreachable, whereupon his central figure either renounced all desire in the manner of the marble faun or sought some form of oblivion through death or sleep. A clear example is Marietta's narcissistic self-absorption with her image in the pool in apparent preparation for drowning herself. The only way Faulkner could conclude his visionary search was through some form of "eternal stillness" in which the yearning for transcendent beauty and ecstasy finally ceases to exist.[21]

One can take this analysis a step further and add to it a cultural dimension by observing how the ideal vision governing Faulkner's poetic work involved not only aesthetics but moral innocence as well. The "transcendent realm" that Faulkner tried repeatedly to realize, writes Stonum, is a place "from which all worldliness and impurity have been purged," where "no ache of longing can arise." Faulkner's favorite symbol for this ideal in his poems soon became a nymphlike girl filled with pure and unquenchable innocence:

> You are so young. And frankly you believe
> This world, this darkened street, this shadowed wall
> Are bright with beauty you passionately know
> Cannot fade nor cool nor die at all.

Faulkner, in short, remained captive to many of the same Victorian values that had come to dominate his great-grandfather's imagination. The vision that had given rise to the angelic Lottie Wallingford was still very much alive for him, reinforced by the imposing presence of his mother, who, Sensibar suggests, was likely the model for the unattainable ideal

woman of his verse. To be sure, forces welling up inside him were pushing him toward challenging the ascendancy of that vision. But it was clear
that he would not be able to mount that challenge so long as his psyche remained locked in a romantic poetic realm amid the poplars and peacocks
— which was why, for the moment, he was keeping it safely locked there.[22]

In retrospect, one can see that Faulkner's career as a poet ended in 1921,
though he would not fully realize it for a few more years. Not only was
most of the verse that would appear in *The Marble Faun* already written
by that time, but nearly all of the additional poems that he would publish,
including those that ultimately filled *A Green Bough* in 1933, now existed
in provisional form. From this point on he would mainly tinker and revise, with some slight improvement in his technical skill in writing verse
and with growing frustration over the impasse his work seemed to have
reached. One can, in fact, date the peak of his poetic efforts quite exactly
to May 1921, when he presented an eighty-eight-page booklet of his best
(and most romantic) works entitled *Vision in Spring* to Estelle, who was
home for a visit. In the course of that work, Faulkner struggled hard to
get out from behind the Pierrot mask he had adopted as a poet, at certain
points going so far as to mock his symbolist persona for seeking to live
in a world of dreams that, Faulkner had now begun to realize, was bound
to lead to solipsism and artistic sterility. But there was no resolution: if
the Pierrot of some of the later poems is drawn to put aside the idealized
female figures of his fantasy in favor of a true sexual relationship with a
real woman, he still falls short of acting on his desires. *Vision*, in Sensibar's
words, may have represented Faulkner's "bid for independence from his
mother's exclusive love and her values," but he was not yet ready to break
free. To outgrow Pierrot, he would need a new literary medium.[23]

Faulkner spent the next four years continuing his wide reading in past
and contemporary masters and searching for an identity that would allow
him simultaneously to survive in his everyday world and to function as
a writer. Somehow, for reasons he sensed but did not yet comprehend,
Oxford was necessary to him. An attempt in late 1921 to take up residence
in Greenwich Village in the hope of making his presence known in literary circles ended after a few months, despite a well-paying job at a bookstore that he seemed to enjoy. There is no clear evidence as to why he
returned home in December of that year, save that Phil Stone, worried by
reports of heavy drinking and little writing, had decided to lure him from

the temptations of Gotham by arranging a sinecure as Oxford's postmaster. One suspects, though, that Faulkner himself had good reasons for the move—that he knew at some level that marshaling and structuring the psychic resources for a literary career would be difficult enough for him in Mississippi but impossible in a strange and demanding urban environment such as New York.[24]

Oxford was less demanding but still required ingenuity. His strategy at this time, he wrote a few years later, was to keep his personality "completely and smoothly veneered with surface insincerity" in order "to support intact my personal integrity." That meant the usual medley of role-playing, as well as maintaining, as one friend put it, his "ability to lose himself in his own private world." Frequently he would seem to retreat into obliviousness for hours, either wandering through the woods, or sitting on the floor of Mac Reed's drugstore absorbed in a magazine "unconscious of anybody's presence at all," or drinking alone in his room. He also continued to collect observations. Reed recalls a 1924 trip to a nearby town that he and Faulkner made on a political errand for one of Faulkner's uncles: "Pretty soon he would be out on the street, looking over the town, looking at the traffic, watching the movements of the people, not talking with anybody." In general, these were melancholic years for Faulkner: an acquaintance remembers him as "wrapped in despair" with "a dark, depressed outlook." But he did not live in unhappiness and isolation all the time. His relationship with Stone persisted, though with Faulkner increasingly restless in the role of pupil. He played baseball with his brothers in a church league, joined in some social activities with contemporaries, enjoyed discussing politics and current events with friends, and served as a highly successful scoutmaster until fired because of his reputation for heavy drinking.[25]

One can gather some idea of what was taking place in his mind during this period through the occasional prose pieces he published, first in the *Mississippian*, and later in the New Orleans *Double Dealer*. Though often filled with confusion and posturing, they reveal in rough fashion where things stood between the two cultures battling inside him. On the one hand, his nineteenth-century sensibility manifests itself in constant complaints concerning "the mental puberty of contemporary American versifiers" who spend their time "sobbing over the middle west" rather than attempting to transcend everyday life and create the kind of otherworldly poetic realm aspired to in his own work. Repeatedly he chides poets such as Carl Sandburg for excessive realism—Sandburg, he fears, would relish nothing more than the chance to take a beautiful poetic drama and set it "in the stock yards, to be acted, of a Saturday afternoon, by the Beef Butchers' Union," while Amy Lowell would stage it amid "broken glass." To Faulkner in the early 1920s, the failure of such present-day American writers to seek transcendent spiritual truth proved how provincial, backward, and unaspiring they were in comparison with the great European masters. "Is not there among us someone who can write something beautiful and passionate and sad instead of saddening?" he asked.[26]

On the other hand, one can detect signs of an emerging Modernist sensibility in these essays. Alongside his bitter complaint of how the United States can claim "no drama or literature worth the name, and hence no tradition," he suggests that American writers possess compensating advantages in the "earthy strength" of the country's language and the abundance of folk cultures with which the nation is endowed. In comparison with American language, "British" seems to him "a Sunday night affair of bread and milk—melodious but slightly tiresome nightingales in a formal clipped hedge." The remark, quite possibly inspired by his discovery of H. L. Mencken's *The American Language*, is, of course, all the more revealing because his own literary imagination to date had been dwelling in that very world of nightingales and formal clipped hedges. Moreover, he insists, for those willing to look in the right places America could supply "an inexhaustible fund of dramatic material" as yet virtually unexploited. "Two sources occur to any one: the old Mississippi river days, and the romantic growth of the railroads," but the only person to have tackled either was Mark Twain, "a hack writer who would not have been considered fourth rate in Europe." These two subjects, one might quickly note, were for Faulkner inextricably linked with the Old Colonel. That was apparently enough to lift them above the threadbare realm of realism and render them "literary," as distinct from Sandburg's grubby stockyards.[27]

At times one even finds a direct critique of the post-Victorian literary mentality, as if Faulkner were taking aim at that part of himself still bound to the nineteenth century. Fellow Mississippi poet William Alexander Percy might display a "passionate adoration of beauty" in his verse and thus escape the censure aimed at Sandburg, but, "like alas! how many of us," he was a man hopelessly "born out of his time" who "should have lived in Victorian England." To Faulkner, Percy seemed a victim of his own romantic illusion, "like a little boy closing his eyes against the dark of modernity which threatens the bright simplicity and the colorful romantic pageantry of the middle ages with which his eyes are full."[28]

In December 1922, he launched a similar attack on that epitome of the post-Victorian American novelist Joseph Hergesheimer, then at the height of his considerable national reputation. Although impressed with the beauty of *Linda Condon*, Faulkner did not consider it a true novel. Rather, it was "more like a lovely Byzantine frieze: a few unforgettable figures in silent arrested motion, forever beyond the reach of time and troubling the heart like music." The trouble, he thought, lay in the fact that Hergesheimer seemed "afraid of living, of man in his sorry clay braving chance and circumstance." "His people are never actuated from within," wrote the author of *The Marionettes*; "they do not create life about them; they are like puppets assuming graceful but meaningless postures in answer to the author's compulsions." With transparent disdain, Faulkner advised Hergesheimer to "spend his time, if he must write, describing trees or marble fountains" instead of human beings—a remark that suggests the growing impatience with which the Modernist part of Faulkner looked upon the works of William Faulkner the fin de siècle poet.[29]

In 1925 came the eruption: forces gathering inside for more than a decade finally burst into the open, releasing the marble faun from his imprisonment. The ostensible catalyst was the loss of his postmaster's job after three years of continuous and justified complaints from patrons. With no further reason to stay in Oxford, he set off for Europe by way of New Orleans and put himself in contact with influences that would help cement his commitment to the new culture that had become established there. Of particular importance was the copy of Joyce's *Ulysses* that he would purchase while abroad. Faulkner, one suspects, had not really known how to respond to Modernist poetry—witness the fact that his early 1920s criticism makes no mention whatsoever of figures such as Pound or Eliot, though he had certainly read them and even on occasion imitated them. But with *Ulysses* he had the example of a Modernist novel that spoke to so many of the dilemmas, artistic and personal, that he was currently wrestling with and that thus gave him access to the new culture in a way that poetry had not.[30]

To be sure, he had shown considerable interest in A. E. Housman's stoic acceptance of an amoral and indifferent universe, which he had for a time believed was "the secret after which the moderns course." But Faulkner's understanding of that new and terrible universe, at least in early 1925, was still filtered (as was Housman's) through fin de siècle eyes that saw only heroism and beauty: "Here was reason for being born into a fantastic world: discovering the splendor of fortitude, the beauty of being of the soil like a tree about which fools might howl and which winds of disillusion and death and despair might strip, leaving it bleak, without bitterness, beautiful in sadness." The courageous endurance of suffering in a world that didn't care could indeed be construed as romantic and splendid so long as it was viewed from the outside; that way it was possible to avoid taking notice of the torment—the pain, disillusionment, and sense of betrayal—going on within the mind. Preserving that externalist perspective, and arming themselves with stoicism, was precisely the tactic that post-Victorians like Housman had devised to be able to accept the new universe that Darwin had decreed yet still shield themselves from its tragic implications. But though Faulkner initially also found that tactic comforting, his emerging Modernist self would not be fully satisfied without probing deeply into the psyche—for, as we shall see, he was to be an inhabitant not only of the post-Darwinian but of the post-Freudian era as well. And for that task Joyce's masterpiece, with its stream-of-consciousness technique, proved a revelation.[31]

Another godsend appearing at this time was Sherwood Anderson. The author of *Winesburg, Ohio*, who had recently moved to New Orleans, recognized Faulkner's talent immediately and took a special and protective interest in him. He was fascinated not only by the tales of Faulkner's war experiences but also by the extraordinary family history that the young man proceeded to invent, complete with an aristocratic great-grandfather who had come over from England to make his fortune and a degenerate present generation that had let the once massive plantation go to seed. Throughout the spring of 1925 the two would usually meet in early afternoon and spend the rest of the day talking and drinking. They might wander about the French Quarter, visit the docks or racetrack, stop in on members of the literary coterie built around the *Double Dealer*, or simply sit in Anderson's living room swapping tall tales and conversing about the craft of fiction. Typically Anderson would do most of the talking, while Faulkner would adopt his preferred role of listener and observer.[32]

For the most part, Anderson's effect on his young disciple was to hasten and confirm tendencies already present. The interest Faulkner had registered back in 1922 in the literary use of American language and subject matter was now greatly amplified by Anderson's insistence on rejecting European models. It was time, Anderson felt, to abjure copses and glades, stilted diction, and mannered narrative techniques in favor of straightforward stories of real people told in everyday language. Even more important, Anderson helped convince Faulkner not only that the South could fall within the ambit of this newly liberated American literature but that it possessed some invaluable materials. Until this juncture in his career Faulkner, like so many other ambitious southerners, had been extremely careful to avoid being labeled a provincial or regional figure; his poetry was almost invariably set in either a European or mythic landscape, and his criticism likewise attempted to intimate that it had been written by a young man of the world. The identity of a southern author had not seemed available to him. But Anderson, with his belief that modern American fiction had to be rooted in specific localities, changed all that. Which locality didn't matter, Faulkner later remembered his saying, "just so you remember it and ain't ashamed of it. Because one place to start from is just as important as any other." As for the South, Anderson told him, "It's America too . . . as little and unknown as it is." That was exactly the advice that Faulkner wished to hear and was primed to act on.[33]

Anderson also helped to enhance the Modernist in Faulkner. Although in retrospect his own work appears restrained and even a little prudish, Anderson in 1925, Wittenberg informs us, "was regarded as a writer whose innovative style and honest probings of sexuality and the subconscious had opened new frontiers for young Americans then beginning to write." In this fashion, Anderson's example strongly reinforced that of Joyce. Moreover, Anderson shared the Modernist tendency toward cultural primitivism. With his poor, rural background and lack of formal education, he had little desire to perpetuate genteel manners, high culture, and bourgeois civilization. Rather, he valued the lives and culture of ordinary people precisely because he saw in them, in Thadious M. Davis's words, "an elemental connection with the earth, with their own feelings and emotions"—a connectedness that deeply appealed to his Modernist desire for wholeness and integration. Blacks held a particular attraction for him because of "what Anderson thought of as the Negro's mystical qualities—intuitive sensitivity to man's innermost life and instinctive perception of human nature." This view of black culture was the basis for his *Dark Laughter*, the novel he and Faulkner researched together in early 1925 through visits to black workplaces and neighborhoods in New Orleans.[34]

Another important influence at this crucial moment in Faulkner's development was William Spratling, a painter and instructor in architecture at Tulane whose French Quarter apartment Faulkner shared for a time. Thoroughly steeped in contemporary art, Spratling was happy to enhance his roommate's knowledge and appreciation of Modernism, performing a function akin to that of Phil Stone in literature. Through Spratling

Faulkner met other young artists such as Caroline Durieux and listened avidly as they debated aesthetics. In an interview years later with Panthea Broughton, Durieux specifically recalled "that Faulkner seemed to consume modernism" during these months. Spratling may have helped in another way. Since childhood Faulkner had toyed with the possibility of becoming a painter, in part because it was his mother's chief ambition for him. One of the main motives for his New York stay in 1921 had been to take courses in drawing in the hope of earning a living as a commercial artist and perhaps doing some serious painting as well. But now, with Spratling's talent before him, he grudgingly realized that his future lay exclusively with literature. Spratling's hand, he wrote, "has been shaped to a brush as mine has (alas!) not." The admission doubtless hurt, for in the hierarchy then existing in his mind he continued, thanks to his mother, to assign first place to the graphic arts, with poetry second and fiction a distant third.[35]

The results of these various influences first became manifest in a series of local-color sketches written for the *New Orleans Times-Picayune* Sunday feature page. Although clearly apprentice work, with too many overwritten passages, contrived plots, and unabashed borrowings from writers such as Anderson and O. Henry, these pieces nonetheless indicate where Faulkner was headed as a writer of prose. They contain his initial attempts to transcribe consciousness by means of interior monologues, to relate the same event through multiple perspectives, and to juxtapose the realistic and symbolic, the prosaic and poetic—all Modernist literary techniques that would become staples of his mature fiction, allowing him to escape that sense of stasis that had bedeviled him as a poet. They also show his growing belief in a universe governed entirely by chance where the only thing a person could count on was change and impermanence, as well as a newfound willingness to puncture rather than celebrate romantic ideals. Instead of peacocks, fountains, and shapely poplars, the world he depicts is filled with people going about their normal, daily business of physical and psychological survival.[36]

Perhaps most significant, one finds in these sketches Faulkner's first experiments with what would soon be a dominant feature of his novels—the dramatic reversal of social and racial stereotypes. Nothing, it seemed, delighted him more than turning conventional perceptions inside out, exploding widely held myths, images, and identities in an effort to establish more complex and authentic ones in their place. In this he was again typically Modernist. Faulkner would shortly turn this mode of perception with scorching intensity on the established social identities of the South and in so doing would make an enormous contribution to revising the region's image of itself. In his New Orleans sketches, one finds him polishing this technique by focusing on the gangsters, racetrack touts, poor blacks, and other social outcasts who inhabited the French Quarter.

Most successful in this respect was "Sunset," which begins with a sensationalized newspaper account of a "black desperado" who had "terrorized" a small town, killing three men, before being machine-gunned to death by the National Guard. We soon learn, however, that this apparent madman, far from fitting the popular stereotype of the savage black criminal, is in fact a simple sharecropper, almost childlike in his innocence, who has left the plantation he had worked on all his life in the hope of returning "home" to Africa. An unscrupulous white boat captain in New Orleans promises to take him there but instead puts him ashore just before nightfall at a Cajun farm. Afraid and bewildered in this strange environment, he is convinced that a farm animal approaching him in the dark must be a lion and shoots it. When the local farmers come after him, speaking their Cajun dialect, he assumes they are cannibals and once more reacts violently in self-defense. "Af'ica sho' ain't no place for civilized folks," Faulkner has the poor man complain, reversing the nineteenth-century presumption of whites as civilized and blacks as savage.[37]

"Sunset" ends with a hail of machine-gun bullets, which the protagonist in his delirium thinks is just a strong wind: "And he, too, was a tree caught in that same wind: he felt the dull blows of it, and the rivening of himself into tattered and broken leaves." The imagery is identical to that Faulkner had employed to describe the "splendor" of stoic fortitude in Housman, except that here we have access to the victim's thoughts and thus to much of the tragedy and injustice of his situation. Instead of protecting us (and himself) from feeling that injustice by having us view the incident solely from the outside in the mode of post-Victorian stoicism, Faulkner has sought to engage our passions by underscoring the vast discrepancy between the protagonist's real intentions and society's treatment of him. In the final paragraph of the story we are reminded once more of the terrible indifference of the cosmos, but instead of finding it all "beautiful in sadness" we are moved to both outrage and pity: "His black, kind, dull, once-cheerful face was turned up to the sky and the cold, cold stars. Africa or Louisiana: what care they?" Faulkner was indeed slowly learning "the secret after which the moderns course."[38]

Experimenting with new perspectives was relatively easy when writing sketches; a far better gauge of the difficulties Faulkner encountered in acquiring a Modernist sensibility is *Soldiers' Pay*, the novel he wrote with Anderson's encouragement between February and May 1925. Although filled with up-to-date literary techniques borrowed from Joyce, Eliot, Woolf, Anderson, and Conrad in a self-conscious effort to appear modern, the novel is still essentially post-Victorian in its basic orientation, with A. E. Housman perhaps the strongest influence. Alongside all the structural and stylistic indicators of cultural rebellion, observes Andre Bleikasten, "one . . . senses Faulkner's persistent fidelity to the mannerisms of *fin-de-siècle* literature, and the proximity of his poetic past," suggesting his equal desire to regress to the security of the Victorian world. From the standpoint of intellectual biography, then, *Soldiers' Pay* appears a strikingly mixed performance—one that often looks back toward the romanticism of his poetry but also clearly indicates his developing talents as a writer of Modernist fiction.[39]

For the most part, the characters in the novel can be divided into two categories: those who have in some fashion directly experienced the recent war, and those who have not. The former include Lieutenant Donald Mahon, an RAF pilot with a mortal head wound who has returned to his hometown of Charlestown, Georgia, to die. Also enrolled among the initiated are Joe Gilligan, the soldier who helps Mahon get home and decides to remain with him, and Margaret Powers, the young war widow who joins them. These three, along with the other returned veterans, have learned at first hand the terrible realities of human existence and as a result have been shorn once and for all of youthful romanticism. They are, like Mahon, "young, yet old as the world," having discovered the hard way that, as Gilligan puts it, "old nature does too much of a wholesale business" ever to care about the plight of individuals. From this knowledge they have acquired a maturity and solidity of character that sets them apart from the rest of their contemporaries. They are "veterans" in the fullest sense of the word. That, Gilligan explains, is why they do not come to visit Mahon or express sympathy over his wounds: "They just kind of call the whole thing off. He just had hard luck and watcher going to do about it? is the way they figure. Some didn't and some did, the way they think of it." "It's a rotten old world, Joe," Margaret declares, and only a thick coat of stoic armor, it would seem, can protect the individual against it.[40]

Those without the benefit of this lesson from the war are doomed to perpetual immaturity and innocence. The foremost example is Cadet Julian Lowe, who, like Faulkner himself, had wanted to be a dashing aviator but never got beyond training camp. Despite his yearning for adult masculinity, he has missed his chance to grow up and so remains a hopeless romantic and a "child" in Margaret's eyes. "As if it were not enough to have wings and a scar," Lowe thinks in his naive envy of Mahon, "but to die." By contrast, Joe and Margaret instantly dismiss "all the old bunk about knights of the air and the romance of battle." Save for the veterans, most of the remaining characters fall into the same category as Lowe. Faulkner saves his special scorn for Cecily Saunders, the flighty girl, "graceful and insincere as a French sonnet," whom Mahon had been engaged to marry, and her circle of overindulged male admirers who had not been old enough to fight. "The boy's ironed face," Faulkner writes with obvious relish of Cecily's Princeton-educated dancing partner, "was a fretted fatuity above his immaculate linen." Self-centered, spoiled, and vacuous, these "jelly-beans" remain deprived of the truths that consume the veterans; to them the world is not "rotten" but a plaything designed solely for their delight.[41]

The book's central theme concerns the way civilian society proceeds to ignore both the veterans and the fateful knowledge they have acquired. To be sure, there is some temporary fuss made over them, but for the most part they quickly become, as Margaret puts it, "the hang-over of warfare in a society tired of warfare." To get a girl's attention during the war a young man needed a uniform, and preferably pilot's wings, but now, in Gilligan's broken English, "uniforms and being wounded ain't only not stylish no more, but it is troublesome." At a dance in Charlestown mounted in their honor the veterans sit alone on a porch railing, conversing among themselves about experiences they alone can understand, while "the agile, prancing youth" on the dance floor treat them with blithe disregard. Having fought bravely and brought back vital knowledge along with their wounds, the soldiers' effective "pay" is to be cast into social and spiritual isolation.[42]

Though Faulkner clearly sides with the veterans against the jellybeans, his depiction of the contrast between the two groups is frequently marked by a most revealing confusion. On the one hand, he is at pains to praise the veterans for their existential encounter with the realities of life and resulting stoic outlook, which he believed to be the essence of being "modern." On the other hand, he cannot help underscoring how outmoded, "provincial," and even innocent their sexual beliefs seem in comparison with those of the jazz age youth. As everyone in the 1920s was aware, mores for the young, especially those in college, had changed drastically right after the war to accommodate the open expression of sensuality in music, dancing, and fashions—a change marking the first major inroad of Modernist values into American popular culture. But to Faulkner's veterans, this new behavior was nothing less than scandalous. "Look at them two: look where he's got his hand," Gilligan bursts out in shock during the dance scene. "This is what they call polite dancing, is it?" "Say the girls don't like it, do they?" another veteran asks. "They haven't changed that much, you know." The nineteenth-century moralism the veterans cling to, Faulkner informs us, had "become inexplicably obsolete over night," rendering the hapless former soldiers "eternal country boys of one national mental state." But if that was so, which of these two groups so continuously contrasted in *Soldiers' Pay* should in fact be considered the more "modern" and which the more sheltered and innocent? Faulkner didn't know.[43]

Faulkner's puzzlement and hesitation about the cultural transition then under way within both his society and his own mind is also apparent in his treatment of Donald Mahon's father, who clearly symbolizes the old culture. At times almost a caricature of the traditional Victorian divine, the Reverend Joseph Mahon spends most of his time in the rectory garden tending his roses and illusions. "I have never been able to do anything well save to raise flowers," he confesses. Although his actual faith has long since given way to agnostic doubt, this warm-hearted and jovial Episcopal minister has continued to observe the empty forms of his religion, maintaining an attitude of innocent optimism regardless of circumstances. His preference if possible is to pretend away the existence of evil or unpleasantness: when visitors engage in blasphemy, blatant insincerity, or sexual misconduct in his presence, he either fails to notice or chides them gently. Given this approach to life, he could not be worse prepared for his son's tragic return. Steadfastly he ignores the evidence when Donald goes blind; repeatedly he insists that Donald will soon recover; with all his energies he attempts to bring about the wedding between Donald and Cecily based on the illusory belief that Cecily herself wants it. At times it seems as if the rector, living in his Victorian dreamworld, has ironically lost more of his ability to perceive reality than has his sightless son.[44]

What is most intriguing is Faulkner's own attitude toward this representative of the nineteenth-century worldview. Though keenly aware of the rector's limitations, Faulkner resists the temptation of making him a fool, as Sinclair Lewis would likely have done, and instead regards him with a compassion that grows, as the novel proceeds, into something approaching admiration. He sees to it that Margaret Powers and Joe Gilligan, although diehard realists themselves, immediately recognize the rector's vulnerability and seek to protect him in his illusions. "Why not let him believe as he wishes as long as he can?" Margaret suggests. Aware that Reverend Mahon will need support to survive his ordeal, they remain in Charlestown after delivering Donald home. However, that decision, one comes to suspect, may involve more than just pity: they may in fact need him as much as he needs them. No matter how obsolete he appears, the rector symbolizes the culture that they—and Faulkner—grew up with but that the war has supposedly forced them to reject. For all their newfound stoicism, they retain a strong underlying affection for the rector's world and do not want to give up the remnant of security it offers. That is why Faulkner has Gilligan move in with the rector at the novel's end: as the dialogue between them makes clear, it is now the older man's turn to provide solace.[45]

The problem, once again, lay in Faulkner's conception of post-Victorian stoicism as the "secret after which the moderns course." Though it might help block the pain of incomprehensible tragedy in a universe now regarded as meaningless, stoicism did so at the price of suppressing a person's whole emotional life—a fact that put it directly at odds with the basic tenets of Modernist culture as found in writers such as Proust or Joyce. Such is the case with Margaret Powers, who is ridden with guilt over the way her husband, "tricked by a wanton Fate," died in France believing that she loved him just before her letter arrived informing him that she did not. "Rotten luck. That's exactly what it was, what everything is. Even sorrow is a fake now," she tells Joe. Her tough, stoic exterior allows her to manage the events leading up to Donald's death in a way that clearly marks her as the strongest and most noble figure in the novel. Yet Faulkner leaves no doubt that Margaret is a deeply damaged woman incapable of making lasting emotional commitments. "Am I cold by nature," she asks herself, "or have I spent all my emotional coppers, that I don't seem to feel things like others?" The prospect of continuing to live in an anesthetized state deeply troubles her: "Can nothing at all move me again? Nothing to desire? Nothing to stir me, save pity?" But there seems no choice. She has become another of the war's many victims, stranded in a spiritual wasteland with no escape in sight.[46]

In time Faulkner would address this contemporary crisis of the spirit through Modernist means, searching for a solution within the psyche, but not in *Soldiers' Pay*. To be sure, he does acknowledge through the Reverend Mr. Mahon that the Victorian God has failed:

> "Circumstance moves in marvellous ways, Joe."
> "I thought you'd a said God, reverend."
> "God is circumstance, Joe. God is in this life. We know nothing about the next. That will take care of itself in good time."

Still, Faulkner's desire for an unimpeded transcendent faith—in his words, "the longing of mankind for a Oneness with Something, somewhere"—persisted. But where could such a faith be found? In the novel's concluding scene we are given an answer. Mahon and Gilligan stand transfixed, listening as the spirituals emanating from a rural black church "swelled to an ecstasy, taking the white man's words as readily as it took his remote God and made a personal Father of Him." Faulkner ends his book with these two men, representing the fading old culture and the stoic, tough-minded new one, both trapped in the symbolic "dust" of mortality while envying the blacks their moment of glorious transcendence:

> They stood together in the dust, the rector in his shapeless black, and Gilligan in his new hard serge, listening, seeing the shabby church become beautiful with mellow longing, passionate and sad. Then the singing died, fading away along the mooned lane inevitable with to-morrow and sweat, with sex and death and damnation; and they turned townward under the moon, feeling dust in their shoes.

Fervently Faulkner hoped that whites like himself might somehow regain the capacity for transcendence and be able to surmount that mundane realm of "sweat" and "sex" and "death" to which post-Darwinian naturalism seemed to relegate them. It was a yearning that would never really leave him.[47]

Further evidence of Faulkner's continuing attachment to nineteenth-century culture appears in his handling of sexuality in *Soldiers' Pay*. Once again he resorts to figures from classical mythology—fauns, nymphs, and satyrs—to distance himself from materials he still perceived as dangerous. Thus the inordinate sexual appetite that Donald Mahon possessed before being wounded is exorcised by giving him, in Duane J. MacMillan's phrase, "the innocence and innate purity of a faun." When he and his devoted friend Emmy, who is clearly typed as a wood nymph, make love by a stream in the moonlight, there is no hint of erotic passion; rather, their liaison is a natural, spontaneous encounter between two wild creatures who can no more be held accountable to moral standards than animals in the forest. With his "wild, soft eyes" and "serenity," the prewar Mahon exudes an almost childlike playfulness and love of life; even his service as a fighter pilot becomes a kind of game for him. He is, in fact, an embodiment of the faunlike sexual hero of the symbolists — sensual and robust yet pure, gentle, honest, and gallant.[48]

Mahon achieves this remarkable feat of maintaining sensuality without corruption by virtue of his selflessness. There is no troublesome ego, no heavy burden of consciousness weighing him down, with the result that he can literally soar up to the sky. Becoming a pilot merely gives concrete form to his spiritual state. He cannot be "soiled" because he lives in a transcendent realm liberated from time and space, far from the contamination of the earth below. "When he looks at you," Emmy recounts, describing their lovemaking, "you feel like a bird, kind of: like you was going swooping right away from the ground or something." There was, of course, no way that Faulkner, working within the naturalistic constraints of a modern novel, could realize this semimythical figure as a flesh-and-blood character. That is why Mahon is present only as a living corpse that has returned from France and why the few glimpses we get of his earlier self come indirectly, primarily through the recollections provided by Emmy and others.[49]

Contrasting sharply with the transcendent Mahon is the corpulent Januarius Jones, a lascivious "fat satyr" whose eyes are not soft and wild but rather "clear and yellow, obscene and old in sin as a goat's." A college Latin teacher who happens to wander into the rector's garden just before Donald arrives home, Jones plays no significant role in the novel except to serve as a spiritual counter to Mahon. Where Mahon is selfless and devoid of desire, Jones is irredeemably self-centered and obsessed with carnal pleasures, particularly food and sex. Where Mahon felt imprisoned within the walls of a schoolroom, much preferring to wander the woods by himself and read avidly on his own, the classicist Jones is steeped in formal and pedantic learning, with a mind more imitative than original — an "aped intelligence imposed on an innate viciousness." Where Mahon soars as an aviator, Jones is repeatedly portrayed as "a worm." More broadly, where Mahon's experience represents a heightened version of that vouchsafed to all the veterans, Jones's hedonism and self-centeredness are shared, on a lesser scale, by the other young men who missed the war. For them, sexuality, and indeed all natural instincts, have become self-conscious and calculated.[50]

The cultural implications again cut two ways. In a sense, Faulkner was reversing the traditional Victorian moral dichotomy by making an animal-like faun embody innocence and virtue, while employing a figure who at first glance appears learned and civilized to represent evil. To that extent Faulkner was clearly rebelling against the old culture. But in other important respects he still clung to it by continuing to insist on pure innocence as his moral standard. Thus in *Soldiers' Pay*, sex is portrayed as either immaculate or filthy; those engaging in it tend to be either radically selfless or narcissistic. The superiority of the innocent, or ethereal, type of sexuality is never in doubt. Even the wretched Jones gets temporarily caught up in a moment of "chaste Platonic nympholepsy" during his pursuit of Cecily Saunders (a tall, slim girl repeatedly associated with poplar trees) and seeks not her body but union with her spirit. "Do you know how falcons make love?" he asks her. "They embrace at an enormous height and fall locked, beak to beak, plunging: an unbearable ecstasy. While we have got to assume all sorts of ludicrous postures, knowing our own sweat." This extraordinary piece of ornithologic fantasy suggests how compelling the ideal of transcendent sexuality still was for Faulkner in 1925.[51]

The falcon imagery also underscores the crucial autobiographical dimensions of the novel once we recall that Faulkner's family name was originally spelled "Falconer" in Scotland. Used frequently in reference to Donald Mahon, who, with his small hands and delicate features, clearly resembles the author who created him, the imagery suggests that Mahon ("Man" as a southerner would pronounce it) is a projection of Faulkner's idealized post-Victorian self—a self that could fulfill the nineteenth-century dream of detaching itself from the flesh, allowing it to soar like an eagle or falcon above common humanity embedded in the mortal "dust" below. That persona, as Faulkner construed it, contained within itself many desirable (and paradoxical) traits, including a faunlike ability to live outside the norms of society in total harmony with nature yet still be well regarded by the community, to seduce women at will but with consummate romance and moral purity, and to engage in masculine military heroics of the first order yet remain essentially gentle and playful. This was the mythic identity of a true "Falkner"—superior, graced with uninhibited motion, yet unquestionably humane and above all innocent. It was the very essence of the southern Cavalier identity bequeathed by the Old Colonel as William Faulkner understood and hoped to incorporate it.[52]

By contrast, Julian Lowe, the callow cadet who never learned to fly, was close to what Faulkner suspected was his actual self, while Jones, the lecherous worm, represented the self he secretly feared he might become. For the fact remains that Faulkner at age twenty-eight was not in reality a gallant war hero or lover but rather a short, slight, shabby, and remarkably unprepossessing social failure with no achievements to his name save for a volume of third-rate poetry brought out by a vanity press and no visible financial future. His childhood sweetheart had married another man, and his conquests of women appear to have been limited to occasional visits to whorehouses in the company of Phil Stone, with Faulkner spending the evening conversing with the "girls" in the parlor and resolutely refusing their entreaties to go upstairs. Far from being a natural faun who swam naked with girls in moonlit pools and spontaneously made love to them, Faulkner, one senses, was beset by a distinct prudery, an inner repression bottling up what was obviously a passionate nature and intense sexual drive. Years later Faulkner would comment on how a young writer inevitably writes about himself "perhaps as he presumes himself to be, maybe [as] he hopes himself to be, or maybe as he hates himself for being." This was precisely what he did in *Soldiers' Pay*, rendering his romantic falcon-like identity the moral victor, while scourging what he saw as his "baser" and less controllable instincts in the persona of Jones.[53]

The crux of Faulkner's first attempt at fiction, then, was a transposition of his immediate experience, especially his failed struggles for romance and heroism. "What one . . . senses so often in *Soldiers' Pay*," notes Millgate, "is the presence of autobiography minimally transferred" in which consequently "the disguises tend to wear thin." Since the purpose of such transposition was to allow Faulkner to vindicate his battered ego, the resonance is more personal than cultural; literature is being used here more as a refuge or prop than a source of broad-gauged insight.* Despite all his yearning for transcendence, Faulkner had yet to learn the vital lesson of how to gain a stable point of external perspective that would enable his

---

*It was also being used to gain revenge on Estelle, who obviously served as the model for the vain and fickle Cecily Saunders. Although tall where Estelle was petite, Cecily as a provincial flapper with a "pretty shallow face" and love for dancing nonetheless closely matches the various accounts we have of Faulkner's temporarily lost love. The giveaway is Faulkner's ploy in making Cecily's family not Republicans like the Oldhams but Catholics—which, he explains, "was almost as sinful as being a Republican" in a southern town. Estelle Oldham Faulkner would later comment in an interview that she immediately recognized herself in Cecily and felt badly wounded by the portrait. See Faulkner, *Soldiers' Pay*, 67–68; Blotner, *Faulkner*, 1:409; Wittenberg, *Faulkner*, 47; Millgate, "Starting Out in the Twenties," 151–52.

artistic imagination to control his ego rather than letting the ego's narrow demands control his art. As he would come to realize, no skill was more essential for Modernist literature, which required an author to perform the delicate balancing act of seeking out experiential materials in his own consciousness and subconscious while still maintaining a high degree of objectivity.[54]

For Faulkner, that stable point of perspective would almost inevitably have to be the South, but there are only minor hints of a southern presence in *Soldiers' Pay*. Though the book is set in Charlestown, a fictitious locale in Georgia, Faulkner informs us that what takes place there could as easily occur "in any small southern town—or northern town, or western town, probably." The only character indelibly southern is Cecily Saunders; as Gilligan observes, "You wouldn't find her in Illinoy or Denver, hardly." Gilligan himself comes from Minnesota, Lowe from San Francisco, while the rector and his church, Millgate remarks, "could be in England almost as convincingly as in Georgia." Margaret Powers does hail from Alabama but with her hard-bitten stoicism is not identifiably southern in the least. Likewise, though the periodic descriptions of Charlestown make reference to its languid atmosphere and its abundance of mules and blacks, Faulkner is at pains to depict the town as typically American. In part this reflects his desire to avoid being labeled a mere regional writer—a widespread concern among aspiring young southerners embarking on literary careers in the mid-1920s. But one suspects another, more important motive that is implicit in the comment by one of his characters on the magnolia blossom, the South's traditional symbol. While beautiful if left alone, we are told, the flowers are "not good for anything if you pick 'em. Touch it, and it turns brown on you. Fades." To Faulkner at this point, the South appears to have existed more as myth than reality—a myth that was best left unexamined lest it fall to pieces.[55]

Also conspicuously absent in light of Faulkner's later work is the Old Colonel. Though Richardson and others are undoubtedly right in connecting Donald Mahon's martial exploits with those of the first William Falkner, it is true that this tale of a gallant warrior returning to his southern home makes no mention of Confederate heroism or hardships—as if the author had never heard of the events of the 1860s. Yet the Knight of the Black Plume was unquestionably present in the depths of Faulkner's mind, waiting for the chance to leap into daylight. We can find him lurking in the novel's descriptive passages, especially those having to do with railroads: "The locomotive appeared blackly at the curve, plumed with steam like a sinister squat knight and grew larger without seeming to progress." The modifiers "blackly" and "sinister" vividly convey some of the hidden feelings Faulkner harbored toward his illustrious ancestor, as does a later image of the train's engine as an "arrogant steel thing." Here was the subject William Faulkner really cared about—the one he would have to confront in order to connect his work to the South, place himself in history, and ascertain his true identity. But, as he may have sensed, he had not yet progressed far enough in his cultural journey to essay such a threatening task.[56]

CHAPTER 3

Fierce, Small, and
Impregnably Virginal

All aspiring American writers in the 1920s knew that they needed to go to Paris, and William Faulkner was no exception, for Paris was more than a good time, the 'moveable feast' that Hemingway and others celebrated. It was, during the first three decades of the twentieth century, the strategic center for the new historic culture that was then sweeping the arts and that would in time pervade every aspect of life in Western society, just as London had earlier served as headquarters of the Victorian world. Paris had been the birthplace of the Modernist sensibility during the latter half of the previous century, when its cafés, studios, and tolerant atmosphere helped nurture the symbolist school in poetry and impressionism in painting. By the start of the First World War, it had sheltered fauvism, cubism, expressionism, vorticism, and a host of other splinter movements through which the emerging culture gradually took shape. Hence, during the 1920s, those attracted to Modernism by exposure to its poems, novels, music, painting, or sculpture descended on France to commune with one another, absorb the new values, and—if they were American—denounce the pall of "Puritanism" that allegedly cloaked their native land.[1]

Faulkner, who arrived in Paris in August 1925, was certainly among those seeking to steep themselves in the new sensibility, but in several respects his pilgrimage to Europe differed from that of the bulk of his literary contemporaries. For one thing, his stay was much shorter than usual:

while most young American writers remained abroad at least two years, and more typically five, Faulkner came home after only four months. It is also striking that Faulkner did not proceed straight to Paris but instead ambled his way on foot across Italy, Switzerland, and the French country-side, stopping to live briefly in two peasant villages. His time in Paris, moreover, was punctuated by similar walking trips to the woods and farm areas. Not only did the calm and simple life of the rural folk impress him, but the landscape seemed to summon up in his mind vivid images of a heroic Cavalier past that he found immensely appealing. In the town of Pavia, he told his mother, he found "old, old walls and gates through which mailed knights once rode, and where men-at-arms scurried over cobble stones." Walking through a French forest on another occasion, he would "sit down and imagine [he] could hear horns, and dogs, and see huntsmen in green jackets galloping past, and then the king and his cavalcade in gold and purple and scarlet." Clearly this was not the same Europe that Fitzgerald and Hemingway had come to find.[2]

In Paris, Faulkner did behave more like a proper 1920s expatriate. He expressed a sharp distaste for rich American tourists, scoffed at "dull middle class very polite conventional people," rented a small flat on the Left Bank among "the working classes," wrote a poem "so modern that I dont know myself what it means," and even grew a beard. He also frequented the appropriate cafés, visited Sylvia Beach's famed bookstore, Shakespeare and Company, and enjoyed himself thoroughly riding buses around the town and sampling urban delights. He did not, however, take advantage of the abundant opportunities to make himself better known in literary circles—his ostensible reason for going to France. Other artists who flocked to the Left Bank during this period sought out fellow exiles for mutual support and valuable contacts, but Faulkner, shy and countrified, appears to have met no other writers, either famous or hopeful, even though he clearly wanted to. "I knew of Joyce," he recounted many years later, "and I would go to some effort to go to the café that he inhabited to look at him," but Faulkner apparently never attempted to speak to the novelist he so admired. Nor could he quite get up the nerve to stop in on Ezra Pound, though he had hiked many miles out of his way to the seaside resort of Rappollo where Pound was then living. Rather than pursue such figures, Faulkner seems characteristically to have spent much of his spare time sitting in the Luxembourg Gardens, observing the children sailing toy boats in a pool.[3]

To be sure, Faulkner did make the rounds of galleries and museums, and his reaction to what he saw was generally enthusiastic. Art indeed became the principal vehicle by which he imbibed Modernist aesthetics during his Paris stay. Nearly all the art of the previous half century intrigued him, with the impressionists and neo-impressionists his favorites. "I have spent afternoon after afternoon in the Louvre . . . and in the Luxembourg [Gallery]," he reported. "I have seen Rodin's museum, and 2 private collections of Matisse and Picasso . . . as well as numberless young and struggling moderns. And Cezanne! That man dipped his brush in light." Most appealing was the work of what he called "the more-or-less moderns, like Degas and Manet and Chavannes." His initial reaction to cubism was more ambiguous and his response to "a very very modernist exhibition" of futurist and vorticist paintings decidedly negative: "I was talking to a painter, a real one. He wont go to the [highly Modernist] exhibitions at all. He says its all right to paint the damn things, but as far as looking at them, he'd rather go to the Luxembourg gardens and watch the children sail their boats. And I agree with him."[4]

What occupied Faulkner most of all in Paris was his attempt to write a novel that would be unmistakably au courant. With Joyce's *Portrait of the Artist as a Young Man* as his obvious model, he commenced "Elmer" almost as soon as he arrived in the city, promising his mother that the book would be "a grand one," and by early September he had accumulated nearly one hundred pages of draft. "I think right now its awfully good," he declared in late August, "—[it's] so clear in my mind that I can hardly write fast enough." But "Elmer" would never be finished; as of mid-September the momentum began to ebb, and though Faulkner would dabble with the manuscript continuously until he left Europe, he could not salvage it. This failure to complete a work was unusual for him: "Elmer" would be the only literary fragment of substantial length that he left behind (though he later claimed there had been two additional book-length apprentice pieces he had destroyed).[5]

Despite its unfinished state, "Elmer" deserves careful attention for several reasons, among them the unmistakable fact that Faulkner was again engaged in spiritual autobiography. Clearly he was dipping into his own experience to create Elmer Hodge, an aspiring southern-born artist in his mid-twenties whom we first meet making his way to Paris aboard a freighter in order to soak up modern culture. Paris, Elmer thinks to himself, "that merry childish sophisticated cold-blooded dying city . . . where

Degas and Manet fought obscure points of color and line and love, . . . where Matisse and Picasso yet painted—all that he had wanted for so long, to permeate himself with becoming one in it." Faulkner did distance himself from Elmer in some respects—Elmer is a painter, not a writer; he comes from a lower-middle-class family with no distinguished forebears; and he is tall and awkward where Faulkner was small and graceful. But the resemblances are far more striking. Like Faulkner, Elmer prefers to be an observer rather than a participant, has a strong-willed mother and an ineffectual father, is beset by a difficult adolescence, and worships girls who are nymphlike and "epicene." Elmer even manages to miss active service during the war, though, badly wounded by a mishap with a hand grenade during training, he enjoys the luxury that Faulkner could only covet of being able genuinely to limp and complain of war injuries.[6]

"Elmer" is also noteworthy because of its extensive reliance on Freudian insights. Almost as if he had kept a textbook of psychoanalysis at his elbow, Faulkner has Elmer proceed through each of the various phases of sexual development that Freud had ordained. Nothing is omitted, including a brief bout of homoeroticism at age fourteen when Elmer falls in love with an older boy. At one point Faulkner even echoes Freud's speculation on how each individual recapitulates the various stages of human evolution. "A boy up to and through adolescence runs the gamut of civilization," he explains, "getting in brief fierce episodes the whole spiritual history of man." It is true that Faulkner would later deny vehemently that he knew anything about Freud: "What little of psychology I know the characters I have invented and playing poker have taught me. Freud I'm not familiar with." But the evidence in "Elmer" leaves no doubt that he had become very well acquainted with Freudian theory by the mid-1920s, though how he had gained that knowledge—through a direct reading of Freud, an acquaintance with other psychoanalytic writers, the influence of Conrad Aiken (one of Faulkner's favorite poets and critics whose work was steeped in Freud), or conversations with friends in the French Quarter—remains unclear.[7]

Perhaps the most intriguing aspect of "Elmer," however, is how astonishingly bad it is. Faulkner's intention, Thomas L. McHaney surmises, was to carry his stylistic experiments well beyond those of *Soldiers' Pay* and, so far as possible, "to translate the innovations of the Impressionist and post-Impressionist painters into literary form, as Gertrude Stein and Sherwood Anderson had done and as Ernest Hemingway was currently doing." But far from constituting artistic progress, this work marks a distinct regress.

The writing is amazingly clumsy for someone with Faulkner's gift for language, most of the symbolism seems contrived, and the author displays virtually no control over plot or characterization. Indeed, even allowing for the fact that it is a draft, anyone reading this disastrous text in 1925 unaware of his first book would surely have told Faulkner that he lacked the wherewithal to become a serious novelist. And yet, less than three years later he would complete *The Sound and the Fury*, one of the great masterpieces of twentieth-century literature, in what Panthea Reid Broughton aptly calls a "quantum leap from apprenticeship to mastery." The central problem that "Elmer" poses, then, is precisely one of accounting for the dramatic contrast between it and Faulkner's subsequent work.[8]

The vital clue for answering that question, one suspects, can be found in the stilted tone that pervades so much of "Elmer," as if the author could not quite bring himself to express what he was seeking to put down on paper. That halting quality assuredly did not stem from a lack of literary skill—*Soldiers' Pay*, after all, had been a model of smooth writing—but from a basic contradiction in objectives. On the one hand, in his effort to stay abreast of Joyce, Faulkner was determined to break with his earlier practice of viewing characters primarily from the outside. Bravely he attempted to journey inside his semiautobiographical hero's consciousness, watching Elmer toy with one piece of moral dynamite after the next, from phallic obsessions, incest, homosexuality, and bisexuality to extramarital affairs. On the other hand, alongside this endeavor to capture the deepest currents of Elmer's psyche ran an equally strong desire—indeed, compulsion—to depict Elmer Hodge as a young man of impeccable innocence. Thus Elmer, when engaged in various forms of perverse sexual behavior, does not display the shame or fear one would normally expect but instead a sort of wide-eyed wonder that he is doing such things or that other people might consider them strange. There is no hint of pathology, of any burning conflict between Elmer's burgeoning desires and the imperatives of his superego—in short, of the psychological themes Faulkner would explore so closely in his mature fiction. As a result, despite its potentially explosive nature the material falls curiously flat.

One sees this approach at work throughout the narrative of Elmer's development. For example, there is his intense fascination with phallic objects. An avid collector of cigar stubs as a child, Elmer becomes mesmerized during early adolescence by smoke stacks, tall vases, and "long tapering whips" on buggies. This obsession, however, is counteracted by his persistent detachment. He is at most an observer, a naive voyeur, who nevertheless vaguely senses how adults "were beginning to expect a certain propriety of conduct of him; that it was no longer permitted to stand before the windows of a hardware store and admire shining nickel joints and slim pipes at the end of which showerbath sprays bloomed like imperishable flowers." His countenance does cloud briefly when another boy, "becoming joyously physiological in the face of Elmer's abysmal innocence," tells him the facts of life. This new knowledge proves painful for a time: "Things that Elmer had heretofore accepted without question now had a terrible soiled significance: why there were different urinals for boys and girls . . . trees, light, his mother and father, his own body had become sinister, dirty." But by the next morning the sun "had made him clean again," and he was once more "charmingly uninterested in his body." For Elmer, "the world was still a continuous succession of happy astonishments, and all mankind including Elmer was admirable."[9]

Even when Elmer indulges in intimate relations with women, Faulkner continues to protect his surrogate by seeing to it that Elmer never initiates the affair. It is always a case of women chasing him: after resisting the efforts of a spinster teacher to seduce him, he loses his virginity to a neighboring farm girl who entices him into a hayloft. He is again lured into sex in Houston by a girl named Ethel, who goes on to marry a convenient local businessman after Elmer makes her pregnant. Through these and other adventures Elmer remains entirely passive, his life "a long blond corridor through which he passed comparatively untroubled." Although technically not a virgin, he is as guiltless as a child. But ironically, Elmer's own child is anything but guiltless. Meeting his five-year-old son for the first time, Elmer is shocked by what he sees: "in a devastating moment Elmer had a vision of it grown, . . . preying on women of all classes, probably diseased and spreading disease with glee." It is as if all the aggrandizing aspects of sexuality that Faulkner had carefully excluded from Elmer's character are suddenly projected onto the boy, catching Faulkner as much as Elmer by surprise. Significantly, Faulkner broke off the manuscript at this very passage.[10]

In this fashion "Elmer" reveals the state of Faulkner's cultural progress as of his stay in Paris. Oscillating between poking fun at his central character's naïveté and safeguarding Elmer's fragile innocence, Faulkner, one senses, was struggling to play the role of avant-garde expatriate author. Attempting a bold leap forward, in both a literary and cultural sense, he fell on his face. The setback would, of course, be only temporary; in a few years' time, he would travel far inside the mind of another "virgin" named

Quentin Compson, with extraordinary artistic results. In "Elmer," however, the Victorian part of his sensibility still managed to prevail, forcing him, as it were, to give his protagonist the prelapsarian moral character of a child rather than portraying him as a young adult with all the psychological complications typical of that stage of life. That is what ultimately rendered the book stillborn.[11]

Why, one might ask, did those residual nineteenth-century beliefs continue to hold such power over him, causing him to cling to the old standard of total purity at a time when he was plainly determined to explore the new vistas opened by Freud? The answer is bound up with the transcendent image of the "fierce proud Dianalike girl, small and dark and impregnably virginal" that dominated Faulkner's writing at this stage of his career and that also haunts the mind of young Elmer Hodge. This slim, chimerical creature, a descendant of the poplarlike "epicene" nymphs that gambol through his poetry, would continue to evolve within his fiction for several more years. After assuming the guise of Elmer's "fierce and dark and proud" older sister, Jo-Addie, she would appear as the "hard and sexless" Pat Robyn of *Mosquitoes*, the sisters-as-mother Narcissa Benbow of *Flags in the Dust* and Caddie Compson of *The Sound and the Fury*, and, finally, as the deceased mother Addie Bundren in *As I Lay Dying*. Two things are especially striking in this sequence: the way all the characters, in one form or another, take on maternal roles toward boys or young men, and the repetition of the disyllable "addie" in so many of the names. Those clues and others suggest that the source of the "Dianalike girl" was almost certainly Faulkner's small, dark-haired, and fiercely proud mother, who, Richard Gray informs us, "haunted the novelist just as his great-grandfather did" and whom he addressed during his youth as "Lady." So long as she was still hovering in her son's psyche, Maud Butler Falkner would prevent him from straying too far from the moral framework she had taught him and powerfully shape his treatment of sexuality and gender.[12]

We see this in the way the "Dianalike girl" functions as a mother substitute for Elmer and, ultimately, as his prime source of artistic creativity. He attaches himself to Jo-Addie, we are told, in an effort to recapture the oceanic sense of bliss he remembers from early infancy after his mother has emotionally rejected him. Why did Faulkner find it necessary to depose the real mother in favor of a sister, as he would do in many subsequent novels? The answer is that a sister figure is much safer from an Oedipal standpoint, especially if, like Jo-Addie, she has a flat chest, a bisexual name (she is sometimes called "Joe"), and a preference for coarse men's cloth-ing. With a figure so marginally female Elmer can pour out his affection without fear of Oedipal retribution. Nothing comforts him more than sleeping in the same bed with her, "the two of them like an island in a dark ocean," and periodically touching her body. Though the love here may be incestuous, it is nonetheless innocent, precisely because it is presexual. As Michael Zeitlin points out, the Jo-Addie to whom Elmer is emotionally attached (as opposed to the "real" Jo-Addie) is associated in his mind not with the usual physical markers of femininity but with that imagined "ma-ternal phallus" that little boys aged three and four assume their mother must possess before they become aware of actual anatomic sexual differ-ences. From Elmer's standpoint, then, their relationship is "safe" because it is not only non-Oedipal but also pre-Oedipal, harking back to that inti-mate, all-encompassing union that exists between mother and son in the first years of life.[13]

Elmer's love for Jo-Addie becomes transmuted into an interest in art when, having abruptly left home, she sends him a box of crayons as a part-ing present (echoing Maud Falkner's attempt to encourage William to take up drawing). Since the crayons have come from Jo-Addie, he immedi-ately invests them with phallic significance, but again, Faulkner makes it clear, they are phallic in the innocent, pre-Oedipal sense, not a true sexual one. That is why Elmer, instead of using them, prefers to keep them pris-tine, carefully preserving "their pointed symmetrical purity." The first set of oil paints he acquires as an adult is likewise associated with his sister and stays "unblemished," though he does enjoy fondling them in a kind of imaginary masturbation: "To finger lasciviously smooth dull silver tubes virgin yet at the same time pregnant, comfortably heavy to the palm— such an immaculate mating of bulk and weight that it were a shame to vio-late them." The symbolism is awkward, reflecting Faulkner's inexperience and great ambivalence about handling this subject matter, but the thrust is clear: art for Elmer proceeds from his yearning for his mother, which must always be kept free of contamination by remaining on the level of fantasy. In time he arrives at the perfect solution for achieving that objec-tive—enshrining his memory of Jo-Addie in his image of the "Dianalike girl" and consecrating his art to rendering that vision on canvas, just as Faulkner was to re-create Lady again and again in his fiction.[14]

To be sure, it was not Maud Falkner herself who caused that image to crystallize in Faulkner's mind in 1925, but a far younger woman who closely resembled her. That spring Faulkner had fallen into Platonic love with Helen Baird, a small, dark-haired, boyish, and beguiling girl whom he had met in New Orleans. The two had spent a fair amount of time together in June, sailing and talking in the coastal town of Pascagoula, where both her family and Phil Stone's had summer houses. Faulkner even proposed marriage to her, but once again his poor financial prospects stood in the way—along, apparently, with her suspicion that he was not so much in love with her as with some ideal vision he saw in her. Though she found him an intriguing companion, she apparently did not begin to regard him as suitable material for a husband. For his part Faulkner became increasingly entranced by what Wittenberg describes as Helen's "child-likeness"—and by the extent to which she seemed to replicate his mother in terms of physical appearance, artistic bent, and outspoken personality.[15]

With the "Dianalike" figure he was able, at least in his imagination, to gain secure possession of both these women and all they symbolized. Because this visionary object of his affections existed primarily in the ethereal realm, there could be no danger of losing her; she was his forever, even though her characteristic behavior toward him in his vision implied rejection, "casting him . . . coppers as if he were a beggar, looking the other way." Moreover, because she was also "epicene" (one of Faulkner's pet words by which he meant, as Brooks notes, not only "sexless" but "unattainable") and "impregnably virginal," all possible moral or Oedipal threat was removed. Both his beloved's purity and his own were safeguarded. Fixed in his consciousness almost to the verge of obsession, the "Dianalike girl" would serve as the starting point in his conception of women, with discernible traces of her remaining in his female characters through the last years of his career.[16]

Faulkner returned to Oxford in late December 1925 to take up his old role as town eccentric and to await publication of *Soldiers' Pay*. Its appearance the following February to predominantly favorable reviews served to boost his national literary stock but had, if anything, the reverse effect on his local reputation. What captured Oxford's attention was not the innovative literary technique but the book's frequent and, for that era, relatively explicit references to sexuality. His mother was predictably the most horrified of all. "Her standards—religious, moral and aesthetic—were all of a piece," writes Blotner, "and they were rigorous." Instead of taking pride in her son's accomplishment, she advised him to leave the country at once. His father also refused to read such an allegedly dirty book. Not only did the university library fail to purchase a copy; it refused to accept one as a gift. Perhaps nothing better illustrates respectable Oxford's state of mind than the remark of a university dean who, on being asked his opinion of Faulkner a few years later, replied, "We don't talk about him around here." All his life Faulkner would pretend to ignore this reaction to his work, but, given his attachment to the community, this response from immediate family and neighbors must have hurt somewhat and may well have spurred on the process of psychic redefinition by which he would separate his authorial self from the self that lived day to day in the rural South.[17]

Faulkner's main preoccupation in early 1926, however, was not his public image in Oxford but rather Helen Baird, who, despite his growing passion for her, was becoming more and more unattainable. To his dismay, she was to leave in February with her mother for a grand tour of Europe and not long after her return would marry a young New Orleans businessman named Guy Lyman. As Judith Sensibar suggests, these facts probably made her all the more alluring to Faulkner, since what mattered most in his love affairs was "not the woman herself but his imaginary vision of her," which could only be "disturbed by her language or movement." If that was true, Helen Baird could hardly be improved upon: he could indulge himself endlessly in pouring out his heart to her, fuel his literary productivity, and still be certain that, while she would pay some attention to him, she would never take his protestations of love seriously. That was doubtless why his literary output in 1926 consisted almost entirely of gifts to her. Though surely not among Faulkner's best writings, they are worth some scrutiny because they mark the conclusion of his apprenticeship stage, which is to say that they are his last works written predominantly in a post-Victorian, fin de siècle mode, as well as providing some insights into the mature fiction that was soon to follow.[18]

The first of these offerings was *Mayday*, a short, hand-bound allegory about the nature of romantic love that he began writing in Paris and gave to Helen in late January 1926. Done in the style of that consummate southern post-Victorian James Branch Cabell, it tells the fanciful tale of Sir Galwyn of Arthgyl, a medieval knight off in quest of the perfect maiden after dreaming that her face appeared to him in "the hurrying dark waters" of a stream. Flanked by the figures of Hunger and Pain, he enters an enchanted forest, meets a hermit called Time, comes across three beautiful, sensual, and willing princesses, but lets each one go to resume his quest. Like a typical Cabellian protagonist, Galwyn discovers that "it is not the thing itself that a man wants, so much as the wanting of it. But ah, it is sharper than swords to know that she who is fairer than music could not content me for even a day." Sir Galwyn, accordingly, carefully cultivates his illusions.[19]

At the book's end, though, he is finally faced with a choice. Having returned to the stream where he had seen his original vision, Galwyn is told that he can cross it and enter human history, becoming "a palpable thing directing [his] destiny in a palpable world," though he will then be subject "to all shadowy ills—hunger and pain and bodily discomforts, and love and hate and hope and despair." Or he can submerge himself in the stream and choose the sweet peace of oblivion. His decision is made when he spies the image of his beloved in the water and plunges in to join her, only to have "good Saint Francis" announce that this visionary creature had all along been "little sister Death." It is a most peculiar ending that leaves one thoroughly puzzled about Faulkner's attitude: does he view Galwyn through romantic eyes as a young man heroically pursuing a worthy vision in the face of a cruel destiny or as a foolish adolescent who prefers to return to the "dark hurrying waters" of the womb rather than accept maturity? Few reliable clues are available, for throughout the narrative Faulkner alternately mocks and exhibits romanticism. In sum, one puts down *Mayday* sensing great confusion in Faulkner's aesthetic beliefs, though it also seems clear that the quest for transcendent beauty continued to tempt him.[20]

Some clearer answers to those aesthetic questions would finally start to emerge in his next work, *Mosquitoes*. Composed during the summer of 1926 for Helen Baird and dedicated to her (though it would appear in print the same month as her wedding), the novel reveals Faulkner more or less thinking out loud about his conception of art, as well as sorting through various influences on his work, in order to firm up his identity as an artist. Though he does not quite succeed, he at least manages to reject a host of unsatisfactory models, most notably that of Sherwood Anderson. Many critics have argued that *Mosquitoes* is Faulkner's weakest published book on the grounds that the novel of ideas, a technique borrowed from Aldous Huxley and much in vogue at that time, was simply not his strength. Once again he was straining to present himself as far more urbane and sophisticated than he actually was, not having yet realized that his best strategy was to do just the opposite. Within a year Faulkner himself would condemn the work as "trashily smart" and later call it outright a "bad book."

Still, despite its flaws, the novel does possess a certain charm and brilliance. And, most important, it appears to have been an essential step in Faulkner's literary growth.[21]

Most of the action in *Mosquitoes* takes place aboard a yacht that has gone aground in shallow water near the shore of Lake Pontchartrain just above New Orleans, stranding together for several days a motley assortment of people with varying involvements in the world of art. The group includes a number of hangers-on and pretenders, who have no understanding of what art truly is but nonetheless seek to be associated with it; a few moderately dedicated writers and critics, who seem to prefer talking about art rather than creating it; and one genuine artist, silent and self-absorbed, who expresses himself almost solely through his work. By aligning his dramatis personae along a spectrum in this fashion, Faulkner was able to separate those characteristics he was coming to view as necessary for an authentic artistic identity from those he was beginning to regard as spurious or false. A close link is established, for example, between creativity and a vigorous sexual drive, with those furthest removed from a true commitment to art portrayed as impotent or perverted, while Gordon, Faulkner's idealized sculptor, stands forth as a paragon of virility.

One suspects that the easiest part of writing the novel for Faulkner—and the most devilishly enjoyable—was composing his sketches of the pretenders. There is Dorothy Jameson, a pathetic figure who, despite two years' residence in Greenwich Village and constant effort, has been unable either to lose her virginity or to learn to paint, and the "sepulchral" Mark Frost, forever stretched out in a lounge chair announcing that he is "the best poet in New Orleans" but barely able to summon the energy to light a cigarette. The most sharply drawn of these portraits, however, are those of Mrs. Maurier, the ship's owner, a wealthy dowager of high Victorian taste who fancies herself a patroness of the arts, and Ernest Talliaferro, a meek, ineffectual man whose chief ambitions in life are to associate with artists and become a bold seducer of women. Significantly, both think of art in stereotyped nineteenth-century terms as the creation of "Beauty," which in turn emanates from genteel refinement and spirituality. "The Soul's hunger: that is the true purpose of Art," Mrs. Maurier declares. "There are so many things to satisfy the grosser appetites." To be sure, Mrs. Maurier does regretfully acknowledge that modern artists often have bohemian tastes and realizes that those like herself entrusted with fostering the creation of Beauty must accordingly exercise tolerance. As she puts it, "one must pay a price for Art."[22]

Talliaferro, an obvious Prufrock figure with "thinning hair" and an effeminate personality, is Faulkner's object lesson on the defects of the Victorian persona in the modern world. Although identified by Mrs. Maurier as a shining "example of the chivalry of our Southern men," we soon discover that he harbors a secret though constantly frustrated preoccupation with sexual conquest. His problems, as one might expect, stem from his repressive upbringing. In Faulkner's words, Talliaferro "had got what is known as a careful raising: he had been forced while quite young and pliable to do all the things to which his natural impulses objected, and to forego all the things he could possibly have had any fun doing." The result is a controlled, genteel exterior—Talliaferro "was a gentleman: he only seethed inwardly"—along with a hopeless urge to recover his lost emotional life. "The sex instinct is quite strong in me," he insists in the very first sentence of the novel, only to have his claim undercut in one misadventure after another. The worst of these is his pursuit of Jenny Steinbauer, a nubile teenager of working-class origin who had inadvertently wandered onto the cruise. Carefully planning his attack, he stands before a mirror, "examining his face, seeking wildness, recklessness there. But it bore its customary expression of polite faint alarm." Finding her asleep in a deck chair, his woeful opening line—"Wake sleeping princess Kiss"—succeeds only in eliciting an obscenity. Faulkner, it would appear, was moving toward associating the nineteenth-century sensibility with emasculation, both in art and real life.[23]

Dismissing such a clear-cut stereotype was simple; handling the likes of Sherwood Anderson, who appears in *Mosquitoes* as the aging novelist Dawson Fairchild, proved far more complicated.* Although they had known each other for a relatively short time, Faulkner owed Anderson a great deal. The older man had helped Faulkner shift from verse to fiction, had reinforced his young disciple's inclination to write about everyday life, and, not least of all, had convinced his own publisher, Horace Liveright, to issue *Soldiers' Pay*. Faulkner genuinely admired some of Anderson's early work, especially *Winesburg, Ohio* and the short story "I'm a Fool" but had increasingly come to recognize important limitations in Ander-

---

*Debate continues as to how closely the various figures in *Mosquitoes* resemble their real-life counterparts. In some cases there are significant differences, as in the character modeled on Helen Baird, but it would appear that in creating Dawson Fairchild Faulkner uncharacteristically made little use of his imagination. As Max Putzel writes, it is "an unmistakable, full-length portrait of Sherwood Anderson painted from life." See Putzel, *Genius of Place*, 78, and Kreiswirth, *William Faulkner*, 92–94.

son's approach to his art—limitations Faulkner knew he could easily fall prey to himself if not careful. Thus he attempted to differentiate himself from Anderson, beginning in mid-1925 with a review essay for the *Dallas Morning News* that mixed praise with biting observations about Anderson's fumbling naïveté and excessive earnestness and culminating the following year with the penetrating—and, at times, devastating—critique of Anderson in *Mosquitoes*.[24]

First on Faulkner's bill of particulars was his mentor's halfhearted embrace of Freud. A half generation older, Anderson, for all his apparent embrace of Modernism, had been too steeped in late Victorian innocence to absorb fully the insights of depth psychology concerning the presence of tragic internal conflicts within human nature that would make moral judgment so problematic in the twentieth century. Faulkner, still shoring up his own grasp on those insights, hammered away at Anderson's inadequacies here through a character named Julius (based on Julius Weis Friend, editor of the *Double Dealer*). The reason Dawson Fairchild's writing seems so fumbling, Julius claims, is "his innate humorless belief that . . . life at bottom is sound and admirable and fine." Fairchild agrees: "I never found anything shadowy about life, people. Least of all about my own doings. But it may be that there are shadowy people in the world, people to whom life is a kind of antic shadow. But people like that make no impression on me at all, I can't seem to get them at all. But this may be because I have a kind of firm belief that life is all right." Fairchild does declare on one occasion that the writer's task is to probe down to the unconscious: "It's kind of like somebody brings you to a dark door. Will you enter that room, or not?" Julius, however, sees right through this talk, telling Fairchild that his problem has always been his inability to pass through that "dark door," that he is still "straying trustfully about this park of dark and rootless trees which Dr. [Havelock] Ellis and your Germans have recently thrown open to the public—You'll always be a babe in that wood, you know."[25]

Fairchild, again much like Anderson, magnanimously admits the truth of these charges, pleading guilty to his own ineradicable naïveté. When an adolescent couple aboard the yacht go off mysteriously into the swamp for a day and return with no explanation, he professes to find it admirable but also observes how members of his generation, given their upbringing, cannot escape a certain censorious moralism: "Only old folks like Julius and me would ever see evil in what people, young people, do. But then, I guess folks growing up into the manner of looking at life that we inherited, would find evil in anything where inclination wasn't subservient to duty. We were taught to believe that duty is infallible, or it wouldn't be duty, and if it were just unpleasant enough, you got a mark in heaven, sure." Various critics have seen *Mosquitoes* as a frontal assault on Anderson—the juncture at which Faulkner made his decisive break with his old patron. That may be true, but his handling of Dawson Fairchild also suggests considerable sympathy for a gifted colleague born too early to evade entrapment by an ebbing culture and misfortunate enough to know it. "There's a man of undoubted talent," Julius says of his friend, "despite his fumbling bewilderment in the presence of sophisticated emotions." That was surely Faulkner's judgment as well.[26]

Along with this critique of Anderson's excessive innocence, Faulkner also found fault with his mentor's midwestern provincialism and especially his failure to distance himself sufficiently from the discredited literary tradition of local color. "You can't grow corn without something to plant it in," Dawson Fairchild declares in support of his contention that art must be rooted in a specific geographic area. Faulkner likewise was coming to believe in using local materials, but *only* when they were set in reference to a larger context and given universal symbolic meaning. As another character informs Fairchild, "You don't plant corn in geography: you plant it in soil. It not only does not matter where that soil is, you can even move the soil from one place to another—around the world, if you like—and it will still grow corn." In other words, the goal was to *integrate* the local and the universal—to pay heed to naturalistic detail by planting one's creative work in the fertile soil of one's home locality, while making certain that its significance knew no national boundaries. "Clinging spiritually to one little spot of the earth's surface," as Julius describes Fairchild's approach, was a snare that constantly beckoned to Faulkner, and that he knew he had to avoid at all costs.[27]

Finally, in this ongoing effort at self-definition, Faulkner took strong exception to Anderson's conception of the artist's vocation. In Faulkner's view, art was a lofty calling indeed, requiring great intensity and a constant willingness to sacrifice conventional pleasures. Dawson Fairchild, we are told, had once subscribed to that standard himself, but no longer. Though he still speaks of creativity as "that Passion Week of the heart, that instant of timeless beatitude," he now seems to regard his own existence as a sort of living comedy, a perpetual tall tale that he milks for earthy humor but does not often penetrate for its underlying meaning. "You can't be an artist all the time," he says. "You'll go crazy." To Faulkner, however, the artist's life was precisely one of controlled insanity; nothing less would permit genius to flourish. Equally problematic is Fairchild's casual approach to the technique of his craft, relying not on fierce discipline but on a hit-and-miss impressionism—"a childlike faith in the efficacy of words." "Words are like acorns," he instructs Julius. "Every one of 'em won't make a tree, but if you just have enough of 'em, you're bound to get a tree sooner or later." To Faulkner that advice, which he had doubtless heard often from Anderson, was unacceptable.[28]

But perhaps nothing disqualified Anderson more as a model than his egotism. In Faulkner's evolving conception of aesthetics, the artist's cardinal obligation was to abnegate his or her self in order to gain access to that part of the psyche from which artistic vision sprang. By the same token, the gravest danger facing an artist was self-absorption—exemplified by the kind of solipsistic concern to which Faulkner had surrendered in his poetry. True creativity, he was beginning to conclude, required two things: delving into and below one's consciousness, but also being able to maintain a degree of objective distance from what one found so that the ego did not distort or crowd out one's vision. Literary artists who had achieved a measure of success faced a special hazard in this regard, it seemed, because of their tendency to batten on their reputations. As Faulkner put it in an essay, they became "pathetically torn between a desire to make a figure in the world and a morbid interest in their personal egos." That was exactly the problem with Anderson, who seemed to be playing the role of leading lion in the French Quarter with all too obvious relish. Faulkner was especially rankled by the way the older man always insisted on dominating the proceedings—just as Fairchild does in *Mosquitoes*. "If Faulkner spoke out of turn or distracted Sherwood's listeners from the conversation," Spratling later recalled, "Sherwood would become annoyed, since he loved to be the center of attention." To Faulkner, this was just the opposite of the self-effacement that genuine artistry required.[29]

The issue was particularly troubling to Faulkner because he was then in the midst of a mammoth struggle to curb his own ego. Even as an adolescent he had sensed that he possessed extraordinary talent, with the result that a strong streak of cockiness soon developed alongside his inherent shyness. As early as 1919, one finds him sending a Memphis acquaintance a drawing that he predicts "will doubtless be quite valuable" after "I have become famous." Such occasional bravado almost certainly served a useful function for a time, propping up his confidence during a period when his literary career was still in doubt, but in the mid-1920s, as his full potential as a novelist became apparent to him, his ego threatened to burgeon out

William Faulkner as a young man in New Orleans, about the time he was writing Mosqui-toes. *(Courtesy Brodsky Collection, Center for Faulkner Studies, Southeast Missouri State University)*

of control. Julius Friend, his associate on the *Double Dealer*, recalls how Faulkner would either "remain silent for hours at a time or talk without interruption for hours, mostly about himself and his ability." There was also his habit of boldly informing people that he was "a genius," as well as the gratuitous cameo appearance he gave himself in *Mosquitoes* as "a liar by profession" who "made good money at it." It would take Faulkner several more years to solve this immense problem of preserving humility in the face of his growing literary mastery, but for the moment he did know that Anderson's example, in this area as in so many others, would need to be rejected.[30]*

At the same time that Faulkner was delineating the sort of writer he did not wish to become, he was also attempting in *Mosquitoes* to set forth his conception of the ideal artist—one capable of maintaining the essential but perilous balance between pride and modesty, intensity and self-abnegation. In sharp contrast to Dawson Fairchild, Gordon, a Modernist sculptor loosely based on Spratling and most likely named after Rodin, does not indulge in endless conversation or attempt to call attention to himself. Rather, he stands aloof, carefully observing life but never actually taking part in it: "Sufficient unto himself in the city of his arrogance, in the marble tower of his loneliness and pride." Unlike Elmer Hodge, Gordon cares little for wealth, women, and comfort, choosing to live an isolated existence in a spartan French Quarter studio. With its bare light bulbs, "unevenly boarded floor," and "rough stained walls broken by high small practically useless windows beautifully set," the room makes one think of a still life by Picasso or Georges Braques, reflecting Gordon's thorough immersion in the Modernist sensibility. For him, art does not entail endless hours of talking in fashionable cafés but rather the incessant "thin fretful flashing" of his chisel and the "faint even powdering of dust" that coats his workplace. "Fool fool you have work to do o cursed of god," he constantly reminds himself.[31]

---

*Faulkner's burgeoning sense of himself can also be found in his correspondence with his mother, in which he insists that she make a scrapbook of all the newspaper sketches and reviews of his work he was sending her ("We must save these things") and reports on his growing fame within New Orleans: "People call to see me, and invite me out, and I sit and look grand and make wise remarks." He clearly enjoyed playing the role of Literary Great Man, which makes it all the more remarkable that he soon deliberately gave it up in order to protect his integrity as an artist. See his letters to Mrs. M. C. Falkner, n.d. [early February 1925] and n.d. [February 16, 1925] in Faulkner, *Thinking of Home*, 180–81, 184.

Another striking feature about Gordon is his unmistakable masculinity. In comparison with the flabby Fairchild, likened at one point to "a benevolent walrus," Gordon is tall, bearded, and hard, with bulging muscles and "a face like that of a heavy hawk." Again and again, almost as a leitmotiv, we are told of his hawkishness—"his lonely hawk's face arrogant with shyness and pride"—indicating his place in that line of Faulkner protagonists beginning with the marble faun, continuing with Donald Mahon, and soon to include John Sartoris in *Flags in the Dust*, who represent idealized self-projections and whose lineage can ultimately be traced to the Old Colonel. One senses that this virile persona was of great importance to Faulkner, allowing him to combat the prevalent nineteenth-century notion, so strong in the South, that, in the words of Louis D. Rubin Jr., it was somehow "unmanly" to become a writer as opposed to "a red-blooded, stalwart man of affairs." By endowing his prototype Modernist artist with the characteristics he so admired in his illustrious ancestor, and by contrasting Gordon with such truly effeminate or impotent types as Talliaferro or Mark Frost, Faulkner was affirming (to himself as much as anyone) that the old stereotype need not hold true in the contemporary world—that writing might now indeed be "man's work."[32]

Given Gordon's status as Faulkner's ideal avant-garde artist, it is worth watching carefully the way his aesthetic principles change during the course of *Mosquitoes*, for the shift parallels the one taking place in Faulkner's mind. At the outset we find Gordon almost predictably the captive of fin de siècle beliefs, fixated on a transcendent vision of eternal innocence. Moreover, the vision is none other than Elmer's fierce and dark "Dianalike girl," but embodied this time in an armless, legless, and headless torso, Gordon's most treasured piece of sculpture. "This is my feminine ideal," he explains, "a virgin with no legs to leave me, no arms to hold me, no head to talk to me." To emphasize its unassailable purity, Gordon casts the work in marble, a substance he chooses "because they have yet to discover some way to make it unpure. They would if they could, God damn them." Thus, from the standpoint of Faulkner's initial philosophy of art, the statue could not be surpassed: it represents "pure" sexuality—impregnable virginity—captured in a form that its creator can possess forever, the instant of "splendid and timeless beauty" made permanent. Little wonder that its presence in his studio is enough to content Gordon with his harsh, self-denying existence.[33]

Or is it? His discipline is put to the test when what he perceives as a flesh-and-blood manifestation of his ideal enters "the dark sky of his life like a star, like a flame," much as Helen Baird had entered Faulkner's. Patricia Robyn, Mrs. Maurier's teenaged niece, in many respects resembles Helen, virtually exuding virginal innocence with her flat breasts, boyish physique, and her face revealing "the passionate ecstasy of a child." Another of Faulkner's fictional wood nymphs, she is "straight as a poplar" and exudes a "clean young odor . . . like that of young trees." At least that is how Gordon sees her, for Faulkner makes clear that the real Pat Robyn, with her brashness, adolescent naïveté, and hint of sexual perversion, falls well short of Gordon's imagined ideal. But that does not matter—the very sight of her calls forth Gordon's latent romanticism, touching "the silver wings in his heart . . . with pink and gold" and forcing him to battle against his own nature. Gordon knows that allowing himself to be diverted from his vision to real life would devastate his artistry, at least by the rules of the visionary poetics to which he still subscribes. Yet it is solely because of Pat Robyn that he agrees to join the cruise.[34]

What little dialogue ensues between the two centers on the marble torso, which Pat wants to buy and Gordon refuses to sell. At first she cannot comprehend either his reluctance to part with the statue or his strange interest in her, but after he tells her how Cyrano in Edmond Rostand's novel had "locked up" the girl he loved in a book, she at last catches on—realizing, much as Helen Baird apparently had, that a complex process of artistic sublimation was taking place. As Minter accurately observes, she comes to comprehend "that he is infatuated with her because she resembles a statue that is in turn but an image of an image." Even so, her quite practical advice to him is to forget his vision, spruce up his appearance, and "get out" of himself more, because "no woman is going to waste time on a man that's satisfied with a piece of wood or something."[35]

It soon becomes apparent, though, that this is not the main reason she finds him repulsive. In fact, given her rebellion against bourgeois propriety, it would seem that Gordon's bohemian appearance and eccentricity would more likely attract than upset her. Rather, the clue to the disquiet he elicits in her comes during their initial meeting when she asks why he is "so black." The question at first seems foolish, since Gordon is a Caucasian with reddish hair. Still, she persists:

"But you. You are black. I mean—" Her voice fell and he suggested Soul? "I don't know what that is," she stated quietly.
"Neither do I. You might ask your aunt, though. She seems familiar with souls."

Both firmly reject the Victorian terminology, but the implication is none-theless apparent: Gordon as an artist must look inward to the very depths of being, to the point where his whole psyche becomes suffused with the "blackness" he finds. His task in life is to journey to places where the mind cannot venture without taking on the indelible hues of human evil—as Conrad had made manifest in *Heart of Darkness*. It is that "blackness" that Pat cannot abide in Gordon; though it causes him to "look so bad," he can never give it up. It seems safe to surmise that the same quality also made Helen Baird reject Faulkner, who refers to himself in *Mosquitoes* as "a little kind of black man."[36]

And it is this very penchant for "blackness," so different from the quest for transcendent innocence that had given rise to the marble virgin, that controls Gordon's artistic vision by the novel's end. It is a major weakness of *Mosquitoes* that we are not really told how this shift takes place. All we know is that his entire approach to art has changed, leading him to create the work he proudly displays in the epilogue—a likeness of Mrs. Maurier's head sculpted in clay, much as Rodin might have cast it, that reveals her face "for the mask it was," capturing a part of her being of which she was not conscious. Instead of employing his imagination to conjure up timeless beauty, Gordon had begun this time by literally laying hands on his subject, feeling the flesh, muscle, and bones in her face in his effort to penetrate the facade of her appearance and reach the inner self below. "There's something in your face, something behind all this silliness," he had told her on that occasion. "I suppose you've had what you call your sorrows, too, haven't you?" As Andre Bleikasten points out, even the choice of material is significant, with the "grey earthiness of clay," so well suited for expressing nuances of emotion, substituted for "the cold purity and hard splendor of marble." Bleikasten sums up the significance of this new sculpture perfectly: "While the virginal torso embodied a private dream of sexless beauty and timeless youth, the mask reveals the humble and poignant truth of a human face; the former sprang from the roman-tic impulse to dissociate art from life, the latter from the wish to relate it back to life." Or, in still broader terms, Gordon (and, through him, Faulk-ner) has put aside the ideal of innocence, accepted his lot of "blackness," and thereby crossed the boundary from a fin de siècle to an authentically Modernist conception of art.[37]

However, it was one thing for Faulkner to have his fictitious sculptor produce an artifact revealing Mrs. Maurier's inner psyche; it was some-thing else to do so himself. In the penultimate scene of *Mosquitoes* he tries to duplicate Gordon's feat, relying for the first time in his career on historical explanation. We are told that Mrs. Maurier's troubles do stem from an earlier trauma, when her father insisted that she marry a wealthy parvenu far older than she was instead of the penniless boy she loved. The story seems far too trite and superficial to be believable, leaving her more of a cliché than the complicated personality Gordon has supposedly discerned. Faulkner did not yet fully know how to lay hands on his characters and sculpt them as if out of clay. Yet there is a familiar and most telling element buried within the story if one looks closely enough. Mrs. Maurier's husband, it turns out, had been a brazen upstart who had risen by dubious means from the status of overseer in the antebellum period to that of "landed gentry" during Reconstruction. A "cold and violent man," he had disappeared in 1863, exactly when the Old Colonel did, to emerge at war's end "with a Union Army Cavalry saddle" on his horse and "a hundred thousand dollars in uncut Federal notes for a saddle blanket." Though he proceeded to compound this ill-got fortune through real estate speculation rather than railroad building, the parallel with William Clark Falkner is again clear.[38]

There was plainly the seed of a novel—in fact, of several—in the tale of Old Maurier, but Faulkner was still not ready to tell it. Not until *Absalom, Absalom!* would he finally attack this subject with the insight and objectivity it required. In *Mosquitoes*, the best he could do to bring the work to a close was to pirate from "Elmer" fragments of an elaborate dream sequence centered on a medieval procession, with priests walking barefoot and a beggar sleeping by a stone wall. This time, however, the romanticism is qualified by having the visionary images interspersed with scenes of Fairchild, Gordon, and Julius drunk and staggering through the French Quarter, with Gordon at one point leaving to enter a brothel, and with Fairchild vomiting in the street. "You want to go into all the streets of all the cities men live in," the narrator incants. "To look into all the darkened rooms in the world. Not with curiosity, not with dread nor doubt nor disapproval. But humbly, gently, as you would steal in to look at a sleeping child, not to disturb it." Slowly, tentatively, Faulkner was now leaving the transcendent realm he had once thought the true province of art and preparing to enter gently what would become the prime locus of his own genius—the darkened rooms and houses of southern history.[39]

CHAPTER 4

Discovering Yoknapatawpha

Once he had completed *Mosquitoes* in September 1926, the exact sequence of Faulkner's literary activities becomes something of a mystery. We do know that he spent that fall in New Orleans, though what he was working on, if anything, is unclear. By Christmas he was back in Oxford, where Estelle Oldham would soon return to await her divorce from Cornell Franklin. The first solid clues as to the progress of his writing appear in a press notice for the *Oxford Eagle* by Phil Stone, issued most likely in late March or early April 1927 and announcing that Faulkner had commenced two novels set in the South. To judge from Stone's descriptions, one was an initial fragment of the Snopes saga entitled "Father Abraham," consisting mainly of material that would eventually be incorporated into *The Hamlet*. The second was a tale of the doomed Sartoris clan that drew heavily on his own family's history. There is no way of telling which was started first, but it is certain that by early summer Faulkner had put aside the Snopeses in favor of the Sartorises and was laboring on the project with great fervor, completing the six-hundred-page typescript in late September under the title *Flags in the Dust*.[1]

Equally certain is that the writing of this book marked the discovery of Yoknapatawpha. Given the central place that this fictional rendering of his home county would occupy in his career, it seems astonishing that virtually no hint of it can be found until this point. Just as astonishing is the way Yoknapatawpha suddenly exploded within his imagination, coming into being all at once and down to the most minute detail, as if it had been lurking there all along. Faulkner himself never explained why this revelation, so obvious in the light of his future work, did not take place earlier, but one senses a prior assumption on his part that the material was simply too familiar and mundane to serve as the basis for Modernist literature, that it belonged to a different universe of discourse. There were some viable Modernist subjects within the South, to be sure, but they tended toward the exotic—returning soldiers consigned by their wartime experiences to a spiritual wasteland, or a group of semibohemian artists galavanting in urbane New Orleans—not the inhabitants of a small Mississippi town going about their daily business. Now, however, the realization dawned that the two worlds of the local and the cosmopolitan could be brought together with enormous profit. Indeed, turning to a familiar setting allowed Faulkner to give his Modernist perspective a firm rooting and thus a degree of depth it had not previously enjoyed—much as Joyce had found when writing of Dublin. One might even say that it proved the final and essential step in establishing his eventual cultural balance, enabling him at last to create a true Modernist or authorial self to counter the still vigorous Victorian sensibility with which he had been endowed.[2]

Just as important, Yoknapatawpha helped resolve the dilemma of excessive egotism that had preoccupied him so much in *Mosquitoes*. No longer would his work be governed essentially by personal needs and obsessions. Now his vision encompassed a whole society, with its preexisting structure, history, and mythology. As his imaginary county came to take on a life of its own within his mind, grounded firmly in the traditions and behaviors he had been carefully observing since his youth, it provided the best possible check on his inclination toward self-absorption, allowing him to gain badly needed distance from issues such as race and southernness that carried such a high emotional charge for him. And since Lafayette County and the South had existed prior to his re-creation of them—since he was, in effect, relying so heavily and consistently on materials he had gathered from outside himself—he could no longer take complete credit for authorship. In this way, as he noted a few years later, his fictionalized cosmos served to moderate his pride, leaving him uncertain whether "I had invented the world to which I should give life or if it had invented me." All he did know was that the effort of completing and articulating those "shady but ingenious shapes" residing "half formed" in his consciousness would enable him to "reaffirm the impulses of my ego in this actual world," but "with a lot of humbleness."[3]

Again, one can only conjecture as to how this dramatic shift in literary strategy took place. However, a manuscript fragment now at the University of Virginia strongly suggests that Faulkner originally intended *Flags in the Dust* as a war story about fighter pilots in France in the mode of *Soldiers' Pay*, focused on the typical "Lost Generation" themes of glamour, fatality, and transcendence. In this initial version of the novel's opening sequence, Bayard Sartoris and his twin brother John (called "Evelyn" in the first few pages) meet in the air over Arras, only to have John shot down by the swarming "Huns." There is a brief mention of Bayard's stay in Memphis, where he was temporarily posted to help train American pilots, and of their "grandfather's home in northern Mississippi," but otherwise one finds no attempt to identify the aviators as southerners. On the contrary, Bayard sports "a thin English veneer," thinks of the Crown as "his adopted government," and evinces "that bleak, hooded falcon expression flying had given him"; we find no hint yet of the Bayard Sartoris who loves to drink moonshine whiskey or hunt possum.[4]

Faulkner must have sensed that the formula of *Soldiers' Pay* was leading him to an artistic dead end, for he soon began again in a very different manner. His new opening was set in the attic of the Sartoris home, with Old Bayard, the grandfather of the two young pilots, sifting among the family's relics and reminiscing about its genealogy. Faulkner's purpose was transparent: to establish unimpeachable aristocratic credentials for this southern planter clan, thereby substantiating the Cavalier myth. The excessive lengths to which he went in that effort reveal the immense allure the myth still held for him. His Sartorises were not merely successful antebellum planters but in fact traced their line back as far as the Plantagenets; the original Bayard Sartoris was said to have fought as a feudal knight at Agincourt during the Hundred Years' War, brandishing the same Toledo blade that now resides in Old Bayard's treasure chest. In time the family found its way to the Carolina Tidewater, where in the early nineteenth century it produced a son who transplanted its swashbuckling traditions onto the Mississippi frontier and became a Confederate hero during the Civil War. His story is strikingly familiar, if heavily embellished. Colonel John Sartoris moved first to Tennessee and then to northern Mississippi, acquired a large plantation, organized his own regiment and took it to Virginia in 1861, was voted out of his command, returned home to lead a guerrilla band that sniped at Federal lines, helped rid his county of carpetbaggers after the war, and fulfilled his lifelong dream of building a railroad, only to be shot down by an angry business associate.

Adorned with the pedigree and status he had been unable to secure in real life, the Old Colonel had at last taken his rightful place at the center of his great-grandson's imagination.⁵

But this new approach, implicating Faulkner so deeply in the perpetuation of the myth, was not right either. More distancing was clearly needed for him to handle the first William Falkner as a literary subject. Thus the long genealogy was soon eliminated (though the Toledo blade remained), the attic scene shortened and shifted inside the novel, and yet another new beginning fashioned in which Colonel Sartoris is introduced by a former member of his partisan band, Will Falls—in Max Putzel's description, "an old soldier whose suspension of disbelief is exceeded only by his lack of critical judgment." The novel now opened with Falls telling Old Bayard a favorite tale of the Colonel's heroic daring, evoking the ghost of John Sartoris as a "definite presence in the room" until he seemed "to stand above them, all around them, with his bearded hawklike face and the bold glamor of his dream." The effect is to present the reader with an initial image of the Colonel as far larger than ordinary life—in Faulkner's words, "like the creatures of that prehistoric day that were too grandly conceived and executed either to exist very long or to vanish utterly when dead from an earth shaped and furnished for punier things." But at the same time, because the narrator is so patently caught up in hero worship, the reader cannot be sure how firmly that image is based in "fact." Perhaps the author of the novel subscribes to everything Falls and the others say about Colonel Sartoris; perhaps not. All the reader can know with certainty is that in Yocona County (an early name for Yoknapatawpha) circa 1919, John Sartoris's outsized memory unquestionably exists as a reality for his descendants.⁶

This strategy of artful ambiguity was a wise one on Faulkner's part, for, taken altogether, the portrait of Colonel Sartoris presented in this novel stops just short of idolatry. We are told (almost invariably through old man Falls) of the Colonel's cool and clever escape from a Yankee patrol; of how he and a subaltern single-handedly took an entire enemy camp prisoner by pretending that their regiment was surrounding it; and of how the Colonel, wearing his Prince Albert Coat and beaver hat, had intimidated would-be black voters during Reconstruction and then dispatched with his derringer two northern abolitionists who had come to organize the freedmen politically—graciously apologizing afterward to the proprietress of their boardinghouse "fer havin been put to the necessity of exterminating vermin on yo' premises." In addition to his heroism and southern patriotism, we are also vouchsafed glimpses of the elegant life he led, "always giving dinners, and balls too on occasion." A man of fine breeding and "innate sociability," he "liked to surround himself with an atmosphere of scent and delicate garments and food and music." A firm patriarch, brilliant military leader, enterprising businessman and generous public benefactor, he emerges as the perfect Cavalier, a man worthy of the ultimate accolade in Faulkner's ornithologic scale of honor—the designation of "an eagle."[7]

The whole Sartoris tradition is likewise invested with aristocratic glamour. As their servant Simon avers, the Sartorises "set de quality in dis country." Their white mansion, with its "colonnaded veranda," is "simple and huge and steadfast"; the fields of their plantation seem to stretch endlessly, filled with loyal tenants who lift their hands "in salute to the passing carriage" as members of the family drive regally by. Symbolic of their innate character is the Toledo rapier preserved among the family's relics—"just such an instrument as a Sartoris would consider the proper equipment for raising tobacco in a virgin wilderness; it and the scarlet heels and the ruffled wristbands in which he fought his stealthy and simple neighbors." The sword epitomizes not only the prestige of the family tradition but also its close and glamorous association with violence. A self-respecting male Sartoris, we are repeatedly told, almost never dies peacefully in bed at an advanced age but rather in some form of reckless combat while still in his prime. To the Sartorises, heaven is a place "where they could spend eternity dying deaths of needless and magnificent violence while spectators doomed to immortality looked eternally on," for, as Faulkner writes in one of the novel's most conspicuously purple passages, "there is death in the sound" of their very name, "and a glamorous fatality, like silver pennons downrushing at sunset, or a dying fall of horns along the road to Roncevaux."[8]

Yet alongside these passages of seemingly complete surrender to the myth there are also occasional criticisms of what at one point is called "the colorful, if not always untarnished pageant" of John Sartoris's career. Typically, the attack is on his war service, and, most strikingly, it is always somehow muffled or retracted. One finds, for example, his younger sister, Virginia Du Pre, speaking of how her brother's regiment had been right to replace him with "a better colonel" and claiming that his guerrilla band was no more than "a bunch of brigands." But Miss Jenny does not repeat or elaborate these charges, and their force is blunted by the obvious pride she continues to take in Sartoris tradition. On another occasion Will Falls recalls the time his hero went home to harvest corn rather than obey orders to join forces with General Van Dorn for a celebrated raid on the Federal supply depot at Holly Springs. That was why the South lost the war, Old Bayard insists, "you damn fellers quit fighting and went home too often." The remark becomes especially pertinent in light of the unauthorized and highly controversial vacation that Colonel Falkner took along with his troops in mid-1863 at a time when they were badly needed— an incident that further estranged him from the Confederate command. Even so, no sooner does Faulkner raise this potentially embarrassing issue than he provides an excuse for his ancestor's conduct through Will Falls. "We wasn't running away," the aging veteran explains; Van Dorn "never needed no help from us, noways."[9]

Beyond these mild reproofs against the Colonel's military record, Faulkner also periodically chides the Sartorises for their excessive pride and violence, describing them as "arrogant" and "haughty." Even the family rapier, he reports, though "itself fine and clear enough," has "become a little tarnished in its very aptitude for shaping circumstances to its arrogant ends." Colonel Sartoris seems especially prone to these traits, as evidenced by the fourteen-foot-high effigy of himself he had built to stand over his grave (just as Colonel Falkner had) with its head lifted in a "gesture of haughty arrogance." But again Faulkner contrives to exonerate his forebear. If Will Falls can be believed, violence and excessive pride became addictive for the Colonel only after "he had to start killin' folks" during the postwar turmoil. "That 'us when hit changed," Falls says, implying that before then John Sartoris had been a far gentler person in effective control of his aggressive instincts (the real Old Colonel had, of course, indulged in murder and mayhem *during his youth* and spent Reconstruction polishing his persona as a refined man of letters, which meant that his violence could not be justified in terms of southern patriotism).[10]

Finally, at one juncture Faulkner goes so far as to disparage the very notion of an American aristocracy. In a remarkable passage he has John Sartoris, a man supposedly descended from medieval knights, announce that "chortling over genealogy" was invariably "poppycock" in nineteenth-century America, "where only what a man takes and keeps has any significance, and where all of us have a common ancestry and the only house from which we can claim descent with any assurance is the Old Bailey." As usual in *Flags in the Dust*, however, the subversive implications of these remarks are almost immediately erased in the two sentences that follow. There we are informed, again by John Sartoris, that "the man who professes to care nothing about his forbears is only a little less vain than he who bases all his actions on blood precedent." What is more, "a Sartoris is entitled to a little vanity and poppycock, if he wants it." Clearly, Faulkner was trying to attack his myth and have it, too.[11]

These verbal double takes suggest how extraordinarily sensitive this material had become for Faulkner, reflecting the cultural crossfire within his psyche. Since early childhood he had regarded the Old Colonel as the identity model whose characteristics he most wanted to imitate and incorporate, mythical or not. Likewise, the notion that the Falkners invariably stood a cut or two above other Mississippians is one he would always relish, even though he knew better. Yet at the same time the Modernist part of him increasingly demanded that he establish his conception of the southern past on the ground of historical actuality, penetrating through family pieties and exploring the full truth of his great-grandfather's life. The result in *Flags in the Dust* is a book that essentially upholds the Cavalier myth but with slight hesitations. Though "a little tarnished," that tradition, as Faulkner portrayed it in 1927, was grounded in a genuine aristocratic ethos transplanted to the South from premodern Europe that in turn became the basis for Confederate gallantry during the Civil War. Perhaps nothing better reveals his state of mind than his strong desire, on finishing the manuscript, to have his Great Aunt Alabama read it. Daughter of the Old Colonel and keeper of the family flame, she was one of the persons from whom he had derived the character of Miss Jenny. *Flags in the Dust*, in other words, was written in large part to please a Sartoris, though it is surely of some significance that Faulkner did not dedicate the work to her or any other relative but to Sherwood Anderson, his mentor in literary Modernism.[12]

Faulkner may have remained devoutly loyal to the Cavalier heritage itself in *Flags in the Dust*, but when it came to charting its devastating effects on the present generation of Sartorises, especially young Bayard, things were quite different. It would seem that this was not the story he set out to tell—in the original opening Bayard appears as a normal enough Sartoris, happily married and expecting his first child, who bravely but unsuccessfully tries to save his brother when the German planes attack. Nor is there any hint of pathology in his relationship with John. On the contrary, Faulkner seems to depict them as paragons of fraternal affection who fly "about each other like playful dolphins in the pale isolation of the mist" when they meet in the air over France. Yet in the finished novel all this changes dramatically. The Bayard Sartoris found there is a deeply troubled neurotic—violence-ridden and drunken, incapable of marital love, and seized by a death wish that he finally fulfills at the novel's end. The playful rivalry with his brother John now verges on homosexual incest, and his pride in being a Sartoris has become a morbid obsession with ancestral ghosts. Crushed by the weight of the past, he seems almost entirely incapable of functioning within his family or society. Why, one might profitably ask, did Faulkner choose to endow his protagonist with such a debilitating neurosis? What might he have been attempting to convey about the terms of modern existence in the South through this device?[13]

Those questions seem especially pertinent if one considers the ironic contrast between Bayard's inherent social standing and his eventual fate. Given the many advantages of his upbringing, intelligence, and courage, Bayard should have taken his place among the South's best hopes—the sort of young man who could lead his community out of its economic and social stasis while preserving its best values. That this is not likely to happen becomes evident immediately in the manner of his return from the war. Instead of coming home to the sort of hero's welcome that greeted Donald Mahon, Bayard sends no advance word of his arrival, jumps off the train before it reaches the station, and heads straight for the cemetery— "sneakin' into de town his own gran'pappy built . . . jes' like he wuz trash," complains Simon Strother, the family's aging retainer. Bayard is not wearing his uniform or any of the medals or decorations he must surely have won. From the outset, then, the reader senses that this Sartoris is markedly different from his predecessors.[14]

That impression is soon reinforced by the description Faulkner provides of him. Though the contour of Bayard's face is "hawklike," as befits a Sartoris, his eyes are "bleak and haunted." Most of the time he displays no emotion whatsoever, though he carries about him an air of "cold leashed violence" that is "like a raw wind" when he enters a room. Lost in "the bleak and lonely heights of his frozen despair," he is "utterly without any affection for any place or person or thing at all." Without warning, moreover, this pent-up violence can break out with a ferocity that is truly bestial. On such occasions his eyes suddenly fill with the "mindless phosphorescence of an animal's," and his "white cruel teeth" veritably "snarl" with "lipless cruel derision." Though aggression certainly belongs to the martial side of the Sartoris tradition, volcanic rage does not. Sartorises are supposed to fly at their foes like great birds of prey, "controlled and flowing for all their violence." But the striking thing about Bayard is that he is at the mercy of instinctual forces he can neither command nor comprehend. He does not at all intend to terrify his old servant Simon or wife Narcissa by driving them at excessive speeds on narrow country roads but literally cannot stop himself from flooring the accelerator. Far from giving him pride, such exploits only serve to make him feel "savage and ashamed." [15]

The ostensible cause of this strange behavior, we are led to believe, is his intense guilt over his brother's death. "I tried to keep him from going up there on that goddam little popgun," Bayard explains to his grandfather the instant he comes home. He seems fixated on the fatal encounter, reliving it in frequent nightmares and telling the story again and again, emphasizing how he had done everything in his power to keep John from getting killed. John, however, had refused to listen, going so far as to fire his machine gun across the nose of Bayard's plane to get his brother to leave him alone. Why, then, does Bayard hold himself responsible for what happened? The answer at first sight would appear to lie in the passionate nature of their relationship, most vividly manifested when Bayard, in his first act after a nearly fatal car accident, kneels on the floor holding John's old hunting jacket caressingly against his face, treating it as an object left behind by his beloved. "'Johnny,' he whispered, 'Johnny.'" Clearly, the bond between them went far deeper than that one would ordinarily expect among brothers. Thus we might assume that Bayard's grief for his dead twin is so intense that it has flowed over into guilt, despite his knowledge that John's death was not his fault. That, certainly, is what Bayard seems to want the world to believe.[16]

But as T. H. Adamowski has shown, there is much more here than initially meets the eye—specifically, a strong current of unconscious hostility toward his twin that makes Bayard's actions far more explicable. In part, that hostility arises from John's air of superiority that leads him to treat Bayard almost like a younger brother. John seems to have invariably been the leader, signaling his primacy through such gestures as thumbing his nose—something, Bayard tells Narcissa, John "was always doing" to him. Still more important is Bayard's fierce jealousy over his brother's carefree personality, with its apparent freedom from neurosis. Though John carries the Sartoris name, he manages to do so with an easy grace that eludes Bayard, for whom the family identity has become a form of virtual imprisonment. Put another way, Bayard takes his place within Faulkner's work as the successor to the marble faun and the comatose Donald

Mahon, both trapped in inanimate coldness, while John is descended from the prewar Mahon, young, faunlike, and exuberantly unrepressed.[17]

One finds this basic opposition between a neurotic, depressed Bayard and a buoyant John stressed throughout *Flags in the Dust*. John's face, according to those who remember him, had been "merry and wild" and "jolly." Looking at a miniature painting of him done at age eight, Narcissa sees in his features "not that bleak arrogance she had come to know in Bayard's, but a sort of frank spontaneity, warm and ready and generous." Even John's violence was, in comparison with Bayard's, "a warmer thing, spontaneous and merry and wild." People are forever comparing the antics of the two, recalling the time John went up in a hot air balloon at the county fair when the regular balloonist took ill, managing simultaneously to soar like a Sartoris and keep the fairgoers from being disappointed. Bayard had also tried to soar, but with far less pleasing results: attaching a rope to a ninety-foot water tower, he had swung out from a rooftop over the freight yard, diving with "a cold nicety of judgment and unnecessary cruel skill" into a "narrow" swimming pool while the onlookers screamed in terror. It was John who always remembered to bring a small gift for the cook when visiting the MacCallum family—and Bayard who forgets. It was John who went hunting with the MacCallums and ended up floating down the river on a log with a fox at the other end—while Bayard is too wrought up to shoot anything. "That 'uz Johnny, all over," one of the MacCallums attests. "Gittin' a whoppin' big time outen ever' thing that come up." Little wonder that Bayard bristles when he hears his brother praised and quickly tries to change the subject.[18]

But jealousy alone will not fully account for the intensity of Bayard's feelings. Rather, it is necessary to follow Adamowski and diagnose Bayard's as a case of severe melancholia. This extreme form of depression develops when an individual, feeling empty and lacking in identity, falls in love with another person and secretly incorporates that person's identity into his or her own ego, only to feel betrayed when the other, in some fashion, goes away. For Bayard, the object of his narcissistic love is clearly his brother, who abandons him by flying heedlessly into an unnecessary death. The mourning that ensues, then, is not normal grief; rather, it consists of a deeply ambivalent reaction made up of continuing love for the one who has been lost, along with a fierce hatred of the love object for having gone away—an ambivalence exhibited when Bayard first clings to Johnny's hunting jacket, then immediately afterward destroys it. But since that element of hatred can never be openly admitted or brought to consciousness, it becomes a source of immense guilt, leading the individual secretly to hold himself responsible for the loved one's loss or death. Thus Bayard, who obviously knows better, cannot help telling himself: "You did it! You caused it all: you killed Johnny." The only source of relief from this inner torment that Bayard can find is suicide—an act that simultaneously allows him to become one with his dead brother and to kill the "Johnny" identity embedded within his ego.[19]*

To understand *Flags in the Dust* fully, it is crucial to realize that this fateful "Johnny" identity that bedevils Bayard does not stem from his brother alone. Rather, there are two ghosts haunting Bayard, both named John Sartoris, for his twin is not only named after the great-grandfather but carries the traits that made their common ancestor so renowned. In Adamowski's words, John "is the attractive one, the heir to the norms of the family's legend" that Bayard both aspires to and constantly falls short of. Like a true Sartoris, Johnny is even transcendent. When he died, "there was no body to be returned clumsily and tediously to earth"; rather, as his epitaph reads, he was borne upward "*on eagles' wings.*" By contrast, when Bayard finally succeeds in killing himself flying an experimental plane that no other pilot dared to fly, the wings and tail section come off, leaving him to plunge unceremoniously to the ground. If "you could only crash upward, burst," he had thought to himself, "anything but earth"; but such was not his fate. In this as in all other aspects of his life, he simply cannot measure up to Sartoris standards.[20]

Again the problem is his ambivalence. On the one hand, the eaglelike identity of a Sartoris has become an integral part of Bayard's psyche and the primary source of his narcissistic self-esteem. On the other hand, he detests the compulsion that identity holds for him, rendering him helpless to break its cycle of repetition and depriving him of control over what he wants to be. But he cannot let that hatred become visible, especially to himself, or act in any way to repudiate the identity directly. Instead, he expresses his conflicted emotions through his strange behavior, which

---

*Adamowski's diagnosis of Bayard's neurotic state is excellent, but he does tend to describe the melancholia almost exclusively in terms of Bayard's hatred of and desire to seek revenge against his brother, rather than a deep-rooted ambivalence. As a result, he fails to see how Bayard, along with gaining revenge, was also trying to perfect his identification with his brother by killing himself in a plane crash. Bayard's death is both a parody of John's, as Adamowski notes, *and* an unsuccessful attempt to replicate John's. On the mechanism of introjection in melancholia and the prevalence of ambivalence, see Freud, *General Introduction to Psychoanalysis,* 434–35.

displays simultaneously a mixture of loyalty and hostility toward his Sartoris heritage. It is striking, for example, that the automobile crash that kills Old Bayard occurs just below the cemetery bluff where the Colonel's statue looks out over the land and that Bayard's celebrated water tower leap takes him out across the railroad yards that his great-grandfather built. In each instance Bayard is performing his feats in John Sartoris's "presence," demonstrating to his ancestor that he still has the audacity of a Sartoris but also evincing by his moral failure his hidden hostility to the tradition with which the Colonel has saddled him.[21]

The situation obviously resembles Faulkner's. Bayard's ambivalence toward his family legend closely mirrors Faulkner's toward his, as exhibited in the carefully wrought combination of genuflection toward and veiled criticism of the Old Colonel found in this novel. There is, of course, one major difference: Faulkner as a Modernist author was slowly becoming conscious of his mixed feelings toward his heritage and thus gaining a degree of control over them, while Bayard's case is portrayed as hopeless. Further evidence of an autobiographical impulse comes in the description of Bayard as "unshaven, in his scarred boots and stained khaki pants, and his shabby, smoke-colored tweed jacket and his disreputable felt hat." That was a uniform Faulkner began cultivating at this time and continued to wear to the end of his life, as when he showed up for a photographic session in the early 1930s unshaven, wearing an "old tweed hoss coat" and "white seersucker" trousers "with red paint splattered all over them." The point should be clear: the dashing young John Sartoris is the person William Faulkner believed his family tradition required him to be, while the repressed and troubled Bayard Sartoris represents, psychologically at least, a projection (magnified several times) of what he feared he might have become had he not been able to work out his relationship to his past through fiction.[22]

This fact almost certainly explains why Faulkner had relatively little trouble realizing Bayard as a complex character but found it almost impossible to bring John Sartoris to life. Whenever he tried to do so, the mythical aura quickly dissipated, allowing a barely concealed bitterness about this idealized persona to surface. In the discarded opening sequence, for example, John seems anything but generous or playful when Bayard tries to warn him about the approaching enemy planes: "What's come over old Bayard? he wondered. Aint any Huns back that way. Wonder what he thought I wanted with him—just to look at his mug? Being in America again did it, I reckon. The land of the kike and the home of the wop, where all men are brave and the women are all virgins through the last reel." Things become worse still in "All the Dead Pilots," a short story written around this time in which John appears with "a face that could be either merry or surly, and quite humorless." Instead of the warm-hearted aristocrat whom everyone loved, we find a ruffian possessing "a working vocabulary of perhaps two hundred words" who could not tell "where and how and why he lived," spending his time drinking, fighting, and woman-izing before finally being shot down. No wonder that in *Flags in the Dust* the reader's impressions of this chimerical creature are derived indirectly, from the stories told after his death by those who knew him and from the miniature painting Narcissa stares at. Only in this way, one senses, could Faulkner preserve his heroic status.[23]

In sum, what Faulkner had discovered in writing this novel was a series of techniques that at last allowed him to render in literary terms the conflicts taking place inside him. By means of narrative indirection, in which a character is depicted solely through the memories that others provide, he was able to start exploring and reshaping his understanding of the Old Colonel, the Cavalier myth, and antebellum southern his-tory. The method would culminate in *Absalom, Absalom!*, a novel in which all the reader knows of the central figure, Colonel Thomas Sutpen, is what he or she can piece together from the often contradictory accounts of four narrators. At the same time, Faulkner, for all his denigration of Freud, was learning to employ psychiatric syndromes as metaphors for significant cultural tendencies in his society. Thus Bayard, as a primary narcissist suffering from the classic symptoms of melancholia, exhibits in heightened fashion a quality that Faulkner detected in those southern-ers like himself who felt compelled to live up to the legends bequeathed them by the Civil War generation. The device permitted him to pene-trate in approved Modernist fashion well below consciousness, providing a strikingly new perspective on the region's experience. Combined with the technique of indirect characterization, it gave Faulkner for the first time the tools he needed for his basic quest of comprehending the inner dynamics of southern culture and diagnosing its ills—while at the same time enabling him to shield himself from all that he was finding.

One finds the same psychoanalytic strategy employed in Faulkner's portrait of the other main character in *Flags in the Dust*, Horace Benbow, whose path to self-destruction is meant both to parallel and to contrast with Bayard's. If the Sartorises embody the Cavalier ethos, the Benbows stand for the more genteel side of the South's cultural legacy, as becomes apparent from their home. Unlike the Sartoris plantation house, standing alone in the countryside with its air of aristocratic splendor, the dwelling Horace and his sister Narcissa inhabit reflects their comfortable, bourgeois neighborhood. Designed by an English architect "in the funereal light Tudor which the young Victoria had sanctioned" and built with materials imported from England, the house epitomizes the transplanted Victorian ideal. With its atmosphere of "gracious and benign peace, steadfast as a windless afternoon in a world without motion or sound," it provides shelter not only from the elements but from life itself. Indeed, the Benbows are so thoroughly walled off from the world's ills, we are told, that their property stays completely free of insects save for "fireflies in the dusk."[24]

Horace, likewise, is presented as a man whose every thought and move has been shaped by his Victorian sensibility. If Bayard is caught up in a family cult of violence and action, Horace is immersed in one of tranquillity and peace, dwelling within the protective confines of "his winged and solitary cage." To be sure, that cage is kept conveniently topless so that "his spirit might wing on short excursions into the blue" — demure, imaginary voyages that contrast sharply with Bayard's sorties into the sky as a fighter pilot. After a brief, pleasant sojourn as a Rhodes scholar at Oxford, a tranquil place "into which the world's noises came only from afar," Horace had hoped to enter the Episcopal ministry, but the early death of his father forces him into the family law practice. This turn of fate, however, causes little distress, since his activities as a lawyer center on "polite interminable litigation that progressed decorously," usually over dinner or golf. While Bayard spends his spare time hunting or driving wildly about in his car, Horace amuses himself by blowing delicate glass vases, with the artifacts standing in his mind for young virgins, "purged and purified as bronze." His favorite, "one almost perfect vase of clear amber, larger, more richly and chastely serene," he keeps on his bedside table and names after his sister, "apostrophising both of them impartially" in the manner of that quintessential Victorian poet John Keats as " 'Thou still unravished bride of quietude.' "[25]

All may seem well in Horace's nineteenth-century utopia, but we soon find out that in reality it is not. Signs of an underlying neurosis appear in his "thin face brilliant and sick with nerves" and in the many hints that his relationship with Narcissa borders on incest. In fact, Faulkner informs us,

Horace is filled with "devious and uncontrollable impulses" that become unmistakably apparent once he falls into the snares of Belle Mitchell, the "preening and petulant" wife of a successful cotton speculator who has grown impatient with her husband's boorishness and sees Horace as the next rung on her climb up the social ladder. With her strong perfume and catlike sensuality, Belle envelops Horace "like a rich and fatal drug." Though he knows full well that Belle is "dirty," he is as helpless in resisting her as Bayard is in forgoing his reckless speeding. "I am immune to destruction," Horace informs Narcissa; "I have a magic. Which is a good sign that I am due for it." By the novel's end, Horace, now married to Belle and living in the jerry-built town of Kinston, presents a picture of utter pathos carrying home a dripping carton of fresh shrimp to satisfy his wife's peevish demands. "Thou wast happier in thy cage, happier," he tells himself, recollecting the existence he has lost forever.[26]

As with Bayard, the psychic flaw that sets Horace on this path to self-destruction is narcissism. According to psychoanalytic theory, such intense love of the self occurs as a normal part of childhood development but is usually attenuated as the maturing individual learns to direct his or her love to objects in the outside world and to gain, through contact with reality, a more accurate, less idealized conception of him- or herself. The adult narcissist, however, insists on preserving the intense gratification of that self-love and devises various strategies for doing so. The most common tactic, writes Freud, is for the person to create an "ideal ego" or "ego-ideal," based on the highest values of his culture, that functions as a "substitute for the lost narcissism of his childhood—the time when he was his own ideal." That essentially is what Bayard Sartoris does, introjecting the Cavalier persona of his great-grandfather and brother into his own ego. But, Freud continues, the "accumulation of narcissistic libido" within the ego may become so overwhelming that it is "intolerable," leading many narcissists (unconsciously, of course) to the alternative of projecting their beloved ego-ideal onto another person and then investing that person with their self-love. In this way, they no longer feel directly responsible for upholding the ego-ideal themselves (the burden that weighed down so heavily on Bayard) but rather can entrust the task to someone they believe more suitable.[27]

Thus Horace has safeguarded his powerful Victorian ego-ideal by projecting it onto his sister (whose name just happens to be "Narcissa"). In loving her incestuously, he is in effect loving his own idealized self, as is evident in the extraordinary scene in which "he sat beside her on the couch and took her hand in his and stroked it upon his cheek and upon the fine devastation of his hair." With her perfect purity (at least in his eyes), she represents and conserves his ideal self, one in which he can readily invest his love. That is why she exercises such extraordinary influence over her older brother—even when she was a little girl of five, we are informed, "people coerced Horace by threatening to tell Narcissa on him." To help sustain his fantasy, Horace sublimates his passion for Narcissa by blowing "lovely," "chaste," and "almost perfect" glass vases—symbolic objects that guarantee him both possession of his sister and her perpetual virginity.[28]

However, as with most neurotic tendencies, this pathological fixation on self-love contains within itself a strong counterimpulse. For the narcissist, Freud reports, the ego-ideal in time comes to seem constricting as well as gratifying, leading to the desire to "liberate himself" from it. More specifically, there is a yearning to recover those primitive impulses that had also proved pleasurable during childhood but that the demands of the ego-ideal have caused to be repressed. That is why male narcissists are particularly susceptible, in Freud's words, to "the charm of certain animals which seem not to concern themselves about us, such as cats and the large beasts of prey"—or to women of a feline disposition. Such creatures offer an alternate model of narcissistic self-regard than that of the chaste and perfect ideal, a model based on indulging rather than extirpating the animal component within the psyche. Belle Mitchell, who snuggles up to Horace "like a great still cat" and whose maid regards her as "some kind of wild animal . . . a dam tiger or something," fits this description exactly. Even her perfume, which both repels and attracts Horace, is said to smell of "tiger-reek." Her name notwithstanding, she is anything but a "southern belle."[29]

To make Horace's transition from his ideal to forbidden ego more dramatic, Faulkner introduces yet another tiger-woman. While Belle is away finalizing her divorce, her sister, Joan Heppleton, unexpectedly arrives to find out, as Horace puts it, "what sort of animal I am." Alternating between "periods of aloof and purring repose" while lying naked on Horace's hearth and bouts of making love to him "with a savage and carnivorous suddenness," she revives his memory of a circus tiger he had watched with rapt fascination at age five. To others, Faulkner notes, the tiger may have seemed old and decrepit, but in Horace "a thing these many generations politely dormant waked shrieking, and again for a red moment he dangled madly by his hands from the lowermost limb of a tree." In short, all the Victorian strictures with which he was raised and that would continue to control his life through his ego-ideal were momentarily stripped away. Joan Heppleton's function, then, is to complete Belle's work in rekindling this part of Horace's nature. Without her Narcissa might still have won and Horace might at the last moment have halted his descent into the abyss. But once Joan appears, Horace finds himself helpless, gravitating to her the way "a timorous person is drawn with delicious revulsions to gaze into a window filled with knives." As a consequence, he is soon reduced to the state of "a fatted and succulent eating-creature," ready for Belle to devour—at which point Joan, her mission accomplished, quickly leaves town.[30]

Like Bayard's, then, Horace's story amounts to an impassioned assault on nineteenth-century southern culture, with narcissism used as a trope to represent in heightened form the dangers Faulkner had come to see as intrinsic to the values he had inherited. Precisely because Horace has been so thoroughly sheltered and encouraged to pursue the goal of self-perfection, he becomes a ready victim for a corrupt woman like Belle. Horace does at one point make a halfhearted effort to comprehend what is happening to him and so avert the debacle that lies ahead. There is, he attempts to explain to Narcissa, "a sort of gadfly urge after the petty, ignoble impulses which man has tried so vainly to conjure with words out of himself" that "you go after; must, driven"—an urge that flouts "that illusion of purification which [man] has foisted upon himself and calls his soul." But in the end Horace is incapable of truly articulating his quandary: "it's something there, something you—you— . . ." By insisting on separating totally the animal and the civilized, and by enshrining the latter as its unalterable ideal, Faulkner is saying, Victorian culture has left Horace defenseless before the realities of human nature.[31]

Again there is an autobiographical element present, though with Horace Benbow Faulkner also drew heavily on his lawyer friends Phil Stone and Ben Wasson to capture a personality type not uncommon among educated southerners of the era. Referred to at times as a "Professor" and "poet," Horace is meant to typify the southern version of the traditional village intellectual, an ineffectual creature who dabbled in literature and learning without making serious commitments to them and for whom the practice of law so often served as a refuge from the world. In sharp contrast to Bayard, who seeks movement for its own sake, Horace in his "solitary cage" is hiding from life and motion, in large part through his intellect. Like the young William Faulkner in the days when he conceived of himself as a poet, Horace enjoys nothing more than allowing his imagination to wander transcendentally "in lonely regions of its own beyond the moon, about meadows nailed with firmamented stars to the ultimate roof of things, where unicorns filled the neighing air with galloping, or grazed or lay supine in latent and golden-hooved repose." It is surely revealing that this fin de siècle rhetoric comes directly from Faulkner's own verse but that this time it is employed ironically, even a touch caustically. Indeed, his deft handling of Horace, always maintaining the necessary distance and control, supplies proof that Faulkner was now moving swiftly toward the point where he would essentially be through with all that.[32]

The same assault on Victorian values informs the treatment of Narcissa Benbow, the first of Faulkner's many attempts to delve beneath the stereotyped figure of the southern lady. That identity, as it developed during the nineteenth century, required women from the respectable segment of society to become paragons of Victorian perfection—free from any sexual desire and devoted only to attending their families, preserving morality, and raising the cultural standards of the community. Narcissa clearly prides herself on fulfilling these expectations and more. Dressed in safe colors such as white or gray, with the "serene repose of lilies" in her face, she zealously guards the boundaries of the "walled and windless garden" she inhabits. She even refuses to read Shakespeare because, unlike a true gentleman, he "tells everything." Nothing, it would seem, could assail the barrier she has erected between herself and the less genteel aspects of life.[33]

Nothing, that is, except Bayard Sartoris. For just as Horace can be lured by the forbidden in the form of Belle Mitchell, Narcissa is obsessed with a "shrinking and fearful curiosity" about the Sartoris twins, watching them from the corner of her gaze with "fascinated distaste" as she might "wild beasts." "All of her instincts," Faulkner tells us repeatedly, were "antipathetic" to Bayard; his "idea was like a trampling of heavy feet in those cool corridors of hers." Yet, though she thinks of him as "the beast," his very animality is what appeals to her, along with the "romantic glamor" of his family that feeds her narcissism. Indeed, her repressed sexual longings are more potent than anyone would suspect from her outward behavior, as we discover when, instead of discarding them in disgust, she carefully stashes away the obscene letters that the bank clerk Byron Snopes has anonymously written her, making it plain that, despite her formal protests, she secretly relishes receiving them. Brooks puts it exactly right in noting how Narcissa "is afraid of sex but also thrilled by it." As with Horace, what her stern Victorian mores have forced her to stifle in her conscious life remains very much alive in her unconscious, ready to exact its claims on her.[34]

It is most revealing, however, that Faulkner does no more than hint at the existence of this hidden flaw in her character in *Flags in the Dust*, permitting Narcissa to emerge from her contact with Bayard "untarnished" — "like a lily in a gale which rocked it to its roots in a sort of vacuum, without any actual laying-on of hands." Clearly, he had not fully overcome his residual reverence for the southern lady. The reason is not far to seek. Ostensibly sexless and unobtainable, with dark hair and an "epicene" figure, Narcissa belongs in that long line of "Dianalike" figures in Faulkner's fiction starting with Elmer Hodge's sister Jo-Addie and ultimately referring back to Miss Maud. By and large still protected by Faulkner in this novel, Narcissa would, however, come under Modernist scrutiny before much longer. In the short story "There Was a Queen," written just a few years later, the distorted nature of her sexuality becomes eminently visible when she first sleeps with a federal agent in order to get back Byron Snopes's letters and then sits in a creek all evening with her son in a primitive attempt to expiate her sin. And in *Sanctuary*, Faulkner's fifth novel, her obsession with maintaining the appearance of moral respectability would be portrayed as nothing less than malignant.[35]

Further evidence of the difficulties that Faulkner was continuing to experience in breaking with nineteenth-century values is the generally upbeat conclusion tacked onto *Flags in the Dust*, despite its previous depiction of a wasteland in which so many of the younger characters are psychologically maimed. With Horace consigned to his purgatory in Kinston and Bayard killed in a crash, we are suddenly introduced to another of their contemporaries, Loosh Peabody Jr. The son of the town's humane but aging doctor who is now completing medical training himself, Loosh Jr. seems too good to be true. Though his face is "ugly," there is "reliability and gentleness and humor" in it; though he is interning with a famous New York City surgeon and learning the ways of the wider world, it is clear from his devotion to his father that he will settle in Mississippi; though schooled in modern science, he cherishes the old ways, too. All too transparently, he is meant to serve as a last-minute antidote to the novel's bleakness, a hope for the future when all else has failed.[36]

Another hopeful note appears on the very last page in the form of Bayard's and Narcissa's baby, named "Benbow Sartoris" by his mother against the wishes of Miss Jenny, who wanted to perpetuate the family tradition by calling him "John." Here the prognosis seems more guarded.

"Do you think you can change one of 'em with a name?" Miss Jenny asks, reminding Narcissa that her son is a Sartoris. But Narcissa has determined "with wave after wave of that strength which welled so abundantly within her" that her child will escape that doom. In the novel's closing scene we find her smiling at Miss Jenny "with serene fond detachment," suggesting that she might just succeed. Despite the ambiguity, this final note seems too auspicious in the context of what has come before, too rapid a shift from the tragic story Faulkner had been telling. It is as if he had taken his reader—and himself—to the edge of the abyss and then flinched.[37]

Nonetheless, Faulkner in *Flags in the Dust* had made several significant steps forward. He had discovered the artistic value, from a Modernist standpoint, of his own roots, both personal and regional. He had learned how provincial materials could be put to cosmopolitan uses. Most of all, through the employment of tropes borrowed from Freudian theory he had acquired the means of dealing directly with the cultural pathology he perceived within himself and the South—with its obsessive attachment to a mythic past, its repression of vital human instincts, its illusive and destructive pursuit of purity, and its incestuous closed-mindedness. For the first time in his career as a writer he was firmly engaged with the subject matter that really mattered to him, the questions arising from southern history and culture. For the first time he was beginning to break apart his society's stereotyped identities—the dashing young Cavalier, the scholarly small-town lawyer, and the immaculate lady—and to diagnose the source of their inherent conflicts. Though still some distance from the insights he would need to complete that quest, with the invention of his fictional county he had at least started.

CHAPTER 5

All Things Become
Shadowy Paradoxical

Outwardly the William Faulkner who sent off the manuscript of *Flags in the Dust* to his publisher in the fall of 1927 did not seem much different from the one the town of Oxford had long known. Having just passed his thirtieth birthday, with no apparent employment prospects and a growing reputation for producing scurrilous literature (a reputation *Mosquitoes* served to augment), he was still the eccentric and floundering offspring of one of the county's more illustrious families. Jack Cofield, arriving in Oxford about this time to open his photographic studio, heard stories of a local character known as "Count No'Count" whose only skills in life were those of a mediocre handyman. As Cofield remembers it, Faulkner's uncle, Judge John W. T. Falkner, was so embarrassed by his nephew that he was barely willing to acknowledge their relationship, while a preacher, at the mere mention of Faulkner's name, launched into a tirade about how "that reprobate should be driven out of town."[1]

Within William Faulkner, however, a crucial transformation was nearing completion. The changes were at once personal, cultural, and artistic, and they were closely interrelated. For one thing, the trial identities on which Faulkner had been relying, such as the persona of the wounded war hero or footloose bohemian, were appearing less frequently and were fast becoming incorporated into a more consistent and permanent identity pattern. Marriage, fatherhood, and homeownership—all about to befall him in the next few years—would cement that new identity and establish a basic style of existence that would continue throughout his career. And in his writing a giant leap into mastery was about to occur that would separate his mature work from the juvenilia that preceded it. To borrow Andre Bleikasten's phrasing, Faulkner was at last becoming Faulkner.

What is most significant is the way Faulkner effected this final step in creating his mature identity. In essence, he was able to move beyond the post-Victorian stage, dampen the battle between two cultures going on inside him, and establish a workable sense of self precisely by arriving at the realization that he would never achieve—and did not want to achieve—a fixed and sure identity in the nineteenth-century sense. Instead, he would define himself henceforth in Modernist terms, relying on a set of interrelated partial identities that would change and develop over time but that, taken as a whole, nonetheless retained a certain degree of continuity and coherence. The solution to his search for identity, in short, was to be found in the process of Modernist integration itself, with its emphasis on fashioning a provisional unity out of continuously shifting fragments. In describing T. S. Eliot's Modernist masterpiece, *The Waste Land*, Michael H. Levenson writes of how the poem "does not achieve a resolved coherence, but neither does it remain in a chaos of fragmentation. Rather it displays a series of more or less stable patterns, regions of coherence, temporary principles of order . . . engaged in what Eliot calls the 'painful task of unifying.' " It is striking how easily one can apply the same modal principle to Faulkner's emerging sense of selfhood. Indeed, that principle applies equally well to Faulkner's work taken as a whole. Again and again critics have remarked on how diverse in style and content his novels are, yet how in different ways they can all be placed within the same matrix— a matrix whose shape nonetheless kept changing throughout his career.[2]

Although Faulkner's mature identity pattern remained fluid, it is also possible to discern a pronounced bipolarity within it corresponding to the two major cultures that had taken root in his psyche, as he more or less compartmentalized the two in separate personae and alternated between them as his artistic and existential needs dictated. As we shall see, this required a continuous balancing act that he was not always able to sustain but could on most occasions keep up sufficiently to achieve his purposes (often using his heavy drinking, it might be noted, as a means of relieving the strain that these conflicting selves inevitably generated). "A divided man," Panthea Reid Broughton writes of him, "he cultivated both sides of his personality at once." The result would be a marked division between his personal and authorial selves. Though from this time onward the Modernist Faulkner was generally dominant when he was at work, it was often by a thin margin and as the result of considerable effort. The Victorian Faulkner remained very much alive in his psyche, acting as a kind of internal censor to block the full realization of his literary intentions when they became too bold or subversive. Whatever distress this must have caused him, he seems to have made his accommodation to it, for, as he must at some level have sensed, it was to be the continuing tension between these two selves that would give such depth and resonance to the great novels he now started to produce.[3]

What precipitated this identity shift was the severe crisis Faulkner found himself in from late 1927 through the early months of 1928. As several biographers have observed, it was a time in his life when everything seemed bleak. Still living with his parents, he was finding it nearly impossible to place his short stories and gain a decent income from his profession. In the past he had been able to shrug off such matters, but his financial responsibilities would soon increase dramatically once Estelle Oldham Franklin obtained her divorce and became available for marriage. Adding to his troubles was a two-hundred-dollar debt, incurred as a result of foolish gambling losses in Memphis, that he owed to his publisher Horace Liveright. But most of all there was Liveright's emphatic decision to reject *Flags in the Dust*, the book on which Faulkner had pinned his hopes for establishing his reputation. On shipping the manuscript Faulkner had boasted that it was "the damdest best book you'll look at this year, and any other publisher"; now he was told that the work was so lacking in coherent characterization and plot structure that it could not possibly be salvaged. According to Faulkner's own account, his reaction was first rage, then intense despair. "I think now that I'll sell my typewriter and go to work," he wrote Liveright, "though God knows, it's sacrilege to waste the talent for idleness which I possess."[4]

In fact, he did just the opposite. Convinced by Liveright's letter and the poor sales of *Mosquitoes* that nothing he wrote would ever be published again, he decided to indulge himself in his craft solely for his own pleasure. He would pour his private visions onto paper, satisfying his personal aesthetic standards, exploring questions about his self, art, and region that preoccupied him without any concern for communicating to a wider audience. Just before making this decision he had drafted a pair of short stories about three children from a once prominent southern family named Compson brushing against the realities of adult life, but the pieces had been written with an eye to magazine sales and so had not really plumbed the family's full literary potential. Now he started a new story tentatively entitled "Twilight," narrated by a fourth Compson child who even when grown would retain the mental status of a five-year-old. This radical device, forcing him to view his subject through a disjointed consciousness, seemed to provide the impetus to liberation Faulkner had been searching for. As the story turned into a novel, in time renamed *The Sound and the Fury*, its composition became an exercise in self-analysis and self-construction in which the medium of literature became his means for gaining control of the conflicting perceptions and experiences that roiled within his psyche, thus enabling him to piece together at last the puzzle of his own identity.[5]

The foremost vehicle for that self-analysis is the book's central character, Quentin Compson, who resembles Faulkner in many ways. The oldest of four children, Quentin possesses a sensitive disposition, has a keen sense of his family's illustrious past, and does not adjust readily to modernity. But he is not by any means a straightforward autobiographical character. Rather, he can most accurately be seen as an extrapolated version of the post-Victorian self Faulkner was then in the final throes of shedding. That William Faulkner, one recalls, had been most evident in the early 1920s, infatuated with Swinburne and writing poetry about a realm of pure transcendent beauty that the artist was destined endlessly to pursue. In similar fashion Quentin, as many critics have remarked, evinces many of the standard characteristics of the late romantic poet and is intent on achieving, in Eric Sundquist's words, a state of "Pateresque purity." To be more precise, Quentin is Faulkner during his fin de siècle stage shorn of all elements of Modernist influence; his tragic trajectory is the one Faulkner sensed might have been his own had he not encountered Eliot, Joyce, Freud, and the other Modernist masters. In turn, the act of externalizing this post-Victorian self in Quentin and thus gaining a measure of control over it proved to be the essential final step in Faulkner's effort to fashion his mature identity.[6]

Quentin, by contrast, finds it impossible to determine who he is. More precisely, he is unable to establish a coherent identity that will allow him to adapt to the historical circumstances in which he has been placed. Burdened with personal roles and values that are no longer viable in the early years of the twentieth century, he can discover no new ones to replace them. Accordingly, his monologue becomes, as Bleikasten so aptly puts it, the record of "a process of derealization" during which "the entire fabric of a self is unraveled and comes apart." There is simply no center around which his various identity fragments can begin to coalesce, no means of fusing together the cultural ideals he has inherited. Instead of exercising the leadership role, whether political or intellectual, that his talents and lineage would indicate for him, he is doomed to an existence fraught with absurdity in a society he can neither relate to nor understand.[7]

The Compsons, with a governor and three generals to their credit, clearly fall within the Cavalier tradition, but it is also apparent that that tradition has become threadbare, with the sad fate of Quentin's father providing a measure of its decline. Far from being able to transmit an aristocratic ethos intact to his children, Jason Lycurgus Compson III has turned into a gloomy advocate of fin de siècle stoicism, a southern A. E. Housman who believes that a person's lot is to bear without complaint the aimless vicissitudes of fate. A scion of the old planter elite whose misfortune it was to come of age amid the desolation of the post-Reconstruction era, he has lost all hope of finding a purpose to life. "Because no battle is ever won," he tells his son, "they are not even fought. The field only reveals to man his own folly and despair, and victory is an illusion of philosophers and fools." The losses suffered by his society and family have shattered his faith in any "higher" or "spiritual" capacity of human nature, leaving him to wallow in sheer materialistic reductionism: "Man the sum of what you have. A problem in impure properties carried tediously to an unvarying nil: stalemate of dust and desire." Consequently his advice to his son runs directly counter to the old Cavalier pursuit of noble ideals: "we must just stay awake and see evil done for a while its not always." In this fashion the trauma of the Civil War defeat has descended to Quentin's—and Faulkner's—generation.[8]

Nor does Quentin receive a usable worldview from his mother. As a Bascomb, her origins lie in a different part of the southern social landscape, the lower middle class, which had long lived under the shadow of planter families like the Compsons. Desperate for status in a culture weighted against them, members of this class in the period after the war often became models of probity, populating the evangelical churches and grasping Victorian morality as their ticket to respectability. Caroline Compson clearly follows this pattern, compensating for her sense of social inferiority to her husband by imposing a repressive moral standard on her children to the point where, as Noel Polk remarks, she virtually turns their home into a prison. Though she has almost totally abdicated her maternal responsibilities, Quentin nonetheless imbibes much of her value system, with its concern for formality and ritual. When she, in her quest for propriety, insists that the youngest child "Benjy" be called "Benjamin," Quentin dutifully complies. And his preoccupation with his sister Caddy's virginity is clearly an extension of his mother's.[9]

The question has frequently been raised as to whether Faulkner was drawing on his own parents in creating Quentin's. There are certainly some resemblances. Like Mrs. Compson, Maud Falkner came from a family well below her husband's on the social scale and was also very much a Victorian stalwart, determined to drum morality and culture into her four sons. Yet there are also important differences: Mrs. Falkner was closely involved with the upbringing of her children, unlike the withdrawn and hypochondriacal Mrs. Compson, who in this regard seems much closer in character to Phil Stone's mother. And although Murry Falkner and Quentin's father were both descended from proud families, the former was plainly far less genteel, learned, and articulate than his fictional counterpart.[10]

In short, although Faulkner may have used his parents as starting points, he went considerably beyond them in creating the Compsons in order to craft literary incarnations of the two most powerful cultural forces in the South at the time—the intertwined Cavalier and Victorian legacies. It was that nineteenth-century heritage, he was in effect saying, that had become so stifling to young southerners of his generation, cutting them off from the world of experience where they could begin to construct a new set of identities for their region.* Faulkner himself had been able to avoid this historical cul-de-sac thanks primarily to his involvement with contemporary literature, which had provided him with a vital arena for exploring new cultural possibilities. That, in fact, was probably the most important factor attracting him to Modernism in the first place. But Quentin has no such escape; through the agency of his parents history bears down on him relentlessly, leaving him no room to maneuver, no space to achieve authenticity as a person.

*At the risk of redundancy, it should again be emphasized that Faulkner was not proceeding consciously here. He assuredly did not pick up his pen with the express intent of engaging in cultural analysis. Rather, as the materials gathered from personal experience, observation, and wide reading circulated in his mind, he instinctively brought them together in a narrative that reflected his intuitive understanding of the cultural dilemmas he and his southern contemporaries faced—exactly as a literary artist is supposed to do.

Foremost among the instruments of that entrapment stands the Victorian moral dichotomy. All of Quentin's thoughts and perceptions are shaped by his underlying belief that a chasm exists between the finite and the eternal. On one side of that gap is a purely spiritual plane of existence, the repository of beauty, virtue, and honor where everything is endowed with lasting meaning; on the other side is the natural world filled with animality, corruption, and transience. To a large extent Quentin's life becomes dedicated to keeping himself and his family on the right side of that dichotomy, fulfilling what he conceives of as an ancestral obligation to make certain that the Compsons remain above the steamy animal passions that characterize mere mortals. He is accordingly devastated when his sister Caddy, whose virginity has become in his eyes the emblem of the family's moral purity, gives herself over to promiscuity. His father wisely counsels against this, warning him that one should never attempt to create "an apotheosis in which a temporary state of mind will become symmetrical above the flesh." But the advice is lost on Quentin, for whom Compson honor is inherently timeless rather than "temporary" and who can envision no greater imperative than to keep it safely "above the flesh." [11]

What makes Quentin's quandary so unbearable, and what stamps him as a post-Victorian instead of a Victorian proper, is his secret realization that his father is right. A keen observer of the world around him, he knows all too well that his values have become outmoded and his defense of them quixotic, but he can envision no alternative standard of meaning. Caught in a cultural no-man's-land and unable to adopt his father's self-protective tactic of stoicism, he is overwhelmed by a profound ambivalence in all realms of life. That paralyzing ambivalence is especially painful for Quentin in light of the Cavalier identity he aspires to, with its traits of firm resolve and courageous leadership. His will never be the sort of personality that gives rise to governors and generals. Rather, beset by forces that constantly pull him in opposite directions, he has become emotionally hamstrung, a psychological cripple cut off from any possibility of decisive action, someone for whom only suicide can finally provide relief.

We can see this powerful sense of division pervading Quentin's life quite clearly in his troubled relationship to time. As a Victorian, he views time as a natural force over which he must establish rational control, leading him to become preoccupied with knowing what time it is and with ordering his life by the clock. But, simultaneously sensing that time, with its rigid order, has imprisoned him, he is equally determined to liberate himself from his fixation on chronology. Thus in the opening scene of his monologue, his first deed on waking is to pull the hands off his heirloom watch so that it continues to run but can no longer tell him what time it is—allowing him, in other words, to remain within time but not be captive to it. That expedient, however, works no better than all the others he has tried to break the spell of time over his imagination. Passing a jeweler's shop a few hours later, he congratulates himself on how he "looked away in time," only to be drawn back to the window as if by a magnet. Staring at the clocks and watches on display, he is struck by how they show "a dozen different hours and each with the same assertive and contradictory assurance that mine had, without any hands at all"—leaving him free (at least within his own mind) to choose whichever time he wants.[12]

relativity!

Part of Quentin yearns to synchronize with the natural flow of time. Those able to do so earn his envy, particularly his college classmate Gerald Bland, whom Quentin pictures rowing "in a steady and measured pull" up the Charles River "like an apotheosis, mounting into a drowsing infinity." Quentin is likewise fascinated by the large trout he spots in the river that, seemingly without exertion, can swiftly snap up a mayfly and resume its previous position, "nose into the current, wavering delicately to the motion of the water above." Spending its days in the midst of onrushing water—an obvious symbol for the Bergsonian flow of time—the trout possesses perfect control over the terms of its existence, to the point where it can "hang" in the water as if flying. Quentin, by contrast, moves fitfully and aimlessly, getting on and off streetcars without knowing where they are headed, dependent on mechanical devices for his locomotion. When he finally enters the river's current, it will not be as an effortless rower or swimmer but with two flatirons attached to his body, causing him to sink to the bottom like a stone.[13]

For the reigning, Victorian part of Quentin's sensibility fears the flux of time and seeks desperately to stop it. Though he knows that it is impossible for humans ever to overcome time and achieve the absolute, he nonetheless makes every effort, as Sanford Pinsker puts it, "to replace an existential flux with an artificial permanence," relying on rituals and abstractions to isolate and rigidify experience. His ultimate aim, much like that of Faulkner himself in the early 1920s, is not only to stop time but somehow to soar above his earthly environment into the "drowsing infinity" of the ether, that realm of spiritual splendor fit only for a Sartoris or Compson—or a Falkner. What is most notable, however, is the shift in Faulkner's own allegiance to that ideal. Where once he had shared his protagonists' urge toward transcendence, he was now clearly detached from it, portraying it in Quentin's case not as romantic and noble but as dangerously self-destructive.[14]

The same framework of beliefs, leading to the same disastrous results, appears in Quentin's relationship to sexuality. At the deepest stratum of his thought, writes James C. Cowan, "love is linked with the saintly ideal and sex with destructive animality." Sexual intercourse becomes the ultimate degradation for him, conjuring up in his mind the sordid images of "the beast with two backs" and "*the swine of Euboeleus running coupled.*" The result is his ironclad commitment to virginity: he will be entirely pure, right down to the neurotic compulsion he develops concerning personal cleanliness. But in an environment where sexual mores are changing, and where his own sister is openly conducting liaisons, the natural human instincts that Quentin seeks to repress will not go away. Sexual desire pervades his consciousness to the point of obsession, just as its symbol, the smell of honeysuckle, becomes so thick for him that he cannot breathe. This crossfire of emotion is visible in his response when Caddy finds him in the barn one rainy afternoon engaged in typical early adolescent sexual play with a young neighboring girl named Natalie. Reminded of his breach of Compson honor by Caddy's interruption, Quentin, who had been thoroughly enjoying himself, feels compelled to jump at once into the hog wallow. In Quentin's contorted thinking, nothing less than a bath in physical filth can atone for his dalliance with moral filth; only a full-scale immersion in animal muck will make him clean again.[15]

As was so often the case during the nineteenth century, this allegiance to the moral dichotomy leads Quentin to a highly warped view of gender relations, in which women typically appear as either delicate and chaste, or oversexed and "filthy." Masculinity becomes indelibly associated for him with control, logic, and order, especially the chronological order of time. Femininity, by contrast, comes to suggest the uncontrollable flow of nature— that river of force that Quentin feels helplessly caught up in, whether it takes the form of the rush of events, the surging stream of his consciousness, or the wild current of sexual energies inside him that he can barely dam up. Given this symbolism, women in his eyes become at once beautiful and terrifying, enticing and repellent:

Because women so delicate so mysterious Father said. Delicate equilibrium of periodical filth between two moons balanced. Moons he said full and yellow as harvest moons her hip thighs. Outside outside of them always but . . . With all that inside of them shapes an outward suavity waiting for a touch to. Liquid putrefaction like drowned things floating like pale rubber flabbily filled getting the odor of honeysuckle all mixed up.

Romantic full moons and used contraceptives, suavity and "periodical filth"—Quentin desperately juxtaposes these divergent images but cannot integrate them into a workable perception of reality. Though he may admire men like Bland and Ames whose ability to cope with the natural flow of time allows them to deal successfully with women, he cannot shake his belief, in James Cowan's words, that they "achieve their masculine virility at the expense of the finer qualities that would make them fully human." To Quentin, nothing is more important than retaining those "finer qualities" that keep him on the "human" side of the dichotomy.[16]

It is precisely his desire to escape this dilemma, to resolve the terrible ambivalence that is tearing him apart, that leads Quentin to his fatal fixation on his sister. Caddy is highly alluring to him; in his fantasies he excitedly imagines himself replacing her lovers:

> *you thought it was them but it was me listen I fooled you all the time it was me you thought I was in the house where that damn honeysuckle trying not to think the swing the cedars the secret surges the breathing locked drinking the wild breath the yes Yes Yes yes*

Yet because she is his sister, she is also unattainable and therefore "safe." Though their relationship is so intimate on the Platonic level that they virtually cohabit the same ego, Quentin can rest assured that she will never surrender to him physically. Given his perverse needs, it is a "perfect" arrangement.[17]

The dynamics of this strange union become manifest in the scene by the branch after Caddy has lost her virginity to Dalton Ames. As they lie beside the stream in the moonlight like two lovers, Quentin first offers to run off with her, then takes out his knife in an attempted double suicide that is filled with erotic overtones. The language is patently sexual throughout, especially when Quentin tries to block her from keeping a late-night rendezvous with Ames:

> Im stronger than you
> she was motionless hard unyielding but still
> I wont fight stop youd better stop
> Caddy dont Caddy
> it wont do any good dont you know it wont let me go

Ostensibly Quentin is engaged in the brotherly task of protecting his sister, yet at the same time their interaction mimics a sexual assault. Their respective roles are just sufficiently blurred to sustain in his mind the possibility of sexual intimacy. But, though he savors his arousal, he is also terrified by it. Breathing hard, he returns to the branch, lying down on the bank "with my face close to the ground so I couldnt smell the honeysuckle" until he finally recovers self-control.[18]

With Caddy's virginity irretrievably lost, Quentin tries one final ploy: a resort to pure fantasy in which he confesses to his father that he and his sister have committed incest. It is a complicated strategy, serving many important psychological functions for him and allowing the reader the deepest possible insight into the workings of his tormented mind. Its most obvious function involves the creation of a comforting alternative reality that can help blot out the hopeless situation he faces—a reality in which he has displaced Caddy's lovers and enjoys uncontested possession of her. At the same time, since he and Caddy have never consummated their love, the admission of incest serves to reverse the fact of her illegitimate pregnancy and restore her virginity. "*Do you want me to say it do you think that if I say it it wont be,*" she asks somewhat incredulously. But that is exactly what Quentin has momentarily succeeded in making himself think. Nor is the fantasy all that implausible, at least from his standpoint, given the intense spiritual incest in which he and Caddy have long been engaged. Even as young children, Mrs. Compson recalls, they were "together too much," and Caddy's possessiveness toward him almost matches his toward her, as is evident from the incident with Natalie. Indeed, if Quentin's account can be believed, Caddy herself is unsure whether or not they have actually committed incest: "*We didnt we didnt do that did we do that.*"[19]

Another key advantage of this fantasy from Quentin's standpoint is the opportunity it provides for realizing his dream of transcendence. Only this time, as Olga Vickery observes, it is a curious sort of reverse transcendence, taking the form of a private purgatory into which he and Caddy are cast to pay for their terrible sin. "*If it could just be a hell beyond that,*" he reflects to himself, "*the clean flame the two of us more than dead. Then you will have only me then only me then only the two of us amid the pointing and the horror beyond the clean flame.*" Here are all of the essential attributes of the spiritual "apotheosis" Quentin has yearned for, including the cauterizing "clean flame" to safeguard innocence. Above all, he and Caddy will be alone together, inviolably isolated from the flow of time and the corruption of human existence. To Quentin even eternal imprisonment in hell is better than mortality—so long as it is the transcendent hell that he has devised in his imagination. That is why he does not really wish to commit incest but only to confess to it; actualizing his fantasy, notes Vickery, would ruin everything "by involving him in the terrible reality of experience." Or, as Quentin puts it to his father, had Caddy in fact consented, "it wouldnt have done any good but if i could tell you we did it would have been so and then the others wouldnt be so and then the world would roar away."[20]

But perhaps the most valuable of the many symbolic comforts that Quentin's incest strategy supplies is the way it permits him to heal his deep-seated psychic division between body and spirit by returning to the oceanic feelings of wholeness associated with earliest childhood. It is clear that Caddy, in addition to being a sister and lover, also represents a mother substitute for Quentin, providing him with the primal maternal love that his real mother is incapable of—a love at once powerful and asexual, all-enveloping yet nonthreatening. To be able to immerse himself in such a safe wellspring of emotion without fear or reservation is the ultimate aspiration of his post-Victorian sensibility. "What Quentin yearns for," writes Constance Hall, "is angelic love—pure, unbounded, unimpeded," which is why incest becomes "the near-perfect vehicle for [his] effort to possess absolutely and to achieve complete oneness." Beyond this, confessing publicly to so terrible a sin offers him the chance to act decisively, to take control of his seemingly purposeless existence and escape from his father's nihilistic philosophy that denies the possibility of meaningful human action. But again, such resolution is possible for Quentin only within his imagination; in the real world events remain intolerably fluid and moral choices uncertain. "If things just finished themselves," he keeps complaining, but, as Faulkner with his Modernist perspective is now at pains to tell us, that is simply not how the universe works.[21]

Equally telling is the degree of detachment Faulkner was able to muster in handling such emotion-laden material. There can be no doubt that he viewed the tragedy of the Compsons from the inside, sharing every stab of Quentin's pain. It was his own story, his own subjective experience, that he was writing from. And yet it is also clear that he had finally managed to surmount that experience, gaining sufficient mastery over it so that he could at last make it serve his artistic purposes as a Modernist writer. In *Mayday* one can not really tell his ultimate verdict on Sir Galwyn's quest for romantic illusion, but in *The Sound and the Fury* there can be no doubt of how he regards the sad plight of Quentin.

His progress is especially evident in his treatment of that "fierce proud Dianalike girl" who served to express his continuing attachment to his mother. With her slender body and dark hair, Caddy Compson surely represents another in this long line of characters, which helps to explain why Faulkner, as he once put it in an interview, always considered her his "heart's darling." Nonetheless, Caddy ends up disgraced and exiled from home as a result of her own moral failings (in the appendix to the novel written in 1945 we are told that she has become the mistress of a Nazi general, a perfectly plausible outcome given what we know of her earlier life). The "Dianalike girl," previously an avatar of innocence who could do no wrong, is now depicted as a creature mired in pathology. At the same time, *The Sound and the Fury* marks the first Faulkner novel providing a full-scale portrait of a mother figure (we see Elmer Hodge's mother only briefly, and those of Donald Mahon, Joe Gilligan, Bayard Sartoris, and Horace Benbow are either dead or absent). Nor is it a flattering picture; on the contrary, in Caroline Compson one finds gathered the worst aspects of late Victorian culture as it had taken hold in the South. What these developments signify is that Faulkner was at last succeeding in disengaging himself from his mother—and from the tradition she symbolized for him. It was a step that Quentin, by contrast, was entirely incapable of taking.[22]

Simultaneously, Faulkner was managing to distance himself further from the Cavalier tradition. In *Flags in the Dust* he had lost no opportunity to cover Colonel John Sartoris with glory, but the Compsons' distinguished ancestors are mentioned only rarely and obliquely, amid hints (later confirmed in the appendix) that their record was characterized more by quixotic failure than legendary exploits. At one point Quentin even drops the astounding suggestion that his grandfather may have somehow been responsible for the Confederacy losing the Civil War. To be sure, there is no real exploration of the ways in which men like General Compson had set the South on the path to ruin; that subversive topic would await the writing of *Absalom, Absalom!* five years later. What we are left with for the moment is the legacy of fatality—the question, as John Irwin puts it, "of whether any male descendant of the Compson family can avoid repeating the General's failure and defeatism and avoid passing it on to the next generation."[23]

The source of that fatality, we discover, lies within the Cavalier identity itself. Whatever virtues it might once have embodied, by Quentin's time it has become a mythic construct almost completely abstracted from the flow of experience. That is why it is so dangerous. A rigid stereotype no longer subject to the influence of history, it chains Quentin to the past, dooming him to a life of endless repetition. His very name, handed down in cyclic fashion through his family, epitomizes this process of imposed identification, as does his grandfather's watch, which, his father warns him, "can fit your individual needs no better than it fitted his or his father's." Again, his response is one of hopeless ambivalence — he is both narcissistically enamored of his Cavalier identity and aware that it is the source of his entrapment. Thus on the day of his suicide we find him desperately attempting to break free of the Compson past by prying the hands off his watch but unable to take the decisive action of smashing it completely. Faulkner's symbolism becomes exquisite: the watch keeps running relentlessly, its constant ticking from Quentin's inside pocket a virtual echo of his heartbeat, reflecting the way the family ethos continues to rule over the innermost core of his being.[24]

As his interactions with other people keep revealing, however, that ethos passed down from the Old South has become virtually emptied of meaning under the conditions of modern life. Faulkner underscores this point through the character of Quentin's Harvard classmate Gerald Bland, a rank pretender from Virginia who manages to set himself up as a gentleman overnight by mastering the required external behavior and acquiring a few basic props, such as Oxford flannels and an English motoring cap. While Bland is employing his store-bought identity to captivate a pair of attractive young women, Quentin, for whom the status of gentleman is bound up with the values of honor and obligation, is doing his best to rescue a maiden in distress — a filthy little girl from an immigrant family who he believes has lost her way home. The final ironic indignity comes when the girl's brother repays Quentin for his noble efforts by pressing charges of child molesting, leaving Quentin to howl with uncontrollable laughter at the absurdity of it all. Clearly, everything he holds sacred has become outmoded; the universe has been turned upside down. *"Father said it used to be a gentleman was known by his books,"* he recalls ruefully; *"nowadays he is known by the ones he has not returned."* [25]

Ironically, the only southerners in the novel capable of achieving the solid sense of self that Quentin desperately seeks are black. In contrast to his plight, they seem able at will to slide in and out of the roles that white society imposes on them, meeting each situation on its own terms thanks to the firm identities with which they are blessed. The various masks they put on are no more than masks—useful for dealing with whites but not their real selves. As Faulkner has Quentin observe, "A nigger is not a person so much as a form of [external] behavior; a sort of obverse reflection of the white people he lives among." No one illustrates this better than Deacon, the obsequious black factotum who befriends southern students at Harvard. As Quentin comes to realize, Deacon is capable anytime he wishes of shedding "that self he had long since taught himself to wear in the world's eye" to reveal his authentic self below. And there are other blacks, like Dilsey Gibson or Louis Hatcher, who wear no masks at all. With his primitive, resolute faith that he can ward off catastrophe simply by keeping his lantern clean, Hatcher, as Thadious Davis remarks, is "a man prepared for living" who continuously "displays a personal integration of self and harmony with the world." He represents, in short, an alternative identity, firmly rooted in physical reality and human community, that white southerners of good family like Quentin covertly crave— which is why Quentin's thoughts keep coming back to him, trying without success to penetrate the barrier of race in order to divine his secret.[26]

Whenever he ruminates on blacks, Quentin's stream-of-consciousness narrative turns almost invariably to his shadow, implying an important link between it and black identity. Clearly, this is no ordinary shadow; in his mind it is nothing less than an autonomous creature that controls its own motions: "I stopped inside the door, watching the shadow move. It moved almost imperceptibly, creeping back inside the door, driving the shadow back into the door." Though never expressing actual hostility toward it, Quentin is forever "tricking" the shadow, as if he could somehow rid himself of it through sheer cleverness, or actively trying to harm it, as when he walks along the sidewalk "trampling my shadow's bones into the concrete with hard heels." Watching it dance on the surface of the river, he wishes he could "blot it into the water, holding it until it was drowned." Dark, lithe, fluid, and "impervious," the shadow simultaneously fascinates and threatens Quentin. He both relishes its presence and seeks intently to destroy it.[27]

That is because Quentin projects onto the shadow a major component of his ego—in Bleikasten's phrase, his "mortal bodily self." This "bodily self" is the part of him that lives in the finite, material world; it possesses the attributes of corporeality and vitality that he admires in men like Louis Hatcher and needs so badly for his survival. But Quentin, following the dictates of his moral dichotomy, also cannot help but consider that physical self dangerous and forbidden—something he must dissociate himself from at all costs. He views it as in the deepest sense representative of "blackness," containing powerful forces and passions that, while enticing, also threaten to undermine his efforts to remain "white" and "civilized." The shadow, in other words, embodies in concentrated form all the traits that southern whites have traditionally projected onto blacks in order to shore up the supposed "purity" of white identity. Hence Quentin's obsession with controlling and punishing his shadow, which becomes for him a kind of psychological punching bag, safely external and containing (since his mind has transferred them to it) all the impulses that he believes might imperil his status as a gentleman. Again, this is a "perfect" arrangement: by tricking and trampling the shadow, he repeatedly demonstrates his moral rejection of his dark self without the risk of either injuring or losing it.[28]

This perverse relationship with his shadow makes clear the extent to which Quentin's post-Victorian culture has served to debilitate him. His mind and body have become foes, functioning as if they were warring entities. One's corporal self can never be trusted, he informs us: "When you don't want to do a thing, your body will try to trick you into doing it, sort of unawares." His body is so detached from his consciousness that he doesn't even realize it when he cuts himself breaking the crystal on his grandfather's watch. Not until he finally notices the blood he has shed, allowing him to conceptualize what has happened, does he experience pain: "There was a red smear on the dial. When I saw it my thumb began to smart." The division between mind and body is that complete. As in other respects, Quentin has taken the Victorian dichotomy to its logical extreme, emancipating his "higher" faculties from his physical being. But, while he may have managed to retain his "purity," the results are hardly enobling. Such, Faulkner was saying, are the wages of transcendence in the modern era.[29]

In the end, Quentin's sense of self has become so weakened, so detached from reality, that everything seems out of kilter for him. His attempts to preserve his Cavalier heritage by defending the chivalric code of honor have not so much failed as collapsed into fiasco. Each such venture—confronting Gerald Bland or Caddy's seducer, Dalton Ames, or protecting the little Italian girl—results not in a clear-cut triumph or defeat but in a muddle of misunderstanding. "Bud," his friend Spoade comments after the fight with Bland, "you excite not only admiration but horror." And in an age when women themselves are overthrowing the old moral standards, the identity of a virgin has become meaningless: "if it was that simple to do it wouldn't be anything and if it wasn't anything, what was I . . ."[30]

The problem, Faulkner is at pains to tell us, resides not in the world itself but within Quentin. The final afternoon of his agony takes place against the backdrop of a peaceful rural setting where a group of care-free boys are enjoying themselves fishing, sunning, and swimming. Those around him go about their activities in a world that they find reasonably solid and hospitable, while for Quentin not even his bed offers a respite from vertigo:

> I seemed to be lying neither asleep nor awake looking down a long corridor of gray halflight where all stable things had become shadowy paradoxical all I had done shadows all I had felt suffered taking visible form antic and perverse mocking without relevance inherent themselves with the denial of the significance they should have affirmed thinking I was I was not who was not was not who.

The passage captures vividly the plight of a person impaled by cultural change, trapped within a major historical value system that he knows is now hopelessly obsolete.[31]

It is precisely to escape this state of psychic limbo that Quentin plans his suicide. With a decisive blow, he will at last set his affairs right; for once things will finish themselves. Thus a slew of conflicting but intricately balanced motives lie behind his leap from the bridge—in Freudian terms, his behavior is "overdetermined." As Sundquist points out, one can see the suicide as a sexual act, consummating Quentin's incestuous love for Caddy in her guise as a water nymph; yet Quentin is simultaneously engaging in a rite of purification by water similar to his earlier jump into the hog wallow. Drowning also represents a return to the maternal womb, with his body "healing" to "the caverns and the grottoes of the sea" to find the uterine peace that has eluded him. "*I will sleep fast*," he promises himself. At the same time, this plunge into the depths will paradoxically permit him to realize at last his quest for transcendence. On Judgment Day, he tells us, the flatirons weighting down his body will rise to the surface by themselves, while his eyes "will come floating up too, out of the deep quiet and the sleep, to look on glory"—suggesting that his spiritual self (symbolized by the eyes) will be rid permanently of the burden of his flesh. His battle against time will be over, and he will be transported to a sort of post-Victorian paradise—a celestial refuge where all his dearest values and desires can be perpetually affirmed, no matter how much they may have contradicted each other here on earth.[32]

Perhaps nothing conveys the dynamics of his mind better than the two extraordinary dream images that appear at the end of his soliloquy. The first centers on a picture of a dungeon he recalls from a children's book—"a dark place into which a single weak ray of light came slanting upon two faces lifted out of the shadow." The two faces, he realizes, are those of his parents, with himself and his siblings "lost below even them without even a ray of light." This nightmare of an existence devoid of identity or hope contrasts diametrically with another childhood vision deeply etched in his memory:

> It used to be I thought of death as a man something like Grandfather a friend of his a kind of private and particular friend . . . I always thought of them as being together somewhere all the time waiting for old Colonel Sartoris to come down and sit with them waiting on a high place beyond cedar trees . . . Grandfather wore his uniform and we could hear the murmur of their voices from beyond the cedars they were always talking and Grandfather was always right.

To Quentin's dualistic mind, the alternatives are stark and simple: the dark and degraded place below, or the "high place" just beyond the cedars where the southern Cavaliers dwell and where firm moral judgments can be had for the asking from a man who "was always right." It is a choice that must be made, for, unlike Faulkner himself, Quentin is incapable of abiding "gray halflight." Dressed in his finest clothes and meticulously groomed, he will be well prepared to meet his grandfather's special friend.[33]

―――――――

Quentin is not the only victim of the deadly pull of the South's cultural past to be found in *The Sound and the Fury*; in their own ways his sister Caddy and brother Jason are also destroyed by inherited tradition. Unlike Quentin, both rebel against that tradition, but in each case the rebellion exacts a terrible price, maiming them psychically and depriving them of the vital thread of cultural continuity they need to advance into the future. By the novel's end they have each arrived at a sort of living death, having lost all hope of generativity (to borrow Erikson's term for the quality that marks a healthy and creative adulthood). As bereft of a viable identity as Quentin, and as thoroughly trapped by compulsive behavior, the two supply further evidence of Faulkner's bleak prognosis for his region in the late 1920s. The planter class, to which southern society had always turned for direction, had now reached a historical dead end, a cultural morass from which it would likely never extricate itself. That is the ultimate meaning of the story of the Compson children.

One sees this in Caddy Compson's dramatic flight from the stereotyped identity of the southern lady, an act of rejection that shapes her whole life. Sensing how the Victorian ethos has disfigured her mother's personality, she adamantly refuses to suppress her emotions for the sake of propriety. Against her mother's orders she continues to lavish affection on her younger brother Benjy and does not hesitate to seek out sexual relationships on reaching adolescence. Her ingrained instinct for rebellion is apparent even at age seven, when she disobeys her parents by getting her dress wet playing in the branch. "I dont care whether they see or not," she tells Quentin defiantly. "I'm going to tell, myself." Likewise she thinks nothing of ignoring her father's injunction against climbing the pear tree to spy out what is taking place at her grandmother's funeral. Faulkner highlights her insurgency by comparing her to Eve in the Garden and to Satan—two figures diametrically opposed to the ideal of the southern lady.[34]

Caddy's tragedy, however, is that she can discover no suitable identity to replace the one she rejects. The only thing she can find in the family storehouse, so to speak, is the legacy of military valor handed down by her Compson forebears—an identity hardly considered appropriate for a female in the social context in which she lives. In their childhood play, Quentin remembers, "she never was a queen or a fairy she was always a king or a giant or a general." Likewise it is Caddy who always insists on being in control, demanding, for example, that her siblings mind her the night of Damuddy's death. While Quentin safeguards his purity as if he were a southern lady, Caddy carries on like an aggressive young man displaying sexual prowess. "*I didn't let him I made him,*" she informs Quentin after kissing a boy for the first time. The two also unmistakably exchange sexual roles when Quentin walks to his "duel" with Dalton Ames while Caddy rides up later on Quentin's own horse, that perennial symbol of planter authority. Galloping to the scene like a Cavalier, she finds her brother lying on the ground, having "passed out like a girl." For these descendants of the antebellum elite, Faulkner is suggesting, the entire process of gender identification has irretrievably broken down.[35]

Here lies the root cause of Caddy's nymphomania. Having repudiated the model of womanhood represented by her mother, she can maintain her fragile hold on femininity only by yielding herself sexually to men as often as possible. Not all men will do. Rather, Caddy is drawn to lovers who act and appear hypermasculine, such as the former soldier Dalton Ames, who can hold her "in one arm like she was no bigger than a child," or the Nazi general whose mistress she in time becomes. They alone are strong enough to overpower her Compson self and force her to submit as a woman. Because her feminine identity is so weak, she must repeat this behavior pattern over and over. Sexuality in this way becomes as compulsive for her as virginity is for Quentin; she has no control over her actions and, in keeping with the clinical syndrome of nymphomania, derives no pleasure or satisfaction from them. On the contrary, she increasingly comes to associate sexual encounters with death. There have been "too many," she confides to Quentin, and "when they touched me I died." [36]

As Faulkner makes clear, Caddy's sexuality has become truly perverted for her. It has turned into an obsession, a kind of specter perpetually haunting her: *"There was something terrible in me sometimes at night I could see it grinning at me I could see it through them grinning at me through their faces."* At each step of her self-degradation she is filled with shame and attempts, in a manner reminiscent of Quentin, to restore her innocence with water. Prompted by Benjy, who senses her corruption, she washes off her perfume after her first date, cleans her mouth out with soap after her first romantic kiss, and, most dramatically of all, bathes herself in the branch the night she loses her virginity. She is obviously in immense pain: Quentin recalls her, accosted by Benjy's bellowing, *"shrinking against the wall getting smaller and smaller with her white face her eyes like thumbs dug into it."* She knows the consequences that will flow from her promiscuity—how it will drive her father to drink himself to death, destroy Quentin, and leave Benjy without anyone to protect him. "I wont anymore, ever," she fervently promises Benjy while holding him and sobbing. But for all her Compson will to dominate, to make the world "mind" her, she is in the grip of forces she cannot master.[37]

Various writers on *The Sound and the Fury* have seen Caddy as a fertility goddess symbolizing the southern land itself, with a bountiful capacity to nurture an entire society. If so, then the dark implication embedded in this novel is that that source of nurturance has now dried up. As Caddy tells Quentin the night before her marriage, she is so emotionally desiccated that she cannot generate a tear: *"I cant cry I cant even cry one minute."* Far from being able to provide the maternal qualities of caring and sustenance that would prevent the Compson household—and, by extension, the region—from succumbing to the wasteland, she has entered a state equivalent to death (when Jason suggests after their father's funeral that she would be better off dead, she instantly agrees). In this sense the "Dianalike girl" had now evolved in Faulkner's imagination well beyond its origins in his own mother to encompass the female ethos itself. At least within the white South, Faulkner appears to have been saying, that feminine spirit had become corrupted, condemning the society to perpetual barrenness.[38]

The glimpse supplied of Caddy's daughter seems to confirm this reading of Faulkner's intent. Though named for her deceased uncle in a last, desperate attempt on Caddy's part to perpetuate the family line, Miss Quentin is endowed with no identity whatsoever. Never told who her parents are, she does not become a Compson, a Bascomb, or even fully a human being, as the description of her room discloses: "It was not a girl's room. It was not anybody's room, and the faint scent of cheap cosmetics and the few feminine objects and the other evidences of crude and hopeless efforts to feminise it but added to its anonymity, giving it that dead and stereotyped transience of rooms in assignation houses." Significantly, it is the same room that once belonged to Damuddy, the family matriarch. Deprived of any sense of self, Miss Quentin is forever "gobbing paint on her face" and dressing like a whore, for that is the only identity left to her. In contrast to her mother, however, her hypersexuality arises not out of deep psychological compulsion but from the simple fact that there is nothing else in her life. If Caddy's eyes show guilt and terror, Quentin's are "hard as a fice dog's." Above all, her vicious treatment of Benjy serves to indicate how the maternal instinct, once so powerful in Caddy, has entirely withered in Quentin. "I'm bad and I'm going to hell, and I don't care," she screams at Jason in an ironic echo of the uncle for whom she is named. Appropriately enough, she runs off with a circus worker, cutting all ties to her family and immersing herself in a tawdry and transient existence where identities can be had through masks and greasepaint.[39]

Just as steeped in pathology is her chief antagonist within the household, Jason. As numerous critics have pointed out, Faulkner's description of Jason in the appendix as "logical rational contained" and "the first sane Compson since Colloden" is true only in the most sarcastic sense. In fact, there are striking resemblances between Jason and Quentin that become apparent as soon as one looks beneath the surface. Both are reacting to the calamity of being a Compson in the modern world—Quentin by clinging to his inherited identity, Jason by violently repudiating his. Like Quentin,

Jason is completely unable to master time, forever racing about behind schedule with no hope of catching up, and has thoroughly repressed his sexuality. Though he does not actually kill himself, his behavior during the period we observe him can only be called self-destructive, culminating in his fight with the hatchet-wielding old man at the circus camp ("What were you trying to do? commit suicide?" the circus owner asks him).[40]

In clinical terms, Jason suffers from paranoia, a psychotic disorder in which a person comes to believe himself the victim of an immense conspiracy whose sole purpose is to persecute him. The paranoiac, we are told, "feels that he is being controlled, observed, influenced, criticized," and often hears voices telling him " 'he is crazy, he is insane!' " Such delusions pervade Jason's monologue, centered on his persistent fear that the rest of the community will think him mentally unbalanced: "All the time I could see them watching me like a hawk, waiting for a chance to say Well I'm not surprised I expected it all the time the whole family's crazy." Everyone, it seems, is responsible for what has befallen him — his ancestors, Caddy, his niece, his servants, his employer, and the "dam eastern jews" on Wall Street who are trying to steal his money. Even the telegraph company shares the blame for his losses on the cotton market: "They're hand in glove with that New York crowd. Anybody could see that."[41]

Indeed, Jason believes that the universe itself takes special delight in harassing him. Like Quentin, he refuses to accept his father's teaching that the natural world operates according to blind chance, with human beings no more than helpless pawns in an indifferent cosmos. To counter that prospect, he ascribes magical powers to nature, convincing himself that rain pours down from the heavens just to drench him and that the brambles and poison oak he encounters while spying on his niece were put there primarily for his torment. "The only thing I couldn't understand," he tells us, "was why it was just poison oak and not a snake or something." The conspiracy extends all the way to the malicious sparrows that victimize him in the courthouse square: "First thing you know, bing. Right on your hat." Of course, in reality it is Jason who is forever placing himself in the path of misfortune, creating his own disasters and then taking inordinate delight in his suffering. He is the one who orders his New York broker to buy after receiving urgent advice to sell and who, in the apt words of Donald Kartiganer, "spends his Good Friday crucifying himself."[42]

Such self-victimization is an integral part of the mechanism of paranoia. As Freud explains, the paranoiac seeks to relieve himself of the burden of his superego by projecting it onto the outside world. What in the normal individual takes the form of a personal conscience, with its incessant promptings and attendant feelings of guilt, in the paranoiac turns into a conspiracy of voices that are forever criticizing him and of sinister forces deliberately out to harm him. Like all neurotic arrangements, paranoia provides certain "advantages." In Jason's case it allows him to escape the enormous weight of moral responsibility from his family's past that fatally crushes his older brother. Jason does not feel obliged to live up to the tradition of Compson honor; on the contrary, he has no apparent scruples and is capable of committing one outrageous act after the next, seemingly without remorse. At the same time he has the psychologically necessary satisfaction of being continuously punished for his sins by a long string of misfortunes (most of which he has brought upon himself). Since he views those punishments as arising from hostile agencies beyond his control, he is spared any sense of self-reproach. "*They*" are always to blame. Through this self-deception, Jason, in contrast to Quentin, can at least go on living in his home community. In effect, he escapes the paralysis of inner division by externalizing his problem into a relatively straightforward conflict between his own ego and everything lying outside it—thus heightening his chances of survival.[43]

In *The Sound and the Fury*, Faulkner began using Freudian concepts not only to get access to his characters at the unconscious level of their minds but also as tropes symbolizing larger trends within the culture. That is again the case here. If Quentin's neurosis serves as a metaphor for the cultural crisis that thoughtful young southerners faced in the early twentieth century (with the symptoms heightened to make the dynamics of the crisis more visible), Jason's derangement illustrates the plight of many ordinary folk within the region swept up in the social and economic turmoil of that era. As Bleikasten puts it, Faulkner was engaged in a "radioscopy of the Southern mind," using Jason to capture latent tendencies that could be found in "all the malcontents of the new South of the twenties: decayed aristocrats, grubbing small businessmen, hard-pressed dirt-farming rednecks, all those whom the hazards of the economic system had condemned to grovel in mediocrity and to boil with chronic frustration." Reality had to a large extent become unbearable for these denizens of a society where military defeat was still a fresh memory and who now sensed that they were being left behind, perhaps irrevocably, as the rest of the country surged forward toward prosperity and modernization. The result was an intensification of the South's long-standing "siege mentality," with its inclination to see other regions as endemically hostile and to blame them for southern backwardness. In this way Jason's paranoia works as a Modernist literary device bringing starkly into view this darker side of the New South mentality in which the South's internal troubles were so often recast into an ongoing battle between "us" and "them."[44]

Faulkner not only depicts that mentality but goes on to unmask it, pinpointing the real forces at work beneath its proffered self-image. For example, Jason, in keeping with the archetypal New South persona, conceives of himself as a man of firm resolve, rational and businesslike, who, as Olga Vickery notes, "alone has a firm grasp on reality." He is likewise at pains to assert his independence. "I guess I dont need any man's help to get along," he boasts; "I can stand on my own feet like I always have." His constant point of reference is his alcoholic father, whose failed stewardship let the family slip into its present state of genteel poverty. Utterly rejecting his father's model—Jason won't touch a drop of whiskey—he sees his mission in life as stopping that slippage: "Somebody's got to hold on to what little we have left, I reckon." "Man enough" to keep the flour barrel full, as he puts it, he will be a strong head of household, restoring some of the family's lost property and status if the world will just give him a fair chance, much as the leaders of the New South movement sought to recoup the supposed failures of their predecessors.[45]

Again and again, however, Faulkner undercuts this posture of autonomy, revealing Jason's claims as mere swagger. Far from being a strong father figure, Jason, we discover, is more like a helpless child. Unable to work steadily at his job, he behaves like a schoolboy playing hooky, dodging up and down alleyways so that Earl, his boss, won't see him. Utterly self-centered, he displays the sort of petty spite one might associate with a five-year-old, as when he destroys a set of carnival tickets rather than give one free to his black retainer, Luster. "A big growed man like you," Dilsey appropriately scolds him. Nor does he truly earn his paycheck; rather, the money is a gift from Earl, who generously supports the family out of an abiding affection for Mrs. Compson—that is what keeps the flour barrel full. Moreover, beyond doubt it is the servants who actually run the household, not Jason.[46]

Most telling of all, Jason has inordinate difficulty handling money—one of the key indicators of a mature sense of autonomy in modern society and an obvious prerequisite for any aspiring capitalist. The basic modalities of autonomy, Erikson explains, are "holding-on" and "letting-go"—which in the realm of finance means that a person has mastered the skills of saving and investing money and also knows how to spend it wisely or give it away when appropriate. But Jason is completely irrational in his attitude toward money. In his mind, it exists not to meet various practical needs but mainly to gratify his ego by giving him a sense of power. He tends to hoard his wealth, locking it away in a strongbox in his closet, and can be tyrannical about small sums, allowing his niece only ten dollars out of the fifty-dollar money order her mother has sent her in order to show who is in charge. "You've got to learn one thing, and this is that when I tell you to do something, you've got it to do," he insists. At the same time, he will impulsively lavish a forty-dollar tip on his mistress, again primarily to establish his control: "Gave it to her. I never promise a woman anything nor let her know what I'm going to give her. That's the only way to manage them." His disastrous ventures in the cotton market are likewise guided not by actual market conditions but by his unquenchable desire to assert himself. He will buy or sell—hold or let go—with no regard to financial consequences, so long as he can maintain the illusion that he is in command: "After all, like I say, money has no value; it's just the way you spend it. It dont belong to anybody, so why try to hoard it. It just belongs to the man that can get it and keep it."[47]

However, the central problem for Jason and the others who share his plight is precisely that their loss of status has left them feeling that they no longer have control over their lives. A member of a family that once ranked among the most powerful in the community, Jason has been relegated to the role of clerk in a hardware store, where he must respond patiently to the trivial demands of hayseed customers, like the "dam redneck" who "spent fifteen minutes deciding whether he wanted a twenty cent hame string or a thirty-five cent one." Nothing galls him more than to hear Earl tell a simple farm woman: "Yes ma'am, Mr. Compson will wait on you." Compsons are not supposed to wait on anyone, but for Jason there is no other choice. As often as he may deny that he cares about his family's former standing, it is clear that the experience of decline has been exceedingly painful for him. When he overhears people talking about the family's dire straits, he assures his mother, "You can jest bet I shut them up [by telling them how] my people owned slaves here when you all were running little shirt tail country stores and farming land no nigger would look at on shares." But, as Jason well knows, virtually all of the Compsons' landed domain has now been sold.[48]

Jason's attempted solution to his predicament takes the shape of what Erikson calls "distantiation." In one bold stroke he seeks to repudiate his Compson heritage altogether: "I haven't got much pride, I can't afford it with a kitchen full of niggers to feed and robbing the state asylum of its star freshman. Blood, I says, governors and generals. It's a dam good thing we never had any kings or presidents; we'd all be down there at Jackson [the state insane asylum] chasing butterflies." Encouraged by his mother, who informs him he is "a Bascomb, despite your name," he attempts to cut all ties between himself and Compsonhood. It will be Jason, we learn from the appendix, who will finally sell the family home, allowing the once gracious mansion to be turned into a boardinghouse. But while such distantiation, like his paranoia, may permit his short-term survival, Faulkner leaves no doubt that Jason's fate is not to be admired. A "childless bachelor," he represents as much of a historical dead end as his ill-fated siblings. Jason has "no human ties with anyone," observes Isadore Traschen, "his family, servants, whore, or employer; he is divorced from the South and its traditions, from nature and God, and finally from himself, as his headaches suggest." By the close of his section he has become not only detestable but utterly pathetic, "sitting quietly behind the wheel of a small car, with his invisible life ravelled out about him like a worn sock." His sad saga becomes a cautionary tale, a reminder to contemporary readers that no shortcuts existed for resolving the crisis of southern identity so poignantly symbolized in the fall of the house of Compson.[49]

Perhaps the most indisputable sign that Faulkner's Modernist authorial self was firmly in charge of writing *The Sound and the Fury* lies in the character of Benjy Compson. Again and again, Benjy stands the Victorian value system on its head: a creature of undiluted moral purity, by far the noblest of the Compsons and the only one capable of genuine religious feeling, he is also a drooling idiot, with skin that is "dead looking" and "dropsical," who walks "with a shambling gait like a trained bear." Unable to care for himself or even to speak, Benjy appears at first sight barely human; in a later interview Faulkner explicitly referred to him as "an animal." Yet Arthur Geffen is surely not alone in describing Benjy as "a holy idiot . . . capable of intuitive acts and knowledge denied to far more 'intelligent' people." Benjy reflects the paradoxical Modernist beliefs that virtue is especially likely to be found among those conventionally dismissed as "savage" or "primitive" and that the kind of knowledge that really matters comes through extensive suffering rather than formal learning. Benjy's function, then, is not to illustrate southern degeneracy, as so many of the book's initial readers believed, but to supply a Modernist standard of judgment. Unimpeachably authentic, he is a device for ensuring that the reader grasps the full moral meaning, the existential truth, of what is happening to the Compsons—which is why the novel begins and ends with him.[50]

He performs that task so well because of the unique way his mind operates. "Benjy," writes Kartiganer, "is perception prior to consciousness, prior to the human need to abstract from events an intelligible order." His soliloquy is made up of a continuous flow of experiential fragments, both immediate and remembered, unimpeded by any effort at rational interpretation. Those fragments are presented in a sequence determined not by logic or chronology but by the emotional associations that the events carry for him. In other words, Benjy's thinking takes place at the level of the mind that Modernist writers on epistemology from William James onward have tended to privilege. Raw sensory perceptions, they have claimed, provide human beings with their most direct access to reality. As those perceptions continue through subsequent stages of the thought process, rising into consciousness and ultimately becoming transformed into abstract concepts, they are increasingly distorted. Each application of the intellect, however valuable it might be for practical purposes, takes us further from the "truth." Benjy, however, avoids such distortion by never engaging in cerebration. In addition, he relies heavily on his sense of smell, which for him is akin to a moral sense. He can, we are told, actually "smell" impending death and Caddy's loss of innocence. Again, this metaphoric device is in keeping with his role as a vehicle for Modernist perspective. As Geffen points out, smell is "the sense least associated with intellectual perception" and is often regarded in folk belief "as the mysterious means which gifted people use to pierce through appearances to truth."[51]

Paradoxically, Benjy can function as such an accurate reporter of events precisely because he has no ego to interfere with or bias his perceptions. Repeatedly he leaves himself out of his own narrative; we often learn he is crying, for example, when others tell him to hush. He is a man totally lacking in self-integration, "shaped of some substance whose particles would not or did not cohere to one another or to the frame which supported it." Castrated after a supposed attack on a schoolgirl and, although an adult white male, subservient to his black servant Luster, Benjy cannot even identify himself in terms of the basic categories of gender and race. Indeed, he has no real name—"Benjamin" was given him to replace "Maury" after his mother, realizing he was abnormal, decided she did not want him to carry the same name as her brother. One cannot imagine a more dramatic rendering of the crisis Faulkner discerned in modern southern identity.⁵²

His fractured and incomplete persona, in turn, makes Benjy acutely sensitive to the lack of identity and integrity surrounding him. In contrast to Quentin, Compson honor and social status as such mean nothing to Benjy; they are abstractions far beyond his grasp. But he can and does register his horror whenever he senses decay, fragmentation, and loss. He does so by the simple expedient of weeping, a direct form of emotional response that in his case serves as a remarkably effective tool of communication. Always exactly calibrated to the moral circumstances at hand, it can range from a subtle whimper to a full-throated bellow that "might have been all time and injustice and sorrow become vocal for an instant." A vivid example comes on Easter Sunday morning when he senses that Miss Quentin has run away, marking the final step in the family's disintegration. Dilsey, realizing that Ben is "smellin hit," correctly predicts that he will stop crying once they "git off de place." But just as predictably he starts again on their return from church as soon as "the square, paintless house with its rotting portico" comes into view. Such scenes of decay are measured in Benjy's mind against remembered occasions when the family was intact and all was peaceful. Of these memories none is treasured more than the one that closes his narrative, when all four Compson children are in bed in the same room: "Caddy held me and I could hear us all. . . . Then the dark began to go in smooth, bright shapes, like it always does, even when Caddy says that I have been asleep." ⁵³

To accentuate this portrait of the disintegration of white southern society, Faulkner toward the novel's end, just as in *Soldiers' Pay*, offers the counterposed image of a black church service. Again, he relies on the Modernist premise that true insight is most often grounded in intense experience and cannot be accurately transmitted through mere words or logic. The church may be dilapidated and the visiting Reverend Shegog so "undersized" and "insignificant looking" that the congregation does not even notice when he enters, but nonetheless, once he has left behind the "level and cold" voice of white intellect for the "sad, timbrous quality" born of his people's tragic lives, his sermon becomes a message of hope and rebirth that moves Dilsey to tears of ecstasy. There is no real narrative or argument to what he says and little order or cohesion—just a montage of phrases and images conveying the sufferings of Jesus, "de resurrection and de light," and the promise of eternal glory to those "whut got de blood en de ricklickshun of de Lamb." As he speaks, his body, with its "shabbiness and insignificance," virtually disappears for his listeners, achieving that transcendence of physical self of which Quentin could only dream. His voice, we are told, utterly envelops them, "until he was nothing and they were nothing . . . but instead their hearts were speaking to one another in chanting measures beyond the need for words." "Yes suh. He seed hit," Dilsey remarks afterward of Shegog's immediate sensory apprehension of religious faith. "Face to face he seed it."[54]

This "oneness of emotion and purpose" that the black churchgoers possess, in Davis's phrase, could not contrast more sharply with the alienation exemplified by the Compsons. It is the sort of all-encompassing integrative experience they and other twentieth-century white southerners desperately need but from which their hopelessly divisive culture has completely shut them off. If the congregation can envision "de power and de glory," there is nothing left for descendants of the old planter class save for Benjy's lamenting sound and Jason's impotent fury. "I seed de beginnin, en now I sees de endin," Dilsey tells her daughter, referring at once to the alpha and omega she has glimpsed in her moment of passion and to the family whose sad saga she is witnessing.[55]

The summary image, encapsulating all that Faulkner had been seeking to express in the book, comes in the final pages when Luster is driving Benjy on his weekly pilgrimage to the cemetery to visit the family graves. The route takes them northward through the town square, at the center of which stands the commemorative statue of a Confederate soldier found in virtually all southern towns. By dint of ritual, the carriage always goes around the square counterclockwise; that way, keeping his head locked to the right, Benjy can entirely avoid seeing the soldier. But this time, on impulse, Luster turns left at the entrance to the square. Suddenly, the heroic past looms directly before Benjy, staring down to remind him of how far the white South has fallen: "For an instant Ben sat in an utter hiatus. Then he bellowed. Bellow on bellow, his voice mounted, with scarce interval for breath. There was more than astonishment in it, it was horror, shock; agony eyeless, tongueless; just sound."* It is indeed "just sound,"

---

*John V. Hagopian, among others, has badly misinterpreted the novel's closing scene by arguing that Benjy's outburst is set off by a violation of "his purely meaningless sense of order." In other words, Benjy is used to going around the monument on the right, and when he finds that Luster has instead gone to the left, he begins screaming until the familiar route is restored.

The approach to the county courthouse in Oxford, Mississippi, the scene Faulkner clearly had in mind while composing the final sequence of The Sound and the Fury. *The Compson family carriage would have turned left at this intersection, placing Benjy directly below the statue of the Confederate soldier looking down with his "empty eyes." (Photograph by author)*

echoing through the reader's ears, forming a sensory bond between author and reader at the most profound level of understanding, capturing in a reverberating instant the anguish that welled up inside Faulkner whenever he contemplated the history of his region and that would now supply the motor force for the balance of his career.[56]

This interpretation ignores several things, including the intensity of Benjy's protest. Throughout the novel his cries have always been finely tuned to the moral outrage of the stimulus that has set them off. He whimpers when Luster mildly mistreats him, but screams in agony when Caddy loses her virginity. Clearly, the bellowing in the town square, with its "unbelievable crescendo," must have a cause greater than a simple flouting of arbitrary ritual. Moreover, in Faulkner's work the appearance of Confederate imagery is never without significance. A clue to its importance in this particular scene can be found in the spiritual kinship that Faulkner carefully establishes between Benjy and the soldier. After telling us how the latter "gazed with empty eyes beneath his marble hand in wind and weather," Faulkner just a few sentences later describes Benjy as sitting with "his gaze empty and untroubled." Throughout the fourth section, in fact, Benjy's eyes are repeatedly described as "empty" and set in a "sweet vague gaze." Finally, when Benjy and Luster turn around and head toward home, they are *again* violating their accustomed ritual. Presumably, if Benjy was the fanatical stickler for order that Hagopian suggests, nothing less than a resumption of the trip to the cemetery (this time going around the square the "correct" way) would finally quiet him.

The crucial phrase for understanding this incident comes in the book's last sentence, when we are told how, as Benjy looks out from the carriage, "cornice and facade [i.e., the houses they are passing] flowed smoothly once more *from left to right*" (italics added). That is the clue that informs us that his head is always turned to the right, avoiding the monument. Further confirmation appears in the map of Yoknapatawpha County that Faulkner prepared a few years later for the first edition of *Absalom, Absalom!*. It includes a notation for the "Confederate monument which Benjy had to pass on his *left* side." The italics this time are Faulkner's own, employed, one suspects, to help ensure that readers would not continue to misread the climactic scene of his Modernist masterpiece.

See Hagopian, "Nihilism in Faulkner's *The Sound and the Fury*," in Kinney, *Critical Essays: The Compson Family*, 203. I am grateful to Carolyn Jerose, my student at William Smith College, for bringing the notation on the map to my attention.

CHAPTER 6

Into the Void

It has become a commonplace among historians of twentieth-century culture that Modernism was essentially an urban affair, a set of beliefs and values that could find sufficient nourishment only in the lively, cosmopolitan environment provided by a large city. "It was in no sense a rural movement," writes Norman Cantor, "nor a frontier movement, but entirely a metropolitan phenomenon whose leading centers were Paris, London, New York, Vienna, Berlin, as well as a number of subsidiary centers like Oslo and Dublin." There is some truth to this, to the extent that many of the seminal figures who helped create the culture happened to live in urban settings. But it is also true that many did not. One thinks of the philosopher Martin Heidegger, who spent most of his life in small provincial towns, or the Irish poet William Butler Yeats. Above all, there are the leading writers of the southern literary renaissance of the 1920s and 1930s, who often grew up in farming villages and did not move to big cities until relatively late in their careers, if at all. And among them, the stellar example of a rural Modernist was surely the novelist who spent nearly all his life in the countrified confines of Oxford, Mississippi.[1]

Whether Faulkner was conscious of this fact or not, there can be no doubt that *As I Lay Dying*, his next published novel after *The Sound and the Fury*, provided indisputable evidence that great Modernist art could emerge from a backwoods setting. The book's central figures, a family of impoverished and uneducated hill farmers named Bundren, could not be more emphatically removed from modern, urban life. Residents of the tiny hamlet of Frenchman's Bend, they seem to occupy a world where time stands still, an archetypal peasant community in which human beings exist just one notch above bare survival. Indeed, they inhabit a landscape so desolate and remote that the little town of Jefferson, with its telephone poles, radios, and automobiles, appears a major metropolis by comparison. And yet there could be no doubt among the initial set of readers in October 1930 that this novel about the deepest reaches of the southern backcountry belonged on the forefront of the international literary avant-garde.

Modernist technique suffuses *As I Lay Dying*. Instead of conventional chapters, there are fifty-nine monologues delivered by fifteen different speakers, some in the stream-of-consciousness mode and others not, creating a veritable montage of conflicting styles and viewpoints. Colloquial and ungrammatical expressions abound throughout to heighten authenticity. In keeping with the basic premises of Modernist aesthetics, Faulkner's objective in these monologues was not straightforward narrative exposition but rather an attempt to apprehend the totality of experience — to flood the reader with sensory particulars until he or she becomes a virtual participant in the events of the novel. *As I Lay Dying* is designed, notes Bleikasten, to be "experienced, not translated; felt, not analyzed." Moreover, since the characters speak from their own limited vantage points, reflecting their needs and biases, the reader cannot possibly arrive at any assured, objective truth about them. Nor was Faulkner attempting to elicit any preordained moral response in the reader. On the contrary, *As I Lay Dying* eschews heroes and villains. All the characters display both good and bad traits, and we are meant to react to them with an equally complex mixture of laughter, puzzlement, empathy, anger, and admiration, to the point where the boundaries between genres dissolve and it becomes impossible to determine if the story in which they are engaged should be accounted a comedy or tragedy.[2]

The novel is also characteristically Modernist in its subject matter, dealing more or less sympathetically with a class of people who appear in Victorian literature only to be ridiculed or held up as a cautionary example of "savagery." It is true that the Bundrens commit a number of outrageous acts that appear to corroborate the prevailing image of dirt farmers as subhuman buffoons. Carting Addie Bundren's rotting corpse for nine days through the steamy July sun before finally laying it to rest is, at first sight, a grotesque enterprise, as is the family's ill-fated decision to set Cash Bundren's broken leg in concrete. Most of all, Anse Bundren, the father, seems to conform perfectly with the traditional stereotype of the poor white as lazy and worthless—his very name, echoing the word "ants," suggests that he belongs among the lower forms of life. When he soliloquizes about how an "honest, hardworking man" like himself is doomed to suffer in such "a hard country," the reader is strongly tempted to guffaw. We know that his neighbor, Vernon Tull, cannot recall ever seeing a drop of sweat on Anse's shirt. As his son Darl explains: "He was sick once from working in the sun when he was twenty-two years old, and he tells people that if he ever sweats, he will die. I suppose he believes it."[3]

As I Lay Dying may confirm the stereotype of the poor white in this way, but it simultaneously undermines it. Anse Bundren, we learn, is a man who has experienced genuine hardship, especially during his childhood, as evidenced by his "badly splayed" feet, with toes "cramped and bent and warped . . . from working so hard in the wet in homemade shoes when he was a boy," and his wife Addie's comment on how, when she first met him as a young man, his back was "already starting to hump." Perhaps he can be partially excused for thinking he has done his share of labor. His disinclination to work may also be related to the loss of his teeth, leaving him unable to eat a normal diet to keep his strength up. In addition, Faulkner makes clear, Anse is not without justice in claiming that the odds are stacked against hill-country farmers like himself. We see this in a vignette that Faulkner pointedly places at the very outset of the novel, when Cora Tull explains how she had gone to considerable trouble and expense to bake cakes ordered by a woman in Jefferson, only to be informed at the last minute that the cakes were no longer needed. "It's not everybody can eat their mistakes," Cora stoically tells her husband. The incident illustrates how poor families like the Bundrens and Tulls, living on the margin of existence, are continuously subject to unforeseeable disasters that negate their best efforts to advance themselves. Given that reality, Anse's self-pitying lament that he is "a luckless man" has a certain ring of truth to it.[4]

Most of the derogatory remarks critics have made about Anse fail to take into account the subtle clues that Faulkner provides about this complicated character. It is said, for example, that even on the occasion of his wife's death Anse fails to display the emotions one would normally expect but rather is selfishly fixated on the prospect of getting a new set of teeth in Jefferson. Anse does want those teeth, but it is also true, as Hyatt Waggoner long ago observed, that he is "sincerely bereaved" over the loss of Addie. This becomes apparent just before her death when Vardaman, the youngest son, comes up to ask him, "Is ma sick some more?" Anse wants to respond but can do no more than perfunctorily instruct the boy to wash his hands. "I just cant seem to get no heart into it," he tells us. A short time later at dinner we find Anse, who cares so much about eating, helping himself to some food and then staring blankly at it. According to his daughter Dewey Dell, he "looks like right after the maul hits the steer and it no longer alive and dont yet know that it is dead." In short, Anse is neither unfeeling or sensitive but a mixture of both—and that is the point. *As I Lay Dying* attacks the stereotype in just this way, allowing poor whites, as Sylvia Cook puts it, "to triumph and sin within the same range of dignity and folly as the rest of humanity." In Anse's words, "I have done things but neither better nor worse than them that pretend otherlike, and I know that Old Marster will care for me ere a sparrow that falls."[5]*

Anse may at times act like the animal-like "ferret" that Cleanth Brooks terms him, but he is more accurately seen as a man living at the outer boundary of civilized existence and struggling to maintain his human dignity. Despite his pathetic awkwardness, he cares about proprieties, even when his self-interest is not at stake. Again and again he chides his children for violating what he regards as the correct forms of behavior toward their dead mother. It troubles him when Jewel insists on riding his horse during the funeral journey because "it wouldn't look right, him prancing along on a durn circus animal." When people outside the family offer help, Anse's standard response is "We wouldn't be beholden" or "We wouldn't discommode you." Critics have assumed that these comments represent a shrewd tactic to weasel food and lodging out of his neighbors, but in fact he accepts the minimum amount of aid necessary to continue his trip under what can only be described as emergency conditions. For example, he could easily take advantage of Samson's offer to put the family up for the night but chooses instead to spend the night "squatting on the ground around the wagon." At Anse's insistence, the Bundrens leave early the next morning so that Samson's wife will not have to fix them breakfast. At Armstid's he likewise decides to spend the night in the barn instead

---

*For a sample of the way most critics have responded to Anse, see Brooks, *William Faulkner: The Yoknapatawpha Country*, 154–55, which speaks of Anse as "one of Faulkner's most accomplished villains," notable for his "essential callousness and cruelty." The most damning evidence usually cited against Anse, it might be pointed out, is the remark he supposedly makes immediately after Addie's passing: "Now I can get them teeth." But we do not know for a fact that Anse ever said this. The scene is recounted in one of Darl's monologues and represents a reconstruction of the event in Darl's mind that may or may not be accurate (Darl is several miles away at the time his mother dies). See *As I Lay Dying*, 51.

of the house in order to "set up with her." What one sees here, then, is a person making every effort to conduct himself so that he can look others in the eye but who is constantly being undercut by his circumstances and severe cultural limitations. His language may be cliché-ridden, his manners clumsy, and his impulses toward self-aggrandizement may keep breaking through, but at bottom Anse's intent is to uphold his humanity as best he knows how.[6]

It is in this sense that *As I Lay Dying* can be viewed as an existential drama akin to the most advanced works of Gide, Malraux, or Beckett—its plot a minimalist quest to preserve identity under the most trying conditions conceivable. The Bundrens, unsophisticated though they may be, are caught up in the typical twentieth-century dilemma of defining themselves in the midst of an indifferent cosmos, of fashioning a basis of being in the midst of nothingness. Their hill-country environment in this sense serves as yet another (and particularly clever) variant of the "wasteland" setting employed by so many Modernist writers to focus attention on existential concerns. What sets off the crisis of self-definition in this case is the death of the mother, Addie, and the subsequent attempt to honor her final wish to be buried with her blood relatives in Jefferson. Her passing, as Eric Sundquist points out, rips away many of the conventional props on which the family's life had been based, leaving its members temporarily exposed to the absurd nature of existence. Each in his own way must adjust his identity to deal with this changed situation or face the threat of personal dissolution. In Kartiganer's words, the "threat of madness and annihilation" always lies at hand during the trip to Jefferson.[7]

Of all the Bundren children, the one with the most precarious identity is Darl, the second son whom Addie never wanted to have. Like Quentin Compson, he has responded to his mother's rejection by taking refuge in pure consciousness, floating about in a world of words and perceptions with no central self to provide stability and direction. His hold on identity is in fact so shaky that he must resort to formal logic to prove his very existence: "I must be, or I could not empty myself for sleep in a strange room. And so if I am not emptied yet, I am *is*." In one respect this lack of firm identity works to Darl's advantage: with no substantive ego to distort his vision, he enjoys a remarkable capacity to penetrate other people's thoughts and motives. Again and again those who know him remark on how his large, "queer" eyes seem to cut through the surface of things like an X ray. As Vernon Tull notes, "It aint never been what he done so much or said or anything so much as how he looks at you. It's like he had got into the inside of you, someway." These special powers come at a price, though, for the intense sensory knowledge that Darl drinks in continually threatens to overwhelm him, causing him to reel with vertigo and break out into those fits of hysterical laughter that "makes folks talk about him."[8]

Here is precisely where Darl differs from Quentin, for if Quentin represented the post-Victorian persona that Faulkner was rejecting, Darl with his acute perceptivity embodies a crucial component of the Modernist self that Faulkner was attempting to fashion. Like a Modernist artist, Darl functions primarily at the level of raw sensory experience, combining his keen responsiveness to touch, sight, and smell with a disposition to express himself in metaphoric rather than conceptual terms. That is why his speech often sounds so much like Faulknerian rhetoric, reflecting the blending of senses, or synethesia, that is a hallmark of the Modernist sensibility: "When I was a boy I first learned how much better water tastes when it has set a while in a cedar bucket. Warmish-cool, with a faint taste like the hot July wind in cedar trees smells." Or again: "The sun . . . is poised like a bloody egg upon a crest of thunderheads; the light has turned copper: in the eye portentous, in the nose sulphorous, smelling of lightning." Likewise it is Darl who describes his mother's coffin sitting on a pair of sawhorses as "a cubistic bug" and who puts on bohemian airs that his neighbors regard as "queer"—which is, of course, how many folks in Oxford had come to regard Faulkner.[9]

Nonetheless, Darl's role in *As I Lay Dying* is more tragic than exemplary, showing how a thoroughgoing openness to sensory experience, that indispensable component of the Modernist mentality, can become a grave danger when it exists by itself. Unless somehow rooted in ordinary life, Faulkner suggests, the extraordinarily sensitive individual like Darl may find himself so flooded by perceptions that he cannot begin to integrate them into a workable pattern of meaning and values. His consciousness may be rich, but, in the absence of a meaningful connection to the actual world such as the one Faulkner was in the process of devising through his deployment of dual identities, it will also be chaotic and out of control. The result is that Darl becomes effectively isolated within his own mind, his primary social role that of a crude existential commentator registering through his harsh laughter the insight that all human endeavor is inherently absurd. His one attempt to act decisively—setting fire to Gillespie's barn in order to burn up his mother's coffin and stop the family's senseless journey—fails because he is totally unable to share his complex motives with others and thus is badly misunderstood. In the end, his pitifully weak self having split entirely in two, he is carted off to the state asylum at Jackson with his vivid perceptive powers now turned on himself: "Our brother Darl in a cage in Jackson where, his grimed hands lying light in the quiet interstices, looking out he foams." Perhaps, all considered, his brother Cash's summary judgment is a fair one: "This world is not his world; this life his life." [10]

Ironically, the same conclusion holds for Darl's mother, Addie Bundren, a figure who, even though she differs from him in many ways, provides another example of a Modernist persona that is fatally incomplete. If Darl embodies that part of the Modernist ethos that insists on intense perception, Addie represents the part that seeks radical self-definition through experience. "I would be I," she declares, leaving no question about her determination to establish her own identity in the face of what she sees as a meaningless existence. Under no circumstances will she allow herself to slip into the conventions of ordinary life like her neighbor Cora Tull, to whom faith, passion, and sin are, in Addie's view, "just a matter of words." For Addie, words are evanescent things that "go straight up in a thin line, quick and harmless," to vanish into the ether, while deeds go "terribly . . . along the earth, clinging to it," constituting the only reality we can know. As a schoolteacher, accordingly, she cares less about the lessons her pupils learn than about the visceral communion she establishes when whipping them: "I would think with each blow of the switch: Now you are aware of me! Now I am something in your secret and selfish life, who have marked your blood with my own for ever and ever." For Addie, being truly alive is that moment of blood touching blood, of breaking through all illusion to confront the "terrible" core of life. Even sin must be embraced with a pure and brutal authenticity: nothing less than a passionate affair with a minister in the woods—a virtual black sabbath—will suffice.[11]

Faulkner clearly admired this kind of existential heroism, just as he admired Darl's impressive powers of consciousness. The ability to accept unflinchingly the absurdity of human existence—understanding, as Addie learned from her father, that "the reason for living was to get ready to stay dead a long time"—was for him a prerequisite to nobility in the modern age, as was Addie's resolve to create an authentic self in the face of that impending oblivion. He could not, however, admire her wholesale rejection of language. Such an absolutist choice ran against the tenets of his evolving belief system, which was predicated on the effective *integration* of words and deeds. Thinking and talking might be evanescent and at times foolish, but they also served the indispensable purpose of helping a person make sense of and respond to the unpredictable flow of events in life. By contrast, as Gary Stonum neatly puts it, a "person who lies immersed in the flux of doing is defenseless against changes in the current." That is certainly the case with Addie, who cannot bring herself to accept Darl when she unexpectedly finds herself pregnant with him. Distrusting words, Addie loses her sensitivity to other people, including her own children, rendering her as isolated in her own way as Darl is in his. In the end she can justly claim to have put aside illusion, but at an enormous price — dying, in Cora's phrase, "a lonely woman, lonely with her pride." Surely that price was too high for Faulkner.[12]

No shining model of an integrated Modernist self emerges in *As I Lay Dying*, but a glimpse of what that persona might look like does appear in the form of Cash Bundren. The name is meant to be ironic, for what concerns Cash is not making money but careful craftsmanship — the urge to create something sturdy and beautiful for its own sake. A carpenter by trade, he subscribes to "the olden right teaching that says to drive the nails down and trim the edges well always like it was for your own use and comfort you were making it." Though he lacks the artistic perceptivity and imagination found in Darl, his handsaw is always "steady, competent, unhurried," even under the most difficult conditions, and his work reflects his central values of precision and balance. As Calvin Bedient explains, Cash invests so much of himself in his craft because it is his sole means for securing a viable identity, for "contesting the amorphousness, the appalling anonymity of existence itself." The coffin he lovingly constructs for Addie represents a perfect example of this sort of existential gesture of self-definition. Though Cash is well aware it will soon disintegrate into oblivion, he insists on taking extra time to bevel all the seams and joints, for that is the only way he knows how, in Bedient's words, "to assert the human in the teeth of its negation."[13]

Most important, Cash is the only figure who, by the novel's end, is able to fuse together thought and action, rationality and emotion. In his first few monologues his mind seems limited to the practical considerations of his craft, but as he proceeds through what Wittenberg calls his "baptism by suffering" on the road to Jefferson, we see him grow increasingly verbal and reflective. Unlike the other members of the family, he is able to learn from experience, and though he never attains the level of true insight, he becomes a far wiser and more fundamentally integrated person than he was at the outset. He alone "functions well on both the horizontal axis of deeds and the vertical axis of words," notes Stonum, making him the only character who can effectively integrate the two realms. With his tolerance and self-effacement, this "good carpenter" is even implicitly associated with Christ (a comparison made explicit in a deleted passage). To be sure, Cash, for all his virtues, never rises to the level of a redemptive or heroic figure: he cannot save Darl, or anyone else; nor does his contribution to the world extend beyond his craftsmanship and the example of stoic courage that he sets. A simple man, he will adopt as his standard what "most folks say is right," rather than exercising any sort of independent judgment. Still, one comes away convinced that Cash's small triumphs over the void of existence are meant to be savored, that he constitutes as positive a vision of southern identity as Faulkner could summon forth at this time.[14]

Indeed, this minimalist perspective offers the best way to comprehend *As I Lay Dying* as a whole, for whatever else it may be, the Bundrens' struggle to reach Jefferson constitutes an undeniable, if minor, triumph wrenched from a hostile world. Faulkner makes this plain in a key passage late in the book when Anse recounts their travail to the marshal in Mottson, compressing into one sentence the full extent of their heroic persistence:

> "We're doing the best we can," the father said. Then he told a long tale about how they had to wait for the wagon to come back and how the bridge was washed away and how they went eight miles to another bridge and it was gone too so they came back and swum the ford and the mules got drowned and how they got another team and found that the road was washed out and they had to come clean around by Mottson. . . .
> "We never aimed to bother nobody," the father said.

The novel may be, as Elizabeth Kerr has argued, "an ironic inversion of the quest romance" in which, instead of a noble knight rescuing a fair maiden, we find a group of illiterate hill farmers struggling to bury a dead mother. The "ironic mockery" Kerr finds was doubtless part of Faulkner's complex attitude toward the Bundrens. But there was just as clearly admiration for them, based on their willingness to plunge gamely into the raging river of experience, to take on "the thick dark current" few others dared to challenge. "I be durn," a neighbor says of Anse, "if he didn't act like he was proud of it, like he had made the river rise himself." In this sense, the work should be seen as both ironic *and* affirmative—as an effort to depict unflinchingly the utter pathos of the human condition, and as an initial step toward reestablishing a basis for heroism in the face of that harsh Modernist revelation.[15]

It seems highly appropriate in retrospect that Faulkner began *As I Lay Dying* the day after the New York stock market crashed in October 1929, for he was entering a period of his career in which he would be dogged by incessant financial troubles. In June of that year he had, with considerable ambivalence, married his childhood sweetheart, the former Estelle Oldham, who had finally secured a divorce from her first husband. Though he felt great pleasure at winning the prize he had long sought, there were also signs that the match was less than ideal. Her heavy drinking did nothing to temper his, and their quarrels, which would in time lead to de facto separations, began almost immediately. An all too valid portent of where the relationship was headed came during their honeymoon when Estelle tried to drown herself in the Gulf of Mexico, walking out through the waves in a fancy evening dress toward a spot where the beach suddenly dropped off into a deep channel. In addition to his uncertainty over his bride, Faulkner had also been reluctant to marry because of the heavy responsibilities it entailed, in terms of not only the normal obligation of providing for his family but also satisfying Estelle's expensive tastes. He must have realized that the need for a steady and sizable income was bound to clash with his literary ambitions.[16]

If Faulkner ever believed he could earn a living as a writer, the events of 1929 swiftly taught him otherwise. *Sartoris*, published in January, fared poorly in the marketplace, as did *The Sound and the Fury* when it appeared in October. The reception of the latter made clear that he was, in his best work, a difficult stylist with an appeal essentially limited to the avant-garde. Sensing this, he began to evolve a two-tiered strategy, consecrating the novel as the primary vehicle of his art and relying on the sale of short stories to high-paying magazines such as *Harper's* or the *Saturday Evening Post* to stay afloat financially. A few of those stories, it is true, had significant artistic merit, and he did occasionally use the medium to play with material that would find its way into novels. More typically, though, he was forced to simplify plot and technique, producing work that fell below his standards. Worst of all were those intervals, such as the one running through most of 1929 and 1930, when this concession to popular taste failed to work—when instead of the continuous stream of checks he had anticipated, the morning mail brought a torrent of rejection slips, making him more and more frustrated.[17]

Such were the circumstances that helped give rise to *Sanctuary*, a book Faulkner was to call "a cheap idea . . . deliberately conceived to make money." One must always be skeptical about Faulkner's statements concerning his work, but in this case his defamation of *Sanctuary* was repeated so often that it appears to be a reliable indicator of how he viewed the novel. Money *was* a major motive for him: the original manuscript, completed during the first five months of 1929, was loaded with sensational material in the hope that it would rake in enough cash to launch his impending marriage. "It will sell," he assured Estelle. And when he undertook an extensive revision of the galley proofs in late 1930—the publisher had initially thought the work too hot to handle and kept it on the shelf for a year—he did so with an eye to movie rights. Although he would claim afterward that his purpose in revising had been to make the book more respectable, the fact is that virtually all of the most horrific material remained, while some new purple passages were added. With a baby soon expected and a house badly in need of repair, Faulkner apparently took the advice of the impressario Leland Heyward, transmitted through Ben Wasson, that film was "where the big money lay" and that *Sanctuary* had good screen potential. That was enough to convince Faulkner, in Gerald Langford's words, "to turn a slow-moving psychological study into a streamlined drama ready for the cameras of Hollywood."[18]

These facts obviously must enter into any assessment of *Sanctuary*, but at the same time one must ask if Faulkner was protesting too much—if his remarks about his commercial intent were also meant to shield, both from others *and* himself, his real attitude toward the book. If *Sanctuary* is at one level a pot-boiling detective story, at another it involves a Modernist-style exploration of human evil that must have been as trying for him to undertake as his voyage of discovery into the southern psyche in *The Sound and the Fury*. What the novel indelibly establishes is the power and omnipresence of the animal component in human nature—that aspect of human character that the Victorians equated with evil and sought to eliminate. More important, *Sanctuary* puts forth this finding in a fashion that is shocking even by late-twentieth-century standards but must have seemed utterly scandalous in 1930. At a time when, as Putzel reminds us, most American newspapers did not allow the actual word "rape" in their columns, Faulkner depicted a young coed from a prominent family appearing to take pleasure in her own sexual corruption. It is a work filled with unremitted pessimism, a nightmare vision of the depravity to be found in the most hallowed precincts of human civilization. No wonder that Faulkner, to placate his Victorian self, felt obliged to disown it by maintaining that it was done out of financial necessity.[19]

By far the most horrific element in *Sanctuary* is the fate of Temple Drake, a delicate blossom of southern civilization attending the University of Mississippi who is sexually assaulted with a corncob and then held virtual prisoner in a Memphis brothel by the notorious gangster Popeye. What makes her rape so sensational is precisely her social background, for according to traditional belief young white southern women of good lineage were assumed to be paragons of innocence, free of instinctual drives, and thus able to serve as agents of moral restraint for men. On the surface level this is true of Temple: she is very much a creature of respectable society who values her reputation above all else. Even before her rape, however, she had displayed a taste for the illicit under certain controlled conditions. She would, we learn, stay out with "town boys" past her weeknight curfew, a piece of mild misbehavior that landed her on probation but did not expose her to any real danger (she would, of course, never consider associating with town boys on weekends, when formal dances were held). If trouble threatened, she would simply invoke her social status through a set of magic words—" 'My father's a judge' "—and the overeager suitor would back off. In this way, the sanctuary of her middle-class southern world allowed Temple to indulge her flirtatiousness, safely sampling a small draft of sensual pleasure while still preserving her claim to purity.[20]

All of this changes abruptly when, through the kind of accidental circumstance that governs the Modernist universe, Temple suddenly moves out of the predictable environment she has always known into one where she stands exposed to the irrational forces of nature, personified by Popeye. Her subsequent behavior has become a hotly debated issue for critics of the novel, with several claiming to find in her a fundamental malevolence, an "affinity for evil" that, David Williams writes, "is absolute" and only waiting for the proper setting to manifest itself. But nothing is ever "absolute" in Faulkner. Temple is not inherently more corrupt than other people; rather, her entry into the criminal underworld serves to unleash a host of natural instincts that she has had little experience in controlling. It is thus not her affinity for evil but her very innocence that makes her so vulnerable, giving rise to the intricate mix of terror and fascination, resistance and surrender that she displays.[21]

Throughout her ordeal Faulkner portrays Temple as torn between her powerful yearning for respectability and her equally powerful unconscious drives toward sexuality and death. The ambivalence begins the moment she and her drunken date Gowan Stevens walk up to the Old Frenchman Place, the ruined mansion that the bootleggers have made their lair. "I dont want to go there," she first informs Stevens, but she then proceeds a moment later to enter the house against his orders. On discovering the bizarre people living there, so different from anyone she had ever known, she starts running aimlessly about in what is at once an act of panic and, in David L. Frazier's description, "an animalistic, feintingly evasive mating dance." Meeting Popeye, she pauses briefly, offering him "a grimace of taut, toothed coquetry," and then speeds off in sheer fright in the opposite direction. Though she could easily escape by continuing down the road to a neighbor's house, she does not. Rather, like a moth fatally attracted to a source of light, she flickers to and from the house, terrified of what may happen but eager to find out what it would be like. Later, after Popeye has deposited her at Miss Reba's, she likewise makes no effort to flee but instead does his bidding as if he were her father, even calling him "daddy," while at the same time taunting him mercilessly about his impotence. Again and again she alternately seeks to regain control and then to surrender it.[22]

In this context, it seems highly significant that Temple's primary tactic for defending herself is a regression to the innocence of childhood. Whenever the situation becomes threatening, she instinctively acts like a helpless, dependent little girl, pulling the bedcovers up to her chin (or disappearing under them), crying "hopelessly and passively, like a child in a dentist's waiting-room," or sitting in an "attitude of childish immobility." It is as if she were saying that, despite all that is happening to her, she cannot be held responsible. No matter if she is filled with "erotic longing" for the lover Popeye has found for her, "hurling herself upon him, her mouth gaped and ugly like that of a dying fish"; no matter if she causes his death and that of other innocent men. By establishing herself as a mere child she keeps her purity intact, while at the same time eliciting a protective response from those around her. The strategy works: after Temple has given the perjured testimony that will cost Lee Goodwin his life, the district attorney restores her image of innocence in the eyes of the community, referring to her as a "ruined, defenseless child." His remark is followed by the peculiar scene in which her father claims her from the witness stand and marches her down the center aisle of the courtroom to where her four brothers are waiting to usher her from the building—enacting a kind of wedding in reverse. Instead of moving forward into maturity, she regresses into the cocoon of her family, thus restoring her sanctuary.[23]

Temple's travail has received much attention in recent years because of its bearing on the hotly debated issue of Faulkner's alleged misogyny. Albert Guerard, for one, supports his claim that Faulkner is an "unrepressed and even undisguised" misogynist by noting the long list of torments that Temple is made to endure and the "insistent denigrative imagery" heaped on her. Ellen Douglas sounds a similar note, claiming that Faulkner is incapable of portraying relationships between men and women as anything other than poisonous: "Over and over he gives us the inevitability of misunderstanding, the cold silence, the eager masochism, the awful sadism, the furious hatred between lover and lover, between man and wife." Surely there is an element of truth here. One cannot help detecting an undertone of sweet satisfaction in the account of Temple, as if Faulkner was finally paying back all those coeds from the early 1920s who, like Temple, danced the night away "in a swirling glitter" while town boys like himself were consigned to watch forlornly through the windowpane. Nor can one overlook the misogynous intent in Faulkner's comment to Ben Wasson that his main purpose in writing the novel was to show how "women are impervious to evil," which, he added, flows off them "like water off a duck's back." [24]

But a crucial question remains: Was Faulkner assailing *all* women, or a specific type of woman highly prevalent in the South of his day? Given the nature of his attack, it is clear that his real target was the southern lady, that transcendent figure whom the region, W. J. Cash tells us, had come to revere as the "mystic symbol of its nationality" and whom so many of the women surrounding Faulkner tried to emulate. Because the southern lady (like her male counterpart, the Cavalier) represented one of the foremost vehicles by which southern Victorian values were passed down to members of his generation, it became almost inevitable that Faulkner in his guise as a Modernist writer would display hostility toward her, exposing her repressed erotic impulses, her obsession with respectability, and her shallowness of character. That was just what he was doing in *Sanctuary*. His belated revenge on the Ole Miss belles notwithstanding, surely his main purpose in dragging Temple Drake out of her sheltered world was to make manifest the tissue of lies on which her persona of false innocence rested.[25]

Moreover, since such a large number of the middle-class women he knew shared that persona, it was again inevitable that this assault on the southern lady would, for a time, spill over into a general aversion toward their sex. That misogyny, like the veneration of the "gentler sex" conditioned into him as a child, would never entirely go away. He would always tend to treat women at arm's length, both in his fiction and in real life, at times striking out against them for their ability to manipulate men by invoking the nineteenth-century mythic ideal, and at other times placing them on a romantic pedestal himself—a pattern that showed up in the way he advised his daughter Jill both to be staunchly independent and, in her words, "to go through the motions of being helpless and female." In time, however, his predominant view of women would change dramatically, to the point where he would begin to populate his novels with intelligent, strong-minded female characters and assign them heroic roles. If anything, Faulknerian women from the late 1930s onward are *more* formidable and admirable than their male counterparts. That is why critics who have cast him as a misogynist are essentially wrong. More precisely, they have fixated on one strand of his multifaceted and constantly evolving attitude toward women while ignoring the other strands, mistaking an attitude that was uppermost during one interval of his career for a lifelong one.[26]

Sanctuary should likewise be seen in terms of this process of evolution that was steadily taking Faulkner in a more Modernist and even feminist direction. One recalls the romanticized "Dianalike girl" of his previous works, originating in the epicene wood nymphs of his poetry and continuing through Caddy Compson in *The Sound and the Fury*, who, despite her nymphomania, still remains a figure of selfless love. With her long legs, thin body, and childlike appearance, Temple clearly belongs within this progression of characters, but she is assuredly not epicene, innocent, or transcendent, and the treatment she receives is starkly naturalistic rather than romanticized. Instead of having her frolic through the woods like a sylvan demigod, Faulkner sends her on an awkward, fear-struck mission into the bushes to go to the bathroom ("Unless you're too pure to have to," the bootlegger's wife pointedly remarks). Caddy's corruption had been visited on her from the outside by an external "doom" that battled against her inherent inner goodness. Temple Drake's innocence, by contrast, is almost entirely a surface matter bound up with cultural conditioning and social image. Beneath that surface, she is a natural human being, replete with animalistic sexual drives, a voracious ego, and other attributes supposedly absent in the southern lady. Even before her rape, Faulkner is saying, Temple's purity was an illusion.[27]

Faulkner reinforces this message by including yet another southern lady among his cast of main characters. In *Flags in the Dust*, Narcissa Benbow seemed benign enough—a delicate flower whose life was so sheltered that she even managed to retain her virginal purity after wedlock. In *Sanctuary*, however, her Victorian mores have turned her into an insidious and vicious woman for whom Faulkner cannot disguise his contempt. Dressed always in white, Narcissa now exudes "that serene and stupid impregnability of heroic statuary" and, as Minter puts it, "speaks consistently for repression." Though still comparatively young, she has become a heartless exponent of blind propriety whose sole concern is her reputation within Jefferson. As she explains to her brother Horace in her "cold, unbending voice," she doesn't care whether his client, the bootlegger Lee Goodwin, is being falsely charged with murder. All that concerns her is "what people in town think" about having a member of her family associated with someone who, by her standards, is not wholly respectable. That is more than she can bear. "Do you think," asks Aunt Jenny Du Pre, "Narcissa'd want anybody to know that any of her folks could know people that would do anything as natural as make love or rob or steal?" Her portrait lacks subtlety and may justly be accounted a weakness of the novel, but it renders unmistakable Faulkner's break with the nineteenth-century ideal of "pure" womanhood.[28]

Although Horace Benbow comes across as a far more sympathetic character than his sister in *Sanctuary*, he represents a rejected identity model as well. With his many Prufrock-like attributes, Horace can best be seen as Faulkner's final settling of accounts with post-Victorian culture, his sharpest articulation of the defects of the "poet" persona he had experimented with just a few years earlier. In several key respects Horace's experience parallels Temple's: a chance contact with Popeye forces him temporarily out of his sheltered existence and into an extended, disastrous confrontation with evil. Unlike Temple, however, Horace consciously seeks that encounter with the "real" world and is able to reflect on what happens to him. Like a true post-Victorian, he senses the constraints his genteel upbringing has imposed and longs to break free but cannot finally muster the resolve. The resulting portrait may again fall short of literary triumph—Faulkner was always at his best when working through new territory, and he had to a large extent covered this ground in creating Quentin Compson. But from the historian's vantage point, what the characterization of Horace lacks in subtlety it makes up for in clarity, providing an unobstructed summing up of the cultural lessons Faulkner had learned in the first stage of his career as a writer.

The root of Horace's problem lies in his simultaneous fascination with and terror of that psychic netherworld of animal drives from which his bourgeois ethos has severed him and that he associates with "reality." Although evident in the published novel, this fact is even more apparent in the original version where Horace functions as the dominant character and his thought processes are set forth in detail. There one sees the complex web of incestuous emotion buried in Horace's unconscious that ultimately derives from his close attachment to his mother. Those illicit desires, transferred to Narcissa when his mother died, have now been reawakened by the sexual coming of age of his stepdaughter Little Belle. The dynamics are readily visible in a passage from the original text in which a photograph of Little Belle's "soft, sweet, vague face" triggers what is at first a blissful reverie in Horace. He begins by dwelling on Narcissa as "a figure enchanted out of all time" and then moves on to his mother, whom he recalls radiating an "abounding serenity as of earth." Suddenly, however, his vision turns into a nightmare. As he watches with alarm, his mother's lace nightgown is transformed into the "shapeless garment of faded calico" worn by Ruby Lamar, the former prostitute he had met at the Old Frenchman's Place, while her mouth unexpectedly becomes the "rich, full mouth" of his wife, out of which "a thick, black liquid welled in a bursting bubble." His fantasy, in effect, shifts from one side of the Victorian moral dichotomy to the other as the image of angelic womanhood he depends on for security is replaced by one of consummate sexual evil. It is both his greatest horror and foremost secret wish.[29]

The same ambivalence runs through his response to his experiences at the Old Frenchman's Place. His initial feelings about the evening he had spent there sitting on the rotting porch and drinking moonshine are positive: this brief contact with the lower depths makes him acutely aware of how limited his genteel existence has been and of how anxious he is to change that. Perhaps, he wonders hopefully (again in the original text), "he had become leavened with a reality which had completely destroyed a world of illusion which he had thought for forty-three years was real." All those years he had been "a man given to much talk and not much else," knowing life "only as a dead parade of words across dead paper." That is why he treasures the chance to commune with people like Ruby and her common-law husband Lee Goodwin. Later, though, in an extraordinary passage that reveals as much about Faulkner as it does about Horace, he realizes what a pathetic figure he must have seemed: "how, having blundered into that reality which he thought he was so hot for, his efforts to establish himself as a factor in it had been like those of a boy watching other boys do things he cannot or dare not attempt, and who performs the dwarfed mimicry of their skill or daring with a sort of raging importunity: Look at me! Look at me!" One suspects that Horace was here expressing Faulkner's greatest fear as an incipient Modernist struggling to surmount his own innocence. To such a person nothing could be more shameful than appearing as a mere "boy watching other boys doing things he cannot or dare not attempt" in the eyes of those who had tasted a full draft of experience (one thinks immediately of young Billy Faulkner sitting in the parlor of the brothel while other men went upstairs). At all costs that weakness, that vulnerability, had to be overcome, or at least kept securely hidden.[30]

Horace, however, cannot get by his Victorian values, which return with a vengeance once he begins to realize what has happened to Temple. Instead of pursuing his desire to explore that tempting "reality" on the other side of the moral dividing line, we now find him marking it off as a realm of absolute depravity radically separated from normal civilized existence. "There's a corruption about even looking upon evil, even by accident," Horace declares; "you cannot haggle, traffic, with putrefaction." To him Popeye appears not as a man who through various circumstances has fallen into the role of a gangster but as a veritable demon who actually "smells black." Anything that is in the least suggestive or untidy now fills him with revulsion, including the sight of a couple embracing in an alleyway or the blossoms that have fallen off the heaven tree outside the jail. "They ought to clean that damn mess off the sidewalk," he mutters as he struggles to keep control of his world.[31]

His intense reaction to Temple's story illustrates how desperately Horace clings to the myth of southern womanhood — the one part of the Victorian cultural edifice he cannot abandon without jeopardizing his very sanity. No matter how alluring the noble qualities of a Ruby Lamar, he must hold tight to his bedrock conviction that young women like his stepdaughter (a "little belle") or Temple are fixed in a state of perpetual innocence. That is why he persists, as did the early Faulkner, in seeing the coeds on the Ole Miss campus as epicene nymphs, "pagan and evanescent and serene." That is also why he at first responds to the possibility that Temple may have been raped by imagining her returning to her dormitory shaken but intact, snuggling in bed with her friends "like puppies in a basket" and sharing the story with them as "a whispered tale over a box of candy." This sort of denial not only allows Horace to evade un-palatable realities but more important serves as a crucial defense against what troubles him most—his unconscious sexual longing for Little Belle, who now starts to meld with Temple in his imagination. If she is not a sexual being, then his dangerous incestuous fantasies (which, one recalls, are Oedipal in origin, harking back to his yearning for his mother) can never be acted upon; but if she is less than totally pure, all of his worst fears might come true. Here, in the last analysis, is the source of the abid-ing power that the myth wields over him.[32]

The more he learns about Temple, however, the more that defense starts to crumble. Faulkner registers the process through Horace's chang-ing perceptions of his photograph of Little Belle, his most prized posses-sion, which also serves as an unerring barometer of the state of his psyche. Soon after he learns that Temple may have been at the Old Frenchman's Place, the "sweet, inscrutable face" in the picture that he had always re-lied on for comfort turns into "a face suddenly older in sin than he would ever be," with "eyes more secret than soft." That is enough to unnerve him, but the truly shattering moment occurs when he discovers during his interview with Temple at Miss Reba's that this supposed paragon of southern womanhood who has been abducted into the netherworld is in fact "recounting [her] experience with actual pride." Returning home, he stares once more at the photo, only to have it set off his worst conceivable nightmare—a vision of Temple, bound naked to a railroad flat car that is speeding through an endless zone of evil (a dark tunnel with "blackness streaming in rigid threads overhead"), watching "something black and furious go roaring out of her pale body."* This image of innocence de-filed, of blackness pouring from the "temple" of a white woman's body, is more than Horace can bear. Reduced to a state of sheer helplessness, he rushes for the bathroom and vomits.[33]

Horace's defeat brings home the central, Modernist point that Faulk-ner was at pains to establish throughout *Sanctuary*—that it is impossible to wall off the darker impulses of human nature, either in society or within the self. In Olga Vickery's fine summary, "Horace's sanctuary, his imagi-native world of moral and aesthetic perfection, has been violated and de-stroyed," demonstrating that "it is only in the verbal universe . . . that evil

---

*One cannot help but wonder if the image of "blackness streaming in rigid threads overhead" contains a subtle echo of the Old Colonel, with his black plume, love of railroads, sexual adventurousness, and (in the eyes of his great-grandson) evil nature.

can be isolated as the antithesis of good." Along with the Victorian dichotomy, Faulkner had also at long last broken his attachment to the image of the "Dianalike girl," evident in both his treatment of Narcissa Benbow and Temple Drake and his exposure, through Horace's fantasies, of the unconscious Oedipal forces fueling the myth of southern womanhood. Freed from viewing women through the distorting lens of his relationship with his mother and her culture, the Modernist Faulkner would henceforth be able to see them in a new, more accurate light. But while Faulkner himself advanced, his post-Victorian character could only retreat. "I found more reality than I could stomach, I suppose," Horace explains to Narcissa in the original text. "Sick to death for quiet," he returns to his meaningless existence in Kinston, a kind of death within life where he can at least remain sheltered from experience.[34]

If Horace remains bound to Victorian moralism, Popeye's immersion in crime, violence, and blackness in general might seem to signal a complete disregard for those same nineteenth-century values, but a close inspection reveals the opposite. All of Popeye's actions are in fact controlled by the Victorian dichotomy, or more precisely his deliberate inversion of it. While those observing the dictates of the dichotomy seek moral purity, Popeye defines himself by ostentatiously placing himself on the wrong side of the dividing line, opting, in effect, for "pure" evil (emblematized by the tight black suit he always wears). His personality, moreover, exhibits many key Victorian attributes. As the half wit Tommy explains to Horace, Popeye does not really fit in at the Old Frenchman's Place: "He ought to have a pair of over-halls. Everybody'll know he haint no business hyer. He looks jest like a durn preacher or somethin." Popeye also *acts* like a "durn preacher"—unlike Lee Goodwin, who for better or worse allows his emotions free play, Popeye carefully controls and hides his feelings, impressing us as inauthentic, abstemious, and repressed. Far from being in touch with nature, Popeye is terrified of it, especially of animals. An owl hooting in the woods causes him to clutch desperately at Horace, and when a dog surprises him one day, he shoots it as if it were a snake. "I be dog if he aint skeered of his own shadow," observes Tommy.[35]

In a final chapter added for the published version, Faulkner attempts in somewhat heavy-handed fashion to account for Popeye's unusual persona through a thumbnail sketch of his childhood. It is a tale of severe deprivation—not only did the father desert the family shortly after Popeye was born, leaving his mother strapped for funds, but the grandmother was a paranoid pyromaniac intent on burning down the family home with

Popeye in it. To make matters worse, Popeye was physically defective, "an undersized, weak child" at first not expected to live. Even after his survival was assured, the doctor warned he would always be stunted in his development and never "a man, properly speaking." As T. H. Adamowski points out, one would generally expect this kind of debilitating childhood to give rise to an enfeebled, helpless adult who would become "everyone's object: an open book before the all-knowing gaze of the world." It is to fend off that horrible fate, Adamowski continues, that Popeye fashions himself into the perfect gangster, hiding his actual, vulnerable self beneath a hard-shelled protective exterior. By adopting a stance of seeming indifference to others, he renders himself virtually opaque, an impenetrable figure of malice who establishes power over others by simultaneously fascinating and terrifying them.[36]

It is a strategy that allows Popeye to regain control of his circumstances by reversing the standing moral code and becoming victimizer rather than victim. If his very life was once threatened by an insane pyromaniac, he will turn himself into a master of fire, learning how to strike a match so effortlessly that his "hand appeared to flick a small flame out of thin air" and to shoot a pistol with a maximum of accuracy and speed. He will anticipate the potential cruelties of nature by a fierce sadistic streak of his own, first manifested at an early age when he methodically cuts up a pair of lovebirds and later a kitten with a pair of scissors. That this violence is directed at animals is no accident; as a Victorian at bottom Popeye detests the creatures and forces of nature most of all. He shoots not only Tommy's dog but also Tommy, who is as much canine as human. Nor does he hesitate to kill humans either, to keep up, in Adamowski's words, his "aura of unpredictability, of being violent by way of his whim." Damaged by chance, he will take no chances, becoming the foremost agent of the void in order to escape the void himself.[37]

In the end, it is the void—that relentlessly random character of the universe—that governs everything in *Sanctuary*, as it did in *As I Lay Dying*. There is no refuge from this elemental fact of life, no dependable oasis of predictability or stability to be found anywhere. The lesson is brought home throughout the novel, but perhaps nowhere more vividly than in the lot of the two small dogs that Miss Reba, the whorehouse madam, acquires the day after her lover's sudden death. Most of the time Miss Reba lavishes on them all the affection she used to give Mr. Binford, but on returning from her periodic visits to his grave she begins to drink heavily and abuse them, venting her fury over the unexplainable, devastating loss she has suffered. In utter fright for their lives — she has gone so far as to throw one out an upstairs window — the dogs hide beneath Temple's bed, "the flatulent monotony of their sheltered lives snatched up without warning by an incomprehensible moment of terror and fear of bodily annihilation at the very hands which symbolised by ordinary the licensed tranquility of their lives." Clearly, it is a harsh existence that Faulkner ordains here, which might just be the reason for Popeye's otherwise astonishing decision to allow himself to be hung for a crime he did not commit. Perhaps, for all his ostensible toughness, he has decided that the game of countering the capricious terms of life is no longer worth the candle.[38]

The bleakness of Faulkner's vision at the start of the 1930s becomes still more evident when one considers the mythic underpinnings of *Sanctuary*. As Thomas L. McHaney notes, the novel makes repeated references to the ancient fertility rite cataloged at the beginning of one of Faulkner's favorite books, Sir James Frazer's magisterial *The Golden Bough*. In that annual ceremony of renewal a virile young man would seek out and slay the King of the Wood (dressed in priestly black) guarding the sanctuary of the virginal goddess Diana at Nemi, thereby becoming the new king and ensuring the success of the coming corn crop. The ironic parallels to Faulkner's novel are obvious. In *Sanctuary*, the challenger (presumably Horace) is not virile, the priest-king (Popeye) is himself impotent and does not get displaced, and the divine virgin is horribly raped with a spent ear of corn. Instead of the promise of cyclic fertility, we are given, in McHaney's words, "a wasteland without rebirth" filled with "unregenerated lives" and "meaningless deaths." That is surely the sense conveyed by the book's closing scene, in which Temple sits with her father in the Luxembourg Gardens in Paris staring at the "discontented and sad" face in her compact mirror and then at a sky "lying prone and vanquished in the embrace of the season of rain and death."[39]*

Given these wasteland conditions, what kind of person could be found who would be tough enough to play the game — to accept the omnipresence of the void and still have the fortitude to press on, avoiding the ever powerful temptation to self-destruction that Faulkner had so elaborately

---

*It also seems pertinent that the sanctuary being guarded in the fertility rite belongs to Diana. One could say that, far from being protected, Diana in *Sanctuary* is conclusively stripped of her innocence — not only within the narrative per se but also within Faulkner's residual conception of her. From this time onward, the "Dianalike girl" would lose her godlike status and have to fend for herself as a mere mortal.

documented in Bayard Sartoris, the Compson children, Darl Bundren, Horace Benbow, and even Popeye? Now that the mythologic and religious beliefs that had sustained people in the past were gone, where could the resources be found that might bolster such existential fortitude in the modern age? And specifically, what within southern life and history might avail? Such were the questions to which Faulkner would soon address himself.

CHAPTER 7

The Making of a
Modernist Identity
Light in August

Aside from his revision of *Sanctuary* toward the end of 1930, that year was to mark a relatively fallow period for Faulkner. Newly married, with a baby expected early in 1931, he spent most of his work time producing short stories for sale to popular magazines in order to meet growing family expenses. These efforts need not detain us. As Frederick Karl observes, Faulkner regarded this kind of writing as "strictly a business proposition" and took a highly "mechanical approach" to it. Though a few of the resulting stories were noteworthy from a literary standpoint, most simply served to pay the rent.[1]

What did engage Faulkner during 1930—and also gave rise to much of the financial burden he now fell under—was his purchase of an antebellum home located just a few minutes from the town square in Oxford. Built in 1844, the old Shegog place could not properly be called a mansion but did partake of the pretensions of its time and place. A moderate-sized wood frame house, it sported four impressive columns in front and was set at the end of a classic cedar-lined drive. The house was decidedly more bourgeois than aristocratic in character—closer to the solid, comfortable Benbow home described in *Flags in the Dust* than the elegant plantation dwelling of the Sartorises. Still, Rowan Oak (a name derived from Frazer's *The Golden Bough* referring to an old Scottish charm for staving off witches) was just grand enough to put the community on notice that this eldest member of the rising generation of Falkners intended to carry on the clan's proud traditions. Faulkner was, of course, highly ambivalent about those traditions, but Rowan Oak was perfect in that regard as well. Decades of neglect had left it in extreme disrepair, from its rotting foundation beams and leaking roof to peeling paint, broken windows, and a total absence of plumbing and electricity. Faulkner did most of the work himself, allowing him to balance his new role as lord of the manor with that of journeyman carpenter, to be a country squire with dirty clothes and hands. Even after the house was restored, visitors would continue to remark on the contrast between its imposing facade and the often shabby appearance of its master.[2]

That need for compensatory balance between conflicting selves was more evident still in the layout of the ground floor at Rowan Oak, which was divided by a spacious main hallway into two separate worlds. To the right as one entered was the world of the Victorian Faulkner and his traditionalist wife, consisting of a formal parlor and dining room that could have graced any respectable American home during the latter half of the nineteenth century. The wallpaper with its large floral print, the full-length draperies, the ornate, sculptured furniture, the baby grand piano, the long dining table where meals were served by a butler—all conspired to create an aura of decorum and taste. But on the other side of the hallway one found a very different ambience in the large room designated the "library" or "study." There, surrounded by books and various artifacts (including several pieces of primitive or abstract art, along with his mother's portrait in oils of the Old Colonel), in a setting that by all reports was usually cluttered and chaotic, the Modernist Faulkner would plunk himself down in a comfortable chair, take up a fountain pen, dig deeply into his subconscious, and pour out all he had dredged up onto paper. Just as his two personae dwelled side by side within the same mind, each appearing at different times and fulfilling different functions, so the two halves of Rowan Oak were to coexist, each part of the same structure but configuring different styles of culture and being.[3]

Sitting in that study, his Modernist self very much in command, Faulkner on August 17, 1931, took up a piece of paper and inscribed the title "Dark House" at the top. Though the exact meaning of the phrase was probably still unclear to him, it was indisputably true that large, decaying antebellum homes held a special resonance within his imagination, symbolizing not only the glory of the mythical Old South but also something hideous and hidden, a forbidden secret lurking just beyond reach in the region's past. A few days later, the title was suddenly changed, apparently as the result of Estelle's casual remark while they were sitting outdoors just before dinner about how "the light in August is different from any other time of year." Faulkner seems to have sensed immediately that the metaphor implicit in her comment was just the one he was searching for. In his text he would speak of that "lambent suspension of August into which night is about to fully come," marking not only the late summer twilight but also the precise time of year when the season of growth and life first gives way to the following seasons of death and dissolution. Counterbalancing imagery of light and darkness would pervade the new novel, supplying a perfect vehicle for expressing the dynamic polarities rapidly coming to the fore in his consciousness—polarities of culture (Victorian/Modernist), history (past/present), gender (male/female), experience (innocence/corruption), and, above all, race (black/white). *Light in August* would be about these warring tensions.[4]

The character who most strikingly embodies that incessant conflict bears the name of Joe Christmas. It is his tortuous quest for a personal identity that constitutes the crux of the narrative, with other important, though less pivotal, plots added as counterpoint. What makes Joe's search so compelling is the inflammatory factor of race: born in the Deep South to a white mother and a father who was probably Mexican but possibly part black, Joe is condemned to a lifetime of uncertainty. As Faulkner later remarked in an interview, Christmas became a man who "didn't know what he was," with "no way possible in life for him to find out." Joe looks white—his skin is "parchment-colored," suggesting Hispanic origins, and most of his features are either Caucasian or racially indistinguishable. Nonetheless the seeds of a black identity are planted in his mind early in life by his fanatical grandfather, Doc Hines, who kills both of Joe's parents, places him in an orphanage, and incites the other children to call Joe "nigger." From that time until his death, Christmas is unable to shake the belief that "black blood" runs through his veins and that blackness, with all its pejorative, shadowy attributes, constitutes an intrinsic part of his being. As a consequence, he is relegated to a ceaseless psychic balancing act, constantly experimenting with different combinations of identity fragments, only to realize in the end that he would never arrive at a unitary sense of self.[5]

What Faulkner was doing here, quite plainly, was drawing on the process of identity formation that he himself had just undergone. In creating Quentin Compson, he had made extensive use of his earlier post-Victorian self in order to raise into view the subconscious psychic legacy from the nineteenth century that he felt was debilitating his generation of white southerners. Now, in *Light in August*, he was again relying on his own inner experience, this time employing the pattern of selfhood based on conflicting identities that he had devised over the past several years as a vehicle for probing the psychological interaction of the white and black races in the South. Though the dual selves that bedevil Joe Christmas would be fashioned out of racial materials rather than broad-scale cultures, the basic structure and dynamics of their interaction would be much the same as within Faulkner. Like Faulkner's, then, his would be the story of the making of a Modernist identity.

Joe's prolonged struggle to achieve identity is in turn closely connected with another central and problematic issue in *Light in August*—that of free will. On the one hand, it is clear that Joe is, in Alfred Kazin's words, "the man things are done to, . . . who has no free will of his own." More precisely, he is the victim of powerful social and psychological forces that largely determine his life, the ultimate example of a man held captive by the interlocking religious, racial, and sexual beliefs of his culture, which lodge in his unconscious during childhood and later dominate him without his ever being fully aware of their power. In the words of Lee Jenkins, "the very thoughts that he thinks about himself have already been determined." To this extent Joe has no control over his identity but rather becomes what his society insists that he be. Viewed from this perspective, he is a helpless pawn of his circumstances.[6]

But at the same time, as Donald Kartiganer convincingly argues, Joe instinctively attempts to rebel against this intense conditioning in an effort to create a genuine identity of his own. Given the complexion of his skin, Kartiganer points out, Joe has the option of "passing" as a white and thus enjoying "a single identity" that would make his life far more comfortable. However, since that choice requires giving up the "black" part of his self, it would be tantamount to a surrender of his authenticity. That is why Joe in the end insists on an identity based on his "doubleness," settling for nothing less, according to Kartiganer, than "a wholeness that serves alike the dual sides of himself" (the language here, one cannot help but note, applies equally well to Faulkner). Attaining this unique identity is anything but easy; it means integrating his white and black identity fragments, joining together personal and cultural characteristics that can never fully merge. As a result Joe's life turns into a "series of alternating roles that seem to divide him" but should more accurately be viewed as "the difficult terms of his wholeness." It is in this regard that Kartiganer sees Christmas's experience as resembling that of Christ, the "man-God" who sought to reconcile within his self the inherently conflicting attributes of the human and the divine. Like Christ, Christmas is doomed to failure, since the degree of wholeness he seeks is not attainable on this earth. Nevertheless, Joe remains committed to his ideal identity, "fiercely defying all attempts to define himself by reduction to less than his awareness of himself."[7]*

Indeed, perhaps the best way to comprehend Faulkner's intentions for *Light in August* is to view the saga of Joe Christmas as an attempt to test the human capacity to achieve personal identity under the most extreme conditions a Modernist author could possibly contrive. Like the Bundrens in *As I Lay Dying*, Christmas achieves a minimal existential triumph, partaking as much of defeat as success, that becomes meaningful precisely because of the awesome doom hanging over him. Only when we recognize *how* fated his existence is, *how* relentlessly he has been victimized by social conditioning, can we adequately calibrate the heroic dimensions of his struggle and appreciate the true significance of his brief and transitory moments of victory.

Faulkner certainly spares no opportunity to establish the repressive nature of Joe's early environment. The critical first years of Joe's life are spent not in a normal family setting but in an institution reeking of impersonality. With its wards dressed in identical blue uniforms and its

---

*Kartiganer's reading of Joe Christmas is truly brilliant, but he does nevertheless overshoot the mark in a few respects. It seems doubtful, for example, that Joe possesses a well-developed or articulated "awareness of himself"; rather, he often seems to grope toward his destiny, relying on subconscious promptings that buffet him about in different directions. Moreover, Kartiganer in his desire to establish a measure of existential freedom for Joe does not always do full justice to the tragic fixedness of Joe's existence that leaves him at the completion of his long journey "still inside the circle." To put this in slightly different terms, Kartiganer seems to suggest that Joe is finally able to achieve a workable identity based on "doubleness," while Faulkner, the cagey Modernist, appears to leave the issue unresolved. See Kartiganer, *Fragile Thread*, 41–43, and Faulkner, *Light in August*, 296, as well as Kartiganer, " 'What I Chose to Be': Freud, Faulkner, Joe Christmas, and the Abandonment of Design," in Kartiganer and Abadie, *Faulkner and Psychology*, in which he takes his argument for Christmas's intentionality one step further, contending that "Christmas chooses to remain within the dilemma of all his possibilities" (304).

compound "enclosed by a ten foot steel-and-wire fence," the Memphis orphanage where he is deposited more nearly resembles "a penitentiary or zoo" than a home for children. However, from the outset Joe, though "sober and quiet as a shadow," acts to transcend his destiny through the limited means at hand. Deprived of maternal sustenance, he secretly finds his way into the dietitian's room (as the person in charge of dispensing food, she is the closest mother substitute available to him) and squeezes her toothpaste into his mouth as if he were breast-feeding (although he had never heard of toothpaste before, he knew instinctively "she would possess something of that nature"). It is at best a fragile expedient bound to end in disaster, which occurs one day when the dietitian and her lover enter the room while Joe is inside. Witnessing their sexual gymnastics from his hiding place in a closet, Joe at the Oedipal age of five becomes aroused, starts swallowing toothpaste faster, and gives himself away by vomiting. Already sensing his entrapment by powerful cosmic forces, he waits behind the curtain "with astonished fatalism for what was about to happen to him" and then tells himself "with complete and passive surrender: 'Well, here I am.'"[8]

The trauma leaves a deeper scar still when the dietitian in her terror hurls at him an abusive racial epithet she has heard other children use. Having his fellow orphans call him "nigger" was bad enough, wounding Joe's fragile self-confidence to the point where he kept exclusively to himself and began questioning a black janitor about what the word meant. But when an adult who had functioned within his fantasy as a surrogate parent tells him at such a critical moment that he is a "little nigger bastard," the effect is to ingrain permanently a conception of himself as black. It is also of great significance that Faulkner has the incident center on oral gratification. In traditional southern culture the servile identity of blacks was grounded in a fundamental oral dependency in which they surrendered initiative and self-assertiveness in return for food and nurture—a relationship symbolized in the image of the childlike slave happily devouring a watermelon provided by the master. Joe's encounter with the dietitian serves to implant in him this latent stereotype, leading him from this moment on to think of a "nigger" as someone who indulges in oral pleasures, especially those proffered by women, only to suffer humiliating ruin. Like the toothpaste itself, such oral pleasure is exceedingly tantalizing for him—it embodies nothing less than the maternal love he has been denied as a child—but the penalty for attempting to obtain it seems to threaten his very existence. For this reason, giving in to his black identity will always represent both his foremost temptation and gravest peril.[9]

The next step in this elaborate process of social conditioning comes at the hands of Simon McEachern, the hard-shell Calvinist who adopts Joe at age five. Dressed in his "suit of hard, decent black," McEachern serves as an archetypal Victorian father, schooling Joe in the stern precepts of the rural South derived from the nineteenth-century moral dichotomy. The "two abominations," he informs Joe, "are sloth and idle thinking, the two virtues are work and the fear of God." Everything in McEachern's world is arranged in terms of such polarized moral choices, with the "right" choice always a certainty. McEachern, Faulkner tells us, is "not unkind," just "cold" and "implacable." In its own way, his house seems as impersonal as the orphanage.[10]

Joe's response to this new environment is twofold. On the one hand, he readily absorbs much of McEachern's dichotomized style of thinking, especially in relation to gender. There McEachern's sexism dovetails perfectly with the distrust of women Joe had developed through his encounter with the dietitian. As a result, Panthea Reid Broughton explains, Joe comes to regard anything feminine as "soft, supine, disordered, unpredictable, and demanding," while viewing masculinity as "hard, erect, ordered, and predictable, demanding no more than simple adherence to a simple code." Given the rampant instability of his life and his need to solidify his attachment to his gender, Joe finds comfort in such firm polarities. He and McEachern come to share a "rigid negation of all compromise" that he associates with being a man, to the point where he actually prefers the certainty of his stepfather's punishments to the moral chaos of Mrs. McEachern's covert kindness toward him. On the other hand, Joe is determined from the outset to preserve his precious sense of self, carving out as large an area for his autonomy as he can in the face of such a totalistic upbringing. For that reason, his time with McEachern, in addition to making him crave order and predictability, also strengthens his resolve to reject any identity imposed on him by outside forces. "*My name aint McEachern. My name is Christmas*," he proclaims.[11]

These contradictory forces shaping Joe's personality, reflecting the basic contradictions Faulkner sensed in southern culture (the "white" obsession with strict morality and the "black" desire for forbidden pleasures), surface unmistakably as he reaches sexual maturity. At age fourteen some neighborhood boys invite him to join in a coming-of-age ritual all too common in the South of that day, a liaison with a black girl in a deserted sawmill. Entering the shed to take his turn (and thus assert his white male identity), Joe panics. The dichotomized moral sense instilled in him by McEachern causes him to see the "womanshenegro" as the abyss itself, "a black well" of sinful female sensuality that can only lead to terrible retribution (a fear heightened by the fact that he is in a sawmill, with its symbolic implication of the Oedipal threat of castration). Simultaneously, however, Joe perceives her as a fellow black whom he must both punish for betraying their race and protect from white assailants. That is why, when his companions try to stop him from beating her, he fights them savagely for reasons they find inexplicable: "None of them knew why he had fought. And he could not have told them." Only afterward does Joe become aware of why he "*struck refraining that Negro girl*," deciding "*that she must know it too and be proud too.*" [12]

The incident makes manifest the precarious state of Joe's sexual identity. All through his life he will feel his manhood is in jeopardy, and since masculinity for him is closely associated with autonomy—being "hard, sufficient, potent, remorseless, strong"—this represents a most serious threat. His anxiety, Faulkner makes clear, is Oedipal in origin. In a normal family situation, Freudian theory maintains, a boy learns to repress his natural longing for his mother in order to escape an imagined punishment from his father that, in the boy's unconscious fantasy, often takes the form of castration. But in Joe's case there has been no mother to love, only a strict father who repeatedly (and often gratuitously) inflicts punishment, leaving Joe in perpetual fear of the ultimate instance of paternal wrath. His secret black identity makes that fear even more pronounced, for in the southern culture of that day the ritual penalty for black men who lusted after white women was the loss of their genitalia. Thus when a friend graphically explains the facts of female physiology, what frightens Joe most is menstruation. In his mind, it suggests that women are in reality castrated men who continue to bleed from their wounds, foreshadowing what might well happen to him. To regain a degree of mastery, Joe shoots a ewe and, "trembling, drymouthed, backglaring," examines its anatomy. "He did not forget what the boy had told him. He just accepted it. He found that he could live with it side by side with it. It was as if he said, illogical and desperately calm *All right. It is so, then. But not to me. Not in my life and my love.*" [13]

Once again, Joe's plight serves to indicate how Faulkner, using his Modernist lens, had come to perceive southern race relations in a radically new fashion. What Joe Christmas really suffers from, when his life is taken in its entirety, is a continuous psychological emasculation at the hands of white society stemming from the stereotyped racial identities embedded in his consciousness during his youth—an effective stealing of his manhood that is appropriately capped by his castration as a supposed Negro rapist just moments before his death. To be black, as Joe understands it, means being unable to exercise one's true powers as a man, and, try as he might, he cannot shed his "nigger" identity. In short, what Faulkner provides here is a damning portrait of the wellsprings of southern racism so advanced in its insights that it was decades ahead of its time.

These problems regarding Joe's sexual identity are readily visible when at seventeen he falls in love with Bobbie Allen, a waitress at a cheap diner who doubles as a prostitute. As her name suggests, Bobbie exists on the bare margin of femininity, a woman with underdeveloped breasts ("it was because of her smallness that he ever attempted her") who earns her living selling food and sex. These attributes make her highly desirable for Joe, whose fear of Oedipal punishment causes him to seek out sexual partners who are as nonmaternal as possible. At the outset of their relationship that fear overwhelms him: on discovering that Bobbie is having her period, he strikes her, runs off to the woods, and vomits. But the next time they meet, he has mastered his anxieties sufficiently to have sex with her, and a month later he listens with "the curiosity of a child" as she lies naked and talks about her body. Significantly, it is at this moment that he informs her he may have "some nigger blood," adding, when she expresses doubt, "I dont know. I believe I have." The encounter represents a rare respite for him during which he is able to achieve sufficient intimacy with another person to be able to disclose honestly his racial predicament.[14]

Almost immediately, though, his vulnerabilities reassert themselves. Contact with Bobbie's milieu introduces him to the pleasures of the urban underworld and to a valuable new role, that of the tough guy. Smoking, drinking, swaggering, and snarling help him not only to mask his underlying rural naïveté but also to reject the identity McEachern sought to impose on him. But, predictably, such rebellious behavior soon sets up a confrontation with the Victorian father, who follows Joe to a dance hall one night in order to punish him. The archetypal Oedipal fantasy of the son killing the father is reenacted as Joe, after knocking McEachern unconscious with a chair, announces, "I have done it! I have done it!" (Faulkner characteristically leaves it uncertain whether McEachern is really dead.) From Bobbie's standpoint, however, Joe's act does not represent a splendid Oedipal victory but a foolish outburst of violence that could land her in trouble. She accordingly stands by while her Memphis friends pummel him senseless. What is remarkable is the passivity with which he accepts the beating, as if playing the stereotyped role of a submissive black man accepting his inevitable retribution from whites for crossing the southern racial divide. And so his relationship with Bobbie concludes in a virtual preview of how his life will end two decades later—with Joe lying on the floor crucified, his racial identity ambiguous. "*Is he really a nigger?*" asks the thug who knocked him out. "*He dont look like one.*" "*These country bastards are liable to be anything,*" Bobbie's pimp replies.[15]

Following this rough initiation into adulthood, Christmas enters what might be termed the middle phase of his life, his journey on "the street which was to run for fifteen years." "It is a street," writes Regina Fadiman, "of sex and violence, of punishment sought, of flight from self and pursuits of self. But always it is a street of color polarities." His travels take him through all parts of the country and a variety of occupations but invariably bring him back to the red-light districts of cities, places filled with marginal, rootless people like himself where he can temporarily feel less estranged than he does in a normal community. Throughout this period his indeterminate identity is symbolized in the clothes he wears—a white shirt and dark pants that, as Davis notes, are invariably "soiled, yet neither worn out nor of poor quality," making him appear "like a tramp, yet not like one." His appearance in this way reflects the agonizing tensions within him that he can neither resolve nor escape for the simple reason that they provide him with his sole basis for self-definition.[16]

The most excruciating tension by far arises from his dual racial selves. Since those coming in contact with him assume he is white, there is an ever present danger that he might slip into an unalloyed white identity, which would violate his most fundamental sense of who he is. To avoid that fate, he must act periodically to assert his equivocal racial status—for example, by goading white men to call him black and then challenging them to a fight for doing so. This kind of tactic works so long as the person he is dealing with is suitably infected with racism. But when a prostitute reacts with indifference to the news that he is black, it threatens the delicate mechanism by which Joe maintains his sanity and he comes close to killing her. Following this incident, he recovers his inner balance by making strenuous efforts to shore up his black identity. Instead of picking fights with whites who call him black, he now takes on blacks who call him white. He also lives for a time with a woman "who resembled an ebony carving," lying beside her at night breathing "deep and hard . . . trying to breathe into himself the dark odor, the dark and inscrutable thinking and being of Negroes, with each suspiration trying to expel from himself the white blood and the white thinking and being." But inevitably his white self fights back. His very nostrils, Faulkner tells us, "would whiten and tauten" in response to "the odor which he was trying to make his own," causing "his whole being [to] writhe and strain with physical outrage and spiritual denial."[17]

What finally enables Christmas to begin pulling together his opposing strands of identity is his relationship with Joanna Burden, a woman who (as her first name suggests) is in many respects his double or mirror image. Although she is no vagabond, having lived her entire life in the same house on the outskirts of Jefferson, the extent of her alienation from society easily matches Joe's, while her sexual ambiguity closely corresponds to his racial ambiguity. A split personality herself—the one half cold and repressed, the other exploding with pent-up sexual energy—she can readily accommodate his duality. The two also share a common Calvinist heritage, along with the need to escape a predestined fate imposed on them by their respective grandfathers. Just as Old Doc Hines set in motion a train of events that severely limits Joe's freedom, Joanna's grandfather, appropriately named Calvin Burden, has in effect controlled her life through the ironclad obligation she feels to carry on his work as an abolitionist. Both are consequently struggling to discover some means of carving out a sphere, however small, of existential freedom and self-definition.[18]

Surely the most puzzling question is why Joe stays with Joanna for more than three years given her insistence on managing every detail of their relationship. Even when she leaves a note on his cot, it is the equivalent of a summons, "an order almost." In the face of this constant threat to his fragile sense of autonomy, Joe repeatedly resolves to leave. Looking out in the dusk at that "savage and lonely street which he had chosen of his own will," which is still there "waiting for him," he thinks to himself, "*This is not my life. I dont belong here.*" But he does not go. On one occasion he waits for sunset and gathers his few belongings, fully intending to reenter the "street." "Yet when he moved, it was toward the house. It was as though, as soon as he found that his feet intended to go there, that he let go, seemed to float, surrendered, thinking *All right All right.*" Finding that Joanna has left only the kitchen door unlocked, in effect requiring him to enter her house as a black man, he is further enraged. But instead of departing, he starts flinging the food she has left him against the wall. Again Faulkner stresses Joe's apparent passivity: "He seemed to watch his hand as if from a distance. He watched it pick up a dish and swing it up and back." To all appearances, he is behaving as "the man things are done to," a creature so bereft of a viable ego that he has become captive to a demented spinster.[19]

A closer look, however, reveals just the opposite. Joe stays not out of passivity but rather because he and Joanna are locked into a fierce contest of wills that he is determined to win—a contest that helps enormously in his effort to build his ego strength and realize a multifaceted identity. In this respect, Joanna, like Bobbie Allen before her, is perfect for him. Almost manlike, even in moments of passion, she can provide the copious quantities of food and sex he craves without triggering his powerful Oedipal fears of castration. Most important, in the ongoing drama she stages he is cast in a series of black roles—as the docile servant living in a slave cabin, eating the traditional field hand's meal of peas and molasses, and the stereotypical "nigger rapist" who steals into her house through an open window—supplying him with the chance to develop and solidify his previously suppressed black self. This is why his interlude with her, for all its obvious pathology, proves invaluable to him, enabling him to make far more progress toward his ultimate goal of wholeness than he could ever have made on the "street."

But once again everything depends on a precise balance, for at the same time that Joe is engaged in strengthening his identification as a black man, he must resist strenuously Joanna's recurrent attempts to fix a full-scale black identity on him. It is one thing for Joe to experiment with being black, gaining access to areas of experience and gratification from which his white Calvinist self had cut him off; it is another for him to be pigeonholed exclusively as either black or white. The only authentic basis on which he can construct an overarching identity is that of multiplicity, with no one racial persona gaining effective domination. Accordingly, every time Joanna threatens the delicate psychic counterpoise that his multiplicity depends on, he must act to reestablish it. Feeling himself becoming too black and subservient, he ostentatiously throws her food against the wall ("woman's muck," he calls it, making clear that he is rejecting her sexual favors as well). For the next six months he shores up his white, independent self by working at a sawmill, using the money he earns to pay for dinners at a restaurant in town, where, like a white man, he always wears his best clothes. But he is careful not to become *too* white:

his job at the mill is to shovel the sawdust pile, a task normally reserved for blacks.* And he is resolute: not until Joanna comes to him on her own initiative and they have fashioned a new ritual designed to sustain his racial ambiguity can their relationship resume.[20]

This strange pas de deux continues until Joanna reaches menopause, at which point the changes within her upset Joe's equilibrium in a way that proves fatal to both of them. As her intense religiosity reemerges, the flow of nourishment she had previously provided him suddenly dries up—no longer does she set out meals for him or even let him touch her. Instead of having him be her black lover she now wants him to become her black lawyer, managing her various philanthropic affairs. With her "cold, remote, and fanatic" face and constant resort to prayer, she increasingly takes on the role of a female McEachern, demanding in effect that he turn into a black Calvinist. For Joe, that is an explosive combination. The more she tries to reshape him along these lines, the more conscious he becomes that his self does have a definite form that he has created almost without knowing it and that he must defend at all costs. "If I give in now," he tells himself, "I will deny all the thirty years that I have lived to make me what I chose to be." It is this determination to define himself, even though he cannot yet fully grasp his ultimate identity, that results in his fateful deadlock with Joanna: "Neither surrendered; worse: they would not let one another alone; he would not even go away."[21]

Although Faulkner, following his narrative strategy, leaves the exact circumstances of her death unclear, he does supply enough detail to establish that it is not a simple murder. Using an old cap-and-ball revolver presumably inherited from her Burden ancestors, Joanna attempts to kill Joe in what seems an intended murder-suicide. After her gun misfires, Joe cuts off her head with his razor. Whether self-defense or not (he may have planned all along to decapitate her), the act amounts to a symbolic castration, enabling him at last to become the castrating father and thus to overcome the Oedipal anxieties he had first felt in the shed with the black girl twenty years earlier. At the same time it cements on him in the eyes of the community the identity of "nigger rapist-murderer"—an identity that will ironically lead to his own castration and death. In this way the

---

*The fact that he works at a sawmill is probably significant, suggesting that his job may also help him in mastering his castration anxieties—yet another example of how his delicate psychological balancing mechanism tends to operate.

deed, like so much else in Joe's life, simultaneously enhances his freedom and spells his doom.[22]

What Millgate calls Joe's "journey toward self-knowledge" vastly accelerates in the following week of his flight and capture. Envisioning himself as a perpetual victim, "being hunted by white men at last into the black abyss which had been waiting, trying, for thirty years to drown him," he makes one final spasmodic effort to cast off the black identity that still carries in his mind a connotation of helplessness before the overwhelming forces of society and fate. Bursting in on a black church service, he ejects the minister from the pulpit, fights off others with a broken bench leg, and curses God before the terrorized congregation. As one can see in both *Soldiers' Pay* and *The Sound and the Fury*, the spiritual communion of the black church represented the essence of black culture for Faulkner, the embodiment of those transcendent Christian virtues that gave southern blacks the characteristics of faith, humility, and stoic endurance he so admired. By his violent interruption of a revival meeting, Christmas is effectively proclaiming his diametric separation from that communal world, delivering the message that he is *not* a black or a Christian (a message duly received: the parishioners see him both as a white man engaged in a vicious racial attack on them and as the Antichrist). To display further his command of the situation and register his defiance he also makes it a point to leave the sheriff an obscene note.[23]

But then a transformation sets in. Living in the woods with no regular food or human contact sets the stage. Day and night, light and dark begin to blend for him until "he could never know when he would pass from one to the other," suggesting that the polarities that had given form to his existence are losing their sharpness and that a fundamental redefinition of identity is now possible. The moment of epiphany comes while he is sitting by a peaceful stream recalling a meal a few days earlier at the cabin of a poor black sharecropper family who had run off in fright after serving him his food. Reconstructing the scene in his consciousness, he suddenly becomes aware that he no longer feels harried and famished but rather "cool, quiet." His obsession with food as such has disappeared, replaced by a craving for "decent food" served in a domestic setting. It is as if his conception of black identity has shifted from one based on simple oral gratification (the "nigger" identity arising out of his traumatic childhood encounter with the dietitian) to one centered on the family gathered around the hearth sharing a communal meal. In his ravenous hunger Joe had taken little notice of how terrifying his presence had been to his hosts, but now he is troubled by it. "And they were afraid," he reflects. "Of their own brother afraid." A few nights earlier he had himself run in alarm from Freedman Town, the black section of Jefferson, construing it in his imagination as "the original quarry, abyss itself" that threatened to swallow him. Desperately he had sought "the cold hard air of white people." But now, following his epiphany, he welcomes the abyss; no longer will he be afraid of his own brother.[24]

Rather than continuing to challenge his fate, he will from this time forth achieve a measure of control over it by willingly submitting himself to it. *"I am tired of running of having to carry my life like it was a basket of eggs,"* he declares. He will end that incessant psychic juggling by the simple expedient of being simply what he is, however fragmented and incomplete his sense of self, however vulnerable to circumstance his ambiguous identity may render him. In part, as R. G. Collins argues, he will assume "the sacrificial role of the Negro" that southern society has sought to fasten on him, becoming symbolically a kind of black Christ who "takes upon himself the guilt of mankind." Even though he knows full well that that blackness will lead to his destruction, and even though he has no intention of defining himself primarily as black, he will proudly wear the oversized brogans for which he has traded his shoes, those "black shoes smelling of Negro" that seem to send a "black tide creeping up his legs, moving from his feet upward as death moves." Whatever the future holds, he will accept responsibility for it as the inevitable continuation of his past. "I have never broken out of the ring of what I have already done and cannot ever undo," he acknowledges. Henceforth he will take control of his destiny by embracing his personal history rather than seeking to escape it, turning his struggle, in Robert Penn Warren's words, into "an image of the existential struggle of all men."[25]

Joe's new sense of identity is manifest in the way he is captured, deliberately placing himself in a situation in which he is sure to be recognized so that he in effect governs the sequence of action. Rather than permitting destiny to work its will on him, he paradoxically takes the initiative by surrendering. Heading to Mottstown, he walks "straight as a surveyor's line," like "a man who knows where he is and where he wants to go." No longer will he haplessly follow the "street." On arriving he at once visits the "white barbershop" for a shave and haircut, replaces his ragged clothes with "a new shirt and tie and a straw hat," and then strolls through the streets "in broad daylight, like he owned the town." He will accept the fate visited on him by society, but on his own terms, cut free of all stereotypes in a virtual parade of his authenticity:

> He never acted like either a nigger or a white man. That was it. That was what made the folks so mad. For him to be a murderer and all dressed up and walking the town like he dared them to touch him, when he ought to have been skulking and hiding in the woods, muddy and dirty and running. It was like he never even knew he was a murderer, let alone a nigger too.

All the time, however, he is wearing the black brogans. And when a man finally does spot him as the fugitive being hunted and gratuitously strikes him in the face, Joe does not fight back. Rather, as one of the townsmen reports, it is a case of "the nigger acting like a nigger for the first time and taking it, not saying anything: just bleeding sullen and quiet." The white devil who a few days before had lacerated the skulls of innocent churchgoers with a bench leg has become the black saint who turns the other cheek.[26]

Does Christmas actually complete his psychological journey? Are we to take the events in Mottstown and his subsequent attempted escape and death in Jefferson as evidence that he has attained the viable personal identity he had been questing toward? Should we see him in Kartiganer's terms as a kind of Modernist Christ, assembling out of the fiercely contradictory elements of his being "a wholeness of identity unknown to human beings"? Or should we regard his saga more as a heroic failure in which true integration of self ultimately eludes him?[27]

The text supplies some clues but no firm answer. In most instances, Faulkner's choice of language suggests both submission to circumstance *and* willfulness on Joe's part. "It was as though he had set out and made his plans to passively commit suicide," the narrator reports. At one crucial juncture, however, it becomes unmistakable that Joe is not simply yielding to "the Player." While being moved from the jail to the courthouse the same Joe Christmas who had virtually turned himself in two days earlier suddenly bolts for freedom. The chase that follows indicates the seriousness of his intent to escape: without Percy Grimm's prodigious pursuit Christmas might well have reached Reverend Hightower's house undetected and from there have been spirited out of town during the night. Why does he do this? Since Faulkner does not admit us into Joe's consciousness during this episode, we can never be sure. But we do know that just prior to this incident his grandmother, Mrs. Hines, had visited him in jail. Presumably, she had informed him about the facts of his birth, telling him that he was more likely part Mexican than part black. If true, it would mean that for the first time in his life he had reliable knowledge not only of his origins but also of how he came into his predicament. From Joe's standpoint this information clearly represents the missing link he had always needed for comprehending his experience.[28]

Does that knowledge arrive in time? The evidence is once again sketchy. We do know that Joe, previously "*tired of running*," takes to flight again in what is probably his most definitive act of will ever. When cornered in Hightower's kitchen, this man who had never shied from violence refrains from firing his pistol, implying that he is now acting from within the moral code of the community rather than as an alienated outsider. And finally, after Grimm castrates his mortally wounded body (thus enacting the ritual that was for Faulkner the modern equivalent of crucifixion), we are told that a motionless Christmas looks up at his tormentors "with peaceful and unfathomable and unbearable eyes." From "unbearable" one might assume that Joe in his dying moment has at last comprehended the tragic nature of his life, from "peaceful" that he has courageously acceded to it, and from "unfathomable" that, as a result, he has gained a vision that surpasses ordinary human understanding. If this interpretation is accurate, one can say that Joe, for this fleeting but ineffable moment, takes on the dimensions of a Christ figure and achieves existential triumph. But without access to Joe's consciousness we can never be sure; Faulkner as a Modernist writer at the height of his powers will not grant us closure.[29]

Indeed, Faulkner muddies the waters even more by introducing the perspective of the community, which does not see Joe's drama as extraordinarily complex and at times inexplicable but rather as quite simple. From its standpoint, a mulatto trying to hide his true identity has been betrayed in the end by his "black blood." To articulate this view Faulkner uses a new character, the lawyer Gavin Stevens, who expounds on the conventional southern belief that whenever "blood" is mixed, the resulting clash will inevitably lead to self-destruction:

His blood would not be quiet, let him save it. It would not be one or the other and let his body save itself. Because the black blood drove him first to the Negro cabin. And then the white blood drove him out of there, as it was the black blood that snatched up the pistol and the white blood which would not let him fire it. . . . It was the black blood which swept him by his own desire beyond the aid of any man, swept him up into that ecstasy out of a black jungle where life has already ceased before the heart stops and death is desire and fulfillment. And then the black blood failed him again, as it must have in all crises in his life.

One suspects that this passage was inserted for two intertwined reasons: to mollify Faulkner's Victorian sensibility, which must have been deeply disturbed by the subversive implications of the novel, and simultaneously to deflect any potential outrage among southern readers by allowing those so inclined to assume (as did many early critics of *Light in August*) that Stevens was functioning as the author's mouthpiece. But, given the glaring contrast between Stevens's crude explanatory scheme based on biology and the complex reality of Joe Christmas's experience, the Modernist Faulkner must surely have also meant the passage to be ironic.[30]

Again and again Faulkner limns a portrait (to be sure, without ever making it definitive) of a white man whose "black blood" has in effect been imposed on him by external forces. Nothing in Joe's appearance indicates that he is anything but white, to the point where he is able throughout the narrative to move easily in white society without anyone suspecting him as black. Even at the barbershop in Mottstown—where the close attention given his face and hair should have made any telltale physical signs of Negro origins detectable—no one recognizes him as the "nigger murderer" carrying a price on his head. "He dont look any more like a nigger than I do," a townsman observes. Another appropriately refers to Joe as a "white nigger"—an obvious oxymoron in the 1930s South. In Robert Penn Warren's words, "Faulkner here undercuts the official history and mythology of a whole society by indicating that the 'nigger' is a creation of the white man."[31]

Hence Faulkner's protracted struggle to bring Joe Christmas to light. It is revealing that, as Regina Fadiman tells us, in the earliest drafts of the novel Christmas was a relatively minor figure who for the most part remained offstage and who, when he finally did emerge as a major character, was at first a man whose "black blood" directly determined his behavior. Also telling is the way the manuscript was at first dotted with gratuitous remarks that can only be described as racist. A black nursemaid unable to read a sign, for example, was said to be exhibiting "that dull stupid and vacuous idiocy of her idle and illiterate race." Beyond dispute, that was the Victorian Faulkner speaking. But then, as the manuscript was revised, key changes set in: prejudiced passages gradually disappeared, Christmas's racial identity went from definitely black to probably white, and a text that had begun as a cautionary tale about the dangers of racial mixing turned into one of the most powerful indictments ever written of the white South's racial sins. One can see Faulkner groping toward Joe Christmas as early as *Sanctuary*, where Popeye, a man with pale skin who is somehow always perceived as "black," goes on to commit an especially repulsive rape of a white woman. But the path to Yoknapatawpha's racial secrets would be tortuous, involving many detours and reversals. The final version of *Light in August* makes clear that by wandering at length through the dark house of his mind he had ultimately managed to unlock them.[32]

There remained one crucial step that Faulkner in 1931 was still not prepared to take: his relentless inquiry into the dynamics of racism in *Light in August* makes no reference to the South's past. To be sure, Joe Christmas is caught up in the familiar southern dilemma of struggling to escape an identity fastened on him by a powerful ancestor. But Doc Hines is hardly a gallant, myth-enshrouded Cavalier. On the contrary, he is presented as something of a freak, a bantam rooster of a man content to live in "filthy poverty and complete idleness" while pursuing his mission of "preaching the superiority of the white race, himself his own exhibit A in fanatic and unconscious paradox." Most important, Hines and his wife have no organic connection to southern society. Rather, Faulkner goes out of his way to describe them as atavistic figures, "two homeless and belated beasts from beyond the glacial period" who, through the accident of their survival, have brought the taint of racial hatred into modern life. Everything about them seems distant and primeval: the townspeople regard them "as if they belonged to a different race, species," while the dingy bungalow they reside in (their version of a "dark house") is "dark and small and rankly-odored as a cave." In this manner Hines functions as a kind of deus ex machina, permitting Faulkner to avoid the question of whether the South and its history must be held accountable for the existence of racism.[33]

However, if the Old Colonel gets off lightly in this novel, he does make an intriguing cameo appearance that suggests Faulkner's conception of him was starting to shift. Joanna Burden's paternal grandfather shares a number of crucial attributes with the first William Falkner, among them the power to haunt and control the lives of his descendants.* We see this when Joanna's father takes her at the age of four to visit the secret graves of her grandfather and half brother, both named Calvin Burden. The two New Englanders had come to Jefferson during Reconstruction to help newly freed slaves register to vote, only to be gunned down by Colonel John Sartoris. Seeing their graves has the same traumatic effect on Joanna's development Joe's encounter with the dietitian had on his. She becomes consecrated to the hallowed spot where her martyred kin lie buried, a Calvinist in a twofold sense whose life will be devoted to fulfilling what she perceives as her grandfather's mission to southern blacks.[34]

Who exactly is that grandfather? At first glance he seems the epitome of Yankeehood, the son of a Congregational minister from New Hampshire who had preached "the bleak and bloodless logic" characteristic of "interminable New England Sundays." But we also learn that young Burden had run away from home at age twelve to seek his fortune, was known for heavy drinking and carrying a gun, had "killed a man in an argument over slavery," and had lost an arm as "a member of a troop of partisan guerrilla horse" during the skirmishing between proslavery and abolitionist forces in Kansas. The giveaway comes when we discover that he sired one son and three daughters—the same configuration as the Old Colonel with his second wife. Also like William Clark Falkner, Calvin Burden seems more of a protean force than an actual human being, especially in the eyes of his granddaughter. His penchant for self-creation and drama-

---

*It could be argued that the Old Colonel makes an additional cameo appearance in *Light in August* in the form of the Reverend Gail Hightower's grandfather, a frontier lawyer who serves as a member of a guerrilla band in northern Mississippi during the Civil War (though not as an officer). Unlike the Colonel, the first Gail Hightower is presented as an earthy and fun-loving backwoodsman, a "not overly particular servant of Chance and the bottle" following the path of least resistance in life. But his ignominious death while attempting to steal chickens from a henhouse, most likely shot by the wife of a Confederate soldier, is at least vaguely reminiscent of the self-serving exploits in which Colonel Falkner was rumored to have engaged during the war. In addition, Hightower leaves behind a damaged set of offspring who prove utterly incapable of creating viable identities, including a son who takes refuge in a double persona, becoming "two separate and complete people, one of whom dwelled by serene rules in a world where reality did not exist," and a grandson so given over to romantic fantasy that he ends up, like Quentin Compson, "a shadowy figure among shadows, paradoxical." Why this "bluff and bold, but kind" man would have such a devastating effect on his descendants seems a puzzle—unless he is in fact the first William Falkner with his less appealing traits sanitized by a great-grandson still under his spell. See Faulkner, *Light in August*, 412–15, 425–26.

tization marks his entire existence, manifested in his decision to change his name from the original "Burrington" to "Burden" (the Old Colonel had changed the spelling of his from "Faulkner" to "Falkner"). Nor is it without significance that the home Burden acquires in Jefferson and bequeaths to his descendants is an old plantation, "a big house set in a grove of trees; obviously a place of some pretensions at one time."[35]

Burden clearly is no Cavalier; rather, he represents the rough-hewn frontiersman—the persona who always stood at the center of the Old Colonel's being, even after he tried to disguise the fact. Both energetic and crude, Burden, we are told, was a man with a "harsh loud voice," with a hand "more apt for a rope or a gunbutt or a knife than a pen." A fanatical abolitionist, he was just as fanatically antiblack. "Damn, lowbuilt black folks," he exclaims to his son Nathaniel, "low built because of the weight of the wrath of God, black because of the sin of human bondage staining their blood and flesh." This streak of racism, we are told, was mixed with a craving for women of melanotic skin color. Of the wives that he and Nathaniel chose, one was a French Huguenot and the other Mexican. "Prurient Puritans," notes Bleikasten, "the male Burdens were obviously attracted to 'dark' ladies and beset with the exotic sin of miscegenation." The Old Colonel, of course, was said to have taken up with a Mexican woman during his service in the Mexican War and to have paid for that dalliance with half the fingers on his left hand (an event echoed when Nathaniel Burden gets in trouble during his stay in Mexico over a horse he had allegedly stolen).[36]

This tactic of camouflaging his great-grandfather as a variant of the Yankee saint and Confederate bête noire John Brown served two essential, if quite different, purposes for Faulkner. First, it allowed him to gratify his southern chauvinism by heaping calumny on the North, much as the Old Colonel himself had done in *The Little Brick Church*. If one looked closely enough at a New England abolitionist, the implication ran, one could find an abundance of blatant racial prejudice and hypocrisy. Lashing out against the Yankees this way was apparently a psychological necessity: the manuscript version of *Light in August*, Fadiman informs us, contained even more scathing references to northern culture that either Faulkner or his editor discreetly combed out.[37]

At the same time, disguising the Old Colonel in this fashion was the only way Faulkner could begin to face the backwoods and racist elements in his forebear's character that stood so sharply at odds with the Cavalier mystique. For it is precisely Calvin Burden's warped values and beliefs, handed down through his son, that ultimately corrupt Joanna, causing her to view blacks not "as people" but in terms of abstract stereotypes—"as a thing, a shadow in which I lived, we lived, all white people." In her mind, that shadow assumes the shape of a cross that white people are doomed to bear from the moment of birth: "It seemed like the white babies were struggling, even before they drew breath, to escape from the shadow that was not only upon them but beneath them too, flung out like their arms were flung out, as if they were nailed to the cross." The imagery corresponds directly to her own experience. If Joe Christmas is crucified at the end of his life, Joanna is impaled on a "cross" of racism at the very start of hers. But in her case the historical agent responsible for bringing about the "crucifixion" is not a relic of primeval times like Doc Hines but rather a stand-in for Faulkner's archetype southerner, the Old Colonel himself.[38]

Given that fact, it seems highly appropriate that Faulkner assigned the task of eliminating Calvin Burden to that mythical Cavalier John Sartoris. For the moment, the legend would prevail over the troubling (though still well-disguised) reality. The casual reader of *Light in August* might easily construe that shooting as just another instance of Reconstruction bloodshed, a case of an unregenerate Mississippian trying to fend off the horde of intruders come to meddle in his region's affairs. However, from the standpoint of Faulkner's ongoing development as a southern Modernist writer, the killing must also be seen as part of an internal civil war—one whose decisive battle was about to take place in his next major work.

CHAPTER 8

The Dark House of Southern History

A long fallow period followed the completion of *Light in August*. Apparently exhausted by the great creative outburst that had resulted in four novels in as many years, Faulkner made no effort to write anything of real literary weight for the next two years, turning his attention instead to his rapidly expanding family obligations. With the death of his father in 1932, he had become responsible for the support of his aging mother, which meant, among other things, paying the taxes and upkeep on her house. The birth of his daughter Jill a year later likewise necessitated a higher income. Added to these unavoidable expenses were others more optional in nature. He could not, for example, resist buying a large parcel of land adjoining Rowan Oak, both to ensure his privacy and to cement further his status as a scion of the old aristocracy. Nor could he resist indulging his penchant for freedom and motion by taking up the costly hobby of aviation. Flying lessons in early 1933 were followed by the purchase of a Waco biplane he could ill afford. And he began contributing to the support of Estelle's family, the Oldhams, whose fortunes had fallen on hard times. Clearly, his carefree bohemian existence of the 1920s was now behind him forever.[1]

Desperate for funds, Faulkner began an intermittent career as a Hollywood scriptwriter. He did it, he kept insisting, in the illusory hope of ending his financial problems once and for all. But the high salaries that

Faulkner the Modernist author at work in his study. He almost always wrote his initial drafts in longhand, either seated in a comfortable chair or at the desk pictured here. He would then prepare a typescript himself, making extensive revisions as he typed in keeping with his exacting standards of craftsmanship. (Courtesy Brodsky Collection, Center for Faulkner Studies, Southeast Missouri State University)

the studios paid represented only part of his motivation. Despite his many complaints over the years about Hollywood, the evidence indicates that it fulfilled his needs on many levels. These included the chance to escape his family and Oxford, engage in a glamorous occupation, explore a new medium that was rife with Modernist techniques such as montage, and, not least of all, pursue sexual adventures in a way that would have been impossible at home. If it was demeaning for a first-rate literary artist to spend his days writing occasional dialogue for grade B commercial entertainments, it was also heady stuff for a country boy from Mississippi to hobnob with the stars and to take home an oversized paycheck (which he and Estelle quickly found new ways to spend).[2]

Nor did working for the studios cut significantly into his productivity as a novelist, as is sometimes alleged. During his first decade as a scriptwriter he composed no fewer than four masterpieces, including *Absalom, Absalom!*, *The Wild Palms*, *The Hamlet*, and *Go Down, Moses*. The situation would be quite different in the 1940s, when he produced almost no significant literature and found himself trapped by a dismal contract at Warner Brothers. However, as Joseph Urgo observes, that experience should not be allowed to color the symbiotic relationship he enjoyed with the film industry in the 1930s, when Hollywood provided him with what in essence was a useful diversion from his real vocation.[3]

Beyond these more or less mundane considerations, there is another, more deep seated explanation for the fallow period after *Light in August* having to do with the journey of cultural exploration on which he had embarked. The next phase of that journey would involve an immense step: the final stripping away of his southern mythological heritage and a direct encounter with that most sensitive of issues, the origins of southern identity. In his previous Yoknapatawpha novels Faulkner had set forth an anguished portrait of the present state of the South. As he acknowledged in an unpublished piece done in 1933, this had been a harrowing task. "We more than other men," he noted of his fellow southern writers, "unconsciously write ourselves into ever[y] line and phrase, postulating our past vain despairs and rages and frustrations." He had encapsulated that despair and rage in Benjy Compson's scream at the very end of *The Sound and the Fury* and in the horrific rush of "pent black blood" attending Joe Christmas's "crucifixion." Now it was necessary to move backward in time to locate the sources of that anguish, an undertaking even more torturous that would involve some of the most difficult writing of his career. No wonder he allowed himself a few years of respite.[4]

Nor should it be surprising that when he did at last resume his journey of exploration in 1934, his initial progress was decidedly slow and fitful, with frequent diversions. In February of that year he started a novel about an antebellum family named Sutpen that would eventually become *Absalom, Absalom!*, but the narrative refused to take shape, and so, after several frustrating months, he reluctantly put it aside. In retrospect it appears that two things had to happen before the voices would speak to him again— he needed to make one last ritual gesture of genuflection to the Cavalier myth before he could break with it decisively, and he needed to fill out the new conception of heroism that had been incubating in his mind since *As I Lay Dying*. Only then would he be fully prepared to embark on *Absalom, Absalom!*.

The task of genuflection he accomplished in a series of six stories for the *Saturday Evening Post* and *Scribner's* depicting the Sartoris family during its Civil War glory days. No doubt Faulkner wrote these stories in large part for the money (in letters to his agent he refers to them as "a pulp series" and "trash"), but one suspects that the chance to exhibit his southern patriotism in print, especially in regard to the fabled courage and nobility of the old planter class, was equally important—that it indeed represented an act of compensation his divided psyche absolutely required before he could go on to deliver what would amount to a devastating blow to that same mythical heritage. This would be the only time in his career that Faulkner would give untrammeled expression to the Old South myth; surely it is no accident that it occurred at the same time he was trying to tell the story of Thomas Sutpen.[5]

Then, having bowed to the myth, he changed direction entirely, leaving the South behind for a short novel about a group of barnstorming aviators that would be published in 1935 as *Pylon*. His motives again appear to have been partly financial—dreams of selling the rights to a film studio undoubtedly danced in his head. But *Pylon*, with its lyricism, complex characterization, and frequent allusions to such contemporary masters as Joyce, Dos Passos, and Eliot, represented much more than a potboiler. Though drafted rapidly, it was a serious work of Modernist fiction that allowed him to revisit the subject of flying—the activity that in his eyes had long offered the best hope of achieving heroic stature under the conditions of twentieth-century existence.[6]

Given the significance with which he invested it, the changes in his treatment of aviation since *Flags in the Dust* are striking. In that work Faulkner had portrayed John and Bayard Sartoris as virtual "knights of the air"—latter-day Confederate cavalrymen performing their feats of bravery from the cockpit of an airplane rather than on horseback. Climbing into the sky had also entailed transcendence, allowing them to enter a pure, ethereal realm far above the dusty world of mere mortals where they could soar effortlessly like hawks or eagles. By contrast, the aviators in *Pylon* are viewed through a Modernist lens that preserves their standing as heroes but strips away virtually all the glamour. Distinctly ordinary men and women from nondescript midwestern backgrounds, they have chosen to risk their lives racing dangerous aircraft in order to escape the humdrum existence to which they would otherwise be consigned. We see them in grease-stained overalls or worn leather jackets moving unrecognized through city crowds, forced to spend their nights in cheap rooming houses because the wealthy businessmen who run the airshows keep exploiting them. Likewise, their planes are no longer great birds of prey that float at will through the heavens but mere "dragonflies" hovering "silently in a vacuum," held up tenuously by their "weightless and terrific speed any momentary faltering of which would be the irreparable difference between motion and mere matter."[7]

It is precisely that fragility that creates the possibility of heroics. The forces arrayed against the fliers are so formidable that one small mistake can prove fatal, yet they persist. Much like Joe Christmas in *Light in August*, they are driven by a powerful internal compulsion to pit themselves against the universe, "shrieking" their "feeble I-am-I into the desert of chance and disaster." Where most people in the urban world that Faulkner depicts evade that struggle by burying themselves in the spiritual "wasteland" of modern life, taking refuge in its deadening routines and comforts, the fliers insist on being truly "alive," even if "only for six and a half minutes a day." To be sure, their victories are at best temporary, since gravity and organized society always claim them in the end. Nonetheless, in their efforts to climb briefly above the mire and assert human initiative in the face of an indifferent cosmos, they illustrate the existential conception of nobility that would dominate Faulkner's remaining novels.[8]

Asked twenty years later, "What character or incident caused you to write *Absalom, Absalom!*?" Faulkner replied instantly: "Sutpen." "The other characters," he explained, "I had to get out of the attic to tell the story of Sutpen." Repeatedly through the years he would insist, "It's Sutpen's story." Yet in the two short stories that served as the germ of the novel, Thomas Sutpen is a relatively minor figure who differs in certain crucial respects from the Sutpen of *Absalom*. Far from being a frontier parvenu who raises himself through his own efforts from poor white to wealthy planter, the Sutpen of "Evangeline" hails from a family "created by long time" that embodies every facet of the aristocratic myth. Likewise the Sutpen of "Wash" appears to coincide with the myth; there is not the slightest hint that he might be self-made. His haughty and bitter disposition, though worrisome, seems to reflect the devastation that the war has visited on his estate and family, not some dark defect of his character.[9]

All of this suggests how hard it must have been for Faulkner to bring to light the far more complex and subversive Thomas Sutpen of *Absalom, Absalom!*. Like Benjy Compson and Joe Christmas before him, Sutpen seems always to have been present in the depths of Faulkner's mind, surfacing from time to time in oblique fashion—as Dal Martin in the 1926 story "The Big Shot," for example, or Joanna Burden's grandfather in *Light in August*—but only through a protracted struggle was it possible to bring him fully into consciousness.

The main reason for this, one suspects, had to do with the threat Sutpen posed to Faulkner's lingering allegiance to the orthodox view of southern history incarnated for him in his great-grandfather. In *Flags in the Dust*, Colonel Falkner had appeared in the guise of John Sartoris, a certified aristocrat whose ghost permeates the novel's opening scene, conjuring up memories of his courage, composure, and glamour. By comparison, when the Old Colonel's shade fills the room at the beginning of *Absalom, Absalom!*, he takes the form of a "demon" with "faint sulphur-reek still in hair clothes and beard." Riding into town "out of no discernible past" and acquiring his land "no one knew how," he proceeds to "overrun suddenly the hundred square miles of tranquil and astonished earth and drag house and formal gardens violently out of the soundless Nothing." The imagery is hardly flattering, yet, as Patricia Tobin points out, by novel's end Sutpen clearly comes to represent "the creator, the founder" who has in some fashion given the South its very identity.[10]

The point is not that Sutpen perfectly replicates the life of Faulkner's notorious ancestor, for that is certainly not the case. Among other things, Sutpen never becomes a lawyer (although he does teach himself to speak like one, replete with the Latinate phrases to which the Old Colonel was addicted); nor does he form a band of partisan guerrillas during the war, found a railroad, or run for political office. Nor would it be accurate to claim that Sutpen typifies the antebellum planter, even in the Deep South of the 1840s and 1850s, where many a prosperous Cotton Snob came from poor backcountry origins. Such men almost invariably worked their way up from an initial log cabin to the eventual "big house"; they did not simply arrive on the scene and proceed to erect a mammoth estate like Sutpen's Hundred. Nonetheless, Faulkner in writing *Absalom, Absalom!* was attempting to locate what he sensed was an essential and tragic truth about the old planter class that the region's reigning mythology had tended to omit or repress—a flaw that had proved of enormous consequence in shaping the South right up to his own day, giving rise to the havoc so vividly depicted in *The Sound and the Fury*. Sutpen thus stands as the founder not so much of the actual, historical South but of the southern psyche.[11]

What is so troubling about Sutpen in turn is not his rapid rise in the world—if anything, Faulkner seems to have admired his great energy and self-reliance—but rather his decision to repudiate his first wife because of the small, virtually undetectable amount of "Negro blood" that she apparently possessed. At the time of their marriage he had not suspected there was anything wrong; not only did Eulalia appear "white" (her skin is described as "parchment-colored," much like that of Joe Christmas), but she came from a wealthy Haitian planting family, supplying just the kind of match Sutpen needed to fulfill his ambition of becoming a great planter himself. As Mr. Compson explains in the course of his narrative, had Sutpen simply "acquiesced" to the situation and ignored the trace of African ancestry in his wife, "it would not even have been an error" for him, since no one on the Mississippi frontier would ever have known about or guessed it, but precisely because he did not acquiesce, the "mistake" became "his doom." Yet Sutpen never really wavered as to what he should do. The very fact that *he* was aware of his wife's infinitesimal racial impurity, he once explained to Quentin's grandfather, would have "voided and frustrated . . . the central motivation" of his "entire design," making "an ironic delusion" of whatever he might accomplish.[12]

Why this should be so is not obvious, especially since Sutpen shows few signs of harboring any notable racial prejudice. Whether working naked in the swamps alongside his field hands, wrestling with them in bloody rough-and tumble matches to secure his dominance over them, or having sex with his female slaves, he is clearly comfortable maintaining the most intimate contact with blacks. Nor is he in the least reluctant to be identified as the father of Clytie, his daughter by a slave woman, or concerned that his first wife's secret might somehow be exposed at a later date had he stayed married to her. What bothers him so much is that *he* would know; that alone would ruin everything.[13]

Sutpen's peculiar behavior here is in fact consistent with all of his other actions. Outward appearances by themselves do not especially interest him. Rather, over and over we find him conducting himself as if each step he takes, large or small, must conform to a script he carries in his head. He believes he is irredeemably obligated to play out every detail of that script, regardless of what the audience that happens to be watching might think. Never once does he pause to consider the likely response of the community as he brings in his twenty Haitian slaves with their strange argot, employs them to erect an oversized mansion in a desolate marshland twelve miles from town, lets it stand empty for three years without so much as a doorknob or windowpane, and then suddenly shows up with six wagonloads overflowing with the finest imported furnishings and accoutrements. In Sutpen's eyes he has simply been laboring as rapidly as possible to complete his design according to the required script. To the town, however, the whole enterprise seems not only bizarre but highly suspicious, leading to his arrest at the hands of a committee of concerned citizens who haven't the slightest idea what crime he has committed. Typically, the arrest fails to register on Sutpen; far from amending his script to take public opinion into account, he goes on pursuing his objectives with "the same singleminded unflagging effort and utter disregard of how his actions which the town could see might look and how the indicated ones which the town could not see must appear to it."[14]

This puzzling behavior begins to make sense when one realizes that what Sutpen is attempting here is nothing less than the creation of a radically new identity for himself. That, at its core, is what his design entails. As we eventually learn, the decisive moment in his life occurred in early adolescence when his father, a lowly overseer on a Tidewater plantation, sent him to the big house with a message, only to have a black servant abruptly turn him away, telling him never to come to the front door again. In the wake of this traumatic encounter Sutpen's entire personhood, by his own report, "seemed to kind of dissolve." Where before he had been blissfully unselfconscious about all aspects of his existence, right down to his dilapidated clothes and hayseed manners, now he suddenly began to see himself and his family "as the owner, the rich man . . . must have been seeing them all the time—as cattle, creatures heavy and without grace . . . who would in turn spawn with brutish and vicious prolixity." Though Sutpen had started to notice the gradations of power on the plantation before this, plainly this incident becomes the fateful catalyst, searing into his mind the belief that, so long as he retains his original identity, the world will perceive him as more animal than human, leaving him open to perpetual victimization.[15]

Retreating to a makeshift cave in the woods, Sutpen is overcome with a feeling of helplessness. His immediate response is to consider shooting the planter, but he soon decides that revenge *"wouldn't do no good."* A well-aimed bullet might dispatch Pettibone himself, but it would have no effect on "*them*," an entity that comprises far more "than all the puny human mortals under the sun that might lie in hammocks all afternoon with their shoes off." Rather, "*them*" refers to a set of distant and nebulous powers who somehow control everything—in a word, the fates, the cosmos itself. They, not Pettibone, have loaded the dice against the Sutpens of this world, and those dice will stay loaded unless he does something drastic to "fix things right." To win that battle—to achieve mastery in the deepest sense of that term—he will need to remake himself as a master, putting aside forever his animal-like vulnerability by attaining the rank of a rich, cultivated planter. He will need to acquire his own mansion, not for the sake of the pleasure it might afford him, but so that he can now be the one who controls the front door. Above all, he will have to establish his own dynasty, assuring his family of immortality by producing a line of "fine grandsons and great-grandsons springing as far as the eye could reach." That alone would erase the shame and vulnerability he feels, allowing him "to look in the face" not only the ancestors who had preceded him "but all the living ones that would come after him." [16]

Most important is the manner in which Sutpen goes about this. He does not, as Faulkner himself had done, enter into a prolonged process of identity formation, first sorting out what might be valuable from his past, then testing various trial identities against experience and juggling the resulting fragments until they had become a viable, if provisional, whole. Instead, Sutpen chooses to jettison his original identity altogether, breaking all contact with his family and previous life. In its place he adopts wholesale the model he had observed in Pettibone. The changeover is not, of course, instantaneous. It takes many years of effort to learn his new self, no doubt following the same methods as his avatar Dal Martin, who, after being turned away at the big house, spent hour after hour telling his shadow on the barn wall, " 'Dont you never come to my front door no more,' " until convinced that he had replicated the planter's very "gestures and tone." But the key point is that his would-be persona is both fixed and complete from the start. Fearful that the smallest mistake might betray him, moreover, he does not dare deviate from it. One could see this "in all his formal contacts with people," Mr. Compson tells us, including the characteristic "florid, swaggering gesture to the hat" that he used to greet other men, even when it was inappropriate and foolish: "He was like John L. Sullivan having taught himself painfully and tediously to do the schottische, having drilled himself and drilled himself in secret until he now believed it no longer necessary to count the music's beat, say." Though the music itself might change, Sutpen's store-bought identity would permit no adjustment.[17]

As Faulkner makes clear, however, the real Thomas Sutpen does not simply vanish. While ruthlessly suppressing what Lee Jenkins calls his "essential and true self," Sutpen simultaneously projects it outward onto Wash Jones, the poor white trapper whom he allows to squat on his land in return for Jones's fawning servitude. Jones, in turn, is most willing to oblige, since he has adopted the gallant figure of Sutpen riding a black stallion as his own vicarious ideal. *"Maybe I am not as big as he is,"* Jones thinks to himself, *"and maybe I did not do any of the galloping. But at least I was drug along where he went."* This relationship, which resembles that of Quentin and his shadow self in *The Sound and the Fury*, suits Sutpen's psychic needs well, allowing him both to keep his "essential self" alive and to demonstrate his superiority over it by treating Jones and his family like animals. Prior to the Civil War Jones is not allowed even to *approach* the back door, much less enter it or the front door, thereby providing Sutpen with the sense of complete mastery he had been seeking.[18]

The culmination comes when Sutpen, having used Jones's granddaughter sexually in a desperate but unsuccessful final attempt to get a son and heir, dismisses her as if she were a beast of the field. "[It's] too bad you're not a mare," he tells her, "[because then] I could give you a decent stall in the stable." The remark seems incredible until one remembers that, as with the "florid, swaggering gesture," Sutpen is doggedly continuing to play his role oblivious to realities. His words partake, Jenkins explains, of a "stereotyped viciousness, as if Sutpen thinks that this is the appropriate manner of contemptuous treatment that the aristocrat reserves for his inferiors." But this is too much for a now disillusioned Wash Jones, who proceeds to mow down Sutpen with a scythe. Faulkner's symbolism is perfect: the repressed makes its inevitable return, with the true self ripping apart the contrived self.[19]

Sutpen's story in this way becomes a kind of mythic allegory of how the southern psyche, as Faulkner construed it, was formed. The standard mythology had, of course, depicted the South's founding fathers as established aristocrats who had automatically inherited their identities and culture along with the family silver. In *Absalom*, Faulkner was offering an alternative myth in which the Cavalier identity was less a direct legacy from a distinguished past than the product of the inherent frontier character of antebellum southern society. That identity was perpetuated, Faulkner's narrative suggests, by children of the backcountry, who, coming into contact with the region's prevailing system of social stratification, had become painfully conscious of their inferiority and cultural coarseness. Their foremost response, however, was not so much envy of the planter class as a devastating feeling of personal shame. Such an experience, writes Helen Merrell Lynd, "may call into question, not only one's own adequacy and the validity of the codes of one's immediate society, but the meaning of the universe itself." So it is with Sutpen. Following his rejection at the front door, his ears ring with the "roaring waves of mellow laughter meaningless and terrifying and loud" that he imagines being directed at him by Pettibone's slaves, epitomizing both his abject status and the decimation of the moral order he has known. Not until he has rendered his planter self immortal by installing himself as the progenitor of a Cavalier dynasty will that maddening laughter cease within his mind and the terror at last subside.[20]

All of this, of course, takes place in a specific cultural context. The model of the gentleman that Thomas Sutpen apes so assiduously is very much a Victorian one. Like the Old Colonel in real life, Sutpen may retain some of his backwoods habits, turning him in the eyes of an outside observer into a strange bundle of cultural contradictions, but from the instant of his transformation one finds him viewing the world through the perspective of the nineteenth-century moral dichotomy, assimilating its values with all the fervor of a recent convert. It is that new perspective that causes him to see his own family as having been ignobly relegated to the realm of savagery. His design is accordingly intended to move them once and for all to the right side of the moral dividing line, where they will be "riven forever free from brutehood." But there is more. Frontier literalist that he is, Sutpen follows the logic of Victorian belief to its ultimate conclusion, deciding, in Adamowski's words, that he must pursue absolute "flawlessness" in his dynastic design if he wishes to transcend the ephemeral flesh-and-blood world into which he was born and attain a level of existence so far above animality that it is possible to "live on" endlessly after death; to accomplish that, "there must be nothing they or he (for he sees with *their* eyes) can see." This explains why Eulalia becomes unacceptable to him. Her taint of "black blood," in his view, would corrupt his progeny, reducing his line to mere mortality. That is also why he marries Ellen Coldfield—she provides "the two names, the stainless wife and the unimpeachable father-in-law, on the license, the patent." With that kind of purity he can stave off the laughter and beat the fates at their own game.[21]

From a Modernist perspective, though, this strategy comes at an extremely high price, for what Faulkner's archetypal self-made planter has done, in effect, is to internalize a stereotype rather than fashion a true identity. Based on a static pattern or ideal to which he rigidly adheres, Sutpen's adult persona contrasts sharply with the supple Modernist style of self created through the vicissitudes of experience. Above all, that persona cuts Sutpen off from his own past. It does not grow naturally out of his ancestry and upbringing but rather is imported entirely from outside. Nothing could be more at variance with Faulkner's own beliefs. As he declared on many occasions, "no man is himself, he is the sum of his past. There is no such thing really as was because the past is. It is a part of every man, every woman, and every moment. All of his or her ancestry, background, is all a part of himself and herself at any moment." But Sutpen has rejected his history, convinced that he can create himself de novo, as if he were an object to be sculpted. In the last analysis, he exists not inside himself but outside, gazing constantly at his handiwork to make sure it is perfect, recounting his life to General Compson with "detached and impersonal interest" as if "telling a story about something a man named Thomas Sutpen had experienced, which would still have been the same story if the man had had no name at all." It is hard to imagine a more fundamental violation of the Modernist tenet of authenticity.[22]

Here, then, Faulkner was saying, lay the origins of that pathological identity that twentieth-century southerners like the Quentin Compson of *The Sound and the Fury* would inherit. Heroic though it might have been in some respects, it was also founded on a mammoth falsehood that transpired when the ambitious offspring of the frontier, ashamed of their heritage, attempted to jettison their actual selves in exchange for a culture and way of life that was not rightfully theirs. By proceeding in this manner, *Absalom* suggests, the Old Colonels, real and fictional, founded not the lasting dynasties they were hoping for but rather a society, to borrow Miss Rosa Coldfield's haunting words, "primed for fatality and already cursed with it."[23]

That curse becomes fate for Sutpen's children. In the usual rendition of the southern myth, the sons and daughters of planter families, whatever their shortcomings, were always firmly grounded in their inherited traditions and obligations, secure in their knowledge of who they were and what role they would play in life. Living in a "simpler" time, they seemed, Quentin's father tells him, "integer for integer, larger, more heroic . . . not dwarfed and involved but distinct, uncomplex who had the gift of loving once or dying once instead of being diffused and scattered creatures drawn blindly limb from limb from a grab bag and assembled." But this is assuredly not the case in Faulkner's revised narrative of how the South came to be. In the Sutpen household prior to the war, no one has a solid sense of self. Unsure who they are, the children attempt, with varying success, to absorb their identities vicariously from others. Far from being the "distinct" and "uncomplex" personalities Mr. Compson envisions, they are presented as "phantoms" desperately searching for definition, density, and wholeness. Their struggle to lift the psychological "curse" their father has placed on them in turn provides the central drama of the novel.[24]

Most anxious of all to achieve an authentic existence is Charles Bon, Sutpen's son by his abandoned Haitian wife who should have become his father's primary heir but does not even receive the family name. The small trace of Negro "blood" that had rendered his mother's skin "parchment-colored" has disappeared in Bon.* To all appearances, he is a dashing

---

*It is certainly the case, as numerous critics have pointed out, that Faulkner nowhere informs us incontrovertibly that Bon is Sutpen's son or has Negro ancestry. That fact has led some to declare that we must refrain from assuming either of these things to be true. Perhaps, it is suggested, the problem was not Eulalia's racial makeup but rather that she had become pregnant by another man, so that Bon was not really Sutpen's child. Such a set of circumstances would explain both why Sutpen put her aside and why he later refused to grant recognition to Bon.

This approach to the novel makes little sense. For one thing, although Bon's possible illegitimacy would account for Sutpen's decision to cast off Eulalia in 1831, it would not explain why he objected so passionately three decades later to Bon marrying Judith that he risked his entire "design" to stop the wedding. After all, if Bon was not his son, incest would not be involved. And besides, Sutpen told General Compson that he had rejected Eulalia "through no fault of her own," which would appear to rule out an illicit pregnancy.

Those who pursue this style of analysis forget that *Absalom, Absalom!* is not a postmodernist exercise demonstrating the impossibility of our ever gaining sure knowledge of reality, but rather a fiction that Faulkner crafted to express certain "truths" that he had intuited about his region's past. That those provisional truths are closely connected to race is demonstrated by how frequently racial issues arise throughout the text, most notably including the tragic story of Bon's mulatto son by his octoroon mistress. The overall architecture of the work, in other words, demands that Bon's "taint"

young aristocrat, wealthy, cultivated, and impeccably white. However, lacking any roots, Bon also lacks any solid center to his being. Having arrived at Sutpen's Hundred "almost phoenix-like, full-sprung from no childhood," he hovers over the scene "shadowy, almost substanceless," a veritable "myth" or "phantom," and when he dies, it is as if he had "vanished, leaving no bones nor dust anywhere." As Mr. Compson limns him, Bon becomes "that mental and spiritual orphan whose fate it apparently was to exist in some limbo halfway between where his corporeality was and his mentality and moral equipment desired to be." What he most desires, with a passion so fervent it can barely be expressed, is to authenticate himself by reestablishing his connection with his father. He yearns for recognition—"the living touch" that will bring him back to life—from the man "out of the shadow of whose absence my spirit's posthumeity has never escaped."[25]

The great irony comes from the fact that, although his father has brutally rejected him, Bon nonetheless represents Sutpen's ideal self. Descended on his mother's side from French planter stock and raised in the cosmopolitan upper-class precincts of New Orleans, Bon is so indelibly aristocratic that Ellen Sutpen immediately wants to obtain him for her household, as if he were an elegant piece of furniture. Far from needing to drill himself at length to master the gestures of a gentleman, he displays "an ease of manner and a swaggering gallant air in comparison with which Sutpen's pompous arrogance was clumsy bluff." Bon swaggers so well in part because he taps into the older continental version of the Cavalier ethos, which, according to Richard Milum, was considered "more 'pure' "

---

be racial and that he be Sutpen's child; otherwise the pieces will not fit into an overall structure, as Faulkner plainly intended.

Beyond this, we know that passages explicitly establishing Bon's racial ancestry and parentage appeared in draft versions of the novel until very late in the composition process, when Faulkner apparently decided for reasons of narrative technique to make the reader play detective and put the story together him- or herself. It is also indisputable that in interviews given after *Absalom* was published Faulkner always spoke as if there was no question that Bon was Sutpen's son and that the problem had been Bon's "black blood." Finally, there is the clinching piece of evidence—a three-word summary of the book that Faulkner provided for a Hollywood producer to whom he was trying to sell the film rights to *Absalom*. "It's about miscegenation," Faulkner wrote.

See Schoenberg, *Old Tales and Talking*, 80–83; Faulkner, *Absalom*, 194; Elisabeth Muhlenfeld, introduction to her edited volume *William Faulkner's "Absalom, Absalom!*," xxvii, xxxi; Ragan, *William Faulkner's "Absalom, Absalom!*," 106, 163; Faulkner, *Faulkner in the University*, 79, 272–73; Blotner, *Faulkner*, 2:946–47.

than its Anglo-Saxon counterpart because it was "less adulterated" by the Calvinist insistence on repressing natural instincts. Free of such repression, Bon enjoys the luxury of being able to indulge himself to his heart's content in earthly pleasures without jeopardizing his genteel status. The rural planters' sons who make up his classmates at the University of Mississippi look on with sheer, dripping envy at this young man who seems to spend his life passing "from the scene of one scarce imaginable delight to the next without interval or pause or satiety." Yet, as Faulkner has his narrators depict him, we discover that Bon is far from fulfilled, craving "the life, the existence" of Sutpen's Hundred in order to complete himself.[26]

No one is more charmed by the charismatic Bon than his half brother Henry, Sutpen's son by his second marriage. If Bon exemplifies the cosmopolite, Henry is "the provincial, the clown almost," who bears a much closer resemblance to the petit bourgeois Coldfields on his mother's side than to his father. Though he tries his best to play the part of worthy heir to such a magnificent estate, sitting his horse "with the same swagger" as his father, something is clearly missing. Heading off to college with his mare and black groom, he is still unmistakably a country boy, "only in the surface matter of food and clothing and daily occupation any different" from the slave who accompanies him. To be sure, he comes from a world where the social landscape is dotted with frequent grand balls and dinner parties, complete with "candles and silk dresses and champagne," but, Faulkner pointedly informs us, on such occasions the rude manners of the backwoods can always be found just below the surface. In the Mississippi of the 1850s, we learn, dancing typically means square dancing, with the music played on "crude fiddles and guitars," while the champagne, though "the best doubtless," is "crudely dispensed out of the burlesqued pantomime elegance of negro butlers who (and likewise the drinkers who gulped it down like neat whiskey between flowery and unsubtle toasts) would have treated lemonade the same way." Given all this, there should be no mystery why Henry would covet Bon's polished aristocratic identity.[27]

As his father had earlier done with Pettibone, Henry, we learn, not only "aped" Bon at college but "caricatured" him, ingesting whole the stereotype that he saw in Bon. "*I am trying*," one of the narrators imagines Henry saying, "*to make myself into what I think he wants me to be*." As "the Coldfield with the Coldfield cluttering of morality," he especially envies Bon's freedom to partake of exotic delights, following his half brother's lead "*even though what he asked me to do looked to me like dishonor*." Indeed, his wish to merge with Bon brings him to the point of sexual desire, only to find himself frustrated by "the insurmountable barrier which the similarity of gender hopelessly intervened." Unable to consummate his love for Bon himself, he does so vicariously by sponsoring a match between Bon and his sister, Judith.[28]

Of all the Sutpen children, in turn, Judith is the one who most resembles the father. A "hoyden" as a girl, who can "outrun and outclimb, and ride and fight both with and beside her brother," she watches with fascination as Sutpen engages in no-holds-barred wrestling with his slaves, while Henry vomits. It is Judith, the daughter, who insists that the family carriage continue racing to church on Sundays, even after her father, who had initiated the practice, stops attending. In time, though, all of this would change. As a result of the terrible suffering she undergoes during and after the war, she matures into one of Faulkner's most admirable characters, filled, as Elisabeth Muhlenfeld puts it, with an "intense determination to *experience* rather than retreat from life." Ironically, it would be the very qualities of frontier energy, persistence, and fortitude inherited from her father, along with his initial egalitarian ethos, that would serve her so well in coping with her drastically changed circumstances. Dressed in simple calico, as opposed to the elaborate wardrobe she had enjoyed while the family's wealth was still intact, she calmly and capably keeps the plantation running while providing whatever food is available to the waves of starved former soldiers straggling home after Appomattox. A woman of immense inner strength, she accepts the terrible things that happen to her with stoic equanimity. "*If happy I can be I will,*" she thinks to herself, "*if suffer I must I can.*"[29]

However, this noble figure emerges only following the war and the death of her fiancé; prior to that the Judith we see is still essentially formless, "the dreamy and volitionless daughter" who exists in a "complete detachment and imperviousness to actuality" akin to "the state before birth." This earlier, adolescent Judith shares an unusually close relationship with her brother Henry, almost as if together they constitute one person, a "single personality with two bodies." "The difference in sex," we are told, "had merely sharpened the common blood to a terrific, an almost unbearable similarity." Although there is no indication of physical incest between them, it becomes clear that, like Quentin and Caddy Compson in *The Sound and the Fury*, this brother and sister are entwined in a Platonic incest derived from their mutual need for self-completion.[30]

Once Charles Bon enters the picture, that incest becomes triangular, giving rise to a situation of incredible psychological intricacy. Far from being the "distinct, uncomplex" men and women that Mr. Compson imagines, the three Sutpen siblings are presented as partial beings attempting to make themselves whole by vicariously incorporating the images they project onto one another. In the house of mirrors that results, we find Henry identifying with Bon in order to be able vicariously to marry Judith, not only to merge with her but also to accomplish his desired fusion with Bon, "the man whom he [Henry] would be if he could become, metamorphose into, the lover, the husband; by whom he would be despoiled, choose for despoiler, if he could become, metamorphose into the sister, the mistress, the bride." Judith, captivated by the elegant Bon, hopes to make "the image hers by possession," meanwhile supplying "the blank shape, the empty vessel" in which her brothers "strove to preserve, not the illusion of himself nor the illusion of the other but what each conceived the other to believe him to be." It almost seems as if Faulkner, in painting this family portrait, was employing the cubist mode, filling his canvas with fragments of human figures, each inchoate and fluid in shape, that overlap and even interpenetrate in places but never come together to form well-defined, substantial persons.[31]

This skillfully constructed incest triangle serves a number of symbolic functions. On one level, it indicates the flawed nature of the cultural legacy handed down by the antebellum South. Heirs to the inauthentic identity authored by Thomas Sutpen, his children become, in Henry's plaintive phrase, *"just illusions that he begot,"* who must couple with one another in order to begin establishing a real, concrete existence for themselves. If Patricia Tobin is correct in observing that the Sutpens stand for "the genealogical family of the South," setting the pattern for southern identity, then the implications Faulkner is drawing here for the region's culture are truly ominous. The implications appear equally foreboding when one moves from the cultural to the social realm. The traditional myth had depicted southern society as quasi-feudal in character, with classes and institutions fitting together seamlessly, leading to a stability and cohesiveness that set it apart from the individualistic, competitive North. The South, in this view, was like one family writ large. "Love for others is the organic law of our society," wrote George Fitzhugh in 1854, "as self-love is of theirs." In *Absalom, Absalom!* Faulkner almost parodies this claim, for the Sutpen children can readily be construed as personifications of the three principal forms of southern settlement in the nineteenth century—Bon, the urbane Tidewater; Henry, the provincial small town; and Judith, the backwoods. However, far from being arrayed in an organic relationship to one another conducive to stability and cohesion, the three are aligned in a most unnatural, incestuous one destined to end in fratricide when Henry kills Bon.[32]

One final incendiary element must be added to the mix before it becomes truly lethal, however. Though the prospect of incest gives Henry considerable pause, causing him to insist that Bon break off all relations with Judith for the duration of the war, he is ultimately able to bring himself to approve a marriage between his half brother and sister. Not until Sutpen plays his "trump card," informing Henry of Bon's racial ancestry, do Henry's objections to the wedding become so strong that he will murder Bon to prevent it. "*So it's the miscegenation, not the incest, which you cant bear*," Bon remarks to him, observing how, in Henry's eyes, Bon's identity has now instantaneously shifted from that of brother to "*the nigger that's going to sleep with your sister*." Surely Bon is correct in this assessment: from the moment Sutpen reveals that Bon's mother was "*part negro*," Henry, who had agonized for four years over the incest, thinks about "*not what he would do but what he would have to do*."[33]

In short, the curse that Thomas Sutpen lays upon his family, and by extension upon the South, consists not only of a deeply inauthentic identity but also of the stipulation that that identity must be based on racial purity. Sutpen may have originally adopted that belief as part and parcel of the planter self he was trying to incorporate, but for Henry, and Judith as well, it becomes an assumption of life instilled in them since birth. While his father deliberates before playing the race card, casting about to make sure he is not committing another "mistake," Henry reacts viscerally once the possibility of racial mixing is raised; as Philip Weinstein notes, the taboo has become embedded in his very "subjectivity." *That* is the essence of the curse for Faulkner—not the noxious practice of turning human beings into property, but an identity model in which the slightest strain of nonwhite "blood" produces an unacceptable level of contamination.[34]

To amplify this tragic insight into southern racial dynamics, which he had first started to develop in *Light in August*, Faulkner introduces the story of Charles Etienne St. Valery Bon, the son of Charles Bon and an octoroon mistress in New Orleans. Like Bon, Etienne appears as if he had been "created without agency of man." An orphan at the age of twelve, this "strange lonely little boy," in a striking echo of Sutpen (who is, of course, his paternal grandfather), is forced to leave his interracial Eden, where the word *nigger* or its equivalent did not exist, for the racist world of Sutpen's Hundred. There he is raised by Judith and her half sister Clytie, Sutpen's daughter by a slave woman. The two make every effort—naively, as Thadious Davis points out—to shield him from knowledge of the South's racial mores, meanwhile consigning him to a limbo status between the races, symbolized by the trundle bed on which he sleeps midway between Judith's regular bed and Clytie's pallet on the floor. Clytie not only chases off strangers before they can speak to him; she attempts to eradicate his trace of Negroid color, "trying to wash the smooth faint olive tinge from his skin as you might watch a child scrubbing a wall long after the epithet, the chalked insult, has been obliterated."[35]

But the women do not reckon with Etienne himself, who, as he grows up, will choose to brandish that "epithet" as a mark of pride. As soon as he reaches adolescence, he begins to confront his identity dilemma, hiding a shard of broken mirror under his mattress, "and who to know what hours of amazed and tearless grief he might have spent before it." A few years later, in a virtual replication of Joe Christmas, he provokes a fight at a "negro ball" and allows himself to be beaten severely. Many more such seemingly inexplicable fights follow with combatants of both races as this "white-colored man" tries to achieve a sense of racial definition through direct, physical means—solidifying his black self by having white men savagely beat him while simultaneously allowing black men to pound his white self into oblivion.[36]

What Panthea Reid Broughton describes as his "final vengeful gesture to make concrete his abstract identity as a black" comes when he takes as his legal wife a "coal black and ape-like woman." Sutpen, one recalls, had abandoned Etienne's grandmother because he feared that her nearly invisible taint of Negro "blood" would subvert his desired identity. In a stunningly ironic reversal, Etienne employs his wife's conspicuous black-ness to declare to the world who he wants to be, "hunting out situations in order to flaunt and fling the ape-like body of his charcoal companion in the faces of all and any who would retaliate." It is not without significance that he emerges from these encounters "neither cursing nor panting, but laughing." If his grandfather, following his rejection at the planter's door, embraced pure whiteness to escape the sound of black laughter ringing in his ears, Etienne now embraces pure blackness in order to be the one who gets to laugh.[37]

It is in large part to indulge that dark, sardonic laughter, one surmises, that Etienne returns to Sutpen's Hundred, throwing his wife and "au-thentic wedding license" in the face of Judith Sutpen. Judith, along with Clytie, had served as his surrogate mother, looking after his welfare as best she could. Yet the racist revulsion inherited from her father always stood as a barrier between them: each time she made physical contact with him, we are told, her hand "seemed at the moment of touching his body to lose all warmth and become imbued with cold implacable antipathy." Now, on his return, she acknowledges her terrible mistake. "*I was wrong. I admit it*," she confesses to him. "*I believed that there were things which still mattered just because they had mattered once. But I was wrong. Nothing matters but breath, breathing, to know and to be alive.*" But the racism, though attenuated by all she has learned, lingers on. Earnestly she counsels him to save himself by moving to a northern city where he can pass for white, while leaving his black family behind. As for "*the license, the paper*," she declares, it is "*between you and one who is inescapably negro*" and can therefore "*be put aside.*" Likewise the child presents no problem: "*Didn't my own father beget one? and he none the worse for it?*"[38]

The irony in this passage becomes nothing short of prodigious, since Judith, who apparently does not know about her father's abandonment of *his* first wife and child (her remark about "*my own father*" being "*none the worse*" for his mulatto offspring strongly suggests that), is advising Etienne to repeat the same grievous error that brought down the House of Sutpen and destroyed her chance for happiness. Etienne likewise seems unaware of Sutpen's actions; he is struggling not to correct a past wrong but to maintain the integrity of the fragile self he has managed to generate in the midst of the wreckage of his life. Still separated from Judith by race — "*she not daring to put out the hand with which she could have actually touched*" him — he turns his back on her and her counsel, "treading the thorny and flint-paved path toward the Gethsemane which he had decreed and created for himself." That she would lose her life three years later ministering to him after he had contracted a fatal infectious disease, touching him even when the consequences might be deadly, does not extenuate her inability, at the crucial moment, to rise above the curse bequeathed by her father. In the late nineteenth century, Faulkner seems to be saying, not even the most noble southerner could do that.[39]

Clearly, *Absalom, Absalom!* was meant as a bleak, tragic work, a fact reflected in its original working title, which once again had been "Dark House." The final title also connotes catastrophe, alluding as it does to the lament of King David over his slain son. That allusion is, of course, ironic. While David weeps unconsolably on learning of Absalom's death,

Sutpen shows no hint of emotion when told of Bon's, demonstrating his fundamental deficiency in human feeling. Indeed, as numerous critics have shown, a bitter irony governs almost all of the parallels between the biblical story and that of the novel. If David goes on to become the classic patriarch, fathering fifty sons and fifty daughters and founding a royal dynasty, Sutpen's sole heir by the turn of the twentieth century is Etienne's son Jim Bond, a mentally retarded mulatto. Instead of creating the Kingdom of Israel, Sutpen ends with his "design" in tatters, his house and family destroyed like that of the House of Atreus. Nothing finally remains of the once magnificent Sutpen's Hundred save for its ashes and "four gutted chimneys."[40]

Yet, amid all the gloom, the saga of the Sutpen children is also graced by important instances of Faulknerian heroism. Charles Bon and Judith Sutpen may begin as "two serene phantoms" who do little more than "watch, hover, impartial attentive and quiet," but in the course of the action we find them managing to surmount their substanceless existences and fashion authentic selves. Like the fliers in *Pylon*, they do so through an existential encounter with harsh experience and with eyes fully open to the absurd circumstances that confront them. Compared with the grandeur of Cavalier-style heroism, theirs may seem diminutive and prosaic, at times no more than a matter of subtle gesture that an inattentive reader could easily miss. But that is now the nature of the heroic in Faulkner. In a reversal of existing literary convention, the episodes most central to this novel's meaning often take place at the margins of the action, in some instances almost hidden from view—just as the defining detail in a Modernist painting can often be found tucked away obscurely in a corner.[41]

That is certainly true of Charles Bon. It is all too easy to retain the initial portrait of him as a jaded, fin de siècle fatalist supplied by Mr. Compson, but if one pays close attention to the narrative provided by Quentin and his Harvard roommate, Shreve McCannon, the story becomes quite different. Their Bon struggles from the beginning against immense odds, raised by a crazed mother concerned only with gaining revenge against the man who had deserted her and by a lawyer scheming to milk the situation for profit. For his part, Bon astutely responds to these circumstances by adopting an attitude of watchful waiting. Though it may look as if he is passively submitting to the vagaries of fate, he is in truth searching for his opening, canvassing the game in the hope of snatching from it some small victory, all the while protecting himself by wearing "that expression which was not smiling but something not to be seen through."[42]

Acutely alert to nuance themselves, Shreve and Quentin together weave the tale of how Bon struggles to seize that victory. Their Bon is seen presenting his father with every conceivable opportunity to flash the crucial sign of recognition that will restore his personhood. Even the barest nod of paternal acknowledgment will suffice: "*He would just have to write 'I am your father. Burn this' and I would do it. Or if not that, a sheet a scrap of paper with the one word 'Charles' in his hand, and I would know what he meant and he would not even have to ask me to burn it. Or a lock of his hair or a paring from his finger nail and I would know them.*" But the father who earlier would not provide him with "an authentic name" will not authenticate him now. Still Bon persists. Taking up his lot as a Confederate soldier, he accepts the responsibility when he is elected an officer, leading his men through four years of hardship and combat to be rewarded only by defeat.[43]

It is at this juncture that we hear Bon's actual voice for the first time. Though his letter to Judith in early 1865 is written in a "faint spidery script" that seems less "something impressed upon the paper by a once-living hand" than "a shadow cast upon it," this ghostly text in fact represents the most vivid communication that has survived from any of the principal players in the Sutpen drama precisely because in it Bon speaks in his own words, sharing the insights he has gleaned from his time at war. The letter recounts how his unit, reduced to "*an assortment of homogeneous scarecrows,*" had succeeded at last in capturing ten Yankee supply wagons, only to find that instead of food or ammunition they were carrying "*box after beautiful box*" of stove polish, "*doubtless still trying to overtake General Sherman with some belated amended field order requiring him to polish the stove before firing the house.*" At first sight this might appear to be Mr. Compson's flippant, sardonic Charles Bon, fatalistically resigned to whatever happens to him or his men, but the next sentence dramatically suggests otherwise: "*How we laughed. Yes, we laughed, because I have learned this at least during these four years: that it really requires an empty stomach to laugh with, that only when you are hungry or frightened do you extract some ultimate essence out of laughing.*" In this context laughter does not stem from derision; it is not a weapon against anyone but rather a vital prop for fortitude, enabling human beings under the most dire of conditions to turn despair into a kind of triumph. No matter how badly fate batters us, Bon is counseling Judith, we can always laugh and in that way preserve our humanity. It is a lesson that the humorless Thomas Sutpen never learns.[44]

Written with stove polish — "*the best (each box said, the very best)*" — on the fine watermarked stationery scavenged from a ruined plantation house, the letter's very physical attributes bespeak an author open to improvisation, one capable of adjusting to the flux of existence and relishing whatever small degree of mastery can be attained in the face of daunting odds. Even if *"you dont have God,"* he tells Henry, and even when there is nothing left *"for honor and pride to climb on and hold to and flourish,"* there remains something that can be called forth inside everyone that will *"decline to sit still in the sun and die."* As Broughton points out, Faulkner's position here corresponds to that of the Modernist theologian Paul Tillich, who argued for the necessity of maintaining "the courage to be" in the midst of a seemingly absurd universe. "With Faulkner," she explains, "that man considers himself to be without God or any sure signposts of meaning and yet still declines just to sit in the sun and die is itself an affirmation of monumental stature." Bon's letter to Judith is suffused with that affirmation: though he reports he must forgo *"thinking"* and *"remembering"* when the bullets start to fly, *"remark that I do not say, hoping."* Patently, he has come a long way from the "expression which was not smiling but something not to be seen through."[45]

It is this existential outlook, blended with his aristocratic ethos, that guides Bon's actions toward the heroic in his final crisis once their father informs Henry about Bon's racial background. Aware that in all likelihood his brother will soon kill him for being a "nigger," an incredible prospect given his long-standing self-identification as white, Bon is composed and solicitous, taking off his cloak and wrapping it around Henry in the early morning chill. Yet he also stands firm in what he will do. In *The Sound and the Fury* Quentin kept bemoaning how things never "finished themselves," but Bon, by his fateful choice to return to Judith, decisively brings matters to a close, affirming once and for all to his father that he exists. At the same time he arranges for one final message to Judith in the event that he dies. Four years earlier she had sent him her picture in a metal case; now he replaces her likeness with that of his octoroon wife and child. As Shreve and Quentin come to realize, this switching of pictures should in reality be viewed as a supreme gesture of love on his part, his "only way" of saying to her: *"I was no good; do not grieve for me."* Again Faulkner turns the ironic screw, since by telling her he was "no good" ("not Bon"), he is declaring unmistakably that he was the Bon she loved. Our last glimpse of him reveals a man who knows himself in the deepest possible sense and has made his peace with an absurd world, speaking to his brother in a voice *"gentler than that first breath in which the pine branches begin to move a little"* while wearing *"that faint expression about the eyes and mouth which might be smiling."*[46]

Judith also learns through her wartime ordeal how to act decisively in a world without meaning. Just hours after Bon's death, an event both shocking and inexplicable for her, Rosa Coldfield finds her calmly giving orders for preparing dinner and building a coffin, the metal picture case resting "casual and forgotten against her flank." With her face "absolutely impenetrable, absolutely serene," she proceeds to direct the family's troubled affairs, from buying tombstones at great financial sacrifice for Bon and his son to remaining a dutiful daughter to her father, despite his complicity in bringing about her tragedy. Except for her failure to rise above her racial heritage in her treatment of Charles Etienne, Judith in fact serves as a model of Christian forbearance and charity. In Muhlenfeld's words, "everything she does is constructive."[47]

Judith also draws the choice assignment of delivering one of the most poignant passages in the novel—the one occasion when she speaks more or less in her own voice.* Faulkner places it within the narrative of Mr. Compson, who, in his inveterate misogyny, consistently misinterprets her serenity as a sign of escapism. For him, she is just another woman responding

---

*Much has been made of the issue of voice in Faulkner's work, with several critics deploring how women and black characters often receive insufficient opportunities to address the reader directly. "Seen from the most part from outside," Philip Weinstein insists, "deprived . . . of their own subjective history, Faulkner's women move through their world as 'wonderful' creatures, but considerably handicapped, from a narrative perspective, when compared with men."

Such complaints reflect a misunderstanding of Faulkner. Again and again, one finds him wrapping his most valuable gifts in small packages, to the point where one can almost posit an inverse correlation between the extent of a character's "voice" and that character's significance. Admirable figures who carry Faulkner's key meanings often speak little but achieve an enormous impact when they do, while those less admirable (Horace Benbow and Gavin Stevens immediately come to mind) are given reams of dialogue with which to hang themselves. Many of those admirable characters who illustrate this tendency, moreover, are women or blacks—one thinks not only of Bon and Judith but also Caddy Compson, Dilsey Gibson, Addie Bundren, Lucas Beauchamp in *Go Down, Moses*, and Linda Snopes Kohl in *The Mansion*. That is why adding up the column inches of "voice" in Faulkner to measure whether or not he has endowed a character with an adequate amount of "subjectivity" is a fruitless enterprise. The issue is not the quantity of that subjectivity but the quality. See Weinstein, *Faulkner's Subject*, 23, 28, 44.

to adversity by fleeing to a dream world, falling back on such "little puny affirmations" as "funerals and graves" to ward off the hard facts of human mortality. Her remarks to Quentin's grandmother on turning over Bon's letter, however, leave no doubt that Judith is capable of facing death head-on: "Then all of a sudden it's all over and all you have left is a block of stone with scratches on it . . . , and it rains on it and the sun shines on it and after a while they dont even remember the name and what the scratches were trying to tell, and it doesn't matter." Far from being rose colored, her vision of existence is a somber one, with men and women little more than puppets whose strings are "all in one another's way like five or six people all trying to make a rug on the same loom only each one wants to weave his own pattern into the rug; and it cant matter, you know that, or the Ones that set up the loom would have arranged things a little better, and yet it must matter because you keep on trying or having to keep on trying." The imagery contrasts pointedly with Mr. Compson's own depiction of people in the past as "integer for integer, larger, more heroic." Judith demolishes that mythic view in favor of an existential realism based on the chilling premise that, in the long run, human aspiration "doesn't matter."[48]

Yet it would be wrong to label her perspective cynical or pessimistic. It is possible to surmount mortality at least for a while, Judith insists, by the simple act of handing down "a scrap of paper" like the letter she is transmitting to the future. The text might or might not "mean anything in itself," but

> "at least it would be something just because it would have happened, be remembered even if only from passing from one hand to another, one mind to another, and it would be at least a scratch, something, something that might make a mark on something that *was* once for the reason that it can die someday, while the block of stone cant be *is* because it . . . cant ever die or perish."

To be effective in pushing back oblivion, she is saying, the "scratch" must somehow be endowed with life itself. It cannot be an inanimate object erected as a tribute, like the thousand-pound marble tombstones that Sutpen ordered from Italy for his and Ellen's graves; those pathetic objects have already started to crack apart when Quentin encounters them. Rather, the "scratch" must be a piece of embedded experience, an instance of thinking or feeling that has somehow been inscribed onto tangible matter such that people in succeeding generations will be able to recapture the better part of that same thought or emotion. Put this way, Bon's letter, as Judith employs it here, sounds like a trope for art in general and literature in particular.[49]

This is what lends Judith's brief comments their immense significance for understanding Faulkner. Art, he had come to believe, represented the sole means available to forestall the annihilation that inevitably awaits us. As he phrased it years later in an interview, the artist's aim is "to arrest motion . . . and hold it fixed so that 100 years later when a stranger looks at it, it moves again since it is life." This, he went on, "is the artist's way of scribbling 'Kilroy was here' on the wall of the final and irrevocable oblivion through which he must someday pass." An enterprising person intent on defeating time, he went on, could always build "a bridge" (or perhaps, like the Old Colonel, a railroad, or an oversized statue of himself to adorn his grave) and "be remembered for a day or two," but "somehow the picture, the poem—that lasts a long time, a very long time, longer than anything."[50]

In his youthful days as a post-Victorian aesthete, one recalls, Faulkner had likewise sought a path to transcendence, a way to move beyond human finitude into a state of absolute permanence. That had been the purpose of art as he first conceived of it—to transport us to that "higher" spiritual realm safely above the flesh. Now, in 1936, the Modernist Faulkner still believed that artistic creation alone could confer immortality, but only provisionally, and only by embracing the very finite realm of experience that it was seeking to transcend. Art was no longer an enchanting, celestial vision of peacocks and poplars that the artist tried strenuously to keep detached from mundanity but rather a deep immersion in the everyday world that should be as dynamic, earthy, and rough-edged as reality itself, relying on concrete images and language that could be passed "from one hand to another, one mind to another."[51]

Here lies the source of the unique system of narration that Faulkner devised for *Absalom, Absalom!*. His overriding goal, writes Daniel Hoffman, was to "replicate in the experience of the reader the experience of the character in all its complexity and confusion." That is why we learn about the House of Sutpen not through conventional literary techniques that have become so familiar that we can virtually disengage our minds as we read, but rather through a narrative format that forces us to stay alert at every moment. The story is literally handed down from one person to another in a series of narrative chains—an especially lively one, for example, runs from Quentin's grandfather to Quentin's father to Quentin to Shreve and then to the reader—so that what reaches the reader is very much a living tale. The sources of this remarkable fictional method lie in a creative blending of the southern oral tradition in which Faulkner grew up and Modernist epistemology. Just as the mind, according to early Modernist theorists like William James, actively selects the data it needs from the sensory flux surrounding it, imposing an order on what is otherwise chaos, the reader of *Absalom* must sort through the welter of detail and interpretation that is presented in order to reconstruct the story anew. For readers willing to engage themselves in this fashion, the book soon takes on the "feel" of actuality, allowing Faulkner's "scratch" to live indefinitely.[52]

That is *not* to say, however, that the reader is free to arrive at any narrative that he or she might wish, as some recent postmodernist critics have claimed. *Absalom, Absalom!* was crafted with painstaking care to perpetuate a specific "scratch"—the fictional history of an antebellum southern family *as it existed* within William Faulkner's imagination, along with the moral and cultural meanings that history carried for him. Although Faulkner, in his effort to augment the sense of actuality, left a number of loose ends and ambiguities in his text (there is no way to determine, for instance, exactly how Quentin learns that Bon had "black blood"), by the final chapter the puzzle does roughly fit together in a predesigned way. One is reminded of the teacher in John Dewey's ideal progressive school who permits students to grope, fumble, and experiment as they try to solve a problem, all the while gently guiding them to a satisfactory solution. Faulkner, too, gives the reader much scope but ultimately employs his skillfully hidden artistic hand to convey his own vision of the Sutpen saga.[53]

Indeed, *Absalom*, for all its twists and turns, arrives at that vision through an underlying progression that corresponds in an approximate way to the transit Faulkner himself had undergone from a Victorian to a Modernist perspective. The book begins with an interpretive approach straight from the mid-nineteenth century, that of Miss Rosa Coldfield, who has been frozen in mental stasis ever since 1866 when Sutpen made his outrageous proposal to her that she should first bear him a son before he would marry her. That insult locked in place the archetypal Victorian worldview she had absorbed as a Coldfield. A prisoner of the nineteenth-century moral dichotomy, she is terrified of sexuality, is intent on preserving racial taboos, and much prefers the ideal world of fantasy over commonplace experience. Her narrative accordingly takes the form of a moral allegory, suffused with purple rhetoric, in which the Civil War becomes an

Armageddon fought to cleanse that demonic scourge named Thomas Sutpen from the earth and return him to the "eternal and abysmal dark" from which he came. Fittingly, though she has authored more than a thousand poems to commemorate the Confederate cause, she leaves behind, James Watson notes, "no scrap of her writing except the epitaph on Judith's gravestone." By Faulknerian standards, she is a monumentalist rather than an artist, suggesting that her version of the Sutpen narrative (though not necessarily the factual detail she supplies) should be viewed as suspect.⁵⁴

If Rosa believes that everything is readily explicable in moral terms, Mr. Compson proceeds from an equally deep rooted assumption that blind chance rules the universe. He is the post-Victorian skeptic par excellence, a figure who freely applies irony and cynicism to cover the pain he feels over the destruction of the Old South. To him Sutpen resembles the hero of a Greek tragedy, bravely, if foolishly, attempting to prevail over circumstance while "behind him fate, destiny, retribution, irony—the stage manager, call him what you will—was already striking the set and dragging on the synthetic and spurious shadows and shapes of the next one." In part his account suffers from his lack of certain vital information, above all the knowledge that Bon is Sutpen's son. But the main limitation remains his viewpoint, which prevents him from either seeking out or intuiting the missing data. Though we gain a much richer grasp of Sutpen thanks to the chapters he narrates, we in time come to realize that, to a large extent, Faulkner is presenting his and Rosa's interpretations in order to be able to demolish them later. For Mr. Compson, the past is "just incredible. It just does not explain." But, we soon discover, history will yield up a serviceable meaning if one approaches it properly.⁵⁵

The task of constructing what Robert Dale Parker calls the "preferred explanation"—preferred because "it matches the incidental details that need explaining"—falls to Quentin and Shreve in the second half of the book.* Sitting in their frigid dormitory room at Harvard, the two young

---

*That the version of the Sutpen story offered by Quentin and Shreve, though not perfect, is nonetheless the preferred one is suggested by three things. First, their narrative provides the best "fit" for the various facts arising from the most reliable evidence. Second, the formal chronology and genealogy that Faulkner appended to the text by and large verify their account. And third, at several points the third-person narrator, who is not omniscient but who, as Hugo Ruppersburg puts it, "occupies a better position to 'know' about events than any of the characters," breaks in to authenticate what Quentin and Shreve are saying. But most important, we know that Quentin and Shreve come closest to the truth because of the basic design of the novel, which moves

men together function like Faulkner's conception of the ideal Modernist novelist, immersing themselves in the story until the characters live again within their minds. In a process governed by the integrative impulse lying at the heart of Modernist culture, things that had previously been separated by time and space are now fused together in a white heat of literary creation to form a nearly seamless whole, a kind of hermeneutic epiphany in which "there might be paradox and inconsistency but nothing fault nor false." Not only do Shreve and Quentin become interchangeable, "both thinking as one, the voice which happened to be speaking the thought only the thinking become audible," but the two soon fuse with their subjects to the point where the distinction between past and present completely dissolves: "Because now neither of them was there. They were both in Carolina and the time was forty-six years ago, . . . since now both of them were Henry Sutpen and both of them were Bon, compounded each of both yet either neither, smelling the very smoke which had blown and faded away forty-six years ago." In this way, as Bernhard Radloff formulates it, "their minds do not create a vision" but rather "give themselves up to one" that has been inscribed in the written and oral evidence passed down to them. "Listening," Radloff writes, "they are allowed to see." [56]

Essential to that exercise is the contribution of Shreve. A Canadian, and therefore even more removed from the traumas of southern history than a Yankee would be, he provides an indispensable measure of critical detachment that Quentin could not conceivably muster on his own. At the same time, in his mounting fascination with the Sutpen tale, Shreve prods his roommate to further exploration, forcing Quentin to confront the more anguishing implications of the story and generating interpretive momentum until the final portrait of interracial fratricide becomes inescapable. However, one must never forget that Shreve originated not as a real person but as a voice within Faulkner's consciousness. He speaks, Ruth Vande Kieft rightly tells us, "for the Faulkner who had traveled, read, seen through other than Southern eyes the fantastic facts and fictions of his homeland," just as Quentin represents the traditionalist Faulk-

steadily toward greater intelligibility and credibility from Miss Rosa's initial effusions to the complex re-creation of experience enacted by the two boys. "Perhaps we ought not to lend most credence to Quentin," Myra Jehlen admits, "but we do, which can only be, after all, because of something Faulkner does." See Ruppersburg, *Voice and Eye*, 95–96; Kuyk, *Sutpen's Design*, 35, 38–39, 44, 101; Ragan, *William Faulkner's "Absalom, Absalom!,"* 128, 137; Christadler, "William Faulkner's *Absalom, Absalom!,"* 163–64; Jehlen, *Class and Character*, 57.

ner "who had lived and felt the Southern past and accepted its full burden of guilt." Shreve, in other words, stands for the Modernist Faulkner that often sparred with its alter ego inside the psyche that held them both. On this occasion, though, the two have merged, making possible a moment of supreme vision.[57]

For Quentin, the other half of that collaboration, things are far more complicated. All his life he has heard the Sutpen story until it has become an elemental part of his cultural memory as a southerner, yet at the outset he would much rather retreat into the comfort of obliviousness than seek out its significance. "Why tell me about it?" he asks his father in the novel's opening pages, shortly after Rosa Coldfield has summoned him. "What is it to me that the land or the earth or whatever it was got tired of him at last and turned and destroyed him?" At the same time, something within him, reinforced later by Shreve, wants to know the "truth" about the problematic past he has inherited, leading to his titanic struggle during the balance of *Absalom, Absalom!*, as Faulkner once put it, to "get God to tell him why." The internal conflict waxes and wanes, with the decisive moment coming in the final chapter during the visit that he and Miss Rosa pay to Sutpen's Hundred. "I just dont want to be here," he thinks to himself as they approach the house; "I just dont want to know about whatever [is] . . . hidden in it." But an hour later when Rosa descends the stairway in shock, having seen the secret residing in the upstairs bedroom, Quentin cannot stop himself from going up as well: "I must see too now. I will have to. Maybe I shall be sorry tomorrow, but I must see." His decision to pursue knowledge whatever the cost is no small matter, qualifying as an act of Faulknerian heroism comparable to those of Judith and Bon.[58]

That heroic act would strongly suggest that the Quentin of *Absalom, Absalom!* has undergone a substantial transformation from the pathetic soul who committed suicide in *The Sound and the Fury*. The earlier Quentin, who dreamed of transcendent purity and struggled to stop the flow of time, had been derived primarily from Faulkner's former post-Victorian self. By contrast, this new Quentin displays no obsession with purity and, thanks to his alliance with Shreve, is able to comprehend and accept the fluid medium of history, even making his peace with the fact that things never finish themselves:

> *Maybe nothing ever happens once and is finished. Maybe happen is never once but like ripples maybe on water after the pebble sinks, the ripples moving on, spreading, the pool attached by a narrow umbilical water-cord to the next pool*

which the first pool feeds, has fed, did feed, let this second pool contain a dif-
ferent temperature of water, a different molecularity of having seen, felt, re-
membered . . . , it doesn't matter: that pebble's watery echo whose fall it did
not even see moves across its surface too at the original ripple-space, to the old
ineradicable rhythm.

Existence may have no more intrinsic pattern to it than the surface of a body of water, but once people act, the consequences of their actions will reverberate across the "narrow umbilical" to future generations, creating a pattern. At odds with his father's teaching, Quentin now realizes that no external fate controls human destiny; rather, we generate fate by what we do, setting in motion an "ineradicable rhythm" much as Thomas Sutpen did when he put aside his first wife and child. In short, in this Quentin a post-Victorian sensibility has gradually and reluctantly become Modern-ist, if just barely, during the course of the novel.[59]

The question immediately arises of whether Quentin's progress is enough to save him. Should we as readers assume that he is able to "work through" the Sutpen story in a Freudian sense and so free himself from its awful psychic burden, or are we to conclude that it crushes him, caus-ing him to fall back into fin de siècle gloom and pushing him toward the suicidal choice he makes in *The Sound and the Fury*?

Here the evidence is incredibly mixed. There can be little doubt that Quentin experiences great agony during his extended séance with Shreve. At first he responds to the more troubling revelations by staying silent; later, after recalling his meeting with Henry Sutpen, he begins "to jerk all over, violently and uncontrollably." It is not clear, however, how we should interpret these convulsions. Are they a sign of his heroic initiative in carrying the narrative forward, equivalent to the body movements that sometimes take place during psychoanalytic sessions when a patient suc-cessfully combats his or her personal demons? Or do they signify a neu-rotic stasis that he cannot overcome, an inner blockage giving rise to the Poe-like "Nevermore of peace" refrain that runs through his mind at the end? Again, it is hard to tell. We do know that Faulkner chose to cut a ref-erence to Quentin's death that had originally opened the second chapter, a possible indication that this reconceived Quentin may not be destined to plunge into the Charles River. Still, we cannot overlook Quentin's morbid complaint on the novel's penultimate page of how he is "older at twenty than a lot of people who have died," followed shortly by the entry in the genealogy that has his life end later that year in Cambridge. As with Joe

Christmas, Faulkner leaves the ultimate disposition of his protagonist unresolved.[60]

Also deliberately left opaque is Faulkner's prognosis for the racial future of southern society. *Absalom*'s final haunting passages, many of them added during the last stages of revision, engage that subject through the enigmatic figure of Jim Bond, Charles Etienne Bon's "idiot negro" son and thus the "scion, the heir, the apparent (though not obvious)" of the dynasty Thomas Sutpen had sought to found. A clear-cut successor to Benjy Compson, whose horrific bellow in the concluding pages of *The Sound and the Fury* registered Faulkner's otherwise inexpressible judgment on the history of his region, Bond dwells amid the ruins of the Sutpen estate howling incessantly at the moral outrage that has attended its rise and fall. What makes Bond so intriguing, however, is the prediction that Shreve hazards concerning him. Though they may be outcasts today, Shreve informs an astonished Quentin, in time "the Jim Bonds are going to conquer the western hemisphere" through interracial procreation with whites. Their offspring, it is true, will likely "bleach out" over the succeeding generations, but "it will still be Jim Bond," so that "in a few thousand years I who regard you will also have sprung from the loins of African kings."[61]

Once more Faulkner masks his intent. Some critics have seen these remarks as no more than Shreve's callow attempt to tease his distressed southern roommate as they disengage from their intense narrative partnership. Supporting that reading is the highly pejorative treatment of miscegenation in many of Faulkner's other works, where it is portrayed as resulting inevitably in degeneracy and misfortune. Bond, with his "slack-mouthed idiot face," would seem to offer evidence for that point of view. But such an approach must contend with the insert that Faulkner composed for *Intruder in the Dust* in 1949, which refers favorably to Shreve's remark (calling it the "tag line" of the novel) and speeds up the timetable for racial amalgamation from "a few thousand" to "five hundred years or perhaps even less than that." Moreover, the entire thematic thrust of *Absalom, Absalom!* would lead one to believe that that "tag line" conveys Faulkner's own position on racial mixing. Why, Charles Bon comments in regard to his octoroon mistress, should anyone care about "a little matter like a spot of negro blood," a phrase drenched with irony when one realizes that it was just such a "spot" that caused Bon's father to disown him, setting in motion the train of events that not only doomed the family but became "the land's catastrophe too." Faulkner, it would appear, was saying that a mentality obsessed with racial purity was primed for de-struction.[62]

To be sure, from the vantage of the late twentieth century, some have argued that Faulkner, in calling for blacks to "bleach out," was surren-dering to the venerable white dream-wish that people of African descent would simply vanish, but that is inexcusably anachronistic. During the 1930s when *Absalom, Absalom!* was written, the vision of an integrated society that Shreve sets forth could only be understood as a fundamental challenge to the South's sacred system of genealogical accounting. From the colonial era onward, perhaps the most potent force motivating south-erners first to preserve slavery and then, in the decades following emanci-pation, to devise a system of legal racial separation had been their fear of a possible "mongrelized" society. Under these circumstances, the impor-tance of Faulkner's attempt to forecast a posterity in which racial blending would be both inevitable and essentially benign must not be discounted. What he was engaged in, writes James Snead, was no less than "a radical attempt to integrate" that which his society had "sundered" by illustrating the "futility of applying strict binary categories to human affairs." Indeed, that a white Mississippian raised during the apogee of segregation would see fit in 1936 to substitute Jim Bond (the very name effuses integration) for Jim Crow might stand as an act of Faulknerian heroism dwarfing all the others.[63]

Anyone doubting the extent of that heroic effort need only consider *The Unvanquished.* This peculiar project, to which Faulkner turned shortly after finishing *Absalom*, involved revising the six stories about the Sartoris family he had published in popular magazines a few years earlier and add-ing a new concluding story in order to achieve the rough semblance of a novel. The original stories had trafficked heavily in chauvinistic south-ern stereotypes. Although Faulkner toned down the pro-Confederate bias somewhat, the narrative continued to celebrate the innate moral superi-ority of the old planter class. Instead of Thomas Sutpen, the menacing reality behind the Old South myth, we go back to John Sartoris, flying like "a hawk" on his great horse Jupiter. It is almost as if Faulkner was deliber-ately trying to recant the more subversive implications of *Absalom*. How, the reader is left to wonder, could the same author who had just risen to the heights of Modernist insight be responsible for such a vintage Civil War potboiler?[64]

Two explanations present themselves. The first is Faulkner's perennial need for money. From the start it appears that he hoped to sell the movie rights to a major studio (as he eventually did for a handsome sum) and that the material was tailored for that purpose. Equally important, however, may have been his need to restore the ever delicate psychic balance between his traditionalist and Modernist selves after writing *Absalom*. Faulkner's goal, one senses, was less literary creation than the appeasement of a very angry set of ancestral gods.[65]

If so, those gods must have been extremely pleased with the results. The loosely connected episodes follow the coming of age of Bayard Sartoris (the Old Bayard of *Flags in the Dust* seen here as a child and adolescent) amid the chaotic conditions of Civil War and Reconstruction. To the degree that a main connecting thread exists, it involves Bayard's character—what we are witnessing, we soon realize, is the emergence of a youthful paragon of moral and social virtue, a possible ideal identity model for the New South. Faulkner accordingly leaves little to chance. When Bayard and his slave playmate, Ringo, fire from close ambush at a Yankee soldier, they run the risk of sullying their boyhood innocence by shedding human blood, so Faulkner conveniently has them hit the man's horse instead. Later, when Bayard does need to kill in order to become a man and warrior in the Sartoris tradition, Faulkner contrives the perfect target for him, a poor white ruffian named Grumby whose band of shabby marauders specializes in "frightening white women and torturing Negroes to find where money or silver was hidden." After Grumby, on top of these cowardly crimes, murders Bayard's defenseless grandmother, there can be no question that Bayard is justified in taking his life, much as one would exterminate a cockroach or rattlesnake. Even so, Faulkner stages the final encounter so that Bayard can be construed as acting in self-defense.[66]

In *Absalom*, as in *Light in August* and *Pylon* before it, heroism required a willingness to accept the task of creating a meaningful identity in the face of the indeterminate nature of existence, but in *The Unvanquished* Bayard is handed his hero's identity ready-made. We see that in the novella's climactic tale when his father is gunned down by a former business partner named Ben Redmond and Bayard is expected to take revenge. Again, Faulkner shamelessly stacks the moral deck for him. "I am tired of killing men," the Colonel had told his son, explaining his decision henceforth to go unarmed in order to help usher in a new era of peace and law. The lesson is reinforced by Bayard's friendly law professor, who reminds him of the biblical injunction "Thou Shalt Not Kill," and by his Aunt Jenny du

Pre. As a consequence of these influences, Bayard does not have to wrestle much with conscience or consciousness in choosing his course of action. "At least this will be my chance to find out if I am what I think I am or if I just hope," he reflects, "if I am going to do what I have taught myself is right or if I am just going to wish I were." Plainly, no doubt exists in his mind about who he should be or what is "right." In a scene that partakes heavily of both myth and melodrama, he walks into Redmond's office with no weapon. His adversary, shamed by Bayard's exemplary courage, fires two shots past him and then leaves town, allowing Bayard to prevail without spilling a drop of blood. His feat establishes him as an updated, much improved version of "The Sartoris," presumably one that will allow the planter class to continue its leadership of southern society for decades to come. In *The Unvanquished*, things are that simple.[67]

The same pertains in the realm of race relations. Ralph Ellison once observed how Faulkner, "more than any other white writer," was able to penetrate to the "human truth" buried in the conventional white stereotype of blacks. In this novel, however, Faulkner capitulates to that stereotype, painting the familiar picture of southern slaves blissfully dependent on their masters who, moved by an "inexplicable" impulse, allow themselves to be deluded by the Yankees' false promise of freedom, only to become trapped in "misery and starvation." The lucky ones find their way back to their old plantations, deeply grateful to be home; those less fortunate end up living "in caves and hollow trees" with "no one to depend on." The smart ones, of course, never leave. This was just the sort of Lost Cause rendition of the southern past that Faulkner had previously made his career challenging, but in this work it is presented as straightforward historical truth.[68]

On the surface, Bayard's childhood companion, Ringo, appears a striking exception to this stereotyped handling of race. The two share an Edenic relationship in which differences in skin color are temporarily put aside, "until maybe he wasn't a nigger anymore or maybe I wasn't a white boy." Far from being helpless, Ringo emerges as well endowed with both initiative and intelligence. Yet he remains a faithful retainer, so attached to the Sartoris family and old regime that, on arriving in Oxford to tell Bayard of Colonel Sartoris's death, his face is streaked with tears. Ringo may know how to outsmart Union soldiers, but he also knows his place, accepting it as perfectly natural when Bayard calls him "my boy" after they become adults. As Lee Jenkins points out, one would think that Faulkner, being Faulkner, would instinctively want to explore the inner contradictions in a character who is at once highly savvy and utterly subservient—a self-assured young black man who nonetheless delivers a lengthy disquisition on the evils of Reconstruction from a white racist standpoint. But not with Ringo. "I ain't a nigger any more," he blurts out after learning of emancipation. "I done been abolished." As Jenkins wryly notes, Ringo "speaks more truthfully than he knows."[69]

To be fair, there are occasional patches of literary and moral complexity in *The Unvanquished*, along with a few characters who sometimes rise above the level of stereotypes, but on the whole this book remains Faulkner's one extended bow toward southern pieties, an act of expiation to atone for a decade's worth of Modernist sins culminating in *Absalom, Absalom!*. It concludes, fittingly enough, with Bayard's encomium for his slain father, who, we are assured, "would always be there," his dream "something which he had bequeathed us which we could never forget." In the same way, the Old Colonel would "always be there" for Faulkner with his unforgettable mythic legacy, demanding homage. Several critics have been struck by the lack of effort Faulkner seems to have put into this book, how little time and care he spent crafting it compared with his usual practice. "There are passages," Myra Jehlen observes, "when Faulkner seems not to be paying attention." But then, this wasn't the usual Faulkner at work.[70]

Ruthless and
Unbearable Honesty

If the majority of critics have come to regard *Absalom, Absalom!* as the most profound of Faulkner's twenty-two novels, and if *The Unvanquished* stands as the most conventional, *The Wild Palms* might distinguish itself as the most controversial. From the time it was published in January 1939, debate has raged about its structure, quality, and meaning. The initial reviews expressed grave reservations about its contrapuntal form, in which two ostensibly separate plots are developed in alternating chapters, as well as its risqué subject matter of adultery and abortion. "Are there any standards of morality left in modern fiction?" asked the *Saturday Review of Literature* in near despair. By the 1960s, that verdict had changed. Readers had acquiesced in Faulkner's use of counterpoint, and, though it was still possible to find complaints that *The Wild Palms* shamelessly celebrated "carnality and lechery," other commentators remarked on how those characters guilty of transgressing moral standards were duly punished. Disagreement now began to center on Charlotte Rittenmeyer, the independent-minded woman in her early twenties who abandons her husband and two small children to run off with a young medical intern on a romantic adventure that ends a year later in disaster. To what extent, scholars have asked, should we regard as noble Charlotte's rejection of a corrupt bourgeois society and fierce determination to create her own style of existence? Or should we see her as a grotesque creature who has abdicated her responsibilities as a mother, forsaken her "natural" role as a woman, and selfishly destroyed the life and career of her lover?[1]

Thomas L. McHaney's highly influential book-length study of the novel clearly adopts the latter perspective. His Charlotte, in essence, is a femme fatale who, on meeting her future lover, Harry Wilbourne, "clamps his wrist like a manacle," brings him under her evil spell, and proceeds to usurp his rightful masculine role. It is Charlotte who earns most of the income, decides where and how they will live, and even assumes the superior position when they make love. Worse still, McHaney's Charlotte is "always making speeches" to Harry and the world in general that, in McHaney's judgment, contain "more sound than meaning," reflecting her prevailing tendency to be "glib and dishonest with herself." Not surprisingly, the art she produces amounts to "either a complete lie or the dilettantish dabbling of a pseudosophisticate." It almost seems inevitable, in McHaney's account, that this scheming, deceitful woman should meet an excruciating death from the complications of a botched abortion that she has pressured her reluctant partner to perform on her after she accidentally becomes pregnant with their child. Faulkner, McHaney seems to be saying, is giving Charlotte what she deserves both for her aggressive sexuality and for insisting on "an act contrary to both nature and moral society."[2]

McHaney's work continues to command great respect for its erudition and perceptive insights, but nonetheless over the years a sharply different reading of Charlotte has emerged. Far from seeing her as immoral, deceitful, and glib, this interpretation paints her, in the words of Sally Page, as "a woman of courage and integrity" who is also "extremely creative." Charlotte, adds William Price Cushman, is a person of true artistic sensibility whose "spirit is exhilarated by the sights, sounds, and smells of the world." She does not make the long-winded speeches with which McHaney charges her but instead speaks with unusual eloquence and precision. Nor does this Charlotte take Harry a helpless prisoner and lead him down the primrose path. On the contrary, Lynn Gartrell Levins explains, she is tutoring him in a "concept of love" that "is as enobling as that celebrated in medieval love lyrics." Even so, many of the authors who take this pro-Charlotte stance continue to fault her for abandoning her daughters, and several cannot help commenting that her decision to abort her third child runs counter to the creative, life-affirming impulse they otherwise find in her. In addition, however enobling her notion of romantic love might be, it has become a common criticism that Charlotte takes it too far, transmuting it into an abstract ideal that becomes detached from everyday reality. Charlotte may display an admirable "deep-rooted strength," Michael Millgate sums up, but with it comes a "sterile fanaticism" that we must not overlook.[3]

By the current rules of literary scholarship, all of these interpretive approaches are, of course, valid—there is no "real" Charlotte Rittenmeyer aside from the one that arises in the minds of individual readers as they encounter the text in which she dwells. And since this novel appears destined to function as a mirror for the values and beliefs of those who write about it, we can rest assured that the debate on Charlotte will persist, perhaps indefinitely. But from the standpoint of intellectual history a different question arises. What, it asks, was *Faulkner's* intention in creating this character? To what extent can we fathom the forces operating in his mind as he summoned up Charlotte to express his own values and beliefs?

One obvious influence was the complex romantic liaison in which he was enmeshed at the time. In December 1935, during a sojourn in Hollywood, he had struck up a relationship with Meta Carpenter, a young woman from Mississippi then employed as a secretary at the studio where he was working. Raised as a proper belle, Meta had decisively broken with her upbringing, choosing instead to indulge her artistic bent by making a career in the film industry. In a word, she was just right for Faulkner—attractive, smart, and independent, open to the latest currents of taste and thought, and at the same time a true "lady," well raised and certifiably southern, who appreciated his enduring attachment to Victorian mores. With her, he could for the first time actually live his Modernist self, letting loose the passions he had long been forced to express only in his fiction. He could ply her with erotic letters, lend her the uncensored copy of *Lady Chatterley's Lover* he had once smuggled in from Paris, and share with her his favorite contemporary poems. Meta took pleasure in satisfying what she later described as his "consuming sexual urgency," but, honoring his complex identity, she also understood his need to hide what he deemed "the grossness of his physical self," which included, among other things, "running the water in the bathroom to cover the evidence of his animality." "He was every inch my mother's definition of a true Southern gentleman," she writes, and in deference to that part of him she would oblige on those occasions during their lovemaking when Faulkner wanted her to assume the role of an innocent maiden "just out of high school."

Faulkner the gentleman bohemian in a snapshot taken at an airshow near Oxford in the mid-1930s, at the time he first became involved with Meta Carpenter. (Photo by Larry Feldman; courtesy Mississippi Collection, John Davis Williams Library, University of Mississippi)

She would willingly become his "sweet, tremulous girl," even though his request "confounded" her. Small wonder that he became deeply attached to her.[4]

In retrospect, Meta Carpenter may well have been the woman William Faulkner should have married, but in 1937 it remained an inescapable fact that he already had a wife and an extensive set of familial obligations. However tempted he may have been to jettison his existing life, much as the fictional Harry Wilbourne would, a powerful undertow pulled him in the opposite direction. There was his attachment to his daughter Jill to consider, along with the preservation of his home base in Oxford, which had served him so well as a counterbalance to the more disorienting tendencies of Modernism. Also important were his feelings toward Estelle. As Judith Sensibar correctly points out, the ties between them ran stronger than might seem apparent. Though he would tell Meta that he and Estelle had not had sexual relations since Jill's birth (a claim that should be met with some skepticism—he also informed Meta that he had been badly wounded in the war and carried a silver plate in his skull), and though the marriage all too frequently deteriorated into mental and sometimes physical warfare, genuine bonds of loyalty and even affection still united the Faulkners, who after all had been tight childhood friends and managed to stay married to each other to the end of their lives.[5]

The available evidence makes it very difficult to reconstruct what transpired during the turbulent years of 1936 and 1937 when Faulkner was torn between Meta and Estelle. Complicating matters was the perverse delight that both Faulkners took in playing out highly charged dramatic scenes with each other—what Sensibar calls their "private theatre." For this reason it is hard to determine how committed Faulkner was in late 1936 when he asked Estelle for a divorce. One cannot discount the possibility that he may have been acting a part, secure in the conviction that she would refuse and so bring the drama to its appropriate conclusion. As Meta astutely acknowledged several decades later, Estelle was probably bound from the start to win: "The pull to Oxford and the Faulkner way of life was greater than to me. Everything at Rowan Oak, even the wife . . . whose weaknesses bound him to her, drew him away from me." What we do know for certain is that Meta, realizing that Faulkner would never leave his wife, agreed to wed Wolfgang Rebner, a refugee concert pianist from Germany. We also know that her decision devastated Faulkner. In 1937 he could not foresee that the marriage would soon prove ill fated, leading to a resumption of their affair; at the time it seemed as if he had lost her forever. Such was the frame of mind in which he conceived *The Wild Palms*.[6]

This backdrop would surely lead one to suspect that the novel served a compensatory function for its author. If he couldn't run off with the woman he loved, he was at least able to write a story imagining himself doing so. That in turn would imply a fairly straightforward transposition between the fictional and real-life characters, with Harry taking the part of Faulkner and Charlotte that of Meta. Reinforcing this interpretive strategy is the fact that Faulkner may have been compensating for yet another failed romance in *The Wild Palms*—his involvement in the 1920s with Helen Baird, who also bears many similarities to Charlotte. Like Charlotte, Helen grew up as the only girl in a house filled with brothers, married a New Orleans businessman, carried a conspicuous burn scar on her body from a childhood accident, and expressed herself artistically by crafting figures out of clay and papier-mâché. Nor did Faulkner forget Helen; in the mid-1930s he was still sending her letters filled with amorous longing, as if he hoped somehow to pry her away from her husband. Again, it would seem that Faulkner was attempting to counter the disappointments of actual life by awarding himself a fantasy elopement in his fiction.[7]

That Charlotte was based on Meta and Helen is surely part of the story; but the other, and perhaps more important, part is that Faulkner, in authoring her, was drawing on a vital aspect of himself. After all, it is Charlotte, not Harry, who faces the dire choice that Faulkner had faced of leaving an established family for the person she loves. Still more crucial, it is Charlotte who labors not only as an artist but as a dedicated practitioner of Modernist art. A sculptor—much like Gordon, Faulkner's surrogate in *Mosquitoes*—she eschews simple realism in the figures she produces. "I dont want to copy a deer," she proclaims. "Anybody can do that." Rather, she seeks to capture "the motion, the speed" of life, its very vitality, just as Faulkner consciously strived to do in his writing. Also like him, she is willing to struggle with her materials, "no matter how hard, how long it took," in order to produce "something fine, that you could be proud to show, that you could touch, hold." The effigies she crafts appear "fragile" and "epicene," as well as "elegant, bizarre, fantastic and perverse"—a set of descriptives that could apply equally well to the work of the surrealist Alberto Giacometti, one of Faulkner's favorite sculptors, or to many of the characters who populate Yoknapatawpha.[8]

The real giveaway as to Charlotte's identity, however, comes when she is cast as "a falcon," capable of soaring into a special realm of grace far above the concerns that afflict ordinary humanity. Mere "crows and sparrows" may "get shot out of trees or drowned by floods," Harry submits, "but not hawks" like Charlotte. As always in Faulkner, a metaphoric comparison to great birds of prey connotes aristocratic status. In his early novels, one recalls, he had embodied that aristocratic persona in male warriors of good lineage like the mythic World War I aviator John Sartoris. Now, a decade later, we find him drastically revising this idealized self-image, shearing away the elements having to do with heredity, masculinity, and martial prowess while retaining the heedless courage, strength of will, and disdain for normal existence. The result is Charlotte Rittenmeyer, a woman with no pedigree who does not fly through the air on horseback or in warplanes but rather immerses herself in that which is concrete and earthy. "I like bitching [her word for physical sex], and making things with my hands," she announces. Yet the paradox is that Charlotte, by embracing the very emblems of common mortality—naked flesh and the dusty clay she works with her hands—succeeds in nobly transcending the mundane. In the "ruthless and almost unbearable honesty" of her gaze, we are told, "the dross of small lying and sentimentality dissolved away." She is the brave Cavalier updated and translated into the terms of a new culture, Faulkner's best approximation of the Modernist as aristocrat.[9]

All of this suggests that *The Wild Palms* should be seen not as a romance novel but rather as a conversion tale in which Charlotte manages, through heroic effort, to save Harry's soul by winning him over to her superior values. In Harry Wilbourne, the intern who shields himself from experience by clinging to a monklike routine in the hospital, Faulkner supplies her with the ideal raw material for that task. As McHaney observes, Harry's surname conveys the essence of his character. Prior to his love affair, he has been borne along almost volitionless by the force of his deceased father's will, which left him a bequest of two thousand dollars for college and medical school tuition. Faced with the need to make the money last, Harry becomes obsessed with every penny; spending even small sums on wine or women is out of the question. In this way, he plays out to the letter the conventional nineteenth-century narrative of self-advancement through thrift, diligence, and self-denial. Faulkner clearly indicates where that narrative would eventually take Harry through the figure of the middle-aged doctor whose beach cabin Harry and Charlotte rent at the end of their journey. Referred to by the narrator as a "puritan," a synonym for "Victorian" among Faulkner's generation, the doctor is depicted as leading a pitifully humdrum, circumscribed existence that he has adopted in deference to his father's wishes. With his "deathless dessicated spirit" he can only look with bitter envy on the young lovers, who, for all their troubles, at least possess the "bright wild passion which had somehow passed him up." "Am I to live forever behind a barricade of perennial innocence like a chicken in a pen?" he asks himself. This is the fate from which Charlotte rescues Harry.[10]

Significantly, Faulkner has Harry and Charlotte meet at the French Quarter studio of a Modernist painter. At first Harry resists going, telling himself in words that echo Horace Benbow's: "*Let well enough alone. You have peace now; you want no more.*" But it is his twenty-seventh birthday, and one of his fellow interns convinces him to celebrate. Once there, he stares hard at the artwork, not because of its content but out of wonder at "a condition which could supply a man with the obvious leisure and means to spend his days painting such as this." The whole style of life fascinates and tempts him, though he is assuredly not about to enter it on his own initiative. That can only happen when Charlotte, apparently seeing in him formless human clay for her to remodel and set in motion, takes him literally into her hands by grabbing his wrist. Their mutual attraction occurs "inexplicably," writes Cleanth Brooks, just "as sometimes in real life such things do happen."[11]

What follows is, in effect, a prolonged schooling in the new culture that Harry had espied in the artist's studio. The first lesson comes when they meet in New Orleans to make love. Harry, still fixated on conserving money, suggests that they walk to their assignation and books a room at a cheap hotel. Charlotte demands that they go by cab and instantly rejects the dingy room. It would have been fine for "somebody with a physique I just leched for all of a sudden," she explains with her characteristic concreteness. "But not us, Harry. Not you. Not you." She continues to be upset not that Harry is poor but that money matters so much to him. In Cushman's words, Charlotte "attaches far more importance to the worth of an experience than to its cost." That is precisely what she means when she instructs Harry, using the economic rhetoric she knows will reach him, on how "the value of love is the sum of what you have to pay for it and any time you get it cheap you have cheated yourself." Like a true Modernist, he will have to learn to measure his world authentically instead of through the mechanical contrivances of money and time.[12]

Harry's education continues when he and Charlotte go off to Chicago

and rent a studio apartment, where she sets up shop as a sculptress. For-
merly entombed in a sterile intern's quarters, he now resides in an artist's
atelier, surrounded by "twists of wire and pots of glue and paint and plas-
ter," the chaotic paraphernalia of creativity. Trying to make sense of his
new world, Harry at first consoles himself with the thought that Charlotte,
like all women, possesses an "infallible instinct" for rendering everything
tame and respectable. What women actually want, he tells himself, is the
challenge of turning illicit love into "the seemly decorum of Monday's
hash and suburban trains." All too many critics have assumed that his ru-
minations reflect Faulkner's own views on women. However, Charlotte
soon makes it clear that Harry is totally mistaken in thinking she favors
bourgeois respectability: "Listen, it's got to be all honeymoon, always. . . .
Either heaven, or hell: no comfortable safe peaceful purgatory between."
To her, "purgatory" means the kind of "seemly decorum" sought by the
middle-aged doctor, who "never had a honeymoon," even after his wedding. Slowly Harry catches on. Though he continues to fret about their
finances, he realizes one day that he is starting to view Charlotte's approach to life with "*the same boundless faith . . . as the Mississippi or Louisiana
countryman, converted last week at a camp-meeting revival, looks upon religion.*" Faulkner's choice of metaphor is just right—Harry is indeed being
"converted" to a new form of religious faith and thereby revived.[13]

Among the most important lessons that Charlotte teaches him is the
need to dispense with traditional gender rules. Although very much a
woman, who takes great pleasure in "bitching," she serves at the outset
of their relationship as a combination seducer, breadwinner, and general
decision maker. From her direct, unsentimental manner, to her "broad,
blunt, strong, supple-fingered" hands, to the whiskey and water she drinks
while working, to her nickname "Charley," Charlotte has no reluctance to
assume characteristics normally associated with men. As Karen Ramsay
Johnson writes, she "stubbornly refuses to fit any category." With her
Modernist instinct for integrating everything, she partakes of both gen-
ders, thus undermining once and for all the old stereotyped division of
women into angels and whores (again she partakes of both). One could,
in fact, see her as yet another rendition of Faulkner's epicene "Dianalike
girl," with that figure's former virginal purity now replaced by a full and
splendid androgyny. Convinced that she is "a better man than I am,"
Harry defers to her wisdom, even when she proposes that they celebrate
the loss of his job by going out and spending all their remaining money.
"We've got forty-eight dollars too much; just think of that," she declares.

It is her way of driving home the point that he should stop trying to be a standard-issue, good providing husband, in line with the conventional expectation for men, and instead focus on the far more crucial goal of opening himself up to experience.[14]

Harry makes further progress during their fall sojourn in a lakeside cabin in Wisconsin, where they are not only alone but able to lead an existence close to nature with its sensory delights. Charlotte fits effortlessly into this idyllic environment, swimming naked every morning, lying in the sun, and heading off to the woods to paint. Harry, still the child of the medical ward and laboratory, feels out of place by comparison but contents himself lying all day "in a drowsy and foetuslike state, passive and almost unsentient in the womb of solitude and peace." He is incubating, preparing to be reborn. Again, the insights that Charlotte is struggling to convey to him begin to sink in. With some effort, he avoids counting the "diminishing row of cans and sacks" in the larder, though he cannot help worrying about what will happen when their provisions run out. Equally important, Harry, who did not even realize he was color-blind until age twenty-seven, starts to regain contact with the perceptual world. Hearing the cry of a loon, he reflects on "how man alone of all creatures deliberately atrophies his natural senses . . . ; how the four-legged animal gains all its information through smelling and seeing and hearing and distrusts all else while the two-legged one believes only what it reads." Such thoughts come straight from Charlotte: though she first encountered her exalted conception of love through reading novels, she as a Modernist knows better than to believe what she has seen in print until she meets Harry and has it confirmed by actual experience. That is the position toward which Harry is inexorably moving.[15]

By the end of their stay at the lake, Harry is at last ready to shift from a passive to an active mode in his approach to life, a change Charlotte strongly encourages. Even McHaney, who tends to portray her as a monster enslaving her helpless victim, must admit that as Harry "begins to assert his manhood," Charlotte "responds appropriately." She is pleased when he makes the decision that they must return to Chicago. Two months later, she takes the satisfaction that all devoted teachers feel in a successful protégé when Harry suddenly uproots them from the city because they are coming to resemble a typical married couple, caring more about earning income than being together. With an indifference to practicality that she surely applauds, he chooses in the middle of winter to move to the mountains of Utah, where he has secured a position as a doctor at a mine.[16]

Best of all, from Charlotte's standpoint, are his reasons for acting. In a long discussion with their journalist friend McCord that can stand as a virtual primer of high Modernist philosophy, Harry explains how he has become aware that the secret is "to be alive and know it." Before he had existed "in eclipse," disconnected from the flow of life — "just on it, nonconductive, like the sparrow insulated by its own hard nonconductive dead feet from the high-tension line, the current of time that runs through remembering, that exists only in relation to what little of reality (I have learned that too) we know." His emotional self had been anesthetized, allowing him to fret about time, money, and respectability but not feel true fear, the energizing kind of fear that comes from facing directly the reality of an indifferent cosmos. "I wasn't afraid then because I was in eclipse," he tells McCord, "but I am awake now and I can be afraid now, thank God." Perhaps, he concludes, "I can be the consort of a falcon, even if I am a sparrow." As McHaney points out, from his first encounter with Charlotte to this moment of "rebirth" takes nine months, leaving him such a complete convert to her belief system "that he has even stopped worrying about money." This explains why he accepts the job as a mine doctor although he knows he probably will not get paid, something the earlier, unawakened Harry would never have contemplated.[17]

Faulkner's choice of Utah as the next stop on Harry and Charlotte's travels itself deserves comment, since it appears to stem in large part from his ongoing subterranean rivalry with Ernest Hemingway. Toward the end of *A Farewell to Arms*, published in 1929, Hemingway has his two main characters, Frederic Henry and Catherine Barkley, stay at a charming mountain lodge in Switzerland. They sleep late in a cozy bed, take pleasant hikes to towns like Montreux and Bains de l'Alliaz, and warm themselves with plenty of beer and vermouth. "It was a fine country," Frederic reports, "and every time that we went out it was fun." One can easily imagine Faulkner reading these scenes, muttering under his breath about Hemingway's blatant pandering to bourgeois sensibility, then providing his competitor with a graphic lesson in existential realism. If Frederic and Catherine get to enjoy sweeping vistas and pristine snow, Harry and Charlotte find themselves in a narrow canyon resembling "a ditch, a gutter," with the snow "scarred and blemished by and dwarfing the shaft entrance, the refuse dump, the few buildings." They camp out in a one-room shack made of sheet iron shared for much of the time with another couple. Coziness is out of the question. "You wont even notice the cold," the manager advises them, "because you will have forgotten what being warm was ever like." For Faulkner's resilient protagonists it is hell but also heaven—a cornucopia of the intense experience they crave in order to know they are alive.[18]

By this milestone in his journey, Harry has made great headway. He had started out as a man who believed that the well-lived life consisted mainly in keeping one's "timing": *"You are born submerged in anonymous lockstep with the teeming anonymous myriads of your time and generation; you get out of step once, falter once, and you are trampled to death."* Less than a year later we find him in a deserted mining camp blissfully out of lockstep, having given up his profession and all his previous values. He and Charlotte have over-come incredible setbacks, proving themselves, in Charlotte's language, "good enough, worthy enough" to keep their love. But now Faulkner sets before them a final obstacle that will prove insurmountable when he has Charlotte accidentally become pregnant and then ask Harry to perform an abortion on her.[19]

The question at once arises of how Faulkner intends us to view Charlotte's resolve to abort her unborn child. Are we meant to brand her actions immoral, or construe them, ironically, as yet another indicator of her farsighted vision and nobility? A second question, closely related, is why Faulkner chooses to subvert his lovers in this fashion. If Charlotte is his epitome of Modernist nobility, why does he contrive to have the story end with a botched abortion and her agonizing, bloody death?

To answer the first question we must consult the historical context in which *The Wild Palms* was written. Thanks to Janet Carey Eldred, we know that American attitudes on abortion were becoming significantly more tolerant in the late 1930s, as sympathy developed for women caught in the ravages of the Great Depression who found themselves expecting children they simply could not afford. Though tough antiabortion laws stayed on the books, they often went unenforced, and when they were, doctors convicted of violating them usually received a minimal sentence. That does not hold true for Harry Wilbourne, but, Eldred reminds us, his grave sin in the public eye is not performing an abortion per se but doing one "on an adulteress who is carrying his child. Had Harry simply performed an unsuccessful abortion on another woman, his chances of prosecution would have been very low, even had the woman died." As

Eldred also convincingly shows, Charlotte's key argument in favor of an abortion—that it would be foolhardy to have a child given their precarious finances—tends to "echo the debates" on the issue taking place at the time. All along she had impressed upon Harry that rising above material circumstances requires a heroic act, fusing together mind and body: "It's more than just training your brain to remember hunger's not in the belly. Your belly, your guts themselves, have got to believe it." But that is far beyond what one can expect from a child. "I can starve and you can starve," she pleads, "but not it."[20]

Just as critical from her perspective is the emotional cost. Children "hurt too much," she explains. By that, Harry soon grasps, she means not the physical pain of childbirth but rather the agony of being torn—as Faulkner himself had been over his daughter—between the necessity of providing the child with a stable, comfortable home and the desire to lead the sort of brave, elemental existence filled with discomfort and danger that Charlotte and Harry attempt. That choice had certainly not been an easy one for Charlotte. When her husband, Rat, accompanies her and Harry on the train to Chicago as far as the first stop, she almost gets off with him. Her relationship with Rat is "not finished," she informs Harry, which is why it and the other ties to her previous life "will have to be cut"—implying that if not severed decisively they will continue to pull hard on her. Later we are struck by the way her hands, "otherwise and at nearly every other human action unhesitating and swift," fumble badly while wrapping Christmas presents for her daughters, betraying her emotion. And when Harry asks after her children following her final visit with them, she finds it too painful to respond. "They were all right," she finally manages to get out.[21]

The evidence, then, would suggest that Faulkner sympathized deeply with Charlotte's dilemma. Although it is likely, given the generation to which he belonged, that abortion carried a definite stigma for him, it also appears that he saw the resort to it as one of those extraordinarily tough choices that people are sometimes required to make. From this perspective the decision to abort becomes yet another test of character that circumstance imposes on Charlotte and that she meets as resolutely as she can. To be sure, this interpretation must remain speculative, yet one additional and highly persuasive piece of proof supports it—the fact that, within the novel, it is that preeminent representative of Victorian hypocrisy, the middle-aged doctor, who most vehemently censures the lovers for seeking an abortion. "If as readers we condemn Charlotte and Harry," Eldred astutely argues, "we equate ourselves with the outraged doctor and his wife." That is surely not something Faulkner wished to encourage.[22]

But if this is true and Charlotte such an exemplary figure, why, one might ask, doesn't her author grant her special dispensation and allow her to survive the abortion? One plausible answer is that Faulkner, responding to his residual Victorian self, felt a need to punish the audacious behavior in which she and Harry had engaged. Since Faulkner had drawn extensively on that Victorian self in creating Harry's initial persona as a medical intern, one suspects that it may have been lingering subconscious guilt—inside *both* Harry and Faulkner—that caused Harry's hand to shake so disastrously while performing the procedure on Charlotte. David Minter puts it just right: "If a part of [Faulkner] wanted to create a novel celebrating love as worth the price it exacts, another part insisted on making the price extreme."[23]

The main reason Charlotte dies, however, is the same one so many of Faulkner's noblest characters depart this world early—the fact that she too closely approaches perfection to remain indefinitely on this earth and thus must be crucified. The parallel that springs to mind is Joe Christmas, who by the final stage of his life verged on becoming a black Christ capable of showing the South a path to possible redemption through the integration of racial identities he had achieved within his own being. In Charlotte, Faulkner was offering something equally original and seditious —a form of female Christ who, with her "ruthless and unbearable honesty," fused together elements of gender in a way few at that time could have imagined and attempted, in order to live by a set of ideal precepts that Joseph J. Moldenhauer correctly identifies as "a religion complete in itself." Although the identification with Jesus is not quite as firm in Charlotte's case (she does not bear the initials "JC" or have "Christ" as part of her surname), she is, like Joe, widely misperceived as evil by the community and dies a horrendous death bleeding profusely from the groin.* The similarities extend to the language with which Faulkner records their death scenes: if Christmas's body at the very end "seemed to collapse, to

---

*For Faulkner, it would appear, a violent excision of the genitalia became the contemporary equivalent of crucifixion—most likely because it was the most appalling physical trauma involving extended bleeding that his imagination could conjure up within a modern-day setting. One sees this not only in Charlotte and Joe but in Benjy Compson, another Christ-like figure who is wrongly considered dangerous and, as a result, castrated.

fall in upon itself," Charlotte likewise undergoes "a collapsing of the entire body as undammed water collapses." It is as if someone had suddenly punctured them, causing their blood to flow out and their larger-than-life spirits to ascend into the air.[24]

It should quickly be added that Charlotte, along with Faulkner's various other Christ figures, was not meant as a literal replica of Jesus, nor were readers being encouraged to imitate her by immediately dropping their conventional lives. Rather, for Faulkner, as for Modernist theologians such as Reinhold Niebuhr and Paul Tillich, the Passion was not an event that happened only once but a basic narrative constantly repeated in both life and art with infinite variations, each time offering, as Faulkner once put it, "a matchless example of suffering and sacrifice and the promise of hope." In whatever guise he (or she) appeared, Faulkner's Christ was meant to serve as an indispensable though impossible ideal, a moral beacon toward which all people should aspire even though it must remain beyond reach. In this schema, human beings are relegated to a permanent tension between that "matchless" image of perfection and the constraining realities of the society in which they live. Those like Charlotte who attempt to transcend that tension by taking on a Christ-like role may succeed in pioneering new social norms and briefly taste the ineffable. But, like Christ himself, they must inevitably pay the "price" of crucifixion by an outraged society that cannot tolerate the revolutionary threat they portend. "If Jesus returned today we would have to crucify him quick in our own defense," Harry laments. That is precisely what happens in *The Wild Palms*.[25]

Faulkner makes it plain that, although Charlotte must die, her teachings will not, thanks to her chief disciple. As part of the religious motif, Harry in jail is presented with a series of temptations, including escape and suicide, but resolutely refuses them, following an inner prompting that he does not yet fully understand. In the sharpest possible contrast to Hemingway's Frederic Henry, who returns to his stoic shell after Catherine hemorrhages to death in a failed childbirth, Faulkner's battered hero opens himself to the world as never before. Although he is confined to a small, dark cell, his senses come alive, savoring every sight and smell and sound available to him. For Frederic Henry, a fickle fate makes human action meaningless: "That was what you did. You died. You did not know what it was about. You never had time to learn. They threw you in and told you the rules and the first time they caught you off base they killed you." Harry Wilbourne had earlier shared that sentiment, believing that "*you get out of step once, falter once, and you are trampled to death*," but paradoxically in the wake of Charlotte's dying and his fifty-year prison sentence he arrives for the first time at the conviction that he can control his own life. "*Not could. Will. I want to*," he declares, making manifest that his will has truly been born.[26]

Appropriately, the insight that finally allows him to achieve this new identity is the central Modernist tenet that, in McHaney's words, "there is no mind-body or spirit/body duality." Charlotte grasped that intuitively, but Harry must struggle at length until he can clearly articulate it. Pondering the situation in which he finds himself, he comes to realize, as did Judith Sutpen before him, that the elaborate gravesite being constructed for Charlotte cannot confer immortality. Though "clipped and green and quiet," it will end up "telling nothing." The only way to cheat death, he decides, is through memory, and the only way to have real, living memory is through "*the old frail eradicable meat.*" After several false tries, Harry reasons it out: "*Because if memory exists outside of the flesh it wont be memory because it wont know what it remembers so when she became not then half of memory became not and if I become not then all of remembering will cease to be.*" By actively choosing to remain alive and in prison, he is continuing the narrative that he and Charlotte began. Perhaps, one imagines, he will write about it (he had for a time produced pulp fiction to earn extra income while they were in Chicago), pushing back oblivion still further, but first he must preserve and cherish "the old wheezing entrails." Once an archetypal "hollow man" like Frederic Henry or the "organless" mannequins Charlotte dressed while working in a department store, Harry has now acquired "guts" and knows it. Though incarcerated, he has at last become free.[27]

To underscore his meaning, and to provide some relief from the intensity of the novel's main story, Faulkner hit upon the ingenious idea of counterpointing the saga of his two primary characters with that of a prison convict who, by dint of circumstance, is handed an opportunity to attain love and freedom but emphatically declines it. The Tall Convict (he receives no name, since by existential standards he is less than fully human) and the woman with whom he travels down the raging Mississippi River during the great flood of 1927 are, as Faulkner later put it, "people in motion doing the exact opposite thing to the tragedy of Harry and Charlotte." Strong similarities do exist—both couples undertake circular journeys that end with the men locked up in the Mississippi state penitentiary at Parchman—but the thematic implications of the two narratives could not be more disparate.[28]

Deploying the Modernist technique of synesthesia, Faulkner uses a variety of sensory contrasts to make the two stories literally feel different to the reader (while simultaneously linking them together by a common reliance on sense impressions). Throughout "The Wild Palms" section the reader is assaulted by the high-pitched, foreboding tone of the "black wind" that sweeps off the ocean, through the streets of Chicago, and down the narrow mountain canyon in Utah, signifying the overwhelming power of nature and inevitability of death. In "The Old Man," earth colors replace black and white as the dominant image becomes the massive, viscous river, "brown and rich as chocolate," a veritable primal ooze. The deep bass rumble it emits suggests a "terrific and secret" force hidden below its seemingly "motionless" surface, capable at the same time of causing immense destruction and of spreading enhanced fertility wherever it goes. In keeping with this imagery, "The Wild Palms" tends to move briskly, with the clipped dialogue typically found in a modern, naturalistic novel or the pulp writing so popular during the 1930s; "The Old Man" rolls along at a slower pace more characteristic of folklore or ancient myth.[29]

Again and again, Faulkner uses these contrasts to heighten his contrapuntal irony. Everything about "The Old Man" seems life-affirming and "brown," while "The Wild Palms" is suffused with an aura of blackness and sterility. In the former, the convict and his companion are placed in a natural environment replicating the primeval conditions under which life first appeared on this planet, with the unnamed woman giving birth to a child on an old Indian mound resembling an "earthen Ark out of Genesis." Harry and Charlotte, on the contrary, are for the most part relegated to the constricted spaces of civilization. Instead of giving birth, Charlotte aborts her baby and then expires on an operating table within the "carbolised" recesses of a modern hospital. All of this would lead one to expect "The Old Man" to be a tale of regeneration and renewal, with "The Wild Palms" centered on stasis and decay. And yet it is in "The Wild Palms" that the life principle emerges victorious, while in "The Old Man" it suffers a dismal defeat.[30]

The irony is compounded by the fact that the convict, at the outset of his adventure, so strongly resembles the early Harry in his determination to separate himself from the chance-ridden world of experience. That resolve stems from his one disastrous venture into that world when, unlike Charlotte Rittenmeyer, he had actually believed what he had read in books before testing it out in real life. Having gathered from paperback crime novels that banditry could be both gallant and easy, he had attempted a daring train robbery, not so much for the money but to prove that he was "the best at his chosen gambit in the living and fluid world of his time." But reality proved unpredictable: at the crucial moment his gun jammed and his lantern went out, leading to his capture. Faced with a long prison term, he puts the blame squarely on the authors who, in his eyes, badly misled him by putting "the stamp of verisimilitude and authenticity" on what was really "criminally false" information. More important, he also blames the young woman whose heart he had hoped to win by showing his mettle as a criminal (that, after all, was how it always worked in fiction). It is true that she did visit him at Parchman, crying "violently for the first three minutes" before starting to flirt with a guard. Seven months later she was thoughtful enough to send him a postcard while on her honeymoon. Wounded by this encounter, he vows to "turn his back . . . on all pregnant and female life forever" by embracing his "monastic existence of shotguns and shackles." Nothing can shake him from that stance. If Harry's travels lead him toward spiritual rebirth, the Tall Convict's unshakable objective is to be able once again to huddle like a fetus in the womblike security of his cell.[31]

Faulkner gives this poor creature what amounts to a series of wake-up calls, but to no avail. Sent to rescue a woman who had been stranded by the floodwaters, he no sooner gets her into his boat than they are carried off by the river. As the warden later observes, the convict "got swept away against his will," providing him with the perfect excuse for escaping from prison, but to him this represents his worst nightmare. Craving more than anything else an orderly, stable existence, he instead finds himself cast adrift in time and space, "toyed with by a current of water going nowhere." In terms of traditional standards he responds heroically, battling mammoth waves, killing alligators with a knife and bare hands, and pulling the skiff by its painter up a steep sixty-foot levee with its human cargo inside. But at no time does the convict display the slightest trace of Modernist-style heroics, taking advantage of his unbounded situation to redefine himself as a person. Far from being able to see the woman as a human being with whom he might establish a relationship, he regards her as an insufferable burden, "one single inert monstrous sentient womb." Nor can he, like Charles Bon, manage to laugh at the absurdity of the cosmos; instead, he is filled with an "amazed and absolutely unbearable outrage." "All in the world I want," he plaintively sobs, "is just to surrender."[32]

The convict also qualifies as a blatant misogynist. His final words—
"Women ———t!"—conclude the novel on an unmistakably sexist note,
generating among critics that seemingly inevitable debate over the extent to which the misogyny can be attributed to Faulkner. As always, the
answer depends on which Faulkner one is talking about. The Faulkner
who lived in the actual world, Anne Goodwyn Jones informs us, most
often "clung to those conventional yet unrealistic definitions of masculine
and feminine within which he and Estelle had been raised." It was that
Victorian Faulkner, with his fear of sexually active women, who found his
way into the Tall Convict, as he had before in characters like Horace Benbow and Quentin Compson. However, Jones goes on, in "his persona as
a writer" Faulkner was willing "to experiment with the pieties of gender
he had inherited," going so far as to "contest the ontological certainty of
the gender dichotomy itself." That Modernist Faulkner, it would seem,
was in control during the composition of both sections of *The Wild Palms*,
looking down on the convict as a pitifully inadequate being who, in running away from women, demonstrates that he is afraid of life. As with the
middle-aged doctor, we are to see in him an utterly negative example.[33]

When all is said and done, that issue—the Modernist imperative to embrace life in all its vicissitudes—lies at the heart of this book. When the
convict voluntarily returns to prison after having been reported killed in
the flood, leaving the authorities puzzled as to how to proceed, one of
them quips, "He's either dead, or free." Those five words neatly sum up
Faulkner's basic existential lesson. When all illusions are stripped away,
Faulkner is saying, being lifeless (although technically alive) or accepting the formidable risks of freedom is the only true choice we have. Thus
when the narrator reports at novel's end that the "Old Man" has gone
"back in [his] banks," having "recovered from his debauch," it becomes
clear that the moniker applies both to the river and to the twenty-five-
year-old who has given up his youth and passion, in dramatic contrast to
Charlotte and Harry, who sacrificed everything to reclaim theirs. In real
life, of course, Faulkner had ostensibly done the same, returning to the
"prison" of his marriage with Estelle rather than pursuing his "debauch"
with Meta. But, one suspects, his decision as he saw it probably came
closer to that of Harry than to the Tall Convict's. He would accept the
pain of his hard but necessary choice and meanwhile keep the memory of
his love affair alive by writing *The Wild Palms* (asking Random House to
send a copy to "Mrs. Wolfgang Rebner"). "*Yes*," Harry affirms, in a final
thought that could not stand in sharper opposition to the convict's closing

line, *"between grief and nothing I will take grief."* Faulkner, in his own way, had made that same choice.[34]

The Wild Palms allowed Faulkner full scope to exhibit his Modernist beliefs, which may help to explain why he valued the novel so highly. In 1946, he even suggested that Random House reprint the story of Harry and Charlotte jointly with *The Sound and the Fury*, the book he always claimed as his favorite within the Yoknapatawpha chronicle. Coupling the two works would, in fact, have made sense thematically. As Gary Harrington points out, Harry Wilbourne's birth in 1910 coincides almost exactly with Quentin Compson's death, making it seem as if Harry picks up where his predecessor left off, plunging into the experiential world and accepting the realities of change and mortality in order to develop the viable identity that had eluded Quentin. Likewise, Charlotte could be considered a successful culmination of the character Faulkner first depicted as Caddy Compson, taking Caddy's incipient Modernist strengths to their potential. *The Wild Palms*, then, together with *Absalom, Absalom!*, can from this standpoint be viewed as Faulkner's most definitive response to the cultural and intellectual dilemmas he had wrestled with since the start of his career, the conclusion of his long quest to come to terms with the riddles of human existence and his native region.[35]

Completing that quest left Faulkner free to take up a quite different project dating from the mid-1920s when he and Phil Stone had spent hours upon hours swapping anecdotes about the so-called rise of the redneck in Mississippi commerce and politics. At Stone's urging, he had attempted to expand this material into a book-length work depicting the progress of a poor white family named Snopes as it conquered first the tiny village of Frenchman's Bend and then the county seat of Jefferson. The original intent could not have been clearer: the sorry tale of chicanery and vulgarity would allow Faulkner (and, vicariously, Stone) to demonstrate superiority over the arrivistes and sound a warning against the insidious threat they posed to southern civilization. One sees this in "Father Abraham," the short fragment of Snopes narrative that Faulkner produced in early 1927 before putting it aside for *Flags in the Dust*. There the main character, Flem Snopes, is snidely dismissed along with the rest of his ubiquitous kin as subhuman: "Cunning and dull and clannish, they move and halt and . . . marry and multiply like rabbits: magnify them and you have political hangerson and professional officeholders and prohibition officers; reduce the perspective and you have mold on cheese, steadfast and gradual and implacable." With such rhetorical blasts, it appears, the peril posed by Snopesism was to be held at bay.[36]

Faulkner toyed with the Snopeses on several occasions over the next decade, placing stories based on them in magazines like *Scribner's* whose northern readers had a seemingly boundless appetite for pejorative, stereotyped treatments of southern poor whites. It was not until late 1938, however, with *The Wild Palms* safely at press and his financial and personal affairs relatively stable, that he was ready to see through to completion the first volume of what was by then a projected trilogy. The plot, he told his editor, would trace the first phase of Flem Snopes's voracious rise, watching "as he gradually consumes a small village until there is nothing left in it for him to eat." Much of the condescending perspective of "Father Abraham" was to persist, with Flem still cast as the founding father of a tribe of rodents set loose to prey on Yoknapatawpha. As in the 1927 manuscript, Flem had "eyes the color of stagnant water" and "a tight seam of mouth" chewing constantly like that of a ruminant cow. But there would also be striking modifications, particularly the "tiny predatory nose like the beak of a small hawk" that stood forth "in startling and sudden paradox" to his other features, implying that there was now more than a little Faulkner in Flem. This and other subtle indicators strewn through the text make it apparent that a significant rethinking of Snopesism was under way in *The Hamlet*. That process would be carried even further in *The Town* and *The Mansion*, the remaining volumes of the trilogy written during the latter half of the 1950s.[37]

What was happening, in effect, was that Faulkner for the first time was looking at the Snopes phenomenon through Modernist eyes. Seen from that perspective, stereotypes dissolved and the story became far more complicated. Where before all Snopeses had looked exactly alike, they began showing up in many different flavors and varieties, from the weasel-faced I.O. with his verbal diarrhea, to the mentally retarded Ike who cannot even speak his name, to the tiny but vicious Mink who kills at the slightest provocation, to the large, "muscle-bound" Eck, described as "unfailingly pleasant and even generous." Most important, although Faulkner would continue to regard Flem and his tribe in conventional moral terms as parasitic opportunists, he would simultaneously start to acknowledge their role as inevitable and even desirable agents of change. In the dynamic Modernist universe, after all, nothing stays the same, whether in New York, Paris, or Frenchman's Bend. Values that had served the community well in its precapitalist, frontier phase might hold strong nostalgic appeal, both to Faulkner and his narrators, but in the first decade of the twentieth century, when the *The Hamlet* takes place, those older values had become a source of devastating entrapment for residents of the rural South and needed to give way. The individual most responsible for challenging those outmoded values is, of course, Flem Snopes, a man who, Richard Gray notes, "does not have to think about change because he *is* change." [38]

"Scratch," remarks Gavin Stevens in *The Town*, "scratch was euphemism indeed for where he started from." When we first encounter Flem, he is living in the "sagging broken-backed cabin" that his father rents from Will Varner, the wealthiest man in Frenchman's Bend. Yet by the end of *The Hamlet* Flem has acquired sizable holdings of land and capital, as well as a partnership in a Jefferson restaurant, and has managed to marry Varner's voluptuous daughter, Eula. A hayseed Horatio Alger, using the time-tested precepts of Ben Franklin to advance himself in a society where almost everyone else is static, he even brings along his own backwoods version of Poor Richard in the form of his cousin, I.O., a man who never met an aphorism he couldn't mangle: "A penny on the waters pays interest when the flood turns. Well well; all pleasure and no work, as the fellow says, might make Jack so sharp he might cut his self." Appropriately, I.O. soon becomes schoolmaster of Frenchman's Bend. [39]

Flem's real secret, though, is his willingness to detach himself radically from the reigning culture. He thinks nothing, for example, of violating traditional mores by dissociating himself from his family if that can work to his advantage. We discover this at the very beginning of the novel when Flem is negotiating with Will Varner's hapless son Jody for a job in the Varner store. As Jody suddenly realizes, Flem is "standing just exactly where couldn't nobody see him" from the family house; he is cutting a separate deal that will benefit no one but himself. Later Flem astonishes the community by his failure to come to the rescue when his destitute cousin Mink is charged with murder. " 'Shucks,' " one of the local farmers remarks. " 'Even Flem Snopes aint going to let his own blood cousin be hung just to save money.' " But Flem does not recognize the concept of "blood" relations. Nor does he especially care about the color line. To the denizens of the community, "the presence of a hired white clerk in the store of a man still able to walk and with intellect . . . was as unheard of as the presence of a hired white woman in one of their own kitchens," yet Flem happily takes the position, using it as the crucial first step in his ascent. [40]

What motivates Flem to jettison customary values this way? Plainly the lure of material gain is never far from his mind, but it is also crucial to recall that Flem is the son of Ab Snopes, a dirt farmer so enraged by the indignities of sharecropping that he specializes in burning down the barns of his landlords. Venting his fierce resentment toward his social superiors has, in fact, become a virtual obsession for him. As *The Hamlet* opens, the county is still buzzing about how Ab, having just taken up residence on the de Spain plantation, had "shoved right past the nigger" guarding the front door of the big house (the contrast with Thomas Sutpen is doubtless intended) and deliberately tracked horse manure onto a fancy rug. When Major de Spain later tried to collect compensation, Ab reached for his matches and gasoline, availing himself of what Faulkner in the short story "Barn Burning" refers to as his "one weapon for the preservation of integrity." Flem, whose eyes are not "fierce and intractable" like his father's but "opaque" and "still," does not expend his energies lashing out at his oppressors, but there is no reason to believe that he has not absorbed his father's sentiments. Instead of trying to get revenge, he will get more than even, earning enough money in time to acquire the de Spain house itself and hire his own black servants. And (again in contrast to Sutpen) he will do it by reversing every facet of the Cavalier ethos, fashioning for himself an identity that is the precise opposite of the old planter ideal.[41]

At the same time, Flem emphatically rejects the other key role model dominating southern life during the nineteenth century, the yeoman farmer. "Aint no benefit in farming," he informs Jody Varner. "I figure on getting out of it as soon as I can." Flem detaches himself completely from the complex culture surrounding the yeomanry, with its existence lived close to nature and its premium on preserving the community's precapitalist rituals and rhythms. In the barter economy of Frenchman's Bend, business is conducted along personal, informal lines, and plenty of time is reserved for leisurely conversation and storytelling. What counts most of all is not the size of a man's bank account but his prowess at trading, especially when horses or other livestock are involved. Skillful contestants square off against each other much as they would in a game of poker, playing "horses against horses as a gambler plays cards against cards, for the pleasure of beating a worthy opponent as much as for gain." Ego enhancement, not dollars and cents, measures the outcome: the winner gets to bathe in the esteem of his neighbors, while the loser suffers a blow to his pride. Sharp dealing and downright deception may take place, but that is part of the game. The point is not to ensure fairness and predictability in economic transactions but to test character—finding out who is a "real" man.[42]

For Flem Snopes, the nascent professional capitalist, none of the ordinary rules of this frontier culture apply. A maven for numbers, he watches every penny and does everything by the book, adhering to the strictest standards of economic rationality. The villagers discover this almost as soon as Flem arrives, when he makes Will Varner pay a nickel for a plug of tobacco at his own store—something hitherto inconceivable in Frenchman's Bend. But that is just the start. Jody Varner, while he ran the store, periodically made mistakes in his own favor when toting up a customer's account to help cover the generous credit he liked to extend, but Flem "never made mistakes in any matter pertaining to money" and gives no credit. Those challenging his figures are treated to a lesson with "pencil and paper," with Flem invariably "proving to them that they were wrong." Moreover, Flem is as stingy with language as with money. In a community that values rich oral exchanges, he almost never speaks, using the fewest possible words when he does. His attempt to separate himself from the agrarian world even shows up in his style of dress—gray cloth cap, white shirt, snap-on bow tie, and gray trousers—which he adopts not only because it is simple and modern but because it is set off from the "unvarying overalls" everyone else wears.[43]

Most important, Flem has completely surmounted the prevailing code of what Bertram Wyatt-Brown terms "primal honor." This age-old ethos, which had become thoroughly entrenched in the southern backwoods by the nineteenth century, centered on a preoccupation with virility. According to Wyatt-Brown, those under its spell could not tolerate the possibility that others might perceive them as weak or inferior. As a result, they felt compelled to prove their courage and strength whenever challenged, responding at hair-trigger speed to any slight and exacting revenge against those thought to have harmed them or their kin. As Faulkner demonstrates throughout *The Hamlet*, however, primal honor by the early twentieth century had become hopelessly archaic, an integral part of the web entrapping the men of Frenchman's Bend in perpetual stasis or worse. By contrast, Flem Snopes, who has broken entirely with the old frontier values, does not exhibit the "emotional brittleness" that Wyatt-Brown finds so widespread among men living in the traditional culture, allowing him alone among the residents of the village to move into the future unencumbered.[44]

Indeed, the novel records instance after instance of men brought to ruin by the pride associated with primal honor. The details vary with each case, but typically there is some connection to the purchase or ownership of horses, which within Frenchman's Bend invariably carries a high symbolic charge for men. To possess a swift and powerful horse suggests both sexual potency and participation in a martial tradition harking back through the antebellum Cavalier to medieval knights and warriors. Horses also connote mobility and freedom, a "bitless masculinity" that boldly casts aside all restraints, particularly those imposed by women. Small wonder, then, that southern tenant farmers would so value horses and cling tenaciously to primal honor. Others in the late 1930s might attribute their plight to the evils of capitalism, but Faulkner, who knew these people well, knew better, describing them as "a race existing in complete subjection not to modern exploitation but to an economic system stubbornly moribund out of the dark ages." And what bound them to that archaic economy, in his view, was their thoroughly outdated, illusory culture.[45]

Faulkner shows us that culture at work right at the outset of *The Hamlet* in an incident involving Ab Snopes, who had initially considered himself more a horse trader than a farmer. Nothing had pleased him more than sitting on his fence, showing off his latest acquisition to the men who happened by. But that was before he ran into the legendary Pat Stamper. What bothered Ab was that Stamper had sold a horse to Ab's neighbor for eight "actual Yoknapatawpha County cash dollars," violating a basic norm of the barter economy: "When a man swaps horse for horse, that's one thing and let the devil protect him if the devil can. But when cash money starts changing hands, that's something else." Ab attempts to gain revenge by souping the horse up (among other things, inserting a fishhook under its skin to make it more lively) and trading it back to Stamper, only to find himself outclassed when the mule team he gets in return nearly expires on reaching Jefferson. Instead of being able to gloat over his triumph, Ab is mortified; not only is he victim rather than victor, but, worst of all, everyone knows it. His humiliation gives rise to an even worse trade with Stamper that leaves Ab with the same horse he had originally but costs him the new cream separator he had just bought for $24.68 — a disgrace compounded when his wife gives Stamper all their livestock to ransom her separator. "Soured," in fact "plumb curdled" by the experience, Ab turns to barn burning as his primary means of defending his fragile honor.[46]

If the frontier ethic can bring a man to ruin through trading, we also soon learn that it can do the same in the area of sexual relations. Like Flem, the schoolteacher Labove is determined to escape the unpromising life of a hill farmer. His means of ascent, though, will not be capitalism but the Jeffersonian route of study at the state university, leading to a legal career and possibly high public office. But just at the point where he is about to be admitted to the bar, "the anteroom to that world he had been working to reach" with its promise of "dignity and self-respect," he is drawn back to Frenchman's Bend by his obsession with Will Varner's alluring teenage daughter, Eula. He sees her not as an actual human being but as a symbol of nature's fertility—a lush, beckoning field that this son of the earth, despite all his efforts to liberate himself, has an irresistible urge to plow. He does not want to marry Eula but to possess her sexually "one time" in order to "leave some indelible mark of himself" on her, which in turn would make everyone aware that he, Labove, was truly a man's man. When he finally attempts to rape her, however, she stops him with the ultimate epithet of impotence: " 'You old headless horseman Ichabod Crane.' " Labove hopes briefly that her brother Jody will kill him so that the community will at least believe he succeeded. When it becomes clear that Eula did not think enough of the incident to mention it, this would-be natural aristocrat flees in shame without even bothering to collect his books, done in by the antiquated values he could not suppress.[47]

The same fate befalls the three suitors who follow Labove, plying Eula's affections with their horse-drawn carriages (a most genteel variant of frontier masculinity). Their courtships are conducted according to backwoods ritual, with a great deal of swaggering and physical combat and razzing from local youth, culminating in a pitched battle at a nearby creek. Eula herself helps to stave off the attackers with a buggy whip before giving herself to the dashing Hoke McCarron. Three months later, when word spreads that she is pregnant, all three of her swains vanish, "secretly and by back roads probably, with saddle-bags or single hurried portmanteaus for travelling fast." McCarron departs "because of what he believed the Varner men would do"; the others go, much like Labove, "in a final and despairing bid for the guilt they had not compassed." Once again, the need to uphold a worn-out concept of honor drives enterprising young men into self-enforced exile from the community.[48]

The most tragic results of the frontier ethic, however, appear in the novel's lengthy and brilliant third section, centering on the characters of Jack Houston and Mink Snopes. Houston, from his first appearance as a customer in the blacksmith shop, is closely associated with horses. As a youth he almost resembles an untamed horse straining at its traces, "possessed of that strong lust, not for life, but . . . for that fetterless immobility called freedom." At age sixteen he runs off to Texas to escape the matrimonial clutches of Lucy Pate, employing the frontier expedient of geographic space as his means of escaping both his past and future. But, Faulkner insists, the freedom obtained that way is only an illusion:

> (Geography: that paucity of invention, that fatuous faith in distance of man, who can invent no better means than geography for escaping; himself of all, to whom, so he believed he believed, geography had never been merely something to walk upon but was the very medium which the fetterless to- and fro-going required to breathe in.)

On reading this passage, one suspects that Faulkner did not have to look far to find a living remnant of the frontier mentality on which to base Houston. His model appears to have been his father, that tall, restless man who loved horses and the outdoors, resisted the middle-class Victorian sobriety of his wife, and dreamed of moving to Texas (the fact that Houston works for a railroad while in Texas makes the connection stronger still).[49]

Houston at last surrenders to his fate after receiving the news that his father has died and he has inherited the family farm. Now "bitted," he returns home to marry Lucy and accept his domestication, at the same time buying "as if for a wedding present to her" a powerful stallion embodying "that polygamous and bitless masculinity which he had relinquished." Much like Murry Falkner, it would seem that he cannot give up the vision of frontier freedom that resides at the core of his male identity; instead he enshrines it in a fiery horse so that it will be constantly at hand. "Bitless masculinity" can be dangerous, however. When Lucy foolishly enters the stallion's stall, recognizing the "transubstantiation" that has taken place but believing herself safe because she is now married to him, it swiftly tramples her. Her death throws Houston into a state of "black, savage" grief, raging not against the values that had led him to want the horse but against the cosmic forces he assumes govern human events. He had thought his return from Texas had placated them, but now, for some inexplicable reason, they have gone out of their way to render him impotent, putting his very honor as a man at stake. "'I dont know why. I wont ever know why,'" he cries out while lying in bed "rigid, indomitable, panting." "'But You cant beat me.'"[50]

Faulkner's most vivid incarnation of the frontier state of mind, though, is found in Mink Snopes, the dirt farmer who kills Houston over a petty financial dispute. The contrast with his upwardly mobile cousin Flem is established from the moment Mink is introduced. "'Your own kin you're

so proud of because he works in a store and wears a necktie all day!'"
Mink's wife taunts him. "'Ask him to give you a sack of flour even and
see what you get.'" Mink, it is obvious, will never work in a store or own
a necktie; rather, he is caught in the downward spiral so prevalent among
southern sharecroppers in the twentieth century. Faulkner conveys the
full extent of Mink's destitution through a set of carefully chosen details:
his lot, we learn, is "foul" and "muck-trodden," his barn leans "away down-
hill," his corn stands stunted because he has no tools or livestock "to work
it properly," and he possesses so little spare cash that he must oil his gun
with bacon drippings. At age twenty-three he had impulsively left home
to find the ocean with its "proffer of illimitable space and irremediable
forgetting," putting his faith, just like Houston, in mere geography and a
vague but potent urge to flee the unacceptable fate he sees in front of him.
But he has no plan for rising above that destiny, which is why before long
he is drawn back to "his native country" and farming on shares.[51]

From Mink's perspective, which Faulkner develops at great length,
there is no question what has caused his plight—a pervasive "conspiracy
to frustrate and outrage his rights as a man and his feelings as a sentient
creature" that has dogged him all his days. That, he believes, is why the
hot summer weather has parched his crop, "as if the zodiac too had stacked
the cards against him." Mink even blames the heavens for making the fatal
shot he fires at Houston "too loud," "as though the very capacity of space
and echo for reproducing noise were leagued against him too." His life has
consisted of one affront after the next, each whittling away his masculine
pride until, in his eyes at least, he has no alternative but to lash out in one
furious destructive act. When he aims at Houston through his gunsight,
he is not so much targeting the man who charged him a one dollar fee for
wintering his steer as, in Melvin Backman's words, "the whole scheme of
his existence."[52]

Though exhausted, starved, and pushed to the limit of his wits, Mink in
the aftermath of the murder conducts himself with a nobility that permits
him at last to transcend his awful circumstances. He is, Faulkner makes
clear, a figure acting out of pride rather than self-interest. We see this in
Mink's resolve not to try to escape (what he really wants, he tells himself,
is "to leave a printed placard on the breast itself: *this is what happens to the
men who impound Mink Snopes's cattle*") and his refusal to help his greedy
cousin Lump salvage money from Houston's corpse. Left with nothing
but "an empty and foodless house which did not actually belong to him,"
he can also lay claim to "that irremediable instant when the barrels had

come level and true and his will had told his finger to contract," and he will do nothing to tarnish it. Still, the portrait of Mink that Faulkner presents is a deeply tragic one of a man done in not so much by a hostile cosmos as by his anachronistic values. As the sheriff's wagon carrying him to jail enters Jefferson, passing "the neat painted gates" and "the clipped and tended lawns where children shrieked and played in bright small garments in the sunset," its prisoner seems a creature left over from another era—a man who, for all his epic willpower and capacity for endurance, could not possibly fit into this modern, middle-class environment. His cousin Flem, of course, will soon prosper mightily in Jefferson.[53]

Against this backdrop of a society whose members are helplessly locked into the past, Faulkner offers a few examples other than Flem of men who have moved beyond the old ethos. One is Will Varner, the wily old entrepreneur who is savvy enough to recognize Flem as the wave of the future and accordingly welcomes him both as a business partner and son-in-law. He and Flem soon become a team, sitting "side by side in outrageous paradox" while Varner, "cheerful as a cricket," watches Flem extract the maximum possible profit out of Varner's assets. Another transitional figure is the traveling sewing machine salesman V. K. Ratliff. As Michael Millgate observes, Ratliff resembles Flem in his ascent from a hill-farmer background and in his ability, so rare in Frenchman's Bend, to view things with a degree of detachment. "Pleasant, affable, courteous, anecdotal and impenetrable," he appears equally adept in a cash or barter economy. He can swap "land and livestock and second-hand farming tools and musical instruments" ad infinitum without any money changing hands or negotiate a complicated financial deal with his Memphis supplier or even Flem Snopes himself and still come out ahead. In the end, though, Ratliff does not prove detached enough. His fixation on beating Flem in a trade frontier-style causes him to fall for the old "salted mine" trick, buying a worthless property after Flem has planted a few sacks of silver coins on it to give the impression that it contains buried treasure. Flem, by contrast, is not trying to fool anyone in particular; he is a cool-headed businessman with no time for personal contests.[54]

Anyone still doubting Flem's mastery over the world of Frenchman's Bend and its dying culture need only consult the final section of *The Hamlet*, in which Flem, with no visible effort, maneuvers his fellow villagers into buying a herd of untamed Texas ponies that, as Cleanth Brooks puts it, "they do not want and cannot afford and will not be able to use." It is the very wildness of the animals that becomes their source of appeal to

Ruthless and Unbearable Honesty [253]

Flem's customers, who identify the "fury and motion" penned up within Mrs. Littlejohn's lot with that "bitless masculinity" at the core of the frontier ideal. The men know on a rational level that purchasing a horse would be tantamount to throwing their money away. "I'd just as soon buy a tiger or a rattlesnake," Ratliff warns them. "And if Flem Snopes offered me either one of them, I would be afraid to touch it for fear it would turn out to be a painted dog or a piece of garden hose." But deception is not at issue here—unlike the participants in the old-fashioned horseswap, these folks can see plainly what they are getting. Despite this, nearly all of them part with "the sparse silver and frayed bills" they had arduously "hoarded a coin at a time," only to have the ponies escape into the night when it comes time to collect their purchases. Flem ends up with his wallet full, while the new horse owners are left to pursue their illusions in a long and fruitless chase.[55]

From the moment Flem emerged in print, critics have taken great delight in construing him and his fellow Snopeses as subhuman. "We watch them," intoned the reviewer for the *New York Herald Tribune* in March 1940, "with the morbid absorption that marks men staring into a pit alive with lizards and nameless crawling things." The subsequent scholarly verdict has been only slightly more restrained. Hyatt H. Waggoner sees the Snopeses as a case of "avarice married to pure animality," while to James Gray Watson they pose "a devastating threat to principled existence that cannot go unchallenged." It is certainly true that a reader can find material within *The Hamlet* to sustain this approach to Snopesism. Faulkner's view of poor white southerners was much like his view of practically everything else—divided. The Victorian part of his consciousness continued to see anyone from a sharecropping background who sought wealth or power as a threat. They "creep" over a town, he told an interviewer in 1939, "lahk mold over cheese and destroy its traditions and whatever lav'liness there was in the place." In this regard, Lewis Lawson is surely right that Faulkner was taking no chances with Flem, rendering him sterile "as an unconscious safeguard against his ultimate triumph."[56]

Besides Phil Stone's influence, family grudges may have come into play here. Several writers have pointed out that Faulkner may have based Flem in part on Joe Parks, the upstart entrepreneur given to wearing bow ties who somewhat rudely displaced Faulkner's grandfather as president of the First National Bank of Oxford and later bought the large house on North Street where Faulkner had spent his happiest childhood years. Another likely source was Richard Thurmond, the man who gunned down the Old

Colonel. Known, at least within Falkner family lore, for his cold personality and lack of scruples, Thurmond had apparently made his fortune lending money at high interest rates and foreclosing whenever the borrower ran into the slightest trouble. By reincarnating Thurmond as Flem Snopes, it would seem, Faulkner was settling an old, vexatious score.[57]

But again, for most of *The Hamlet* Faulkner was looking at Snopesism through a Modernist lens. If certain passages give the impression Flem is a monster, Alan Friedman rightly points out, that fact in almost every instance arises from "the panic-filled responses others make to him." Examined dispassionately, Flem comes across less as an evil aggressor than an opportunistic historical scavenger, ready to batten on the weaknesses of others, especially their failure to make the necessary cultural transition from the nineteenth to the twentieth century. Where others remain in thralldom to primal honor in all its manifestations, Flem shrewdly capitalizes on it, allowing those intent on bolstering their egos by outsmarting their trading partners to outsmart themselves. No wonder Faulkner once expressed a measure of admiration for the early Flem Snopes. It was not, Faulkner added, "until he was bitten by the bug to be respectable" in the later novels of the trilogy that Flem finally "let me down."[58]

The closing scene of *The Hamlet* captures this perfectly. On his way to Jefferson, Flem pauses to watch Henry Armstid, the destitute hill farmer who, in his utter desperation to escape his lot, has fallen for Flem's salted mine stratagem. Convinced that there *must* be buried treasure on the Old Frenchman's Place, which he has bought from Flem with his last penny, Armstid steadily digs himself into a hole while the other residents of the community sadly and silently bear witness. His figure, disappearing into the niggardly soil that has imprisoned him all his life, serves as a trope for the fate of all the men of the village. Flem, by contrast, has decisively broken with the old ways. He is a southern Babbitt who succeeds, not because Babbitry or Snopesism is either good or bad but because his time has come. With his proceeds constantly reinvested in new ventures, his progress is linear and upward. And as Flem says, "There's a right smart of country."[59]

CHAPTER 10

Diminished Powers

The Writing of *Go Down, Moses*

The years 1940 and 1941 marked a watershed in Faulkner's career, a great divide separating an initial period of continuous, intense creativity from a later era during which both the volume and quality of his writing sharply declined. During the following years, observes Andre Bleikasten, it was as if "another, much less stringent Faulkner appeared," one "sufficiently altered for us to wonder about the nature and significance of the change." Since the mid-1920s he had published thirteen novels—almost a book a year. In the remaining two decades of his life there would be only seven book-length titles, of which *The Mansion* alone can compare with his earlier work in terms of artistic merit, and then only toward the bottom of the range, with four of the remaining six distressingly weak by his previous standards. If the dedicated Faulknerian can find occasional flashes of the old splendor in *Intruder in the Dust*, *A Fable*, *Requiem for a Nun*, or *The Town*, these efforts of the late 1940s and 1950s seem minor achievements when set beside *Light in August* or *Absalom, Absalom!*. Had someone other than William Faulkner written them, they would probably be entirely forgotten today and deservedly so. Likewise *The Reivers*, which appeared just a few months before his death in 1962, is, despite its charm, lightweight Faulkner.[1]

Most striking of all, a very different kind of tone began to appear in his texts. Throughout the major phase of his career Faulkner had made a practice of listening to the voices speaking deep within his mind and re-producing them as faithfully as he could on paper. As he once explained, "When I put down what the voices say, it's all right. Sometimes I don't like what they say, but I don't change it." The result was a narrative told largely from within the consciousness of his characters—a format that immersed the reader directly in the experiences being described while affording an extraordinarily nuanced rendition of the tensions and forces at play. That distinctly Modernist mode of narrative now gave way to one more charac-teristic of nineteenth-century writing, in which an apparently omniscient narrator controls the text and delivers moralistic pronouncements on what is happening. Though Faulkner at times attempted to disguise what he was doing (from himself as much as from the reader, it would seem), again and again, as Richard Gray puts it, one finds his "authorial voice" coming "dangerously close to a public address system" as it flatly and mo-notonously argues in favor of "some universal, and implicitly unalterable, 'truth.'" If, with the writing of *The Sound and the Fury*, Faulkner had at last become Faulkner, now he was turning into something else again, shifting, in Judith Wittenberg's apt phrase, "from a novelist of consciousness to one of conscience."[2]

Over the years Faulkner scholars have made numerous attempts to pin down the causes of this sea change. One explanation holds that Faulkner's lengthy and demeaning service as an underpaid scriptwriter for Warner Brothers in the early to mid-1940s broke his spirit and fatally interrupted the momentum of his career. That may have been true, but the fact re-mains that the problematic changes that would become so noticeable in his writing started to manifest themselves *before* he signed his contract with the studio. Moreover, Faulkner's stays in Hollywood during the 1930s had demonstrated that he was perfectly capable of producing first-rate litera-ture there; his legendary powers of concentration allowed him to write in virtually any environment. Another hypothesis is that he had more or less exhausted his material. "His essential story having been told," writes Richard King, "the rest tended toward stale repetition." Again, there is surely some truth to this, but one cannot help recalling that the fore-most characteristic of Faulkner until this point in his life was always his incessant originality—that driving instinct to invent new literary forms, tackle new subject matter, and overturn accepted thinking. "Even when he wishes to settle into some conventional or trite assumption," Irving Howe reminds us, "a whole side of himself—committed forever to restless inquiry—keeps resisting this desire." Why, we must ask, did that spark of intellectual vitality dim so dramatically after 1940?[3]

Although many factors were doubtless at work, ranging from his ongoing family difficulties to his preoccupation with the outbreak of war in Europe, the most important probably lies in the realm of physiology. From the Old Colonel onward, male Falkners had invariably become heavy drinkers on reaching adulthood, and William was no exception. At the outset, his tolerance for liquor appears to have been as extraordinary as his literary gifts. Friends marveled not only at the vast quantities he consumed but also at the way he was able to drink while writing. Although alcohol usually impairs brain function, making it harder to sustain a high level of verbal craftsmanship, it is abundantly clear that it had no such effect on Faulkner at first. In his case it is possible that alcohol consumption actually aided his artistry, helping to dampen inhibitions and so facilitate the liberation of his authorial self. However, by the mid-1930s, Tom Dardis informs us, Faulkner entered the "middle stage" of addiction, and things started changing rapidly. Owing to shifts in his internal chemistry brought on by a combination of aging and excessive drinking, his body "now demanded an increased dosage of alcohol in order to feel 'normal,'" leading to self-perpetuating cycles of drunkenness that almost always ended with a prolonged stay in a hospital for the painful process of drying out.[4]

To Faulkner none of this seemed out of the ordinary or especially worrisome. He had, after all, watched his father and grandfather follow the same path, and given the tensions in his life and psyche, he valued the anesthetic properties of alcohol so much that he was determined never to give it up. Equally important, all through his life he would exhibit a high degree of recklessness toward his body, treating it with what can only be called Cavalier abandon. Even in his final years, when his medical troubles began to mount ominously, he would ignore the advice of doctors and family by continuing to take horses over high jumps, despite the severe injuries to his back and rib cage that resulted from his all too frequent falls. It was as if he believed himself bound by his family tradition to dismiss such physical perils as inconsequential. If a Faulkner wished to risk his neck, or drink to excess, that was his prerogative.

In retrospect, though, one can see that the addiction that was steadily tightening its grip on him was bound to have significant long-term consequences for his health and art. Liquor, ingested in massive quantities, will begin to circulate through the body as a poison, doing progressive damage to all major organs, including the comparatively fragile tissues of the brain. It is a virtual certainty that anyone drinking as heavily as did Faulkner, decade after decade, will in time suffer some degree of neurological deterioration, which by itself could account for some of the decline in talent one finds in his later novels. Even more important, though, is the way severe alcoholics put themselves at risk for medical traumas, such as a fall or extensive bleeding, that can inflict greater harm to the brain. Because that damage occurs inside the cranium, one of the least accessible areas of the human body, it often goes undetected, even by the attending physician. Nonetheless, the consequences can be very real. Intricate circuits of molecular cells that provide the basis for thinking and remembering and imagining can be wiped out in sufficient quantities to render the individual a different person from what he or she had been before.[5]

There seems a high likelihood that this is what happened to William Faulkner in November 1940. Having traveled to a remote location in the Mississippi Delta with a group of friends for their annual hunting expedition, he had all too characteristically drunk himself into a stupor as his way of putting himself to sleep. The next morning his companions found him, in Blotner's description, "unconscious and ashen." Deeply alarmed, they rushed him back to the hospital in Oxford, which involved hours of difficult travel along a wilderness river and backcountry roads. Although complete medical details are not available, we do know that he was suffering from internal hemorrhaging stemming from alcohol abuse and, according to his doctor, had been just a few hours from death. We also know that in the ensuing years this author for whom words had flowed so easily would be filled with complaints that he had "gone stale" and could no longer write, and that by the mid-1940s he would complain of convulsive seizures and bouts of amnesia. Michael Grimwood, who first called attention to the 1940 incident, has argued that it had a major psychological impact on Faulkner, leading to "the onset of a spiritual menopause." "Though still forty-three years old," Grimwood writes, "he was beginning to think like a man whose time was running out, whose cupboard of talent was bare." Evidence drawn from Faulkner's writing, which we will consider shortly, makes it clear that the event did leave a deep and lasting psychological scar. But that same evidence, coupled with the known medical circumstances, suggests a neurological scar as well, one consequential enough to affect his mental and verbal agility, cutting into his capacity to work his usual literary magic and portending the greater loss that lay ahead as the disease of alcoholism followed its predictable course.⁶*

To be sure, at no point did this process reach the stage where it became truly disabling. Even in later years, Faulkner had enough left of his once immense reservoir of talent to compose polished, competent novels. Rather, the problem lay in the area of artistic vision and control. In his prime, Faulkner had always performed a virtuoso juggling act for the reader, keeping several themes and narrative lines aloft without the slightest mishap—a feat that in turn gave his writing its great energy and power. At the same time, much like a cubist or expressionist painter, Faulkner felt an obligation to bring the diverse elements he had set in motion to some kind of aesthetically suitable resting point, avoiding full resolution but providing just enough sense of closure to indicate to the alert reader where his meaning lay. Whether a novel or a collection of short stories, he once wrote Malcolm Cowley, a book of fiction should always be "set for one pitch, contrapuntal in integration, toward one end, one finale." But now, with the edge taken off his genius, as it were, that juggling act became harder to perform. As Joseph Reed puts it: "It is as if Faulkner [had]

---

*Since this medical event took place more than half a century ago, it is impossible to arrive at a precise diagnosis of what happened. Many scenarios suggest themselves, ranging from a small blood clot in the brain perhaps arising from a fall to an elevated level of neurotoxins in the blood owing to a temporary suppression of liver function. The most likely possibility, though, would be hypoxic encephalopathy, which occurs when extensive bleeding reduces the volume of blood in circulation and thus blood pressure. In essence, the flow (or "perfusion") of blood through the brain is not sufficient to sustain its vulnerable tissues, leading to irreversible damage. Given the considerable length of time that Faulkner was apparently unconscious and the amount of blood he must have lost (his doctor believed he was near death), the chances that he suffered some neurological deficit through hypoxia would be extremely high.

Moreover, the part of the brain most susceptible to damage from hypoxia involves the tissues lying between the major blood vessels, which, among other things, tend to control "global cognitive functions" such as the manipulation of broad-scale intellectual patterns. In one case, to take an illustrative example, an academic who had experienced low blood perfusion during prolonged surgery found that he could no longer recognize themes and symbol systems in the texts he assigned to students, even though his intellectual capacities were normal in all other respects. That kind of impairment would be in line with the changes that were soon to appear in Faulkner's writing. In subsequent years he would complain, as Frederick Karl puts it, of "how the clarity of his mind was sometimes clouded" and conjecture that "something had happened to his brain" as the result of a fall from a horse. Perhaps he did injure his head later on, but the problem in all probability had its origin in his medical emergency of November 1940. See Karl, *William Faulkner*, 762, 821–22.

lost the key to his structure in which parts fit other parts and the whole, in which all parts are timed and measured." Characters, symbols, and even whole scenes tossed up into the air in his accustomed manner would come crashing to the ground, despite his best efforts to prevent it. In response, he would steadily cut back on his juggling, settling for plots and imagery that were comparatively obvious in their intended meaning and resorting to extended passages of long-winded moralistic rhetoric to pull his materials together. His writing came to resemble less a daring collage by Picasso than the comparatively tame canvas of a late-nineteenth-century realist with periodic patches of impressionist technique added in an effort to make it look up to date.[7]

As one might expect, this shift also expressed itself in terms of the cultural balancing act within Faulkner's psyche. A weakening of his intellectual powers could not help but lead to a weakening of his Modernist authorial self in favor of the traditional Faulkner, the self he had evolved to live in the world of rural Mississippi. That Victorian Faulkner accordingly started to encroach more and more on his literary productions and public pronouncements. "I have been writing all the time," he informed Professor Warren Beck in mid-1941, "about honor, truth, pity, consideration, the capacity to endure well grief and misfortune and injustice and then endure again," adding, "there is only one truth and endurance and pity and courage." But of course he had *not* been writing about those old-fashioned virtues at the height of his career. Characters such as Quentin Compson or Horace Benbow or Henry Sutpen who had clung tenaciously to the abstract principles of "truth and endurance and pity and courage" had repeatedly gone down to flaming ruin in comparison with those who had learned how to negotiate the morally complex and ever changing universe that the Modernist Faulkner had ordained. For that Faulkner, truth had been multiple, not monolithic, and post-Victorian stoicism ("endurance") a poor substitute for existential awareness and initiative. The Faulkner who was speaking to Warren Beck had never gained such complete command of the typewriter before, save for potboilers like *The Unvanquished*, but with his Modernist rival in disarray he was about to enjoy a long reign banging out his preachy messages at the keyboard.[8]

Go Down, Moses, a work undertaken during those crucial years of 1940 and 1941, sits precisely astride this watershed in Faulkner's life, which accounts for its puzzling nature. Part of the time brilliant, but in places conspicuously flawed, it almost seems to consist of two books, written by the same author at different stages of his career. During the final decade of his life Faulkner would take to describing *The Sound and the Fury* as his "most splendid failure," but in reality that designation should belong to this often quite moving book that nonetheless falls short of holding together.[9]

The idea for it first entered Faulkner's mind in the spring of 1940, when he wrote his publisher about using four "stories about niggers" he had recently tossed off for the popular magazine market as the basis for a loosely structured volume like *The Unvanquished*. That book had done extremely well financially, netting enough profit to allow him to buy Greenfield Farm, a small plantation near Oxford, and to enjoy a year of relative peace from economic woes while writing *The Hamlet*. But now his bank account was pushing empty once again, and he was anxious to duplicate *The Unvanquished*'s success. By summer he had added two more stories, but there his progress stopped. Then, in late November, came his close brush with death, leading almost immediately to a new story about a hunting party much like his own entitled "Delta Autumn," which in turn marked an abrupt shift in his plans for *Go Down, Moses*. The pages already piled up had dealt primarily with black life in the South; those he would now compose focused on the ritual of the hunt and the encroachment of modern civilization on the wilderness. Their central character, who had not appeared in any of the six existing stories, would be Isaac McCaslin, an expert woodsman based loosely on Faulkner's real-life hunting companion, "Uncle Ike" Roberts. Most important, they would mark the introduction of that new rhetorical voice that was to become Faulkner's virtual signature in the years ahead.[10]

Throughout 1941 Faulkner struggled to bring these two blocks of material together. As of early May, he was still telling Random House to expect a volume of "collected short stories, general theme being the relationship between white and negro races here." By the summer, however, he was devoting the bulk of his time to reworking two previously written hunting stories, "The Old People" and "Lion," both set in northern Mississippi in the late nineteenth century before logging had decimated the forests there. "Lion," much expanded, would turn into "The Bear," a novella in its own right destined to become the dominant section of *Go Down, Moses*. As he labored on the project, yet another new pattern emerged that would soon become familiar to his friends and editors. "Moments of extraordinary self-confidence," observes Gray, would "be followed by attacks of profound uncertainty about his work and abilities" as he became filled with "the suspicion that what he had said was not quite what he had wanted to say." To judge from the final text, what may have troubled him most was the question of whether he was ending up with a reasonably integrated work by Modernist standards, one in which the race and wilderness themes marched "toward one end, one finale." As he must have sensed, they did not. "No one can doubt that Faulkner worked to connect these stories so that they would form a coherent whole," John Pilkington comments, "but in the end they proved too dissimilar." [11]

The portion of *Go Down, Moses* that does show impressive integration, exhibiting all the strengths of Faulkner's writing at its best, is the material centered on race—in essence, the chapters drafted before his medical emergency of November 1940. Its antecedents can readily be traced to the closing scene of *Soldiers' Pay*, where two white characters stand outside a black church overcome by the transcendent beauty of the spirituals the congregation is singing, but are prevented by a racial barrier from fully sharing the experience. That distinctly Modernist conception of black culture as more authentic and fulfilling than white culture, yet inaccessible to anyone with white skin, pervades *Go Down, Moses*. What had been a somewhat vague afterthought in 1925 becomes a concrete and overpowering insight in 1940 as we survey the graves in a black cemetery "marked off without order about the barren plot by shards of pottery and broken bottles and old brick and other objects insignificant to sight but actually of a profound meaning and fatal to touch, which no white man could have read." The passage bespeaks a realm of profound faith and emotion that this son of the segregated South hoped to make visible to his white readers, to the point where they could at least see the grave markers, even if they could not "read" them. [12] *

---

*Controversy abounds over Faulkner's portrayal of black culture, with the main complaint, as one might predict, his alleged failure to surmount his own cultural perspective as a southern white. "The story does not offer what it promises," writes Walter Taylor of "Pantaloon in Black." "It is no slice of Negro life, but rather another, more skillful, interpretation of Negro life on white terms." Others, such as James Baldwin, charge Faulkner with political conservatism, arguing that his black protagonists are too submissive—that they show no willingness to band together and challenge white domination but rather content themselves with seeking some kind of spiritual salvation. Faulkner, in this view, fears true racial equality.

Given the historical context in which Faulkner worked, such criticisms seem extremely unfair. They ignore the state of white opinion throughout the nation in the decades prior to the Second World War, which clung to the racist assumptions that not only were blacks genetically inferior to whites and closer to animals than humans,

Of the three main glimpses Faulkner gives us into that culture, all concerned in one fashion or another with burial, the most poignant by far is "Pantaloon in Black." Its protagonist is Rider, an impoverished black mill worker whose beloved wife, Mannie, has suddenly died a few months into their marriage. At first sight, this physical giant of a man, with his taste for moonshine, gambling, and sex (his friends had apparently named him after "Easy Rider," the blues song hero who "rides" women easily), could pass for Thomas Dixon's "black beast." But the more we are shown of Rider, the more we are struck by his indelible humanity. On falling in love with Mannie, we learn, he had jettisoned his vices and devoted himself to her with a passion that can only be called breathtaking. Equally breathtaking is his grief-stricken desire to be reunited with her. Unconstrained by white notions of rationality or empiricism, he is able to see Mannie's spirit still "wawkin" after her funeral and approaches it with consummate gentleness

---

but their way of life was so worthless that it could be entirely ignored. Faulkner, at least in his Modernist guise, clearly stood among the tiny minority of white thinkers who took issue with such attitudes. For that contingent, the great task in the 1920s and 1930s was not encouraging southern blacks to rise up against their oppressors, which would have been suicidal, but rather rendering black life *visible* to whites for the first time and combating the noxious yet pervasive belief that people of African ancestry were somehow subhuman.

The overwhelming objective, in other words, had to be changing the image of blacks that whites held in their minds, which meant above all eradicating the stereotyped, pejorative identity of the "nigger" that most whites automatically transposed onto blacks. Not until that happened would it be possible to muster the broad-scale support needed to launch an effective civil rights movement in the United States. Faulkner may not have grasped this on a conscious, strategic level, but he did sense intuitively that white racist assumptions were terribly wrong and had to be challenged, a fact reflected again and again in his writing. That is the target he was aiming at, and it was surely the right one. To suggest that he should have chosen some other target more appropriate to the 1960s or subsequent decades makes no sense under the circumstances.

In addition, Faulkner remained convinced, as Blotner points out, that white southerners of his generation could never successfully penetrate the inner world of their black contemporaries, in part because of the masks that blacks wore to conceal and protect that inner world and in part because "their modes of thought and feeling were often different and therefore difficult for a white person to understand." In a word, Faulkner had too much respect for the intricacies of black culture and the obstacles preventing him from apprehending it in 1940 to presume to offer a "slice of Negro life." See Walter Taylor, " 'Pantaloon': The Negro Anomaly at the Heart of *Go Down, Moses*," in Budd and Cady, *On Faulkner*, 66–68; Werner, "Tell Old Pharaoh," 714, 719–21; Blotner, *Faulkner*, 2:1038–39.

so as not to lose her again: "He didn't breathe nor speak until he knew his voice would be all right, his face fixed too not to alarm her. 'Mannie,' he said. 'Hit's awright. Ah aint afraid.' " The stereotype may have had it that black men were prisoners of uncontrollable lust and poor candidates for a civilized institution like marriage, but Faulkner here presents a depiction of marital love so moving that it is hard to match in all of world literature.[13]

To make certain that the reader catches his meaning, Faulkner falls back on one of his favorite devices, an alternate narrator who relates events from what is patently the highly prejudiced point of view of the white community. A deputy sheriff recounts to his wife how Rider, instead of mourning, had reported to work bright and early the day after Mannie's funeral, only to walk off the job, down a gallon jug of whiskey, slash the throat of a white man who was running a rigged crap game for blacks, and then allow himself to be captured and eventually lynched without putting up a struggle. "Them damn niggers," the deputy concludes, lack "the normal human feelings and sentiments." "They look like a man and they walk on their hind legs like a man, and they can talk and you can understand them and you think they are understanding you," but in fact "they might just as well be a damn herd of wild buffaloes." The reader, however, having just seen the same events through Rider's eyes, knows that Rider went to the mill in the hope of temporarily drowning his sorrow in his work and, when that tactic failed, tried strong drink. Killing a white man had been his way of indirectly committing suicide in order to rejoin Mannie while at the same time striking back at the race that seemed to control the cosmos and thus was in some manner responsible for her death. What propels Rider, the reader comprehends, is not animalism but the unbearable intensity of his grief, a "normal" human emotion with which any responsive person should be able to empathize.[14]

Once again it is necessary to take note of how radical such sentiments were in 1940 and how extraordinary it was for a writer from a small town in Mississippi to be expressing them. In *Light in August* and *Absalom, Absalom!*, Faulkner had attacked the southern system of racial perception at its core, exposing the tragic consequences of his society's commitment to racial purity. But he had done so through two characters, Joe Christmas and Charles Bon, whose African lineage was either nonexistent or undetectable. By contrast, not only is Rider unequivocally black, but he is portrayed as a superior human being on that account, privileged with a range of emotion and a nobility of character that repressed whites can only envy. Moreover, if the racial message in the previous novels was to a degree obscured by the opacity of the text, in "Pantaloon" it is very much out in the open, even though it is conveyed not by an authorial spokesman but through ironic juxtaposition and exquisitely chosen detail. As Rider passes the "sandy ditch where he had played as a boy with empty snuff-tins and rusted harness-buckles and fragments of trace-chains and now and then an actual wheel," we apprehend viscerally the injustice he has suffered. At the end, as we watch him "laughing, with tears big as glass marbles running across his face" while musing how "hit look lack Ah just cant quit thinking," we grasp the full complexity of this supposedly primitive man. "And what do you think of that?" the deputy asks on finishing his tale. Faulkner, at the peak of his skill, ensures that we know exactly what to think.[15]

"Pantaloon in Black," it seems, was the catalyst for Faulkner's initial conception of Go Down, Moses. Once he had written it in March 1940, he suddenly saw where he wanted to go with the rest of the project. Even though it has almost no formal connection to the other stories that make up the novel, "Pantaloon" was paradoxically to be the book's thematic centerpiece, which explains why it alone took its place in Go Down, Moses without any substantial revision. By contrast, the earlier "stories about niggers," which had been told largely from the standpoint of a white plantation owner, now had to be recast into narratives emphasizing the dignity and mystery of black life and the hopeless inability of whites to penetrate it. Instead of exploiting racial stereotypes, as he sometimes reluctantly did in his potboilers when desperate for cash, he would return to the mode of his serious writing and once more demolish them.[16]

In line with that aim, Faulkner moved back to the ever explosive issue of antebellum miscegenation he had last dealt with in Absalom, Absalom!. The three commercial stories done before "Pantaloon" had followed a stock format, deriving their humor from the schemes concocted by Lucas Beauchamp, an uppity black tenant on the plantation of Roth Edmonds, to bamboozle his long-suffering landlord. Nothing had especially distinguished Lucas from the huge corps of "Negro" figures that had appeared in such fiction for decades. That changed dramatically when Faulkner, revising this material into the composite "The Fire and the Hearth" chapter of Go Down, Moses, arranged to have planter and tenant descended from the same family. There had, in fact, been hints of such a relationship in the original stories, suggesting that an embryo vision of the McCaslin clan had reposed in Faulkner's mind from the beginning. Drawing for what would prove to be the last time on the Old Colonel, he now created another lusty and ruthless progenitor in Lucius Quintus Carothers McCaslin. "Old Carothers," as he was known, would have three lines of descent, each leading to a major character in *Go Down, Moses*—one through his son "Buck," which would end with the childless Isaac McCaslin; another through his daughter Mary, who would marry an Edmonds and eventually become the great-great-grandmother of Roth; and a third through his black slave Eunice, which three generations later would produce Lucas. As a result, the wrangling between Roth and Lucas turned into a contest between cousins of different races, endowing it with momentous implications it had not carried before.[17]

Once more it is imperative to take note of the historical context in which the revised Lucas Beauchamp was created. Putting forward such a character in the early 1940s, Richard King reminds us, "was artistically and morally daring for a white writer, Southern or not." In part this stems from the depiction of Lucas as a successful mulatto, a man whose "mixed blood" does not follow the expected course and debilitate him but rather aids him in the task, always problematic in Faulkner, of coping with the psychic burden handed down from the past. "Instead of being at once the battleground and victim of the two strains," the narrator tells us, "he was a vessel, durable, ancestryless, nonconductive, in which the toxin and its anti stalemated one another, seetheless, unrumored in the outside air." His white cousins, Roth Edmonds and Isaac McCaslin, struggle in different ways to free themselves from that burden, Isaac by the radical step of re-pudiating his claim to the family plantation. But Lucas, with his balance of racial identities, is able to rise above the struggle. If Isaac ends up dis-connected from society and hopelessly ineffectual, and if events again and again reduce Roth to a "grim and seething white man" (his very name, Annette Bernert remarks, is "emblematic" of how "he is always 'wroth' at somebody"), Lucas stays solidly rooted on his land, very much in control of his existence and "seetheless."[18]

The main reason Lucas represented such a daring innovation, however, lies in his unique status as a black man endowed with a Cavalier persona. According to the region's most treasured myth, dark skin was a surefire indicator of bestiality, while whiteness signified incipient nobility. But Lucas, like the "white nigger" Joe Christmas before him, is something that never should be, an authentic black aristocrat—suggesting, as Lee Jenkins points out, that the ideal self-image white southerners had long prized was essentially "raceless." Black pseudoaristocrats, in the form of servants who put on fancy airs by imitating their white masters, were, of course, staples of plantation fiction. Faulkner himself had once produced a perfect example in Simon Strothers, the subservient, conniving major-domo of the Sartoris household in *Flags in the Dust*, but that had been a decade and a half earlier. In Lucas he was presenting the very opposite of Simon, a black man who had incorporated into his being the traits of pride, self-assertion, and independence previously ascribed to the old planter class. *"He's more like old Carothers than all the rest of us put together, including old Carothers,"* Roth reflects. One sees this in the way Lucas comports himself crossing the town square. Where Sutpen, the instant aristocrat, betrayed his origins through his "florid, swaggering gesture," Lucas strides "with that unswerving and dignified deliberation" that Roth, "with something sharp at the heart, . . . recognised as having come from his own ancestry." A true "black gentleman," in John Bassett's phrase, Lucas carries the Cavalier ethos deep in his bones.[19]

Given Faulkner's stance on the South's racial dilemma, it is hard not to surmise that Lucas took shape as much for prescriptive as for narrative purposes—that he was intended as a model transitional identity for blacks, a figure who could help smooth the path from Jim Crow to the racially amalgamated society Faulkner was convinced would evolve. With an evenhandedness that can be construed as either courageous or naive, Faulkner during the next two decades would attempt to help that process along by telling both races the unpalatable truths he believed they needed to hear. For whites, his message included continual reminders of the essential humanity of blacks and of the need to end segregation as quickly as possible. Writing in 1956 in the wake of the Supreme Court's Brown decision, he came out definitively for integrating public schools and for equality in general: "To live anywhere in the world today and be against equality because of race or color, is like living in Alaska and being against snow." Neither death threats nor social ostracism within Oxford caused him to waver from this stand, which represented the cutting edge of racial liberalism among southern whites in his day. At the same time, he repeatedly advised blacks to prepare themselves to deserve the equality they would soon receive. As a minority group they would be wise to adopt a strategy of conducting themselves "better than white people," of being "*more* responsible, more honest, more moral, more industrious, more literate and educated." Though the law would finally grant them equal rights, he was convinced it would prove an empty victory unless they had the attributes necessary to take advantage of their hard-won freedom.[20]

Hence the utility of Lucas Beauchamp. A man of great inner strength who keeps his own counsel, Lucas tends his land "when and how" he sees fit, but always diligently, "taking a solid pride in having good tools to use and using them well, scorning both inferior equipment and shoddy work." He even insists on a "quality copper-lined kettle" for his illicit distillery, not the cheap, used equipment on which most rural moonshiners rely. In all these ways and more, Lucas applies the attributes of pride and self-reliance he has inherited from Old Carothers to the everyday routine of a southern tenant farmer. It is certainly true, as some writers have charged, that Lucas, for all his nobility, hardly provides a model relevant to the urban environment in which most blacks have lived since World War II. We must recall, though, that Faulkner was writing at a moment when the massive exodus of African Americans out of the South had not yet become visible to contemporary observers. From the perspective of 1941, it still appeared that the overwhelming majority of blacks would be locked indefinitely into sharecropping, as they had been for three generations. Under those circumstances it is not difficult to see why having them acquire some of the old nineteenth-century virtues might have struck Faulkner as a logical next step in bettering their lot.[21]

Equally exemplary, from Faulkner's standpoint, is Lucas's style of dealing with whites. We find him constantly pushing against the system, creating as much space for himself as he can but always knowing when to pull back. On visiting the big house he does not head for the rear kitchen entrance as any other tenant would, nor does he attempt the unthinkable and knock at the front door like a white man. Rather, he stops "beside the gallery" and raps "with his knuckles on the edge of it," avoiding a confrontation while ensuring that he does not have to demean himself by going to the back. He is also skilled at manipulating forms of address, an important element in the South's racial etiquette. Roth in his fury recalls how Lucas had "always referred to his father as Mr. Edmonds, never as Mr. Zack, as the other negroes did, and how with a cold and deliberate calculation he evaded having to address the white man by any name whatever when speaking to him." In the same manner, Lucas eloquently expresses his feelings toward the white-run legal system by failing to take his hat off in court and refusing to address the judge as "sir." One senses in all these encounters that Faulkner strongly approved of what Lucas was doing. He *wanted* blacks to push—to keep chipping away at the South's racial oppression—but at the same time to calibrate their gestures carefully to avoid violent encounters.[22]

That, Faulkner makes clear, would not be easy. Lucas may understand whites much of the time, and they may think they understand him, but even in this exceptional case where a black man acquires a sizable part of his persona from a white ancestor, there are formidable barriers to communication between the races. Roth, for instance, cannot begin to comprehend his elderly cousin's persistence in hunting for buried treasure in an old Indian mound after finding a gold coin in it. How, he wonders, could a level-headed man like Lucas neglect all his regular obligations for such a foolhardy escapade. Lucas, however, is the product of his black heritage as well as his white, giving him entry into that noumenal world whose existence lies far beyond Roth's imaginative grasp. For him the mound did not collapse and reveal its bounty as the result of gravity but rather through "a sort of final admonitory pat from the spirit of darkness and solitude, the old earth, perhaps the old ancestors themselves." (In fact, it was Lucas's daughter Nat who, for her own reasons, salted the coin in the mound and set off the miniavalanche that causes it to surface in front of her father, but Lucas does not know this.) His perspective on what has happened stems directly from his sensibility as a black man: the ancient spirits have "vouchsafed him one blinding glimpse of the absolute," and now he must pursue it. Appropriately enough, he obtains a *divining* machine to locate the treasure, handling it "as if it were some object symbolical and sanctified for a ceremony, a ritual," in the hope that its magical powers can bring forth a miracle. In his eyes, his quest is as much sacred as economic, which is why he becomes so obsessed with it.[23]

If Roth cannot fathom Lucas, he is even more puzzled by Lucas's wife, Molly, a woman of infinite love and patience who suddenly decides she wants a divorce after forty-five years of marriage. She does not care that her husband has been staying out night after night for no good reason. That is his business. What worries her is that he might actually come upon the treasure and wrest it from its consecrated site where a nonwhite people once buried their dead. "Because," she tries to explain to Roth, "God say, What's rendered to My earth, it belong to Me unto I resurrect it. And let him or her touch it, and beware." When Lucas offers as a compromise to give the divining machine to their son-in-law, Molly becomes so terrified that she runs off into the woods with the device, risking her life to keep "the curse of God" from falling on her daughter. Her tactic directly threatens the perpetual fire that she and Lucas have kept burning on their hearth since the day they were married, symbolizing the powerful emotional bond that unites black families in this novel. That is enough to bring Lucas to his senses. As a black man, Faulkner is telling us, Lucas will value that sacred fire above a possible fortune in gold (one of the original stories

Faulkner drew on for "The Fire and the Hearth" had been entitled "Gold Is Not Always"). To Roth, of course, all of this remains inexplicable. "Aunt Molly," he believes, is getting old and has "some curious notions." [24]

Of the many episodes in "The Fire and the Hearth" dramatizing the impediments to understanding between the races and the consequent difficulty of calibrating how they should relate to each other, none can compare to the confrontation that had once erupted between Lucas and Roth's father, Zack. The two had grown up "almost as brothers," fishing and hunting together and sleeping "under the same blanket before a fire in the woods," and yet in early adulthood they had found themselves facing off across a bed with a loaded pistol between them, daring each other to grab it and shoot. What brought them to this point, on the surface at least, had been Zack's decision to import Molly into his house as a wet nurse after his wife had died giving birth to Roth, a common enough practice in the South at that time. Lucas was at first willing to tolerate the arrangement, but as the months went by, his anger grew to fever pitch as he came to suspect, almost surely incorrectly, that Zack had been using Molly sexually. The charge had dumbfounded Zack, leaving him at a total loss to explain how his childhood friend and cousin could ever imagine him doing such a thing. The reader is also initially mystified by Lucas's response, which runs counter to the known facts. As best we can discern, we are witnessing a case of primal honor at its worst, a man whose pride has become so touchy that he has lost contact with reality. [25]

Although Lucas *is* overreacting, we learn before long that his motives are readily comprehensible in light of the family's history. Watching the plantation owner summon Molly to the big house triggers powerful and conflicting memories of the series of sexual encounters involving Old Carothers and his female slaves that had produced Lucas's father. On the one hand, Lucas remains loyal to Old Carothers, his flesh-and-blood ancestor who has bequeathed him an invaluable psychological legacy. On the other hand, he knows that he is descended from black women who were shamelessly violated by their white master. It is these inheritances that combine to overdetermine his fury at Zack. His pride as a "man-made McCaslin" and as a black man are *both* at stake, which is why his emotions have become so volatile. "I am a McCaslin too," he reminds Zack as they square off across the bed, and thus must defend his honor exactly as Old Carothers would have by challenging his adversary to a duel. But, he goes on, "I am a nigger too," and so he must act at whatever the cost to protect a black woman. As Lucas sees it, all that Zack has to do is to beat him, while "I got to beat old Carothers." He means that in the doubled sense of rising to the occasion as "old Carothers would have told me to do" and of avenging himself against the man whom he sees as a stand-in for his lecherous ancestor. It is a hopelessly tangled web of causation, arising directly from the South's tangled racial past, that Zack, for all his good intentions, could never hope to decipher.[26]

Again, what makes this scene so poignant is the enormous wellspring of affection that had existed between the two. To stress that fact, Faulkner has Zack finally leap for the gun only after Lucas threatens to commit suicide, risking his own life to save his black cousin's. Yet that affection, we are aware, cannot help Zack overcome the limitations of his white perspective that have led to such a terrible impasse. This time Faulkner lets them off the hook by having the pistol misfire. Convinced that he has beaten Old Carothers by demonstrating his willingness to pull the trigger, Lucas can back down. However, it is clear that his relationship with Zack will never be the same. Just as clearly, the underlying forces of racial separation and consequent distrust will continue to poison the attempts of southern whites and blacks to bond with each other for years to come. "How to God," Faulkner has Lucas ask in conclusion, "can a black man ask a white man to please not lay down with his black wife? And even if he could ask it, how to God can the white man promise he wont?" Old Carothers will not be so easy to beat, after all.[27]

The final story in *Go Down, Moses*, which is also the title story, serves as a kind of exclamation mark to this theme of interracial miscomprehension. "Go Down, Moses" concerns Molly Beauchamp's impassioned campaign to have her grandson, Butch, receive a proper funeral after he is executed for the cold-blooded murder of a policeman in Chicago. With her numinous powers, Molly senses without actually knowing that Butch is slated to die. Since she as a black woman views burial as a sacred rite, the one means through which the dead may transcend mortality, it matters tremendously to her that her grandson, despite his criminal record, come home for his funeral. Perhaps even more impressive is how Butch himself, although so deracinated that he has lost his native accent, still feels the need to be laid to rest amid the shards and broken bottles of the McCaslin plantation's "nigger" graveyard. After having lived under an alias in Chicago, he goes out of his way to divulge his true name and address to a census taker just before going to the electric chair to ensure that his body will be sent to Jefferson. His real self, down below the thick veneer of the hardened criminal, remains that of a southern black who apprehends the sanctity of the earth. When his interlocutor professes astonishment, Butch sets him straight: "It was another guy killed the cop."[28]

Again, a wide gap is shown to exist between how whites and blacks perceive these events. To register the extent of that gap, Faulkner resurrects Gavin Stevens, the Harvard-educated lawyer with a gratuitous Ph.D. from Heidelberg who had supplied the racist explanation of Joe Christmas's tragedy at the end of *Light in August*. This time Stevens emerges as a sympathetic paternalist who, within reasonable limits, will do everything he can to help Molly but cannot credit her with a full human subjectivity or "read" her culture. Indeed, it is almost as if they spoke different languages. That becomes apparent in the scene when Stevens dutifully pays a mourning call on her at her brother's house. There, sitting before "the brick hearth on which the ancient symbol of human coherence and solidarity smoldered," even in July, he finds Molly chanting in her sorrow how she holds Roth Edmonds responsible for Butch's fate. "Done sold my Benjamin," she intones. "Sold him in Egypt." Stevens, with his well-trained empirical mind, tries to correct her: "No, he didn't, Aunt Mollie. It wasn't Mr. Edmonds." Then it suddenly dawns on him that "*she cant hear me. . . She was not even looking at him. She never had looked at him.*" Feeling his utter alienation from the circle of mourners, he rushes for the door, desperate to return to his own world. He leaves with an apology and, one imagines, with genuine regret that he will be forever precluded from experiencing the emotional warmth of that inner circle.[29]

For that brief moment, Faulkner has permitted Stevens, and his readers, to witness the culture of southern blacks as he, Faulkner, believed it really was. We are no longer standing outside the church, listening to the music from a distance, but inside by the hearth, watching a family grieve for a lost child and for the sad destiny of a people. Though surely romanticized in keeping with the Modernist veneration of the primitive, it is also a crucial passage in Faulkner's exploration of race and possibly one of the most insightful treatments any white author had given the subject up to that time.

The symbolic meaning of Molly's biblical chant may be lost on Gavin Stevens, but it need not escape us as readers, given the context that Faulkner's narrative provides. Although Roth Edmonds never sold Butch to anyone, he did apparently evict him from the plantation after catching him breaking into the commissary as an adolescent. Technically, Roth cannot be blamed for the boy's subsequent descent into a career of crime; Stevens could well be correct that Butch was merely following in the footsteps of his father, who had spent most of his adult life in prison. But perhaps Roth is guilty after all in his role as conservator of a system that had oppressed young blacks for generations, causing more and more of them to flee to the "Egypt" of the North. Perhaps, as Thadious Davis suggests, Butch was helping himself to goods in the commissary as "a form of rebellion," taking what would rightfully have been his as a McCaslin descendant except for his skin color. Faulkner hints strongly in this direction, giving us a glimpse of Butch making no effort to avoid detection while burglarizing a store in Jefferson as if he were engaged more in a political act than a crime. Lying on the ground after a police officer has subdued him, with "his teeth fixed into something like furious laughter through the blood," he reminds one of Joe Christmas in his contempt for the white social and legal codes that are destroying his life.[30]

For Gavin Stevens, that "designated paladin of justice and truth and right," none of this is visible. Fulfilling his obligation to what he doubtless views as the inferior and helpless race that is part of his community, he perfects the funeral arrangements, soliciting contributions from local merchants "to bring a dead nigger home." In tandem with his friend, the county newspaper editor, he even accompanies the cortege as far as the town limits, bringing his car to a halt where the pavement turns to gravel. Given all that has gone before in Go Down, Moses, his choice seems just right: a black graveyard is no place for him. Should he ever succeed in penetrating beyond those sacred shards to the cultural realm they portend, it might prove fatal to everything he believes about "justice and truth and right."[31]

Had Faulkner stopped his novel at this point in its composition, that might also have been a wise decision. After completing "Go Down, Moses" in the late spring of 1940, he had in hand the makings of an evocative short work on southern race relations viewed from a Modernist perspective that eschewed the format of a conventional linear novel yet still managed a high degree of thematic coherence, driving steadily "toward one end, one finale." Stepping back from the manuscript like a painter from his canvas, he might well have decided that it needed a bit more contrast—possibly a few additional tales told from a white perspective—but he would surely have felt that his project was on track. Whatever he may have been thinking, we know that as of June 1940 he put the manuscript aside for a few months. If he was suffering from writer's block or in doubt as to how to proceed, he made no mention of it in his correspondence. Rather, it appears that he was taking advantage of the summer weather to tend to chores at Greenfield Farm, sail on a nearby reservoir, and indulge his love of flying, while producing a few potboilers to assist his ailing finances. He would not go back to *Go Down, Moses* until December, soon after he had recovered from his disastrous hunting trip and subsequent hospitalization.[32]

When he did return to the book, his approach underwent an enormous change. Not only was race displaced as the central focus by a new absorption with hunting and the wilderness, but the concern with overcoming stereotyped modes of vision by heightening the reader's perceptive capacities (always one of the essential aims of Modernist fiction) began to give way to the overt expression of moral sentiments. To be sure, some of the material he now produced on hunting did connect reasonably well with the chapters on race relations already on hand, though that was most likely to occur when he was working from previously published short stories. In the material drafted de novo after November 1940, however, the altered, more traditionalist Faulkner who would become so visible in the ensuing years was all too likely to come to the fore. Though the prose of this new Faulkner might contain all the "familiar words and cadences" of his former authorial self, Bleikasten declares, it would in truth be "Faulknerian to the point of self-travesty, . . . far removed from that unique, highly idiosyncratic and at the same time flexible and multiple voice that we have come to identify as Faulkner's." Whatever the underlying cause — actual neurological injury or psychological shock—Faulkner in the wake of his close encounter with death was becoming a different writer.[33] *What crap!*

"Delta Autumn," the first story he wrote on resuming work, does deal with the earlier theme of racial misunderstanding to some degree. In its original version, a character named Don Boyd asks the aging Ike McCaslin to deliver an envelope of guilt money to his mistress when she comes by their hunting camp, along with the message that he does not want to see her or their newborn son again. Ike, already unhappy at serving as the intermediary in such a sordid transaction, becomes especially perturbed when he suddenly realizes that the woman is not white. "You're a nigger!" he bursts out, counseling her to go back to the North where she has been raised and find a black man who will admire her light-colored skin, just as, he claims, she must have coveted Don Boyd's. These insulting remarks suggest that Ike views the woman in racist terms rather than as a person with normal human feelings, a point Faulkner foregrounds through her devastating rejoinder: "Old man, have you lived so long that you have forgotten all you ever knew or felt or even heard about love?" In this regard the episode falls into line with the existing text that Faulkner had piled up for his new book. Revised for the novel, "Delta Autumn" would fit even better, with Don Boyd converted into Roth Edmonds and the young woman made a great-niece of Lucas Beauchamp so that their unhappy liaison carries a faint echo of those between Old Carothers and his female slaves.[34]

However, although prominent, the racial issue in "Delta Autumn" is ultimately overwhelmed by another concern—the destruction of the wilderness through capitalist greed, which itself becomes a metaphor for a more general doomsday sentiment that everything of value or beauty in the world is about to vanish. Once "tremendous, primeval, looming, musing downward upon this puny evanescent clutter of human sojourn," the woods have been "retreating year by year before the onslaught of axe and saw and log-lines and then dynamite and tractor plows" until there is precious little left of them. Though the tone at times seems nostalgic, arising more from a fundamental conservatism than modern ecological awareness, few could object to the message being conveyed here. But the same cannot be said of the long, rambling racist screed in which Ike blasts away at the twentieth century: *"This land, which man has deswamped and denuded and derivered in two generations so that white men can own plantations and commute every night to Memphis and black men can own plantations and even towns and keep their own town houses in Chicago, where . . . Chinese and African and Aryan and Jew, all breed and spawn together until no man has time to say which is which, or cares."* This is a note not heard before in Faulkner, save perhaps for Rosa Coldfield's hysterical monologue in *Absalom, Absalom!*. Although it is true that the words ostensibly belong to Ike rather than Faulkner himself, the reader has been led to presume that Ike serves as the author's mouthpiece on the issue of the vanishing wilderness, making the passage more than a little worrisome.[35]

Reinforcing that concern is the strange story he generated the following month. Taken altogether, "The Tall Men" seems less a literary effort than a right-wing diatribe against the New Deal, that "fine loud grabble and snatch of AAA and WPA and a dozen other three-letter reasons for a man not to work." Especially noteworthy is the appearance of what would soon become one of Faulkner's favorite practices, the stringing together of abstract moral virtues as the answer to all social problems. It's "honor and pride and discipline that make a man worth preserving, make him of any value," Faulkner's folksy protagonist declares. "That's what we got to learn again." To be sure, Faulkner in his guise as a resident of Oxford had periodically voiced complaints about Roosevelt administration programs sapping individual initiative. However, the only time those sentiments had ever shown up before in his fiction had been in *Pylon*, where the wicked capitalist Feinman delivers a protracted blast against federal regulation of business. On that occasion there had not been the slightest degree of doubt that Faulkner, far from sharing Feinman's opinions, was engaged in a scathing caricature of the attacks on FDR then being mounted by the corporate rich. In "The Tall Men," by contrast, the rhetoric is deadly serious, suggesting that the real-life Faulkner who took pleasure in castigating the New Deal to friends in the town square was usurping the place of the authorial Faulkner. That was not a good sign.[36]

Now that he had introduced the wilderness motif in "Delta Autumn," his initial plan, it appears, was to employ it within *Go Down, Moses* as a kind of obligato to his main theme concerning race, much as the story of the tall convict provides a contrasting accompaniment to the tragedy of Charlotte and Harry in *The Wild Palms*. His apprehensions for the fate of the wilderness appear to have come from his experience a quarter century earlier hunting at the camp owned by Phil Stone's family in the Big Bottom of the Tallahatchie, where he had witnessed large tracts of virgin forest being sold off to lumber companies. The ensuing devastation made such a strong impression on him that he kept revisiting it in his writing — in the account of the "brigands" who level the cypress swamps near Kinston in *Flags in the Dust*, for example, or the "stumpocked scene of profound and peaceful desolation" surrounding Lena Grove's hometown of Doane's Mill in *Light in August*. In *Go Down, Moses*, this ecological rape of the South's woodlands would parallel the region's racial sins as evils stemming directly from the rapacious spirit of men like Old Carothers. Ike, in this schema, would be set in tandem with Lucas Beauchamp as two cousins, white and black, who were destined to struggle with the tainted heritage of their common ancestor.[37]

Two problems soon arose, though. First, the more Faulkner played with his contrapuntal material, the more it seemed to acquire its own momentum, until it became a virtual runaway. As a result, the final manuscript mailed off in December 1941 would have Isaac McCaslin as its protagonist and the hunting story, if anything, dominating the one centered on race, which would in turn throw the design of the novel well out of kilter. The second problem concerned his inability to gain sufficient artistic control over the wilderness segment itself, especially in regard to maintaining continuity and plausibility within Ike's tangled narrative. A brief review of the sequence in which he wrote that narrative will make evident how these difficulties developed.

Searching for additional material on the wilderness in what he liked to call his literary "lumberyard," Faulkner began by dusting off two stories he had done for popular magazines in the 1930s about a young boy's initiation into the world of the unspoiled forest. What he was seeking, it appears, was a return to the Edenic beginnings of the big woods in order to establish the most vivid possible contrast with their ruined state in "Delta Autumn." Along with ten-year-old Ike McCaslin the reader is transported to a mystical realm of giant trees looming "profound, sentient, gigantic and brooding" in the "gray and fading light," separated from the tamed land "where the hand of man had clawed for an instant" by a "line as sharp as the demarcation of a doored wall." It is a Paradise free from the contamination not just of civilization but of time itself, a place where endings are also beginnings and where mortality dissolves into a recurrent cycle of death and rebirth.[38]

Presiding over this domain is Sam Fathers, the mixed-breed son of a Chickasaw chief and quadroon mother, who acts as Ike's mentor, teaching him the essentials of hunting and woodcraft. But the lessons Ike learns from this "old dark man sired on both sides by savage kings" go far beyond practical skills. As Susan Donaldson points out, Sam is no less than "a guardian of the sacred" who instructs Ike in the art of "vision." A nonwhite who forgoes "servility or recourse to that impenetrable wall of ready and easy mirth which negroes sustain between themselves and white men," he stands as a unique guide, ready to lead his willing pupil into that noumenal domain that was part of humanity's aboriginal condition but that whites had long since abandoned in favor of law and logic. When Ike kills his first deer, Sam baptizes him with the animal's blood, marking him "not as a mere hunter, but with something Sam had had in turn of his vanished and forgotten people." Thus consecrated, Ike is able to see the magnificent totem buck that arises from the corpse of a slain yearling "walking out of the very sound of the horn which related its death," much as Rider could see the spirit of his dead wife "wawkin." Here, then, was a possible link to "The Fire and the Heart" and "Pantaloon in Black." In the young Ike McCaslin there is at last the promise of a white southerner who may in due course break through the limitations of his racial heritage and help lift the curse on his native land.[39]

Ike's special capacity to commune with the spiritual realm at the heart of nature becomes especially manifest in his relationship with Old Ben, the great bear who had "loomed and towered in his dreams" long before he ever saw it. It is Ike who, thanks to Sam's tutelage, comprehends that the annual hunt for Old Ben is not just an attempt to kill a large and fierce animal but a hallowed ritual centered on a totemic figure. To him the bear is less "a mortal beast" than a symbol: "an anachronism indomitable and invincible out of an old dead time, a phantom, epitome and apotheosis of the old wild life which the little puny humans swarmed and hacked at . . . like pygmies about the ankles of a drowsing elephant." To see this mythic creature at close range, Ike sheds his gun, watch, and compass, divesting himself of those last corrupting symbols of civilization and, more important, leaving behind completely the human-created dimensions of time and space. Only then will the magical forest divinity reveal himself, allowing Ike to follow his evanescent paw prints that dissolve in the wet ground as soon as they are formed (as though "shaped out of thin air") until Ike at last comes to a small clearing where he is vouchsafed his moment of epiphany. It is an overwhelming transcendent experience for Ike, one that would provide him, notes Donaldson, "with a Center of sorts, a touchstone," for the remainder of his life.[40]

Based on these experiences, one might even say that, in "The Old People" and the first three sections of "The Bear," Faulkner had embarked on fashioning Ike into a potential Modernist hero, an ideal identity model for the South who this time would be a white male. If the forest and bear signify the archetypal human unconscious, as several authors have claimed, then it would be fair to conclude that Ike by age sixteen has journeyed far into that psychic interior, garnering extensive knowledge of its subterranean forces. Like Dilsey Gibson during the Easter sermon in *The Sound and the Fury*, he has been granted the privilege—more extraordinary still for a white man—of staring divinity in the face. The "profound sensitivity" with which he emerges, observes Carol Clancey Harter, would seem to make him "the prototype of the much-needed reformer" for whom Faulkner had long been searching.[41]

Moreover, like a true Modernist, Ike at this juncture in his narrative seems to realize that Eden must inevitably be lost—that innocence must always be surmounted as one moves into adulthood. Even when he first entered the big woods, we are told, he had sensed that the ancient trees would be no match for the "little puny humans" (a phrase almost certainly indebted to Gulliver's Lilliputians) with their relentless swarming and hacking and that Old Ben as "a mortal animal" would finally succumb when the right dog was found to bay him. But Ike is portrayed as resigned to all this. After the fateful dog Lion has turned up and it has become apparent that Old Ben's days are numbered, Ike continues enthusiastically to join in the hunt, knowing full well that the drama in which he has invested so much is moving toward its finale. "So he should have hated and feared Lion," Faulkner informs us on three separate occasions. "Yet he did not." Presumably because of the wisdom with which Sam has endowed him, Ike accepts the inevitability of change and death in nature and so "would not grieve. He would be humble and proud that he had been found worthy to be a part of it too." This would appear to be an Adam actually prepared for the Fall.[42]

But now Faulkner faced the immense challenge of connecting this Isaac McCaslin with the shrill, pathetic backward-looking old man of "Delta Autumn," that superannuated Adam who had stubbornly based his existence on his outmoded memory of the Garden. How, to borrow Alan Friedman's formulation, was Faulkner to account for a character who had managed to "go so wrong" after "such a propitious beginning"? Moreover, he needed not only to address this vital issue of continuity within Ike's story but simultaneously to shore up the contrapuntal structure of the novel as a whole. Making his task more daunting still was the deadline pressure from his publisher to complete the book by the end of the year. Such were the conditions under which he suddenly decided to create a new section for "The Bear" that was unlike anything he had previously done.[43]

Despite his comment to Robert Haas at Random House that section 4 would require "careful writing and rewriting to get it exactly right," the available evidence indicates that it was done in a frantic rush. It is possible that Faulkner started it as early as the first week in November, though in all probability he did not. If by chance he did, he soon put it aside for other things, including a treatment for a film script that was dashed off for Warner Brothers, a popularized version of the wilderness sections of "The Bear" for the *Saturday Evening Post*, and, most likely, his regular two-week-long November hunting trip. Since the final manuscript of *Go Down, Moses* went off to New York in mid-December, it appears that section 4 was completed in less than three weeks in the midst of numerous distractions and interruptions (among them Pearl Harbor). In the past Faulkner had often done his best work under similar conditions, scribbling away at a white heat, but that was when his talent was intact. In 1941 it was not. Section 4 would contain spurts of ingenious writing, most notably the series of ledger entries detailing how Old Carothers had shamelessly fathered a son by his own mulatto daughter and then casually left a bequest for the child, as if money could atone for his crime. But it would also fail to fulfill its raison d'être of tying together the two strands of the Isaac McCaslin narrative and bringing a modicum of unity to the book as a whole. Since it now became the fulcrum on which *Go Down, Moses* rested, its flaws would, in turn, leave the novel seriously flawed.[44]

The new section takes place in the commissary of the McCaslin plantation and consists of an extended dialogue between Ike and his older cousin, Cass Edmonds, over Ike's decision to repudiate his inheritance of the family's land. Theirs is not, by and large, an inspiring debate but rather one filled with insipid moralism and political preachments, resembling nothing so much as, in Joseph Reed's apt phrase, "college freshmen grown heady on the panoply and scope of the Saga of Western Man." To Ike the overriding objective is to free himself completely from the legacy of sin handed down from Old Carothers. In a manner reminiscent of Horace Benbow, he confesses why he feels he must do this: "because I have got myself to have to live with for the rest of my life and all I want is peace to do it in." For his part, Cass acknowledges the moral horrors committed by Old Carothers but also calls attention to their ancestor's feat in carving out of "a wilderness of wild beasts and wilder men" a thriving enterprise that continues to supply a livelihood for so many people. In contrast with Ike's moral idealism, Cass adopts a pragmatic position, stemming from the premise that "man was dispossessed of Eden" and must as a consequence learn to make do with an imperfect world.[45]

Over the years, critics have reached a near consensus that the debate ends in a draw, primarily because Faulkner was himself so deeply divided on the key issues. "I think a man ought to do more than just repudiate," he told an interviewer in 1955 in regard to Ike's decision. "He should have been more affirmative instead of shunning people." Two years later, however, he completely reversed himself, insisting that even if Ike did not achieve worldly "success," he had attained "serenity" and "what would pass for wisdom," which are "a lot more important." Ambivalence had always been endemic to Faulkner's thinking, but where he had once made it serve his artistic purposes, he now in essence surrendered to it, content simply to reproduce the argument between the "realistic" and "idealistic" approaches to the southern dilemma without any attempt to move beyond it as he had done in the final chapters of *Absalom*.[46]

What is so disheartening about the debate, though, is the virtual disappearance of Faulkner's Modernist self. Neither of the two cousins can be said to represent it. In the case of Ike McCaslin, a total cultural about-face inexplicably occurs, with the young man who had learned through Sam Fathers how to accept a cosmos that was both mysterious and forever changing replaced by a nineteenth-century sage who contends sententiously, much as Faulkner had to Warren Beck, that "there is only one truth and it covers all things that touch the heart." For this good Victorian moralist, the wilderness has come to serve not as a locus for encountering those hard realities of existence that civilization tries to evade but rather as a refuge from the corruptions of human society where he can sustain his purity. Instead of Adam prepared for the Fall, he becomes Adam clinging to his innocence. Presumably it is his newfound knowledge of his family's racial sins that brings about this change, but everything we have learned about him up to this point in "The Bear" would suggest a disposition to allow for human frailties, not the flight into moral perfectionism that he undertakes. Cass, it is true, offers an appealing practicality, to the point where the reader almost sympathizes with him. Yet he is very much a Lost Cause apologist with typical late Victorian views on race. His arguments, Carl Rollyson astutely observes, "would surely seem static and unimaginative" if they were not set beside Ike's.[47]

Especially regressive is the long-winded passage in which Ike and Cass discuss the lessons of the Civil War and Reconstruction. Here we witness a return of the neo-Confederate Faulkner who wrote *The Unvanquished*, speaking first through the voices of Ike and Cass and then as a highly agitated narrator who virtually hijacks the text. Though God in his wisdom brought about the war to eradicate slavery, Ike claims, the southern men who fought in it were motivated not by political or economic considerations but "just love of land and courage." Why the same Ike McCaslin who had been so outraged by what he had learned of the southern past in his family's ledgers that he relinquished his legacy would look so charitably on the Lost Cause is never explained. The low point comes in the narrator's account of how a horde of intruders, consisting of carpetbaggers, speculators, and Jews, descended upon the region during Reconstruction. It was the descendants of this "third race" — one "even more alien to the people whom they resembled in pigment" than the freed blacks — who would fill the ranks of the Ku Klux Klan in the 1920s, we are informed, with the grandchildren of Federal "Quartermaster lieutenants and Army sutlers and contractors" supposedly leading "lynch mobs against the race their ancestors had come to save." If Ike McCaslin was repudiating his land, William Faulkner seems in moments like this to be repudiating much of his hard-won understanding of the complexities of southern history for a mindless chauvinism.[48]

That upsurge of chauvinism could only mean one thing: a revival of the influence of the Old Colonel within his great-grandson's imagination. In actual life, Faulkner had been moving closer and closer to the model provided by his haunting ancestor, becoming by this time the foremost landholder in Lafayette County. Although living so extravagantly used up financial resources that might have gone to support his art, it was essential, Karl Zender argues, for allowing him to be "what he evidently very deeply needed to be: a paterfamilias, the owner of a mansion, the master of a plantation." Within the fictional world of Yoknapatawpha, however, Colonel Falkner and all that he stood for had been under incessant bombardment since the late 1920s. After taking a devastating blow in *Absalom, Absalom!* (followed by a brief compensatory gesture of homage in *The Unvanquished*), he had left the scene completely in *The Wild Palms* and *The Hamlet*, almost as if for the first time he no longer mattered. Now, with the Modernist Faulkner severely weakened, the Colonel was back in force. That is why the dominating thematic image of *Go Down, Moses* in the end was not to be Lucas Beauchamp's devotion to the fire on his hearth but the profound loneliness of Ike McCaslin, deprived of the son he desperately wanted by his disobedient act of repudiating *his* patriarchal inheritance. Having crossed Old Carothers, he would be "father to no one."[49]

Anyone doubting this return of the Old Colonel need only consult Faulkner's treatment of Old Ben. On two separate occasions that regal creature with two toes on its "trap-ruined" left paw (Colonel Falkner had lost all but two fingers on his left hand when he ran into a trap of sorts in Mexico) is described tearing through the forest "with the ruthless and irresistible deliberation of a locomotive," a strange enough image until one remembers the Knight of the Black Plume. No wonder Old Ben "loomed and towered" so persistently in Ike's dreams. No wonder that Faulkner has Sam Fathers triumphantly declare: "He's the head bear. He's the man." And no wonder, given the trajectory its author was now following, that it would prove impossible to mesh the two halves of this novel.[50]

CODA

David Minter is surely on target in calling the 1940s through the early 1950s the "dark years" of William Faulkner's life. Following the completion of *Go Down, Moses*, everything seemed to fall apart for him. Six years would elapse before he mailed another manuscript to Random House, and when he did, it would be an inferior work, marked by a sharp drop-off in his imaginative powers and by that apparently unstoppable virus of moral preaching that had started to infect section 4 of "The Bear." "I am free," Ike McCaslin had bravely declared in that story, but for Faulkner the word best describing his existence soon became "bondage" — to Warner Brothers through the terms of a disastrous contract signed in 1942, to an ill-conceived would-be magnum opus that he would not abandon even though he sensed it was "no good," and of course to his drinking. There would be unhappy affairs with younger women, more ugly scenes with Estelle, and continuing neurological troubles that were alarming enough by 1953 to cause him to seek professional help (the doctor, Faulkner wrote a friend, had decided that "my brain is normal, but it is near the borderline of abnormality"). Occasional bright spots did exist, including his periodic travels as a cultural ambassador for the State Department and the growing acclaim for his earlier achievement, most notably the award of the Nobel Prize for Literature in 1950, but overall the downward spiral continued. Saxe Commins of Random House, rushing to Oxford after an emergency call for help in October 1952, witnessed the very worst. He found Faulkner helpless and delirious, with a body "bloated and bruised from his many falls." "This is more than a case of acute alcoholism," Commins reported. "It is a complete disintegration of a man."[1]

Then, in the mid-1950s, the clouds suddenly began to lift, ushering in a new stage of his life in which he would succeed in exorcising some, though not all, of his most irksome demons. "Pappy really changed," his daughter Jill recollects. "He became so much easier to live with," a "different man" who "was enjoying life." Her marriage to a West Point graduate, Paul D. Summers Jr., helped to raise his spirits, as did the arrival soon afterward of two grandsons, one of whom was named after him. A common interest in those grandchildren also helped to produce a modus vivendi with Estelle. But most of all he discovered Virginia. An invitation to become writer-in-residence at the University of Virginia brought him to Charlottesville at the start of 1957, and once there he never wanted to leave. It offered not only a mutually beneficial association with the university and the chance to be near Jill and her family but also the opportunity to play the role of gentleman as never before. Virginia was fox-hunting country, which to Faulkner meant donning the habit of an English squire and riding powerful horses across the landscape at breakneck speed like a Sartoris. Though he loved the sport for its own sake, he appears to have been equally drawn by the social circle that came with it. Surrounded by fellow horse lovers with long pedigrees and genteel accents, the Old Colonel's great-grandson could at last feel in his element. All he lacked was a grand estate, which he was in the midst of purchasing at the time of his death in July 1962.[2]

Along with this improvement in his state of mind came a partial resuscitation of his literary career. After his decade-long struggle with *A Fable*, a dubious allegorical tale about the second coming of Christ in the trenches of World War I that he confessed was done by "deliberate will power" rather than true inspiration, it must have been a relief to return to Yoknapatawpha in late 1955 for the second volume of the Snopes trilogy. Nonetheless, his instinct as a writer kept telling him that *The Town* was not going well. "I still have the feeling that I am written out," he informed his editor in January 1956, "and all remaining is the craftsmanship, no fire, force. My judgment might be extinct also, so I will go on with this until I know it is no good. I may even finish it without knowing it is bad, or admitting it at least."[3]

Unfortunately, Faulkner's premonition would prove all too accurate. If *The Hamlet* brilliantly reverses the conventions of the 1930s sharecropper novel, its successor lamely repeats the attack on small-town hypocrisy that had been the centerpiece of American fiction back in the 1920s. We watch with flagging interest as Flem Snopes uses his wife Eula's affair with Mayor Manfred de Spain to blackmail his way up the socioeconomic ladder while the citizens of Jefferson pretend not to see what is happening.*

---

*About the only intriguing thing in *The Town* is the mischievous mayor of Jefferson, Manfred de Spain—a character based in part on Faulkner's maternal grandfather,

Nor do they allow the sheriff to close down Montgomery Ward Snopes's pornography shop, since that, too, would make public the existence of corruption and threaten the town's self-image. Faulkner's message is tediously apparent, but to be sure that not even the most benighted reader misses it, he has Gavin Stevens deliver a lengthy soliloquy on the subject:

> That was it: the very words *reputation* and *good name*. Merely to say them, speak them aloud, give their existence vocal recognition, would irrevocably soil and besmirch them, would destroy the immunity of the very things they represented, leaving them not just vulnerable but already doomed; from the inviolable and proud integrity of principles they would become, reduce to, the ephemeral and already doomed and damned fragility of human conditions.

Cleanth Brooks compares *The Town's* place within the Snopes trilogy to that of "a rather frail and limber board placed across two firmly based stools" and counsels readers to "omit" it entirely. Most Faulkner scholars would heartily second that advice.[4]

By contrast, a number of critics would join Brooks in describing *The Mansion* as "excellent," at least by the standards of late Faulkner. Written in 1958, after he had established his base in Charlottesville, it easily surpasses any of his novels since *Go Down, Moses* in terms of energy and originality. Significantly, the complaints about writer's block that had filled his correspondence from the early 1940s onward do not appear in the letters he sent while working on *The Mansion*. Moreover, as his zest for living and productivity returned, it appears that his alcohol intake tapered off, which may have led to a limited reversal of the cerebral damage done by his earlier heavy drinking. Whatever the causes, the result was a book with its share of defects but also, as Joseph Gold observes, with an abundant store of "splendid writing and storytelling." It was, in a sense, a final, brief

---

Charles E. Butler, an official of Oxford who in 1888 had absconded with the town's tax revenues. As Joel Williamson notes, Faulkner had always acted as if this nonpatrician side of his family did not exist. In 1956, however, Charlie Butler finally got his moment in the Yoknapatawpha sun, only to be put down sharply by a local matron in the story who harps on his lowly status: "The mayor of a town is a servant. He's the head servant of course: the butler. You dont invite a butler to a party because he's a butler. You invite him in spite of it." Butler's departure had left Faulkner's beloved grandmother and mother in the lurch financially; at long last, it would appear, Faulkner was avenging them. See Williamson, *Faulkner and Southern History*, 165, 116–17; Faulkner, *The Town*, 57.

William Faulkner wearing his standard riding attire in the late 1950s, just a few years before his death. With his formal dress and impeccably groomed hair and moustache, he now looked the very image of the well-born Virginia squire. (Courtesy Brodsky Collection, Center for Faulkner Studies, Southeast Missouri State University)

rekindling of Faulkner's imagination, a last hurrah for his long quiescent Modernist self.[5]

In his initial plan, set forth twenty years earlier while he was writing *The Hamlet*, the Snopes dynasty would fall prey to degeneration, much like the Compson and Sutpen lines before it. Having become the wealthiest man in Jefferson, Flem was to have as sole heir a Snopesian version of the idiot Jim Bond with a brain rotted by syphilis. That, however, changed dramatically by the time he began *The Mansion*. Instead, the surviving member of the family who dominates the action of the novel is the daughter born of the momentous union between Eula Varner and Hoake McCarron and raised by Flem as if she had been his child. To be sure, some scholars, especially those of a conservative political bent, have viewed Linda Snopes as a deranged pariah figure. Brooks finds her "an almost clinically pure example of a woman who is restless, alienated, and disturbed"; Millgate is struck by "the pathos implicit in the contrast between what . . . she might have been, and what she has in fact become." Increasingly, though, this conception of Linda has given way to an opposite one in which she is viewed as among the most positive characters Faulkner ever created—his only protagonist, in Keith Fulton's words, who manages to achieve "an act of justice that settles her conflict with the past and empowers her move into the future. Simone de Beauvoir would call it transcendence." By Faulknerian criteria, that is the highest possible accolade.[6]

In keeping with the existentialist notion of authenticity, Linda's arrival at her state of grace is anything but quick or easy. She begins under the tutelage of Gavin Stevens, who provides her with a literary education much like that which Phil Stone had given Faulkner. To ensure her escape from provincialism, Stevens ships her off at age nineteen to Greenwich Village, again as Stone had Faulkner. There in the citadel of American Modernism she enters into a passionate relationship with Barton Kohl, a young sculptor of Jewish descent and an ardent Communist. This "virile, alive" man, "who loved what the old Greeks meant by laughter," completes her immersion in contemporary culture. Later, the two, now married, go off to fight against Fascism in the Spanish Civil War, one of the few political causes of his lifetime that Faulkner deeply cared about (donating one of his most prized possessions, the manuscript of *Absalom, Absalom!*, to a relief fund for the Loyalists). It is in Spain that Linda confronts tragedy directly: not only is her side defeated and her husband killed in a plane crash, but she permanently loses her hearing when a shell explodes beneath the ambulance she is driving. Thus by the time of her return to Jefferson as the town's first "wounded female war veteran," Linda has garnered more than her share of meaningful experience. Yet she is anything but battle-weary or dejected. Buoyantly she speaks "of hope, millennium, dream; of the emancipation of man from his tragedy, the liberation at last and forever from pain and hunger and injustice, of the human condition." Moreover, having encountered the "abyss" at first hand, she is tough and savvy enough to act effectively on those dreams.[7]

What Linda represents, in short, is the culminating example of Modernist heroism in Faulkner, a protagonist in whom he fused together significant traces of all his noblest characters from four decades of writing. With her dark hair and tall, willowy figure, as well as her inner strength and assertive manner, she resembles the many luminous "Dianalike" women who populated his imagination from his early poetry through Judith Sutpen in *Absalom, Absalom!*, carrying the traits he most admired in his mother. Separated from the tumult of reality by her deafness, Linda also becomes a living embodiment of the virginal figure who so obsessed Faulkner in Keats's "Ode on a Grecian Urn." Over and over she is depicted in language paraphrasing Keats as "the bride of quietude and silence striding inviolate," a woman "forever pure" who is "absolved of mundanity." Though rendered incorruptible by the "thunderclap" that took away her hearing, Linda is at the same time unmistakably earthy. Like Laverne Shumann in *Pylon* or Charlotte Rittenmeyer in *The Wild Palms*, the androgynous predecessor from whom she is most directly descended, she is fully capable of preserving her femininity while holding her own in spheres of activity traditionally allotted to men. Her hand is "hard and firm like a man's," and shaking it, you knew at once that "she really had driven that ambulance and apparently changed the tires on it too," yet her eyes are "beautiful, and more than just the eyes."[8]

Again like Charlotte Rittenmeyer, Linda can be seen as a female Christ who integrates in her being attributes that most ordinary mortals would find it impossible to combine. In full experiential contact with the world, she lives as well in a state of celestial serenity after having undergone and survived her transforming crucifixion on the battlefield. If Faulkner's previous Christ figures from Benjy Compson onward were all in some way castrated, Linda is "castrate of sound." "The Lord touched her," an elderly black man attests, "like He touches a heap of folks better than you, better than me." One narrator, sitting across from her at dinner, is struck by both her physical contentment and the sense of beatitude she seems to exude as he watches her eating her meal "soundly" and "heartily": "Yes, by God, that was exactly the word: happy. Happy, satisfied, like when you have accomplished something, produced, created, made something." With her queer, lifeless "duck's voice" Linda may barely be able to communicate by speaking, but that, we are meant to understand, is irrelevant. She teaches by serving as a living embodiment of what Faulkner believed was the Christian spirit at its finest, fulfilling his definition of Christ as "a matchless example of suffering and sacrifice and the promise of hope."[9]

But there is more. Returning home from her job as a welder in the naval shipyard at Pascagoula at the end of World War II, Linda sports "a fine, a really splendid dramatic white streak in her hair running along the top of her skull almost like a plume"—a "white plume collapsed in gallantry." The imagery is unmistakable. Though a woman, a Communist, and, at least in name, a Snopes, Linda also represents Faulkner's final literary incarnation of his most revered ancestor, the man whom he was still trying so hard to emulate in the late 1950s. A much improved, thoroughly Modernist version of the Old Colonel who preserves all his best attributes and reverses his defects, she is truly the Knight of the White Plume.[10]

In this way, she can also be said to represent William Faulkner's final version of his Modernist ideal self. Her Hemingway-like wound is, after all, located toward the back of her skull, exactly where he had claimed his imaginary steel plate was inserted. Likewise, her habit of walking alone "through the back streets and alleys of the town or the highways and lanes and farm roads and even the fields and woods themselves" dressed in old khaki and immured in silence resembles his own self-absorbed rambles around Oxford. In 1927, at the outset of his career, Faulkner had incorporated that Modernist self in Bayard Sartoris, another returned combat veteran who had roamed the countryside wearing old khaki. But Bayard, as a young man from a legendary planter family, was so heavily burdened by his cultural inheritance that his only viable option became self-destruction. The same would be true for such successors as Quentin Compson and Ike McCaslin. By the late 1950s, however, Faulkner had worked his way through to a very different outcome. Following Modernist principles, he knew that the only way to gain liberation from the weight of the past was to overturn all conventions and stereotypes. The vehicle he needed to realize his ideal self would not be a male Sartoris or Compson or McCaslin but a maimed female Snopes.[11]

Freed of that paralyzing ambivalence born of conflicting cultural values that destroys characters like Bayard and Quentin, Linda displays the capacity for direct, immediate action that Faulkner had long been seeking in his protagonists. We see this not only through her service in Spain but also in her response when war engulfs Europe in 1940. Unlike so many others, Gavin Stevens notes, she does not go around saying " 'I must do something to help, I've got to do something, I can't just sit here idle.' " Rather, she announces that she has secured a job in a defense plant and spends the next five years working until her fingernails are "worn off" in order "to say No to people like Hitler and Mussolini." Likewise there is her campaign against racial segregation in Jefferson. A full two decades before the civil rights era would reach Mississippi, Linda attempts to break the color line by getting white teachers appointed in black schools, literally besieging the school board and town supervisors until they "didn't dare unlock their door." When that does not work, she begins teaching Sunday school classes at a black church, persisting even when her front yard is adorned with the epithet "Nigger Lover" and a burning cross. Where the real-life Faulkner advocated gradualism and caution, the Modernist Faulkner was busy creating what at the time must have seemed the very model of an impatient militant, anticipating in an uncanny way that small legion of activists who in the 1960s would overthrow the South's oppressive racial traditions once and for all.[12]

Linda's greatest contribution to the community, however, is her effort to rid it of her stepfather. As president of the bank and owner of the de Spain mansion, Flem has become something far worse than a mere money-grubber; he has turned into "not only a conservative but a tory too: a pillar, rock-fixed, of things as they are." To a Modernist, history is always dynamic, and any attempt to block its course is bound to end in tragedy. As Jay Watson points out, through much of his life Flem had, in fact, fulfilled an important historical purpose by breaking down the embedded social distinctions between "insider and outsider, the lawful and the outlaw, 'gentility' and 'trash'" that had allowed the old "moribund elite" to retain their dominance over poor whites. But now Flem belongs himself to that "moribund elite" and must be removed. Linda contrives to do just that by arranging the release from prison of Mink Snopes, a man who has spent his life being victimized by others, including his cousin Flem. She acts with the knowledge that Mink, if set free, will not rest easy until he has gained revenge on Flem. In effect, she is consciously plotting her stepfather's murder, yet to Gavin Stevens's amazement she does not hesitate an instant. Her "crime," writes Sally Page, "fosters life, for it accomplishes justice, destroys Flem, and frees Jefferson from the evil he embodies."[13]

Stevens tries to believe that Linda has been motivated solely by the desire to help her impoverished, desperate uncle get out of jail, but after the murder he can no longer sustain his illusion. The clinching evidence comes when she leaves Jefferson in a brand-new Jaguar that had been ordered months in advance, making it clear that her action was premeditated. Though the name of her car brings to mind Faulkner's tendency at the outset of his career to associate women with great beasts of prey (one thinks of Joan Heppleton, the tiger-woman who worked her wiles on Horace Benbow in *Flags in the Dust*), Linda cannot remotely be deemed a vicious predator, even if she has just assisted in killing a man. On the contrary, she is a woman with a remarkable talent for steering her way through dense moral thickets, all the while heading toward the future. As a Modernist, she is aware that no immutable laws exist to govern behavior but that we must constantly scramble to construct provisional rules and ethics to fit the historical context in which we live, standing ready to make tough-minded and even distasteful choices when necessary. At the conclusion of the novel, Faulkner neatly sums up this fundamental insight about the nature of human existence through an exchange between Stevens and his friend V. K. Ratliff as they set out to deliver the escape money Linda has left for Mink:

"So maybe there's even a moral in it somewhere, if you jest knowed where to look."

"There aren't any morals," Stevens said. "People just do the best they can."

"The pore sons of bitches," Ratliff said.

"The pore sons of bitches," Stevens said. "Drive on." [14]

That Faulkner could have summoned up Linda Snopes from within his consciousness in the late 1950s seems all the more astonishing given the decidedly traditionalist direction in which he was moving in actual life. Having drawn fire from both his fellow Mississippians and some black leaders for his stance on the South's racial crisis, he now pulled back, making his statements on civil rights both less frequent and more conservative. "As long as there's a middle road, all right, I'll be on it," an exasperated (and, to be fair, partially inebriated) Faulkner told a British interviewer in 1956. "But if it came to fighting I'd fight for Mississippi against the United States even if it meant going out into the street and shooting Negroes." Clearly, a different Faulkner was speaking here than the one who the following year would create Linda. It was also a different Faulkner who became increasingly absorbed with his hunt club activities and who soon afterward wrote *The Reivers*, a novel depicting Yoknapatawpha County at the turn of the century as a mellow land free of all social division and tension, where, as Richard Gray points out, fathers calmly passed on to sons the invaluable lessons of "patriarchal power and obligation." It was as if Faulkner's Modernist self, having reached in Linda the objective toward which it had always been tending, could now "break the pencil," give up the struggle, and quietly depart from the scene.[15]

So ended one of the most stunning journeys of cultural exploration of this century. It had begun tentatively enough with gentle probings of Victorian moralism through the techniques of the French symbolists and early Modernist poets. Then, leaving behind Pierrot and his nymphs in their autumnal garden, Faulkner as of the mid-1920s had embarked on a far more serious pursuit—an unearthing of the darkest secrets buried in the subconscious strata of what might figuratively be called the southern psyche. Employing insights derived from Freudian theory, he had dug deeper and deeper into the culture of his region, exposing the root sources of its mythic self-images as well as its racial and gender stereotypes. Examining the South's past from a Modernist perspective, he had found an alternative history sharply at odds with the accepted tale of Cavalier glory, one that more closely reflected the society that actually existed below Mason and Dixon's line. Continuing his quest, he had sought out a new style of heroism to serve as the basis for a model southern identity better adapted to the conditions of modern life than that his own generation had inherited—a search starting, in effect, with Quentin Compson and ending with Linda Snopes Kohl. From his initial transfixing vision of John Sartoris soaring eaglelike through the heavens, utterly removed from the concerns of common mortals, to the "pore sons of bitches" struggling in the face of harsh existential circumstance to "do the best they can," Faulkner the Modernist author had traveled a great distance, indeed.

Today one can visit the gravesite of William Faulkner in St. Peter's Cemetery in Oxford. It is located not in the Falkner family's large, prominent plot, with its protective iron fence and tall obelisk reaching toward the sky, but in an unobtrusive spot down a steep hillside, with little to distinguish it from the other graves in the vicinity. The flesh-and-blood Faulkner is buried here. There is "a block of stone with scratches on it" to mark where his remains lie, and much of the time one finds it covered with leaves and other debris, but as Judith Sutpen knew so well, "it doesn't matter." What does matter are the other "scratches" he left behind, the ones still surging with the motion of life, that year after year continue to pass "from one hand to another, one mind to another." They represent the monument of the Modernist Faulkner, and although by the nature of the cosmos they cannot survive forever, one feels sure that they will last "a long time, a very long time, longer than anything."

NOTES

INTRODUCTION

1. Ricks, *William Faulkner*; Brooks, *William Faulkner: Toward Yoknapatawpha*, xiii; Arthur F. Kinney, introduction to his edited volume *Critical Essays on William Faulkner: The Compson Family*, 34.
2. Slatoff, *Quest for Failure*, 253; Gold, *William Faulkner*, 188; Meriwether and Millgate, *Lion in the Garden*, 108, 169, 191.
3. Gresset, *Fascination*, 3.
4. Howe, "American Victorianism," 508, 511-14, 521; Clark, *Making of Victorian England*, 20-21, 36-38; Himmelfarb, *Victorian Minds*, 283, 291, 303; Hall, "Victorian Connection," 562-63; Burn, *Age of Equipoise*, 57-58, 60, 64-66, 106.
5. Houghton, *Victorian Frame of Mind*, 14, 144-45, 420; Cominos, "Late-Victorian Sexual Respectability," 21-25; Haller and Haller, *Physician and Sexuality*, 126-28; Nancy F. Cott, "Passionlessness: An Interpretation of Victorian Sexual Ideology, 1790-1850," in Cott and Pleck, *A Heritage of Her Own*, 166-68; Kern, *Culture of Love*, 402. For a fuller exposition of the Victorian dichotomy, see Singal, *War Within*, 5-7.
6. Miyoshi, *Divided Self*, xv; Cominos, "Late-Victorian Sexual Respectability," 235; Rosenberg, *Beyond Separate Spheres*, xiv.
7. Arnold, *Culture and Anarchy*, 57; Meyer, "American Intellectuals," 601; Houghton, *Victorian Frame of Mind*, 266, 297-300, 356, 303, 305-9; Williamson, *Crucible of Race*, 307; Gay, *Education of the Senses*, esp. 328-402. Gay documents widespread eroticism and sensuality among middle-class Victorians, but it is of interest that many of his examples involve surreptitious behavior and date from the late nineteenth century, when various individuals were beginning to challenge what they saw as the repressive nature of their culture. On the limitations of Gay's argument, see also Kern, *Culture of Love*, 401.
8. Houghton, *Victorian Frame of Mind*, 13, 336; Meyer, "American Intellectuals," 591; Miyoshi, *Divided Self*, 129-30; Robert Browning, "Pauline; A Fragment of a Confession," in Browning, *Robert Browning: The Poems*, 31; Singal, *War Within*, 24-26; Clayton, *Savage Ideal*, 32; Arnold, *Culture and Anarchy*, 37, 55, 47, 11.
9. On the strong appeal of Victorian culture in the South, see Howe, "American Victorianism," 519-20, though he errs somewhat in describing the antebellum planter class rather than the postwar, small town bourgeoisie as its main constituency. It should be noted, however, that an earlier version of Victorianism could be found in the Old South, as Drew Gilpin Faust has shown. All of its essential characteristics appear in the "sacred circle" of proslavery writers whose work she so admirably explicates, including the striving for innocence and purity, the zeal for moral reform, and, in her words, "the search for certainty that preoccupied the wider intellectual world and has been seen as a defining trait of the Victorian frame of mind." Faust, *Sacred Circle*, 64, 50, 59, 88-89, 130-31.
10. Gaston, *New South Creed*, 7, 25, 63, 68, 86, 93-95; Paul M. Gaston, "The 'New South,'" in Link and Patrick, *Writing Southern History*, 319-20.

11. Gaston, *New South Creed*, 160, 162–63, 173; Briggs, *Victorian People*, 11–12.

12. Taylor, *Cavalier and Yankee*, 69, 124, 301–2; Singal, *War Within*, 11–21; Cash, *Mind of the South*, 16–17, 21, 36, 65–67, 71.

13. Ronald F. Howell, "Education for the Uncommon Man," in Rubin and Kilpatrick, *The Lasting South*, 147; Williamson, *Crucible of Race*, 26.

14. Woolf, *Mr. Bennett and Mrs. Brown*, 4; Malcolm Bradbury and James McFarlane, "The Name and Nature of Modernism," in Bradbury and McFarlane, *Modernism*, 20, 28, 34–35; Gay, *Freud, Jews, and Other Germans*, 21–22; Bruce Robbins, "Modernism in History, Modernism in Power," in Kiely, *Modernism Reconsidered*, 231–32, 234–39; Singal, *War Within*, 3–4. On postmodernism, see especially Jameson, "Postmodernism"; Wolin, "Modernism vs. Postmodernism"; and Singal, "Definition of American Modernism."

15. Gay, *Freud, Jews, and Other Germans*, 22–26; Trilling, *Beyond Culture*, xiii, 3, 30; Howe, *Decline of the New*, 3–5, 9–10, 21–25; Krupnick, *Lionel Trilling*, 135–36, 143–45; Bell, *Cultural Contradictions of Capitalism*, 46–48.

16. Robbins, "Modernism in History," 231–39; Peter Faulkner, *Modernism*, 19; Ricardo Quinones, "From Resistance to Reassessment," in Chefdor, Quinones, and Wachtel, *Modernism*, 6–7; Kuspit and Gamwell, *Health and Happiness in Twentieth Century Avant-Garde Art*. For a more extended discussion of this newer conception of Modernist culture, see Singal, "Definition of American Modernism," 7–8, 10–22; for an intriguing example of a recent application of this concept of Modernism to the study of American popular culture, see Watts, *Magic Kingdom*.

17. Faulkner, "Elmer," 432. For a sense of the diverse ways in which Modernism found expression as it reached across academic disciplines from philosophy and literary scholarship to physics and biology, see Ross, *Modernist Impulses in the Human Sciences*.

18. Bradbury and McFarlane, "Name and Nature of Modernism," 31; Lunn, *Marxism and Modernism*, 42–43; Clive Scott, "Symbolism, Decadence, and Impressionism," in Bradbury and McFarlane, *Modernism*, 219; Gay, *Freud, Jews, and Other Germans*, 275; Kern, *Culture of Time and Space*, 204; James, quoted in ibid., 204; Schwartz, *Matrix of Modernism*, 5–6, 12, 17–19.

19. Bradbury and McFarlane, "Name and Nature of Modernism," 46, 48–49; James McFarlane, "The Mind of Modernism," in Bradbury and McFarlane, *Modernism*, 80–81, 83–84, 92. Alan Wilde expresses this tension between the acknowledgment of fragmentation and the desire for integration in somewhat different terms, contending that the essence of Modernism lies in "the articulation of disconnection" through irony but that this tendency calls forth a countervailing "vision of wholeness" that Wilde calls the "anironic." In his view, the anironic remains a "secondary" phenomenon—what Modernists really care about, he believes, is calling attention to the massive disorder of the modern world. Yet Wilde describes his one extended example of a Modernist writer, the British author E. M. Forster, as pursuing a "moral design" in his major novels that centers directly "upon the possibility of integration"—in this case, the attempt of his characters to fuse themselves with the physical world they inhabit. One wonders if Wilde is undervaluing the role of the anironic in Modernist thought. See his *Horizons of Assent*, 29–32, 50, 70–72.

20. Panthea Reid Broughton, "The Cubist Novel: Toward Defining a Genre," in

Fowler and Abadie, *"Cosmos of My Own,"* 48–52; McFarlane, "Mind of Modernism," 84–85; Kern, *Culture of Time and Space,* 219–20, 199–201, 75–79; Lunn, *Marxism and Modernism,* 35.

21. Singal, *War Within,* 7–8; Trilling, *Sincerity and Authenticity,* 6, 11, 143–47; Halttunen, *Confidence Men and Painted Women,* xvi–xvii, 51–54; Kern, *Culture of Love,* 5; Baumeister, *Identity,* 92–93, 259; Taylor, *Ethics of Authenticity,* 63; D. H. Lawrence quoted in Ronald Bush, "Modern/Postmodern: Eliot, Perse, Mallarme, and the Future of the Barbarians," in Kiely, *Modernism Reconsidered,* 197.

22. Bradbury and McFarlane, "Name and Nature of Modernism," 50; McFarlane, "Mind of Modernism," 82–89; Sontag, *Susan Sontag Reader,* 212; Bruner, *On Knowing,* 62–63. McFarlane, in his otherwise excellent essay, does err in describing the "logic" of the dream as the guiding sensibility of Modernism. He notes, for example, how "a great many of the artists and writers of the first two decades of the twentieth century" found in the dream a "paradigm of the whole *Weltbild* in which reality and unreality, logic and fantasy, the banal and the sublime form an indissoluble and inexplicable unity." But surely this is an early and more extreme version of Modernism and not necessarily a characteristic of the more mature culture. The latter involved not simply an attempt to assimilate the fiery processes of the unconscious but also an effort to integrate them with those of rational thought. The unity sought may have been "indissoluble" but not "inexplicable." That is why metaphor provides a more accurate representation of the "logic" of Modernism than does the dream. See McFarlane, "Mind of Modernism," 86.

23. Susman, *Culture as History,* 273–74; Erikson, *Identity and the Life Cycle,* 26–31.

24. Jerome H. Buckley, "Toward Early-Modern Autobiography: The Roles of Oscar Wilde, George Moore, Edmund Gosse, and Henry Adams," in Kiely, *Modernism Reconsidered,* 1–3; Baumeister, *Identity,* 251; Trilling, *Sincerity and Authenticity,* 11; Langbaum, *Mysteries of Identity,* 148; Ryan, *Vanishing Subject,* 20.

25. Ryan, *Vanishing Subject,* 2–4, 12–13, 21–22; McFarlane, "Mind of Modernism," 81; Langbaum, *Mysteries of Identity,* 9–10; Bush, "Modern/Postmodern," 214, 196–201. Robert Langbaum captures this shift nicely in terms of two central figures in Anglo-American literary culture. Matthew Arnold, he observes, "never fails to believe that he has a true self even though it is buried," while for T. S. Eliot the self, "if it exists at all, is changing and discontinuous." See Langbaum, *Mysteries of Identity,* 84, 97.

26. Baumeister, *Identity,* 226–27.

27. Skura, "Creativity," 141; Gwynn and Blotner, *Faulkner in the University,* 268; Laing, *Divided Self,* 95, 73–76; Langbaum, *Mysteries of Identity,* 193–202; Kaplan, *Mr. Clemens and Mark Twain,* 18, 43–45, 80–81, 96.

28. Estelle Faulkner to Saxe Commins, n.d., "Sunday night" [March 1954], in Brodsky and Hamblin, *Faulkner,* 2:136; Wilde and Borsten, *Loving Gentleman,* 79; Panthea Reid Broughton, "Faulkner's Cubist Novels," in Fowler and Abadie, *"Cosmos of My Own,"* 87–88; Taylor McElroy, quoted in Bezzerides, *William Faulkner,* 30; Faulkner to Joan Williams, n.d. [April 29, 1953], in Faulkner, *Selected Letters,* 348.

29. Gresset, *Fascination,* 89; Wilde and Borsten, *Loving Gentleman,* 225–27, 230; Minter, *William Faulkner,* 76, 248.

30. Webb and Green, *William Faulkner of Oxford,* 78, 111, 66, 172, 183, 72, 92, 141, 172, 187, 191; Wilde and Borsten, *Loving Gentleman,* 62, 130; Wasson, *Count No 'Count,*

47; Emily Stone, quoted in Snell, *Phil Stone of Oxford*, 244. This self-division in Faulkner resembles that which Louis D. Rubin Jr. has described as characterizing the writers of the southern literary renaissance. According to Rubin, such authors were caught in a double pull, at once alienated from their home communities by the demands of their profession while still retaining "strong emotional and intellectual ties" to those communities. Rubin's observation is certainly convincing, though in Faulkner's case it is necessary to add that the creative tension was so intense as to result in the formation of two distinct personal identities. Also, those identities were not based on a clash between agrarian and industrial values, as Rubin would have it, but on Faulkner's allegiance to the two major historical cultures with which he had been endowed. See Rubin, "The Dixie Special: William Faulkner and the Southern Literary Renaissance," in Fowler and Abadie, *Faulkner and the Southern Renaissance*, 65, 72, 74–75.

31. Faulkner to Mrs. M. C. Falkner, n.d. [November 22, 1918], and Faulkner to Mr. M. C. Falkner, n.d. [October 17, 1921], in Faulkner, *Thinking of Home*, 133, 149; Faulkner, *Sound and the Fury*, 86; all references will be to the "corrected edition" of *The Sound and the Fury* published in 1984 unless otherwise indicated.

CHAPTER ONE

1. Blotner, *Faulkner*, 1:14–17, 21–24, 31–32, 37–39, 42–44; Duclos, "Son of Sorrow," 310, 344–45; John Wesley Thompson Falkner quoted in Wittenberg, *Faulkner*, 14.

2. Murry C. Falkner, *Falkners of Mississippi*, 6; Minter, *William Faulkner*, 18; Faulkner to the Four Seas Company, September 9, 1924, in Faulkner, *Selected Letters*, 7; Duclos, "Son of Sorrow," 373–75, 412. Other evidence of his interest in and reverence for the Old Colonel abounds. For example, interviewers over the years almost invariably found Faulkner laconic and unwilling to volunteer information, but the mere mention of his famous forebear's name, Robert Cantwell discovered in 1938, "ended the long silence" and elicited what was for Faulkner a torrent of dialogue. Cantwell, "The Faulkners: Recollections of a Gifted Family," in Hoffman and Vickery, *William Faulkner*, 55.

In a highly speculative essay, David Wyatt claims that previous scholars "have overemphasized Faulkner's tendency to identify with the figure of the Old Colonel" and that the more important model was Faulkner's grandfather, J. W. T. Faulkner. This contention, however, runs contrary to all the testimony from Faulkner's family and acquaintances and to the central and recurring role that the Colonel plays in many of Faulkner's novels, especially *Absalom, Absalom!*. See Wyatt, *Prodigal Sons*, 76–100.

3. Duclos, "Son of Sorrow," 7, 31, 333; Cantwell, "Faulkners," 56; Minter, *William Faulkner*, 4. It is worth pointing out that, in a technical sense, the Old Colonel was not the first William Falkner, since the name "William" had been recycled within the family for generations. Nonetheless, in the eyes of his descendants he represented the founder of the family in modern times and the first William about whom they had direct and detailed knowledge, allowing him to exist as a real person in their recollections.

4. Duclos, "Son of Sorrow," 20, 9, 240, 22–24, 32, 37–40.

5. Duclos, "Son of Sorrow," 47, 76, 52–62; Williamson, *Faulkner and Southern History*, 18, 21; William C. Falkner, *The Siege of Monterey*, quoted in Blotner, *Faulkner*, 1:16; William C. Falkner to J. W. Clapp, March 18, 1863, in Duclos, "Son of Sorrow," 432.

6. Duclos, "Son of Sorrow," 71–73, 78–81; Blotner, *Faulkner*, 1:17–18.

7. William C. Falkner, preface to *The Siege of Monterey*, in Duclos, "Son of Sorrow," 421; Duclos, "Son of Sorrow," 58, 83–85; Robert Cantwell, introduction to William C. Falkner, *White Rose of Memphis*, xv–xvi.

8. Blotner, *Faulkner*, 1:21–23; Duclos, "Son of Sorrow," 123–25, 132–34.

9. Duclos, "Son of Sorrow," 135–36, 138–40, 144, 153–82; Williamson, *Faulkner and Southern History*, 42–44; Wittenberg, *Faulkner*, 12. Duclos, in his otherwise fine, detailed account of Falkner's war service, disparages his two-year campaign for an officer's commission, referring at one point to the Colonel's "neurotic fever for promotion and for recognition." But given Falkner's excellent record of service in 1861, and the strong recommendations he procured from the generals he fought with, it is something of a mystery why the Confederate War Department did not grant his request. Perhaps the problem was, as Falkner himself believed, that he had no political friends in Richmond, but it is also possible that War Department officials saw something in Falkner's character that made them mistrust him. The question merits further investigation. See Duclos, "Son of Sorrow," 168, 431–38.

10. Duclos, "Son of Sorrow," 296–98, 307–13, 304, 202–3, 286–87.

11. Williamson, *Faulkner and Southern History*, 24–25, 28, 65–67.

12. Ibid., 298–301, 319–26, 330, 334–37; Cantwell, "Faulkners," 56; Williamson, *Faulkner and Southern History*, 60.

13. Cantwell, introduction to Falkner, *White Rose of Memphis*, v, xxv–xxvi.

14. Falkner, *The Siege of Monterey*, quoted in Duclos, "Son of Sorrow," 90, 109, 94–95; Duclos, "Son of Sorrow," 90–95. In his poem, Falkner also chose to make his two lovers Mexican, a device that may have rendered his quasi-erotic descriptions of their relationship more palatable to his audience than if the couple had been American.

15. Falkner, *White Rose of Memphis*, 23, 3–4, 394, 492.

16. Ibid., 430, 319, 37, 291, 503, 133.

17. Ibid., 314, 316, 92, 86, 71, 133, 56, 197.

18. Ibid., 344, 272, 287–88.

19. Duclos, "Son of Sorrow," 219–20; Cantwell, introduction to Falkner, *White Rose of Memphis*, vi, xvi, xviii–xxi; Sallie Ada Malone, review of Col. William Falkner, *The White Rose of Memphis*, quoted in Duclos, "Son of Sorrow," 246.

20. Falkner, *White Rose of Memphis*, 21, 503–4.

21. Ibid., 148, 213–14, 217–18, 275–77, 338, 539.

22. Ibid., 13–14, 344, 503–4, 518–19.

23. Ibid., 198, 446, 486–89.

24. Halttunen, *Confidence Men and Painted Women*, 40–41; Falkner, *White Rose of Memphis*, 416.

25. Halttunen, *Confidence Men and Painted Women*, 60–61, 27–31, 116–18. One of Halttunen's most valuable contributions is the perspective she provides on the perennial question of Victorian hypocrisy. Viewed through the lens of twentieth-century culture, the Victorians' effort to achieve sincerity and consistency while

in the process of transforming their own selves seems highly hypocritical, but regarded in terms of their historical circumstances, it appears an appropriate psychological response to changing objective conditions.

26. Ibid., 31–32; Falkner, *White Rose of Memphis*, 455, 447.

27. Ibid., 83–84, 66–67, 262, 334, 370–71, 398, 477, 535.

28. Ibid., 370–73, 378, 385, 387, 140–41, 317, 527–28.

29. Falkner, *White Rose of Memphis*, 24–25, 343, 355–56, 538, 540. On the reconciliation theme in post-Reconstruction southern fiction, see Buck, *Road to Reunion*, 220–35.

30. Duclos, "Son of Sorrow," 250, 262–63; Falkner, *The Little Brick Church*, quoted in Duclos, "Son of Sorrow," 250, 263, 265, 267–68.

31. Duclos, "Son of Sorrow," 268–69; William C. Falkner, *Rapid Ramblings in Europe*, 449, 99–100, 105, 417–18; Cantwell, introduction to Falkner, *White Rose of Memphis*, xxiv.

CHAPTER TWO

1. Blotner, *Faulkner*, 1:58, 62–64, 67–68, 150; Minter, *William Faulkner*, 6–8.

2. Wittenberg, *Faulkner*, 15–19; Minter, *William Faulkner*, 5–9, 17; Blotner, *Faulkner*, 2:1762. Judith Sensibar speculates that J. W. T. Falkner had no financial reasons for selling the railroad (it was turning an exceedingly high profit at the time) but rather acted out of Oedipal "malice" toward his son—in effect signaling to Murry who had the real power in the family. She also argues that Murry did not dare express his subsequent anger to his father directly, since he remained dependent on him, but redirected that inner rage toward his wife and children. Her hypothesis seems both plausible and intriguing, but in the absence of the requisite archival evidence there is no way to ascertain what J. W. T.'s real motives were in the sale of the Gulf and Chicago (he might, to take one possibility, have been gathering up capital for his own venture of starting a new bank in Oxford, which came a few years later). Also, although Murry could on occasion be nasty to his sons, especially William, by all accounts his primary personality trait was not a bad temper but a profound retreat into himself, almost to the point of permanent mourning—though in this case that might well be interpreted as a form of passive aggression. See Sensibar, *Origins of Faulkner's Art*, 48–50.

3. "Classroom Statements at the University of Mississippi (1947)," "Interviews in Japan," "Interview with Simon Claxton," and "Interview in University of Virginia *College Topics*," in Meriwether and Millgate, *Lion in the Garden*, 55, 181, 276, 280, 17; Minter, *William Faulkner*, 10–12; Blotner, *Faulkner*, 1:92, 104, 110, 146; Falkner, *Falkners of Mississippi*, 10, 17.

4. Minter, *William Faulkner*, 11–12; Blotner, *Faulkner*, 1:119–20, 140, 154–55; "Interview with Dan Brennan," in Meriwether and Millgate, *Lion in the Garden*, 49; "Interview with Simon Claxton," 273.

5. John E. Fontaine, "Never the Ordinary Genius," in Webb and Green, *William Faulkner of Oxford*, 35; Minter, *William Faulkner*, 12–13; Blotner, *Faulkner*, 1:124.

6. Wittenberg, *Faulkner*, 27–29; Blotner, *Faulkner*, 1:159–60, 175, 179–80; Minter, *William Faulkner*, 14–16, 19–20, 27–28.

7. Snell, *Phil Stone of Oxford*, 2, 111–12, 68, 82, 57–58; Blotner, *Faulkner*, 1:161–62, 164, 168–70, 173, 336–37; Richardson, *William Faulkner*, 27, 39; Minter, *William Faulkner*, 26–27.

8. Richardson, *William Faulkner*, 28; Richard P. Adams, "The Apprenticeship of William Faulkner," in Cox, *William Faulkner*, 83–88, 112–13; Blotner, *Faulkner*, 1:164; Philip A. Stone to Richard P. Adams, October 4, 1961, Stone to Carvel Collins, August 16, 1954, in Brodsky and Hamblin, *Faulkner*, 2:296–97, 154; Mick Gidley, "One Continuous Force: Notes on Faulkner's Extra-Literary Reading," in Wagner, *William Faulkner*, 59–63; Carvel Collins, "Biographical Background for Faulkner's *Helen*," in Faulkner, *"Helen,"* 55–56; Millgate, *Achievement of William Faulkner*, 289–90.

9. Wittenberg, *Faulkner*, 29–30; Minter, *William Faulkner*, 28–33; Blotner, *Faulkner*, 1:193–97, 206–7, 209–11, 222–26; Faulkner, *Soldiers' Pay*, 7.

10. Blotner, *Faulkner*, 1:229–33, 224 26; Emily Whitehurst Stone, "Some Arts of Self-Defense," and William Evans Stone V, "Our Cotehouse," in Webb and Green, *William Faulkner of Oxford*, 96–98, 77; Minter, *William Faulkner*, 31–32; Anderson, *Sherwood Anderson's Notebook*, 103, 109–10. A vital prop for the wounded pilot persona was Faulkner's RAF trench coat, which he continued to wear, even when it was in tatters, for the rest of his life. See Stone, "Our Cotehouse," 77.

11. Erikson, *Identity and the Life Cycle*, 23, 89–92; Erikson, *Identity: Youth and Crisis*, 15–17, 87, 212; Baumeister, *Identity*, 21–22, 104, 202–6; Kegan, *Evolving Self*, 100–101, 240.

12. Minter, *William Faulkner*, 33–37; Fontaine, "Never the Ordinary Genius," 34; Blotner, *Faulkner*, 1:232, 236, 238, 251–53, 289–90.

13. Blotner, *Faulkner*, 1:184–85, 247, 262–65; Minter, *William Faulkner*, 36; Richardson, *William Faulkner*, 61–66; Brooks, *William Faulkner: Toward Yoknapatawpha*, 2–3, 8, 11, 17–18; Kreiswirth, *William Faulkner*, 4–7; Stonum, *Faulkner's Career*, 43–44; William Faulkner, untitled poem, quoted in Blotner, 1:309.

14. Ilse Dusoir Lind, "The Effect of Painting on Faulkner's Poetic Form," in Harrington and Abadie, *Faulkner, Modernism, and Film*, 131–32; Brooks, *William Faulkner: Toward Yoknapatawpha*, 68 69; Lewis Simpson, "Faulkner and the Legend of the Artist," in Wolfe, *Faulkner*, 77; Patrick Samway, "Faulkner's Poetic Vision," in Fowler and Abadie, *Faulkner and the Southern Renaissance*, 222–23.

15. Faulkner, *Marble Faun*, 46 and passim; Richardson, *William Faulkner*, 48, 55–60; Wittenberg, *Faulkner*, 30–31; Samway, "Faulkner's Poetic Vision," 223–26; Stonum, *Faulkner's Career*, 49; Brooks, *William Faulkner: Toward Yoknapatawpha*, 4–6; Minter, *William Faulkner*, 37, 35.

16. Minter, *William Faulkner*, 28.

17. William Faulkner, "A Poplar," in Faulkner, *William Faulkner: Early Prose and Poetry*, 60.

18. Faulkner, *Marionettes*, 1–2, 24–25, and passim; Noel Polk, "William Faulkner's *Marionettes*," in Meriwether, *Faulkner Miscellany*, 14–17, 23–24; Judith L. Sensibar, introduction to Faulkner, *Vision in Spring*, xvi n, xvi.

19. Ilse Dusoir Lind, "Faulkner's Uses of Poetic Drama," in Harrington and Abadie, *Faulkner, Modernism, and Film*, 71; Lind, "Effect of Painting," 131–34; Wasson, *Memory of Marionettes*, vi; Blotner, *Faulkner*, 1:298.

20. Stonum, *Faulkner's Career*, 43–44, 46–48, 50, 53–54; Lind, "Faulkner's Uses of Poetic Drama," 73; Samway, "Faulkner's Poetic Vision," 205, 239; Faulkner, "Nympholepsy," in Meriwether, *Faulkner Miscellany*, 150–54.

21. Stonum, *Faulkner's Career*, 42, 45, 50–53, 56, 59; Samway, "Faulkner's Poetic Vision," 242–43.

22. Stonum, *Faulkner's Career*, 43, 49–50; Richardson, *William Faulkner*, 73, 75; Faulkner, "After the Concert," in Faulkner, *Vision in Spring*, 34; Sensibar, *Origins of Faulkner's Art*, 31.

23. Blotner, *Faulkner*, 1:356, 799, 307; Brooks, *William Faulkner: Toward Yoknapatawpha*, 7; Minter, *William Faulkner*, 34, 41.

24. Blotner, *Faulkner*, 1:318–19, 325–26; Minter, *William Faulkner*, 41. That his home base in Oxford served Faulkner well becomes clear when one compares his experience with that of his southern literary contemporary Thomas Wolfe. Convinced that he had "outgrown" his hometown of Asheville, North Carolina, Wolfe was certain he could become a successful writer only by moving to such fashionable intellectual venues as Cambridge or New York. One wonders about the wisdom of that strategy in his case. Faulkner, in his backwater refuge in Mississippi, was able to absorb new cultural and literary influences at his own pace through his prolonged tutorial with Stone. By contrast, David Herbert Donald tells us, when Wolfe "encountered complex modernist ideas and sensibilities" at Harvard, he "had difficulty in dealing with them" and as a result, one suspects, never assimilated them as thoroughly as Faulkner did. Likewise, it seems clear from Donald's account that becoming a rootless wanderer for the remainder of his life destabilized Wolfe, helping to ensure that he would fall short of realizing his true potential as a novelist. While Wolfe was scurrying about aimlessly in his travels and career, unable to devise a new center for his life to replace the one he had lost in Asheville, Faulkner avoided the problem of not being able to go home again by the simple expedient of never having left in the first place. See Donald, *Look Homeward*, 80, 77, 90.

25. Faulkner, "Verse Old and Nascent: A Pilgrimage," in Faulkner, *William Faulkner: Early Prose and Poetry*, 114; Blotner, *Faulkner*, 1:334, 339, 347–49, 366; Calvin S. Brown Jr., "Billy Faulkner, My Boyhood Friend," and W. McNeill Reed, "Four Decades of Friendship," in Webb and Green, *William Faulkner of Oxford*, 45, 182–83.

26. Faulkner, "Books and Things: *Turns and Movies* by Conrad Aiken," "Books and Things: *Aria da Capo: A Play in One Act* by Edna St. Vincent Millay," and "Verse Old and Nascent: A Pilgrimage," in Faulkner, *William Faulkner: Early Prose and Poetry*, 74–75, 85, 118.

27. Faulkner, "Books and Things: American Drama: Eugene O'Neill" and "Books and Things: American Drama Inhibitions," in Faulkner, *William Faulkner: Early Prose and Poetry*, 87, 89, 94–95; Gidley, "One Continuous Force," 57.

28. Faulkner, "Books and Things: *In April Once* by W. A. Percy," in Faulkner, *William Faulkner: Early Prose and Poetry*, 71–72; Brooks, *William Faulkner: Toward Yoknapatawpha*, 19.

29. Faulkner, "Books and Things: Joseph Hergesheimer," in Faulkner, *William Faulkner: Early Prose and Poetry*, 101, 103; Blotner, *Faulkner*, 1:343–44.

30. Blotner, *Faulkner*, 1:366, 352; Hugh Kenner, "Faulkner and Joyce," in Harrington

and Abadie, *Faulkner, Modernism, and Film*, 21–22. Kenner is skeptical that Faulkner could have read through and understood *Ulysses* in 1925 without devoting "weeks of full-time concentration" to the job, but he seems unaware that Faulkner had earlier read the chapters published in the *Little Review* and spent, in Stone's words, "endless hours" discussing them with his mentor. As a result, Faulkner was unusually well prepared to comprehend and absorb the book when he finally got his hands on it. Besides, given Faulkner's work habits, there is no reason to think that he did not devote a period of intense concentration to the novel. It does appear that *Ulysses* did not make its full impact on Faulkner until this 1925 reading (or, in the case of several chapters, rereading); only then did he grasp the scope of Joyce's accomplishment and realize how it might relate to his own career. See Kenner, "Faulkner and Joyce," 22, and Phil Stone to Carvel Collins, August 16, 1954, in Brodsky and Hamblin, *Faulkner*, 2:154.

31. Blotner, *Faulkner*, 1:366, 352; Faulkner, "Verse Old and Nascent," 117.

32. Faulkner, "A Note on Sherwood Anderson" in his *Essays, Speeches, and Public Letters*, 3, 7; Anderson, *Sherwood Anderson's Notebook*, 116, 118; Minter, *William Faulkner*, 50.

33. A. Wigfall Green, "First Lectures at a University," in Webb and Green, *William Faulkner of Oxford*, 135; Davis, *Faulkner's "Negro,"* 43–44, 34, 36; Faulkner, "Note on Sherwood Anderson," 8.

34. Wittenberg, *Faulkner*, 37–38; Davis, *Faulkner's "Negro,"* 39–40; Blotner, *Faulkner*, 1:369.

35. Blotner, *Faulkner*, 1:401–2, 315–16; Lind, "Effect of Painting," 128; Pamela Reid Broughton, "Faulkner's Cubist Novels," 74–75; Faulkner, "Out of Nazareth," in his *New Orleans Sketches*, 102; Stonum, *Faulkner's Career*, 69. As Lind notes, Faulkner seems to have absorbed still more knowledge about contemporary painting from Sherwood and Elizabeth Anderson, both of whom had brothers associated with the Modernist movement in art.

36. Carvel Collins, introduction to Faulkner, *New Orleans Sketches*, 9, 25–26; Brooks, *William Faulkner: Toward Yoknapatawpha*, 103, 106; Wittenberg, *Faulkner*, 39; Minter, *William Faulkner*, 49–50.

37. Faulkner, "Sunset," in his *New Orleans Sketches*, 147, 152–55. Further evidence that Faulkner was beginning to break with southern stereotypes about race appears in "Peter," an unpublished sketch about the mulatto child of a black prostitute that was undoubtedly too controversial for the *Times-Picayune* to use. In it Faulkner refrains from his culture's traditional moralizing about racial mixing, referring to Peter simply as "an incidental coin minted between the severed yet similar despairs of two races." See "Peter," in Faulkner, *Uncollected Stories of William Faulkner*, 490.

38. Faulkner, "Sunset," 157; Faulkner, "Verse Old and Nascent," 117. Cleanth Brooks correctly identifies the many flaws of "Sunset," including Faulkner's error in making the main protagonist far too simple-minded to be credible. Also, the reversal of stereotypes in a lynching plot is not nearly as effective as it would be in later works such as "Dry September" or *Light in August*, since the black victim in a sense causes his own downfall, rather than becoming the victim of persecution by white society. But these shortcomings should not be allowed to obscure the way the story evidences Faulkner's "cultural" progress in breaking loose from his nineteenth-century values. I would add that "Sunset" does have some artis-

tic merit, especially if one remembers that the tragedy in it is not meant to be attributed to the community (as Brooks suggests) but to the chance workings of circumstance. See Brooks, *William Faulkner: Toward Yoknapatawpha*, 107-13.

39. Bleikasten, *Most Splendid Failure*, 18.

40. Faulkner, *Soldiers' Pay*, 22, 24, 210, 104, 29.

41. Ibid., 36-37, 73, 50, 30, 133, 141; Michael Millgate, "Starting Out in the Twenties: Reflections on *Soldiers' Pay*," in Cox, *William Faulkner*, 150.

42. Faulkner, *Soldiers' Pay*, 136-37, 23, 30, 130-31.

43. Ibid., 136-38; Fass, *Damned and the Beautiful*, 261-62, 269-72, 301-6.

44. Faulkner, *Soldiers' Pay*, 43-44, 76-77, 80, 48, 51, 58, 198, 116-17.

45. Ibid., 82, 106, 219-20.

46. Ibid., 26-27, 31, 29, 104-5; Millgate, "Starting Out in the Twenties," 150; Linda W. Wagner, "Faulkner and (Southern) Women," in Harrington and Abadie, *The South and Faulkner's Yoknapatawpha*, 129-30.

47. Faulkner, *Soldiers' Pay*, 220-21.

48. Duane J. MacMillan, "'Carry on, Cadet': *Mores* and Morality in *Soldiers' Pay*," in Carey, *Faulkner*, 48; Faulkner, *Soldiers' Pay*, 47, 58; Kreiswirth, *William Faulkner*, 59.

49. Faulkner, *Soldiers' Pay*, 87-89; Brooks, *William Faulkner: Toward Yoknapatawpha*, 69.

50. Faulkner, *Soldiers' Pay*, 98, 47, 64, 49, 171; Brooks, *William Faulkner: Toward Yoknapatawpha*, 71; Bleikasten, *Most Splendid Failure*, 21.

51. Faulkner, *Soldiers' Pay*, 156-58.

52. Blotner, *Faulkner*, 1:3; Wittenberg, *Faulkner*, 44, 46; Richardson, *William Faulkner*, 158-59, 161.

53. Putzel, *Genius of Place*, 33, 44; Wittenberg, *Faulkner*, 29; Snell, *Phil Stone of Oxford*, 98, 127-28; Gwynn and Blotner, *Faulkner in the University*, 25.

54. Millgate, "Starting Out in the Twenties," 152-53; Richardson, *William Faulkner*, 159; Bleikasten, *Most Splendid Failure*, 24.

55. Faulkner, *Soldiers' Pay*, 78, 74, 18, 25, 162-63; Brooks, *William Faulkner: Toward Yoknapatawpha*, 98-99, 79 n; Millgate, *Achievement of William Faulkner*, 66.

56. Richardson, *William Faulkner*, 162; Faulkner, *Soldiers' Pay*, 212-13.

CHAPTER THREE

1. Hoffman, *Twenties*, 43-44, 52-53; Malcolm Bradbury, "The Cities of Modernism," in Bradbury and McFarlane, *Modernism*, 102-3; Cowley, *Exile's Return*, 102-3. On Paris as a center for the development of Modernism, see especially Shattuck, *Banquet Years*, and Seigel, *Bohemian Paris*.

2. Blotner, *Faulkner*, 1:448-50; Hoffman, *Twenties*, 47; Faulkner to his mother, August 6, 1925, August 13, 1925, October 3, 1925, in Faulkner, *Selected Letters*, 8-11, 27.

3. Faulkner to Mrs. Walter B. McLean, n.d. [postmarked September 10, 1925], Faulkner to his mother, August 16, 1925, n.d. [August 30, 1925], n.d. [postmarked September 10, 1925], n.d. [postmarked September 6, 1925], in Faulkner, *Selected Letters*, 19, 12, 15-17; Blotner, *Faulkner*, 1:432, 452, 447-48; Gwynn and Blotner, *Faulkner in the University*, 58. Faulkner seems to have been especially drawn to the

Luxembourg Gardens because they had been a favorite haunt of George Moore, whose *Memoirs of a Dead Life* Faulkner had once greatly admired. See Collins, introductory essay to Faulkner, *Helen*, 52–53.

4. Panthea Reid Broughton, "Faulkner's Cubist Novels," 75–76; Faulkner to his mother, n.d. [postmarked September 22, 1925], August 18, 1925, in Faulkner, *Selected Letters*, 24, 13; Lind, "Effect of Painting," 138–41.

5. Blotner, *Faulkner*, 1:453, 455, 466, 479–80; Brooks, *William Faulkner: Toward Yoknapatawpha*, 115, 119; Faulkner to his mother, August 23, 1925, n.d. [postmarked September 10, 1925], August 26, 1925, September 13, 1925, in Faulkner, *Selected Letters*, 13–14, 17, 22.

6. Faulkner, "Elmer," 432; Minter, *William Faulkner*, 56–57.

7. Faulkner, "Elmer," 365–66; Gwynn and Blotner, *Faulkner in the University*, 268; Sigmund Freud, *General Psychological Theory*, 30–31; Sensibar, *Origins of Faulkner's Art*, 117; Michael Zeitlin, "Faulkner and Psychoanalysis: The *Elmer* Case," in Kartiganer and Abadie, *Faulkner and Psychology*, 219. For an intelligent discussion of Faulkner's attempt to disguise Freud's influence on him, see Irwin, *Doubling and Incest*, 5.

8. Thomas L. McHaney, "The Elmer Papers: Faulkner's Comic Portraits of the Artist," in Meriwether, *Faulkner Miscellany*, 53; Broughton, "Faulkner's Cubist Novels," 59–60.

9. Faulkner, "Elmer," 375–77, 369–70.

10. Ibid., 374–75, 434–35, 443, 447.

11. Thomas L. McHaney, in his otherwise excellent essay on "Elmer," argues that "what seems to have spelled the doom of 'Elmer' " is Faulkner's decision to introduce a family of down-at-heels English aristocrats midway through the existing text—a judgment that has been echoed by so many subsequent critics that it is now almost a cliché. But the English aristocrats are contained within one short section of the manuscript that has no necessary connection to the plot. Since that section could easily have been cut, it is hard to see why it "spelled the doom" of the whole project. Rather, it seems more sensible to seek the cause of failure in the conception of Elmer Hodge himself. See McHaney, "Elmer Papers," 52.

12. Faulkner, "Elmer," 374–75, 434–35, 443, 447; Faulkner, *Mosquitoes*, 194; Gray, *Life of William Faulkner*, 68. For instances of Faulkner addressing his mother as "Lady" (or "Miss Lady"), see his letters to her of August 16, 1912, and April 5, 1918, as well as his letter to his father of April 6, 1918 (in which he writes, "Be sure and tell Lady that I shan't starve") in Faulkner, *Thinking of Home*, 39–40, 44, 46–47. "Lady" may not be the only source of "Addie"—it may also owe something to "Callie," the nickname of Faulkner's black mammy, Caroline Barr, who was also very small physically and notably strong minded.

13. Faulkner, "Elmer," 346, 348–49, 351–53; Zeitlin, "Faulkner and Psychoanalysis," 225–28. It should be noted that, although Jo-Addie's name is always shortened to "Jo" in the published version of "Elmer," it often appears as "Joe" in the typescript. Compare, for example, "Elmer," *Mississippi Quarterly* 36 (Summer 1983): 351, and the typescript of "Elmer" in the William Faulkner Papers, Alderman Library, Charlottesville, 11.

14. Faulkner, "Elmer," 355–56, 345; McHaney, "Elmer Papers," 42; Minter, *William Faulkner*, 56, 58. Judith Wittenberg, in her attempt to link Faulkner's biography

and his fiction, convincingly suggests that 1907, when Faulkner was ten, became "a psychically pivotal year" for him closely reflected in his later account of Elmer's childhood. For Elmer, the chief trauma was the loss of his sister, Jo-Addie, and the last link to maternal love that she provided. For Faulkner, the precipitating incident was the birth of his youngest brother, Dean, who, for a number of reasons, came to monopolize his parents' affection, leaving William, in Wittenberg's words, feeling "emotionally deserted." One might carry this analysis a step further and speculate that Dean's birth may have created an even deeper shock for young William by making obvious to him that his mother was *not* "impregnably virginal"—that the image he had held of her (and that she, with her Victorian mores, may have fostered) as exempt from physical sexuality was untenable. What likely did not occur to him at a much earlier age when his two other brothers were born may now have become an inescapable realization, shattering much of what he held dear. The repeated use of "impregnable" would appear to be a revealing clue. See Wittenberg, *Faulkner*, 23–25.

15. Wittenberg, *Faulkner*, 18–19, 51; Martin, " 'Whole Burden of Man's History,' " 614–15, 620; Collins, introductory essay to Faulkner, *Helen*, 22–23, 10; Minter, *William Faulkner*, 54, 64.
16. Faulkner, "Elmer," 378; Brooks, *William Faulkner: Toward Yoknapatawpha*, 125–26.
17. Blotner, *Faulkner*, 1:505–6, 494; Webb and Green, *William Faulkner of Oxford*, 75.
18. Collins, introductory essay to Faulkner, *Helen*, 11–12; Sensibar, introduction to Faulkner, *Vision in Spring*, xxv.
19. Brooks, *William Faulkner: Toward Yoknapatawpha*, 48–49; Faulkner, *Mayday*, 71. On Cabell as a southern post-Victorian, see Singal, *War Within*, 87–91.
20. Faulkner, *Mayday*, 52, 83–87; Brooks, *William Faulkner: Toward Yoknapatawpha*, 47–48.
21. Blotner, *Faulkner*, 1:514, 523; Bleikasten, *Most Splendid Failure*, 24–25; Kreiswirth, *William Faulkner*, 81–82, 85–87; Faulkner to Horace Liveright, n.d. [mid- or late February 1928], in Faulkner, *Selected Letters*, 40; Meriwether and Millgate, *Lion in the Garden*, 92.
22. Faulkner, *Mosquitoes*, 84, 37, 28, 15–16, 151, 9, 55.
23. Ibid., 27–28, 15, 9, 105–6.
24. Wittenberg, *Faulkner*, 41–42; Blotner, *Faulkner*, 1:415–16; Putzel, *Genius of Place*, 74, 81.
25. Faulkner, *Mosquitoes*, 200, 190–91, 205, 208.
26. Ibid., 188, 199; Wittenberg, *Faulkner*, 57; Putzel, *Genius of Place*, 74, 81–82.
27. Faulkner, *Mosquitoes*, 151; Faulkner, "Note on Sherwood Anderson," 8; Rubin, "Dixie Special," 68; Brooks, *William Faulkner: Toward Yoknapatawpha*, 143–45.
28. Faulkner, *Mosquitoes*, 280–81, 53, 43, 206, 173.
29. Faulkner, "Books and Things: American Drama Inhibitions," 93; Spratling, *File on Spratling*, 22.
30. Faulkner to Estelle Lake, n.d. [received September 2, 1919], in Faulkner, *Selected Letters*, 4; Julius Weis Friend, quoted in Brooks, *William Faulkner: Toward Yoknapatawpha*, 379; Blotner, *Faulkner*, 1:428, 554; Faulkner, *Mosquitoes*, 119.
31. Faulkner, *Mosquitoes*, 126, 19, 9–10, 39.
32. Ibid., 29, 11, 39, 24, 68, 221, 125–26; Wittenberg, *Faulkner*, 53; Rubin, "Dixie Spe-

cial," 72–73; Louis D. Rubin Jr., "William Faulkner: The Discovery of a Man's Vocation," in Wolfe, *Faulkner*, 46–47, 61–62, 64–65.

33. Faulkner, *Mosquitoes*, 11, 22–23, 272.
34. Ibid., 126, 21, 19, 24, 68, 223, 154.
35. Ibid., 223–24; Minter, *William Faulkner*, 67.
36. Faulkner, *Mosquitoes*, 22, 223. There may be yet another level of reference to the "blackness" imagery: in June 1925, while he was simultaneously engaged in courting Helen in Pascagoula and drafting *Mosquitoes*, Faulkner wrote home that he had a tan of "a grand mahogany color." Faulkner to Mrs. M. C. Falkner, n.d. [postmarked June 25, 1925], in Faulkner, *Thinking of Home*, 212.
37. Faulkner, *Mosquitoes*, 266, 127; Bleikasten, *Most Splendid Failure*, 29–30.
38. Bleikasten, *Most Splendid Failure*, 31; Faulkner, *Mosquitoes*, 267–70.
39. Faulkner, *Mosquitoes*, 269–70, 277–81.

CHAPTER FOUR

1. Blotner, *Faulkner*, 1:524–26, 531, 557; Meriwether, "Sartoris and Snopes," 36–39; James B. Meriwether, introduction to Faulkner, *Father Abraham*. Stone's press release was written to inform the citizens of Oxford of the forthcoming publication of *Mosquitoes*, though it does not provide an exact publication date. Since that novel was issued by Boni and Liveright on April 30, it seems a reasonable guess that Stone's piece was composed about a month earlier.
2. Pilkington, *Heart of Yoknapatawpha*, 3, 32; Kreiswirth, *William Faulkner*, 105, 107.
3. Bleikasten, *Most Splendid Failure*, 35–36; Faulkner, "William Faulkner's Essay on the Composition of *Sartoris*," 124; Putzel, *Genius of Place*, 297. Malcolm Cowley would later describe Faulkner as both "the proudest man" he knew and, at the same time, as "almost lacking in vanity—except in such minor concerns as riding jackets." See Cowley, *Faulkner-Cowley File*, 175.
4. Faulkner, "Rejected Manuscript Opening," 371, 375–78, 382–83.
5. Blotner, *Faulkner*, 1:532–34. Blotner contends that Faulkner wrote the genealogical material first, then the fragment detailing the aerial combat over France. However, the fact that the dead pilot's name was initially Evelyn strongly suggests that Faulkner had not yet arrived at his fundamental decision to pair a John and a Bayard in each Sartoris generation—something that was clearly in his mind by the time he turned to the family genealogy and wrote of the Civil War Sartorises.

It is striking that Faulkner's "discovery" of the South as a literary subject in early 1927 came at almost exactly the same time as that of the Nashville Agrarians. Both he and his Nashville contemporaries were struggling with the transition to Modernism and found their region's history the perfect medium for resolving that struggle—although they would do so in very different ways. See Singal, *War Within*, 200.
6. Blotner, *Faulkner*, 1:557; Faulkner, *Flags in the Dust*, 3–5; Putzel, *Genius of Place*, 118; Faulkner, *Sartoris*, 20. Because this novel was originally published in a severely cut version as *Sartoris* in 1929, with Faulkner's final typescript apparently used for the cutting, it has proved next to impossible to establish a firm text for it. Douglas

Day attempted to do so in 1973 when he edited the first published edition of *Flags in the Dust*, but he was working from an earlier typescript than the one Faulkner ultimately sent to Harcourt Brace. There is no perfect solution to this problem unless and until that final typescript someday reappears; in the meanwhile it seems best to use the 1973 edition supplemented with those passages that appear only in *Sartoris* (on the assumption that such passages were either present in the missing final typescript or were added by Faulkner on the galley proofs).

For a summary of the (often acrimonious) controversy over the authenticity of the 1973 text, see Merle Wallace Keiser, "*Flags in the Dust* and *Sartoris*," in Fowler and Abadie, *Fifty Years of Yoknapatawpha*, 47–53.

7. Faulkner, *Flags in the Dust*, 3–5, 250–52, 263–64, 59–60, 427.
8. Ibid., 121, 315, 11, 94–95, 427.
9. Wittenberg, *Faulkner*, 70; Faulkner, *Flags in the Dust*, 60, 258, 248–49, 252; Duclos, "Son of Sorrow," 173–74.
10. Faulkner, *Flags in the Dust*, 94–95, 263, 427, 7.
11. Ibid, 96–97.
12. Faulkner to Mrs. Walter B. McLean, n.d. [probably late September 1927], and n.d. [probably spring 1928], Brodsky and Hamblin, *Faulkner*, 2:7–8.
13. Faulkner, "Rejected Manuscript Opening," 375–77, 380; Kerr, *Faulkner's Gothic Domain*, 77–78.
14. Faulkner, *Flags in the Dust*, 10, 34, 44–45.
15. Ibid, 44, 330–31, 80, 278, 323, 76, 123–24, 279, 281–82, 291, 125–26.
16. Ibid., 44, 46–47, 134–35, 280, 368–69, 240.
17. Adamowski, "Bayard Sartoris," 150, 154–55; Faulkner, *Flags in the Dust*, 280; Bleikasten, *Most Splendid Failure*, 36.
18. Faulkner, *Flags in the Dust*, 74, 407–8, 76, 72–73, 361, 379, 323.
19. Adamowski, "Bayard Sartoris," 152, 154–55; Freud, "Mourning and Melancholia," in *General Psychological Theory*, 170–73; Fenichel, *Psychoanalytic Theory of Neurosis*, 400–401; Faulkner, *Flags in the Dust*, 240, 359; Bleikasten, *Most Splendid Failure*, 37.
20. Adamowski, "Bayard Sartoris," 153, 155–56; Faulkner, *Flags in the Dust*, 74, 426, 419; Faulkner, *Sartoris*, 170.
21. Faulkner, *Flags in the Dust*, 351, 76.
22. Ibid., 396; Jack R. Cofield, "Many Faces, Many Moods," in Webb and Green, *William Faulkner of Oxford*, 109.
23. Faulkner, "Rejected Manuscript Opening," 381; Faulkner, "All the Dead Pilots," in Faulkner, *Collected Stories*, 517, 514.
24. Faulkner, *Flags in the Dust*, 177–79.
25. Ibid., 190–94, 141, 179–80; Minter, *William Faulkner*, 85.
26. Faulkner, *Flags in the Dust*, 210, 182, 170, 191, 196, 284–85, 223, 185, 403–4, 399.
27. Freud, *General Psychological Theory*, 69, 74–75; Freud, *Introduction to Psychoanalysis*, 428.
28. Faulkner, *Flags in the Dust*, 186, 179, 188, 191; Faulkner, *Sartoris*, 141.
29. Freud, *General Psychological Theory*, 76, 70; Faulkner, *Flags in the Dust*, 211, 223.
30. Faulkner, *Flags in the Dust*, 343, 345, 347, 341, 348.
31. Ibid., 337–38.
32. Blotner, *Faulkner*, 1:546; Faulkner, *Flags in the Dust*, 402, 187, 203; Wittenberg, *Faulkner*, 71; Minter, *William Faulkner*, 85.

33. Scott, *Southern Lady*, 4, 7, 9–10; Kerr, *Faulkner's Gothic Domain*, 80, 84; Faulkner, *Flags in the Dust*, 31, 77, 185–86.

34. Faulkner, *Flags in the Dust*, 77, 143, 158, 431, 164, 79; Kerr, *Faulkner's Gothic Domain*, 84; Jehlen, *Class and Character*, 37; Brooks, *William Faulkner: Toward Yoknapatawpha*, 173.

35. Faulkner, *Flags in the Dust*, 431; Brooks, *William Faulkner: Toward Yoknapatawpha*, 167; Faulkner, "There Was a Queen," in Faulkner, *Collected Stories*, 739–41; Faulkner, *Sanctuary*, 61, 66, 104.

36. Faulkner, *Flags in the Dust*, 429–30.

37. Ibid., 431–33.

CHAPTER FIVE

1. Cofield, "Many Faces, Many Moods," 108.

2. Levenson, *Genealogy of Modernism*, 190–93.

3. Panthea Reid Broughton, "Faulkner's Cubist Novels," 87–88. On Faulkner's use of drinking to relieve internal tensions, see the excellent discussion in Karl, *William Faulkner*, 131–32.

4. Blotner, *Faulkner*, 1:559–62; Wittenberg, *Faulkner*, 76; Kreiswirth, *William Faulkner*, 128; Faulkner to Horace Liveright, n.d. [October 16, 1927], November 30, [1927], and n.d. [mid- or late February 1928], in Faulkner, *Selected Letters*, 38–39.

5. Faulkner to Alfred Harcourt, February 18, 1929, in Faulkner, *Selected Letters*, 43; Blotner, *Faulkner*, 1:570, 565–67; Minter, *William Faulkner*, 93; Faulkner, "An Introduction for *The Sound and the Fury*," *Southern Review*, 710.

6. Rubin, "Dixie Special," 73; Jackson J. Benson, "Quentin Compson: Self-Portrait of the Young Artist's Emotions," in Kinney, *Critical Essays: The Compson Family*, 222, 214–17, 220; Donald Kartiganer, "Quentin Compson and Faulkner's Drama of the Generations," in Kinney, *Critical Essays: The Compson Family*, 400 n; Sundquist, *Faulkner*, 22; Irwin, *Doubling and Incest*, 158; Putzel, *Genius of Place*, 143–44.

7. Bleikasten, *Most Splendid Failure*, 133, 95.

8. Faulkner, *Sound and the Fury*, 76, 124, 176; all references will be to the "corrected edition" of *The Sound and the Fury* published in 1984 unless otherwise indicated.

9. Ibid., 66, 102; Noel Polk, " 'The Dungeon Was Mother Herself': William Faulkner, 1927–1931," in Fowler and Abadie, *New Directions*, 62.

10. Davis, *Faulkner's "Negro,"* 98; Benson, "Quentin Compson," 215–16; Snell, *Phil Stone of Oxford*, 8, 15, 32.

11. Bleikasten, *Most Splendid Failure*, 193; Stonum, *Faulkner's Career*, 82; Faulkner, *Sound and the Fury*, 116, 177.

12. Faulkner, *Sound and the Fury*, 76, 80, 88, 83–85; Pilkington, *Heart of Yoknapatawpha*, 70; Slater, "Quentin's Tunnel Vision," 7.

13. Faulkner, *Sound and the Fury*, 120–21, 116–17, 86, 89, 105; Broughton, *William Faulkner*, 114; Slater, "Quentin's Tunnel Vision," 10–11.

14. Stonum, *Faulkner's Career*, 82; Olga Vickery, "Worlds in Counterpoint," in Cox, *William Faulkner*, 189; Sanford Pinsker, "Squaring the Circle in *The Sound and the Fury*," in Carey, *Faulkner*, 119; Slater, "Quentin's Tunnel Vision," 7–8; Bleikasten, *Most Splendid Failure*, 139–40.

15. Cowan, "Dream-Work in the Quentin Section," 98. 101; Faulkner, *Sound and the Fury*, 78, 148, 134–36; Bleikasten, *Most Splendid Failure*, 98–99, 101.

16. Slater, "Quentin's Tunnel Vision," 6, 8–11; Faulkner, *Sound and the Fury*, 128; Cowan, "Dream-Work in the Quentin Section," 94–95.

17. Bleikasten, *Most Splendid Failure*, 108, 224 n; Faulkner, *Sound and the Fury*, 149; Faber, "Faulkner's *The Sound and the Fury*," 331, 335.

18. Faulkner, *Sound and the Fury*, 150–56.

19. Ibid., 148–49, 122.

20. Ibid., 116, 148, 177; Olga Vickery, "Worlds in Counterpoint," 188–89.

21. Irwin, *Doubling and Incest*, 43; Hall, *Incest in Faulkner*, 42–43, 45, 49; John Earl Bassett, "Family Conflict in *The Sound and the Fury*," in Kinney, *Critical Essays: The Compson Family*, 421; Faulkner, *Sound and the Fury*, 79.

22. Gwynn and Blotner, *Faulkner in the University*, 6.

23. Faulkner, *Sound and the Fury*, 101, 82; Irwin, *Doubling and Incest*, 69; Sundquist, *Faulkner*, 17.

24. Kartiganer, *Fragile Thread*, 185; Bleikasten, *Most Splendid Failure*, 94, 129–31, 217 n; Faulkner, *Sound and the Fury*, 76.

25. Faulkner, *Sound and the Fury*, 90–91, 146, 130, 81.

26. Ibid, 86, 97–100, 114; Davis, *Faulkner's "Negro,"* 94–96, 98. I would take issue with Davis's superb analysis of Quentin's attitude toward blacks on one minor point. She suggests that the "model for living" provided by Louis Hatcher, Deacon, and the Gibson family is "incomprehensible" to Quentin. My reading of the text (particularly his remarks on Hatcher) leads me to believe that he does at some level understand that model but realizes that it will always remain inaccessible to him.

27. Faulkner, *Sound and the Fury*, 81–82, 90, 92, 95–96, 112.

28. Bleikasten, *Most Splendid Failure*, 124–25; Faber, "Faulkner's *The Sound and the Fury*," 338.

29. Faulkner, *Sound and the Fury*, 83, 80.

30. Ibid., 167, 147.

31. Ibid., 170.

32. Irwin, *Doubling and Incest*, 122–23, 90–91, 151; Sundquist, *Faulkner*, 17–18; Brown, "Language of Chaos," 549; Faulkner, *Sound and the Fury*, 90, 112, 173, 116, 80; Bleikasten, *Most Splendid Failure*, 119, 140–42.

33. Faulkner, *Sound and the Fury*, 173, 176, 81, 178–79; Slater, "Quentin's Tunnel Vision," 5.

34. Faulkner, *Sound and the Fury*, 9, 63, 19–20, 39, 45; Hall, *Incest in Faulkner*, 39.

35. Faulkner, *Sound and the Fury*, 24–27, 46, 74, 173, 133, 159, 162.

36. Gwynn and Blotner, *Faulkner in the University*, 263; Faulkner, *Sound and the Fury*, 155, 115, 149, 123–24; Faulkner, *The Sound and the Fury* (1946), 12–13; Brooks, *William Faulkner: The Yoknapatawpha Country*, 334; Fenichel, *Psychoanalytic Theory of Neurosis*, 244. In recent years the Freudian concept of nymphomania has come under attack from feminists who regard it as yet another example of the alleged misogyny to be found at the heart of psychoanalytic theory. The fact remains, though, that Faulkner in the late 1920s was very much aware of Freud's work on sexuality and appears to have drawn heavily on nymphomania, as it was understood in his day, in fashioning the character of Caddy. To date, moreover, we do

not have an equivalent gender-neutral term to describe the hypersexual behavior that can become compulsive for some women (as it can for some men)—hence the employment of "nymphomania" here in an effort to stay close to Faulkner's universe of meaning.

37. Faulkner, *Sound and the Fury*, 112, 148–50, 40–43, 47–48, 124.

38. Bleikasten, *Most Splendid Failure*, 60; Adams, *Faulkner*, 218; Pilkington, *Heart of Yoknapatawpha*, 37; Faulkner, *Sound and the Fury*, 124, 203.

39. Faulkner, *Sound and the Fury*, 282, 180, 48, 187, 70, 189.

40. Faulkner, *Sound and the Fury* (1946), 16; Kartiganer, *Fragile Thread*, 15–16; Millgate, *Achievement of William Faulkner*, 101; Bleikasten, *Most Splendid Failure*, 173–74, 151–52, 158–60, 167; Brooks, *William Faulkner: The Yoknapatawpha Country*, 328; Hall, *Incest in Faulkner*, 51; Faulkner, *Sound and the Fury*, 311, 313.

41. Fenichel, *Psychoanalytic Theory of Neurosis*, 430; Sigmund Freud, "Certain Neurotic Mechanisms in Jealousy, Paranoia, and Homosexuality," in *Sexuality and the Psychology of Love*, 163; Longley, *Tragic Mask*, 222; Faulkner, *Sound and the Fury*, 233, 191, 227.

42. Faulkner, *Sound and the Fury*, 305, 240–42, 248; Bleikasten, *Most Splendid Failure*, 235 n; Kartiganer, *Fragile Thread*, 15–16.

43. Fenichel, *Psychoanalytic Theory of Neurosis*, 431–34; Sigmund Freud, "On the Mechanism of Paranoia," in *General Psychological Theory*, 41.

44. Bleikasten, *Most Splendid Failure*, 169–70. On the southern siege mentality, see F. Sheldon Hackney, "Southern Violence," in Graham and Gurr, *Violence in America*, 496–97.

45. Vickery, "Worlds in Counterpoint," 192–93; Faulkner, *Sound and the Fury*, 206–8, 211, 257; Stonum, *Faulkner's Career*, 87.

46. Faulkner, *Sound and the Fury*, 216, 235, 196, 254–55; Davis, *Faulkner's "Negro,"* 84.

47. Erikson, *Identity and the Life Cycle*, 69–70, 107–8; Faulkner, *Sound and the Fury*, 277, 211–15, 193–94, 244, 264.

48. Faulkner, *Sound and the Fury*, 194–95, 239; Davis, *Faulkner's "Negro,"* 89–91.

49. Erikson, *Identity and the Life Cycle*, 96; Faulkner, *Sound and the Fury*, 230, 233, 182, 313; Faulkner, *Sound and the Fury* (1946), 17; Traschen, "Tragic Form of *The Sound and the Fury*," 807; Hall, *Incest in Faulkner*, 54.

50. Faulkner, *Sound and the Fury*, 274, Jean Stein, "William Faulkner: An Interview," in Hoffman and Vickery, *William Faulkner*, 74; Arthur Geffen, "Profane Time, Sacred Time, and Confederate Time in *The Sound and the Fury*," in Kinney, *Critical Essays: The Compson Family*, 234; Waggoner, *William Faulkner*, 44.

51. Kartiganer, *Fragile Thread*, 8; Traschen, "Tragic Form of *The Sound and the Fury*," 800–801; Schwartz, *Matrix of Modernism*, 12–21; Millgate, *Achievement of William Faulkner*, 91; Gail M. Morrison, "The Composition of *The Sound and the Fury*," in Bleikasten, *Faulkner's "The Sound and the Fury,"* 50; H. P. Absalom, "Order and Disorder in *The Sound and the Fury*," in Kinney, *Critical Essays: The Compson Family*, 144; Geffen, "Profane Time, Sacred Time, and Confederate Time," 235.

52. Bleikasten, *Most Splendid Failure*, 71; Absalom, "Order and Disorder in *The Sound and the Fury*," 147; Faulkner, *Sound and the Fury*, 10, 274.

53. Faulkner, *Sound and the Fury*, 288, 285, 298, 75.

54. Ibid., 293–97; Davis, *Faulkner's "Negro,"* 119–21.

55. Davis, *Faulkner's "Negro,"* 109, 116, 112, 126; Faulkner, *Sound and the Fury*, 297, Geffen, "Profane Time, Sacred Time, and Confederate Time," 240.
56. Faulkner, *Sound and the Fury*, 319–21.

CHAPTER SIX

1. Cantor, *Twentieth-Century Culture*, 124. Thomas Bender avoids the error of describing the Modernist movement as indelibly urban only to move to the opposite extreme of seeing it as detached completely from any meaningful connection to society. In his words, "the modernist impulse was to interiorize," focusing increasingly on the self rather than "the public world." That contention may hold true for much of the Modernist art of the 1920s, a decade when writers and intellectuals, revulsed by World War I, did look inward. However, when one considers the entire history of the culture, one finds that its predominant impulse was precisely to integrate the private and public so that interior experience was tied directly to social setting, either urban *or* rural—as Faulkner did in *As I Lay Dying*, or as Bender himself does so admirably in his work. See *New York Intellect*, 251–52.
2. Bleikasten, *Faulkner's "As I Lay Dying,"* 12–13, 27–29, 67–69, 133–34; Pilkington, *Heart of Yoknapatawpha*, 90–91; Calvin Bedient, "Pride and Nakedness in *As I Lay Dying*," in Brodhead, *Faulkner*, 136–38, 152; Waggoner, *William Faulkner*, 79.
3. Faulkner, *As I Lay Dying*, 104–5, 30–31, 16–17.
4. Ibid., 12, 162, 6–9, 18; Bleikasten, *Faulkner's "As I Lay Dying,"* 75.
5. Waggoner, *William Faulkner*, 77–78; Faulkner, *As I Lay Dying*, 37, 58; Cook, *From Tobacco Road to Route 66*, 41–42, 44–46.
6. Brooks, *William Faulkner: The Yoknapatawpha Country*, 154; Faulkner, *As I Lay Dying*, 95–99, 81, 109–11, 176.
7. Waggoner, *William Faulkner*, 73; Bleikasten, *Faulkner's "As I Lay Dying,"* 27–29, 108–10; Sundquist, *Faulkner*, 31–33; Kartiganer, *Fragile Thread*, 24.
8. Bleikasten, *Faulkner's "As I Lay Dying,"* 89, 95; Olga W. Vickery, "The Dimensions of Consciousness: *As I Lay Dying*," in Hoffman and Vickery, *William Faulkner*, 240; Faulkner, *As I Lay Dying*, 76, 115, 119, 99; Kartiganer, *Fragile Thread*, 25; Bedient, "Pride and Nakedness," 142–45.
9. Faulkner, *As I Lay Dying*, 10, 39, 209, 23.
10. Palliser, "Fate and Madness," 628–29; Vickery, "Dimensions of Consciousness," 233; Faulkner, *As I Lay Dying*, 186, 244, 250.
11. Faulkner, *As I Lay Dying*, 165–66, 168, 161–62; Vickery, "Dimensions of Consciousness," 240; Gwynn and Blotner, *Faulkner in the University*, 114; Brooks, *William Faulkner: The Yoknapatawpha Country*, 148–49, 152.
12. Faulkner, *As I Lay Dying*, 161, 164, 21; Stonum, *Faulkner's Career*, 106–8.
13. Faulkner, *As I Lay Dying*, 224, 49, 72–73, 77–78, 82; Bedient, "Pride and Nakedness," 147–49; Melvin Backman, "Addie Bundren and William Faulkner," in Carey, *Faulkner*, 21.
14. Wittenberg, *Faulkner*, 108–10; Stonum, *Faulkner's Career*, 118–19; Faulkner, *As I Lay Dying*, 4, 223; Vickery, "Dimensions of Consciousness," 233, 239–40.
15. Faulkner, *As I Lay Dying*, 194, 134, 108; Elizabeth M. Kerr, "*As I Lay Dying* as Ironic Quest," in Wagner, *William Faulkner*, 230–33, 241.

16. Minter, *William Faulkner*, 111–16; Blotner, *Faulkner*, 1:633, 630; Wittenberg, *Faulkner*, 91.

17. Blotner, *Faulkner*, 1:612, 601, 633, 643–50.

18. Faulkner, *Essays, Speeches, and Public Letters*, 176–78; Meriwether and Millgate, *Lion in the Garden*, 53–55; Blotner, *Faulkner*, 1:604–6, 617, 672–73; Bleikasten, *Ink of Melancholy*, 214, 219; Wasson, *Count No 'Count*, 102; Millgate, *Achievement of William Faulkner*, 115; Langford, *Faulkner's Revision of "Sanctuary*," 7.

19. Putzel, *Genius of Place*, 285; Guerard, *Triumph of the Novel*, 121.

20. Creighton, "Self-Destructive Evil in *Sanctuary*," 262; Fowler, *Faulkner's Changing Vision*, 29; Pilkington, *Heart of Yoknapatawpha*, 123; Philip M. Weinstein, "Precarious Sanctuaries: Protection and Exposure in Faulkner's Fiction," in Canfield, *Twentieth Century Interpretations*, 130–31; Faulkner, *Sanctuary*, 31.

21. Weinstein, "Precarious Sanctuaries," 132; Williams, *Faulkner's Women*, 142; Brooks, *William Faulkner: The Yoknapatawpha Country*, 131; Bleikasten, *Ink of Melancholy*, 235, 238.

22. Faulkner, *Sanctuary*, 43–45, 51, 57, 97, 243–45; Minter, *William Faulkner*, 109; David L. Frazier, "Gothicism in *Sanctuary*: The Black Pall and the Crap Table," in Canfield, *Twentieth Century Interpretations*, 52; Olga Vickery, "Crime and Punishment: *Sanctuary*," in Warren, *Faulkner*, 130.

23. Faulkner, *Sanctuary*, 75, 152, 166, 56, 156, 303–5, 250–52; Aubrey Williams, "William Faulkner's 'Temple' of Innocence," in Canfield, *Twentieth Century Interpretations*, 62.

24. Guerard, *Triumph of the Novel*, 109, 126–27; Ellen Douglas, "Faulkner's Women," in Fowler and Abadie, *"Cosmos of My Own,"* 160; Faulkner, *Sanctuary*, 30; Wasson, *Count No 'Count*, 115; Blotner, *Faulkner*, 1:613. On Faulkner's alleged misogyny, see also Fiedler, *Love and Death in the American Novel*, 319–24.

   Judith Wittenberg is probably right in suggesting that the portrait of Temple may also have reflected his ambivalent feelings toward Estelle, a slim and notoriously fickle former college belle whose father was a judge. See Wittenberg, *Faulkner*, 102.

25. Cash, *Mind of the South*, 89.

26. Jill Faulkner quoted in Rollyson, "'Counterpull,'" 224. Ellen Douglas supplies a good sample of the argument for casting Faulkner as a misogynist, contending, erroneously in my opinion, that he "has accepted without examination or question his own society's evaluation of women." Perhaps the one truism that can be ventured about Faulkner, however, is that he never accepted *any* of his society's conventional attitudes "without examination." See her "Faulkner's Women," 164. Linda Welsheimer Wagner, by contrast, claims that "what is most striking about his depictions of women is his almost unrelieved admiration—and sympathy—for them," and she depicts him as a protofeminist in "Faulkner and (Southern) Women," 128–46.

27. Wittenberg, *Faulkner*, 100; Faulkner, *Sanctuary*, 95.

28. Faulkner, *Sanctuary*, 110, 121, 192–93, 123; Minter, *William Faulkner*, 125.

29. Langford, *Faulkner's Revision of "Sanctuary*," 11–12, 14–15, 82–83.

30. Ibid., 82, 74, 88–89; Faulkner, *Sanctuary*, 14, 123.

31. Langford, *Faulkner's Revision of "Sanctuary*," 84; Faulkner, *Sanctuary*, 134, 232, 140; Vickery, "Crime and Punishment," 135.

32. Faulkner, *Sanctuary*, 180, 168, 186; Langford, *Faulkner's Revision of "Sanctuary,"* 101, 104.

33. Faulkner, *Sanctuary*, 174–75, 226, 234–35; Sundquist, *Faulkner*, 51.

34. Vickery, "Crime and Punishment," 135–36; Langford, *Faulkner's Revision of "Sanctuary,"* 116; Faulkner, *Sanctuary*, 232, 274.

35. Langford, *Faulkner's Revision of "Sanctuary,"* 73; Faulkner, *Sanctuary*, 7, 20–21. In the original text Faulkner goes even further in connecting Popeye to Victorian culture, among other things underscoring his latent sentimentality and Oedipal ties by having him secretly carry a lock of his mother's hair inside a silver watch fob. See Langford, *Faulkner's Revision of "Sanctuary,"* 74.

36. Faulkner, *Sanctuary*, 319, 323–24; T. H. Adamowski, "Faulkner's Popeye: The 'Other' as Self," in Canfield, *Twentieth Century Interpretations*, 33–34, 39, 41–42; Bleikasten, *Ink of Melancholy*, 243.

37. Faulkner, *Sanctuary*, 324–25; Adamowski, "Faulkner's Popeye," 43–44.

38. Faulkner, *Sanctuary*, 163.

39. Thomas L. McHaney, "*Sanctuary* and Frazer's Slain Kings," in Canfield, *Twentieth Century Interpretations*, 79–81, 83–84, 88, 91; Frazer, *Golden Bough*, 1–4, 9; Faulkner, *Sanctuary*, 333.

CHAPTER SEVEN

1. Karl, *Faulkner: American Writer*, 401, 506.

2. Blotner, *Faulkner*, 1:651–53, 657; Minter, *William Faulkner*, 122.

3. These observations on Rowan Oak are based on a personal visit to the house in November 1988. I am grateful to Howard Bahr, the curator of Rowan Oak at that time, for the helpful information he supplied.

4. Blotner, *Faulkner*, 1:701–2; Faulkner, *Light in August*, 430; Phyllis Hirshleifer, "As Whirlwinds in the South: An Analysis of *Light in August*," in Wagner, *William Faulkner*, 256.

5. Gwynn and Blotner, *Faulkner in the University*, 72; Faulkner, *Light in August*, 242.

6. Millgate, *Achievement of William Faulkner*, 137; Alfred Kazin, "The Stillness of *Light in August*," in Warren, *Faulkner*, 148, 151; Carl Benson, "Thematic Design in *Light in August*," in Wagner, *William Faulkner*, 263–64; Tully, "Joanna Burden," 356; Jenkins, *Faulkner and Black-White Relations*, 65–66; Blotner, *Faulkner*, 1:763–64.

7. Kartiganer, *Fragile Thread*, 41–45, 48–49; Andre Bleikasten, "*Light in August*: The Closed Society and Its Subjects," in Millgate, *New Essays on "Light in August,"* 83–84; John L. Longley Jr., "Joe Christmas: The Hero in the Modern World," in Warren, *Faulkner*, 166–67; Davis, *Faulkner's "Negro,"* 148. See also Jenkins, *Faulkner and Black-White Relations*, 93–95, 98–99, where he appears to agree that Christmas *does* achieve an original and integrated racial identity.

8. Faulkner, *Light in August*, 104–7.

9. Ibid., 107, 336–37; Erikson, *Childhood and Society*, 241–43.

10. Faulkner, *Light in August*, 124, 126, 130.

11. Broughton, *William Faulkner*, 96; Faulkner, *Light in August*, 130, 139, 147; Bleikasten, "*Light in August*: The Closed Society," 84.

12. Faulkner, *Light in August*, 137–38, 154; Jenkins, *Faulkner and Black-White Relations*, 81. In an earlier draft of the novel, Faulkner makes the connection between Joe's reaction at the sawmill and his black identity even more explicit, informing us that all the while he is fighting, Joe hears in his head the "falsetto voices" of the children at the orphange calling him "nigger." See Fadiman, *Faulkner's "Light in August*," 82, 111.

13. Faulkner, *Light in August*, 140, 161–62; Fenichel, *Psychoanalytic Theory of Neurosis*, 77–81; Rosenzweig, "Faulkner's Motif of Food," 102.

14. Faulkner, *Light in August*, 150, 163–65, 170–71; Kartiganer, *Fragile Thread*, 44–45.

15. Faulkner, *Light in August*, 156, 160, 173–74, 178–80, 190–91; Fadiman, *Faulkner's "Light in August*," 102.

16. Faulkner, *Light in August*, 195–96; Fadiman, *Faulkner's "Light in August*," 112; Davis, *Faulkner's "Negro*," 134–35.

17. Faulkner, *Light in August*, 197. Kartiganer construes Joe's tottering between two racial poles as a kind of triumph, an indication of his ability to sustain a life filled with "deliberate reversals" and "contradictory actions" out of which he bravely fashions "a single seam of personality." However, Faulkner's language seems to suggest a different interpretation. Verbs such as "writhe and strain" point to fierce psychic turmoil rather than deliberateness. It is not a vision of transcendent wholeness that drives Joe down his long "empty" street but "the courage of flagged and spurred despair." Kartiganer is certainly correct that Christmas's odyssey is taking him toward a state of "wholeness," but to say that Joe has reached that destination at this point or even come close enough to realize where he is headed would appear decidedly premature. For now the "street" runs continuously from one place to another, but "in none of them could he be quiet." See Kartiganer, *Fragile Thread*, 45; Faulkner, *Light in August*, 197.

18. Collins, "*Light in August*: Faulkner's Stained Glass Triptych," 123, 125.

19. Faulkner, *Light in August*, 234, 225, 207–8; Kazin, "Stillness of *Light in August*," 151.

20. Faulkner, *Light in August*, 208–10; Collins, "*Light in August*: Faulkner's Stained Glass Triptych," 120; Kartiganer, *Fragile Thread*, 46.

21. Faulkner, *Light in August*, 234–35, 241, 232, 243–44; Davis, *Faulkner's "Negro*," 137.

22. Faulkner, *Light in August*, 246–47, 250–51; Fadiman, *Faulkner's "Light in August*," 167; Hlavsa, "Mirror, the Lamp, and the Bed," 41–42.

23. Michael Millgate, "'A Novel: Not an Anecdote': Faulkner's *Light in August*," in Millgate, *New Essays on "Light in August*," 38; Faulkner, *Light in August*, 282–85, 289; Fadiman, *Faulkner's "Light in August*," 134.

24. Faulkner, *Light in August*, 291–93, 100–101; Jenkins, *Faulkner and Black-White Relations*, 100. The reverence that Faulkner displays here for the communal dimension of black rural life in the South is also reminiscent of the scene in *Flags in the Dust* in which Bayard Sartoris has Christmas dinner with a family of black sharecroppers and looks with envy on their domestic warmth. See Faulkner, *Flags in the Dust*, 391–94.

25. Faulkner, *Light in August*, 294, 296–97; Collins, "*Light in August*: Faulkner's Stained Glass Triptych," 95, 100; Robert Penn Warren, "Faulkner: The South, the Negro, and Time," in his edited volume *Faulkner*, 261. For further details on Faulkner's attempt to portray Christmas as a black Christ, see McCormick, *Fiction as Knowledge*, 102–5.

26. Faulkner, *Light in August*, 295, 306–7.
27. Kartiganer, *Fragile Thread*, 41, 48–49.
28. Faulkner, *Light in August*, 388, 405; Kerr, *Faulkner's Gothic Domain*, 123.
29. Faulkner, *Light in August*, 407. On castration as the equivalent of crucifixion, see chapter 9 below, page 238.
30. Faulkner, *Light in August*, 393.
31. Richard H. Brodhead, introduction to his *Faulkner*, 8–9; Faulkner, *Light in August*, 306, 302; Robert Penn Warren, "Faulkner: The South, the Negro, and Time," 259; Davis, *Faulkner's "Negro,"* 130–32; Karl, *Faulkner: American Writer*, 448–49; Nilon, *Faulkner and the Negro*, 73.
32. Fadiman, *Faulkner's "Light in August,"* 24–25, 42–43, 36, 56, 111, 202; Karl, *Faulkner: American Writer*, 466 n.
33. Faulkner, *Light in August*, 298–99, 301, 305.
34. Tully, "Joanna Burden," 361; Bleikasten, *"Light in August*: The Closed Society," 86.
35. Faulkner, *Light in August*, 211–13, 197.
36. Ibid., 212–14, 216–17; Bleikasten, *"Light in August*: The Closed Society," 86.
37. Fadiman, *Faulkner's "Light in August,"* 90–91.
38. Faulkner, *Light in August*, 221; Tully, "Joanna Burden," 362, 365.

CHAPTER EIGHT

1. Wittenberg, *Faulkner*, 132–34; Blotner, *Faulkner*, 1:803, 805, 795–97; Williamson, *Faulkner and Southern History*, 321; Zender, *Crossing of the Ways*, 69.
2. For information on Faulkner's initial encounters with Hollywood, see Blotner, *Faulkner*, 1:771–81, 792–94, 800–802, 850–53; and Karl, *Faulkner: American Writer*, 473–74, 482–87.
3. Urgo, *"Absalom, Absalom!*: The Movie," 57.
4. Faulkner, untitled draft introduction to *The Sound and the Fury*, n.d., Rowan Oak Papers, University of Mississippi Library.
5. Faulkner to Morton Goldman, n.d. [August,1934], in Faulkner, *Selected Letters*, 84. As Joanne V. Creighton points out, Faulkner toned down the chauvinism and sentimentality considerably when he later revised the stories for *The Unvanquished*; see her *William Faulkner's Craft of Revision*, 74–78.
6. Minter, *William Faulkner*, 143–46, 149.
7. Brooks, *William Faulkner: Toward Yoknapatawpha*, 179, 183; MacMillan, *"Pylon*: From Short Stories to Major Work," 207; Faulkner, *Pylon*, 238, 15.
8. Faulkner, *Pylon*, 119, 53; MacMillan, *"Pylon*: From Short Stories to Major Work," 192, 212.
9. Gwynn and Blotner, *Faulkner in the University*, 73; Hunt, "Keeping the Hoop Skirts Out," 38; William Faulkner, "Evangeline," in his *Uncollected Stories*, 584, 609; William Faulkner, "Wash," in his *Collected Stories*, 539–40.
10. Faulkner, *Flags in the Dust*, 3–5; Faulkner, *Absalom, Absalom!*, 4–7; Patricia Tobin, "The Time of Myth and History in *Absalom, Absalom!*," in Budd and Cady, *On Faulkner*, 80.
11. On the experience of the typical Deep South planter, see Oakes, *Ruling Race*, 81–87.

12. Faulkner, *Absalom, Absalom!*, 268, 41, 211.

13. On the lack of racial prejudice in Sutpen, see Weinstein, *Faulkner's Subject*, 132; Brooks, *William Faulkner: The Yoknapatawpha Country*, 299; Sabiston, "Women, Blacks, and Sutpen's Mythopoeic Drive," 17.

14. Faulkner, *Absalom, Absalom!*, 56.

15. Ibid., 185–86, 190, 192; Parker, *"Absalom, Absalom!,"* 102; King, *Southern Renaissance*, 123.

16. Faulkner, *Absalom, Absalom!*, 191–92, 178, 218; James Guetti, *"Absalom, Absalom!: The Extended Simile,"* in Muhlenfeld, *Faulkner's "Absalom, Absalom!,"* 77–78, 82; Friedman, *William Faulkner*, 56; Irwin, *Doubling and Incest*, 99; Garzilli, *Circles without Center*, 53.

17. Faulkner, *Absalom, Absalom!*, 34–35; Faulkner, "The Big Shot," in his *Uncollected Stories*, 509.

18. Jenkins, *Faulkner and Black-White Relations*, 197; Faulkner, *Absalom, Absalom!*, 99, 226, 231.

19. Jenkins, *Faulkner and Black-White Relations*, 195; Faulkner, *Absalom, Absalom!*, 229.

20. Lynd, *Shame and the Search for Identity*, 57; Faulkner, *Absalom, Absalom!*, 188–89. It is also noteworthy that Faulkner here reverses the prevailing literary and cultural imagery associated with the "laughter" that African Americans directed toward whites. The conventional view held that such laughter was benign, an expression of general amusement at the pretensions of civilization by a people who supposedly lived close to nature. As Sherwood Anderson put it in *Dark Laughter* (1925), a novel written at the time Faulkner was virtually a member of Anderson's household in New Orleans, "They are like children looking at you with their strangely soft innocent eyes. White eyes, white teeth in a brown face—laughter. It is a laughter that does not hurt too much." By a decade later, Faulkner, through his journey of exploration into the southern psyche, had learned that such laughter was far darker and more sharply barbed than Anderson, and most other white writers, ever realized. See Anderson, *Dark Laughter*, 260.

21. Faulkner, *Absalom, Absalom!*, 210, 39; Andre Bleikasten, "Fathers in Faulkner," in Davis, *Fictional Father*, 140; Martin Christadler, "William Faulkner's *Absalom, Absalom!*: History, Consciousness, and Transcendence," in Coy and Gresset, *Faulkner and History*, 160; T. H. Adamowski, "Children of the Idea: Heroes and Family Romances in *Absalom, Absalom!*," in Muhlenfeld, *Faulkner's "Absalom, Absalom!,"* 144; Radloff, "Fate of Demonism in William Faulkner," 27.

22. Gwynn and Blotner, *Faulkner in the University*, 84; Faulkner, *Absalom, Absalom!*, 201, 199.

23. Faulkner, *Absalom, Absalom!*, 14.

24. Ibid., 71, 77; Weinstein, *Faulkner's Subject*, 92–93; Broughton, *William Faulkner*, 137.

25. Faulkner, *Absalom, Absalom!*, 268, 74, 82, 58, 98, 254–56.

26. Ibid., 58–59, 253, 75–77, 86; Milum, "Faulkner and the Cavalier Tradition," 581, 584, 589.

27. Faulkner, *Absalom, Absalom!*, 76–78, 95, 56, 86.

28. Ibid., 81, 264, 75–78.

29. Ibid., 52, 21–22, 17–18, 126, 96; Elisabeth Muhlenfeld, " 'We Have Waited Long Enough': Judith Sutpen and Charles Bon," in Muhlenfeld, *Faulkner's "Absalom,*

Absalom!," 176–77; Sabiston, "Women, Blacks, and Sutpen's Mythopoeic Drive," 23–24.

30. Faulkner, *Absalom, Absalom!,* 55, 73, 139.

31. Ibid., 77, 85, 83, 75, 95. On Faulkner's appropriation of the sensibility of cubism for literary purposes, see the two excellent essays by Pamela Reid Broughton, "Cubist Novel" and "Faulkner's Cubist Novels," 36–94.

32. Faulkner, *Absalom, Absalom!,* 277; Tobin, "Time of Myth and History," 89; Irwin, *Doubling and Incest,* 59; George Fitzhugh, "Sociology for the South," in Erik L. McKitrick, *Slavery Defended,* 46. For further analysis of the incest triangle in *Absalom, Absalom!,* see Singal, *War Within,* 192–194.

33. Faulkner, *Absalom, Absalom!,* 220, 285–86.

34. Weinstein, *Faulkner's Subject,* 94.

35. Faulkner, *Absalom, Absalom!,* 158–61; Davis, *Faulkner's "Negro",* 202–4.

36. Faulkner, *Absalom, Absalom!,* 162, 164, 167.

37. Ibid., 166–67; Broughton, *William Faulkner,* 72.

38. Faulkner, *Absalom, Absalom!,* 166, 160, 168.

39. Ibid., 169.

40. John V. Hagopian, "The Biblical Background of *Absalom, Absalom!,*" in Muhlenfeld, *Faulkner's "Absalom, Absalom!,"* 131–34; Stephen M. Ross, "Faulkner's *Absalom, Absalom!* and the David Story: A Speculative Contemplation," in Frontain and Wojcik, *David Myth,* 138–41; Schoenberg, *Old Tales and Talking,* 48; Rose, "From Genesis to Revelation," 220, 225; Levins, *Faulkner's Heroic Design,* 37–38, 4; Faulkner, *Absalom, Absalom!,* 301.

41. Faulkner, *Absalom, Absalom!,* 77.

42. Ibid., 243, 245–49.

43. Ibid., 261, 213.

44. Ibid., 102–3.

45. Ibid., 104, 279, 249; Broughton, *William Faulkner,* 178; Muhlenfeld, " 'We Have Waited Long Enough,' " 181. Broughton, an exceptionally astute reader of Faulkner in most instances, does make the error of attributing the *"decline to sit still"* passage to Henry rather than to Bon. On the affinity with Tillich, see also Hunt, *William Faulkner,* 127.

46. Faulkner, *Absalom, Absalom!,* 284–87; Faulkner, *Sound and the Fury,* 79; Jenkins, *Faulkner and Black-White Relations,* 217; Price, "Shreve's Bon," 332; Friedman, *William Faulkner,* 72; Hunt, *William Faulkner,* 133.

47. Broughton, *William Faulkner,* 178; Faulkner, *Absalom, Absalom!,* 114, 121, 155–56, 101; Muhlenfeld, " 'We Have Waited Long Enough,' " 179, 184–85; Ragan, *Faulkner's "Absalom, Absalom!,"* 80–81.

48. Faulkner, *Absalom, Absalom!,* 156, 100–101, 71; Parker, *"Absalom, Absalom!,"* 50–51.

49. Faulkner, *Absalom, Absalom!,* 101, 153–54.

50. "Interview with Jean Stein Vanden Heuvel," in Meriwether and Millgate, *Lion in the Garden,* 253; Faulkner quoted in Reesman, *American Designs,* 50; Faulkner, "Albert Camus," in his *Essays, Speeches, and Public Letters,* 113–14; Christadler, "William Faulkner's *Absalom, Absalom!,*" 163.

51. Minter, *William Faulkner,* 37. On Faulkner's early aestheticism, see chapter 2 above, pages 48–53.

52. Hoffman, *Faulkner's Country Matters*, 11; Parker, *"Absalom, Absalom!,"* 156; Porter, *Seeing and Being*, 242, 259; Schwartz, *Matrix of Modernism*, 17–20; Myers, *William James*, 312, 324–26.

53. For examples of recent writers on *Absalom* who maintain that there is no preferred interpretation within it, allowing the reader to decide on whatever interpretation he or she might wish, see Reesman, *American Designs*, 85–86, 102; Morris, *Reading Faulkner*, 210; and Matthews, *Play of Faulkner's Language*, 118–19. On Dewey, see his *Child and Curriculum*, 17–18.

54. Jehlen, *Class and Character*, 58–59; Wittenberg, *Faulkner*, 144–45; Faulkner, *Absalom, Absalom!*, 115, 139; Kartiganer, *Fragile Thread*, 73; Walter Brylowski, "Faulkner's 'Mythology,'" in Muhlenfeld, *Faulkner's "Absalom, Absalom!,"* 120–21; Ragan, *Faulkner's "Absalom, Absalom!,"* 51, 71–74, 77–78; Watson, *William Faulkner*, 138.

Given Rosa's tiny body, dark hair, and strong-mindedness, it is tempting to think of her as another variant of the "Dianalike" woman of Faulkner's earlier fiction. If so, one cannot help but notice how that figure has turned from an object of desire into one of pity as Faulkner achieved more and more emotional distance from his mother and her culture. The character of Rosa Coldfield, though, may owe less to Maud Falkner than to Phil Stone's mother, a die-hard Confederate loyalist who, though her name was Rosamond, was called "Miss Rosie."

55. Jehlen, *Class and Character*, 59; Ragan, *Faulkner's "Absalom, Absalom!,"* 95; Millgate, *Achievement of William Faulkner*, 154; Faulkner, *Absalom, Absalom!*, 57, 80; Levins, *Faulkner's Heroic Design*, 16–21.

56. Parker, *"Absalom, Absalom!,"* 162–63; Rollyson, *Uses of the Past in Faulkner*, 92–93; Faulkner, *Absalom, Absalom!*, 243, 253, 237, 280; Kartiganer, *Fragile Thread*, 100–102; Tobin, "Time of Myth and History," 87; Johnson, "Gender, Sexuality, and the Artist," 11–12; Radloff, "Dialogue and Insight," 270–71.

57. Ragan, *Faulkner's "Absalom, Absalom!,"* 90; Schoenberg, *Old Tales and Talking*, 146; Waggoner, *William Faulkner*, 158; Rollyson, *Uses of the Past in Faulkner*, 38; Vande Kieft, "Faulkner's Defeat of Time," 1107.

58. Faulkner, *Absalom, Absalom!*, 7, 293, 296; Gwynn and Blotner, *Faulkner in the University*, 275; Hunt, "Keeping the Hoopskirts Out," 43.

59. Faulkner, *Absalom, Absalom!*, 210; Lensing, "Metaphor of Family," 116; Singal, *War Within*, 194–95.

The argument that we see the same Quentin in *The Sound and the Fury* and *Absalom, Absalom!* has been developed most extensively by John Irwin in his *Doubling and Incest* (especially pp. 25–30). In the opinion of the present writer, Irwin runs roughshod over the textual evidence in order to sustain what he admits in his subtitle is a "speculative reading" of Faulkner, and his book should be used with great caution as a result. There are many points of divergence between the two novels that Irwin conveniently ignores, ranging from the fact that Caddy, Benjy, and Jason are never mentioned in *Absalom* (it is almost as if Quentin has become an only child) to the way Quentin and Shreve have separate rooms in *The Sound and the Fury* (as we learn on p. 172) but share the same room in *Absalom*. For the contention that the two Quentins are different, see Gresset, *Fascination*, 235; Kuyk, *Sutpen's Design*, 93, 110–11; Parker, *"Absalom, Absalom!,"* 39; Ragan, *Annotations*, 70; Rollyson, *Uses of the Past in Faulkner*, 80–81; and Guerard, *Triumph of the Novel*, 311.

60. Faulkner, *Absalom, Absalom!*, 259-60, 288-89, 298-99, 301, 309; Ragan, *Faulkner's "Absalom, Absalom!,"* 89-90, 104, 124, 146, 152; Schoenberg, *Old Tales and Talking*, 117, frontispiece, 4, 15; Zender, *Crossing of the Ways*, 163 n.

61. Faulkner, *Absalom, Absalom!*, 300-302, 296; Langford, *Faulkner's Revision of "Absalom,"* 40-41; Blotner, *Faulkner*, 2:936.

62. Bluestein, "Faulkner and Miscegenation," 154-57, 160-61; Faulkner, *Absalom, Absalom!*, 296, 247, 58; Patrick Samway, "New Material for Faulkner's *Intruder in the Dust*," in Meriwether, *Faulkner Miscellany*, 107-12; Sabiston, "Women, Blacks, and Sutpen's Mythopoeic Drive," 25.

63. Faulkner, *Absalom, Absalom!*, 302; Jordan, *White over Black*, 144, 542-43; Snead, *Figures of Division*, ix, 14. Noel Polk has claimed that what is really at stake in this closing passage of *Absalom*, which Polk refers to as "Shreve McCannon's nonsense," is "the extinction of the black race." However, that would hold true only if one believes that all races are pure. When Shreve contends that "in time the Jim Bonds are going to conquer the western hemisphere," he is saying, in effect, that the majority of the population will someday be made up of individuals whose ancestry is a mix of European and African strains—which would make them "black" by the standards of racial identification prevailing today. It is true that Shreve goes on to predict that "as they spread toward the poles they will bleach out again like the rabbits and the birds do, so they wont show up *so* sharp against the snow" (emphasis added). The key word, however, is "so," which suggests that the racially amalgamated Americans of the future *will* still show up against the snow—presumably because their skin color will be at least a few shades darker than white. If that means that "the black race" will have become extinct, then it entails the extinction of the white race as well in favor of a radically new genetic blend representing the ultimate stage in racial integration. Far from being "nonsense," Faulkner's effort to peer into the future would seem to have been extraordinarily prescient and courageous. See Polk, "Man in the Middle: Faulkner and the Southern White Moderate," in Fowler and Abadie, *Faulkner and Race*, 143-44, 132.

64. Millgate, *Achievement of Faulkner*, 170; Reed, *Faulkner's Narrative*, 180; Faulkner, *Unvanquished*, 57; Backman, *Faulkner*, 118-19.

65. Porter, *Seeing and Being*, 219; Jehlen, *Class and Character*, 48-49.

66. Faulkner, *Unvanquished*, 29-32, 117, 128, 138-41.

67. Ibid, 175, 170-71, 164-65, 178-81, 186-88.

68. Ralph Ellison, quoted in Lowe, "*The Unvanquished*: Faulkner's Nietzschean Skirmish," 424; Faulkner, *Unvanquished*, 68, 64, 121.

69. Faulkner, *Unvanquished*, 16, 68, 99, 104, 164, 28, 162, 152; Jenkins, *Faulkner and Black-White Relations*, 114, 128-29.

70. Faulkner, *Unvanquished*, 190-91; Reed, *Faulkner's Narrative*, 180; Pilkington, *Heart of Yoknapatawpha*, 193, 197; Backman, *Faulkner*, 113-14; Jehlen, *Class and Character*, 54.

CHAPTER NINE

1. Blotner, *Faulkner*, 2:1014; Banning, "Changing Moral Standards," 1; Richards, "Sex under *The Wild Palms*," 330; Joseph J. Moldenhauer, "Unity of Theme and

Structure in *The Wild Palms*," in Hoffman and Vickery, *William Faulkner*, 305, 309, 313; Faith Pullin, "Faulkner, Women, and Yoknapatawpha: From Symbol to Autonomy," in Lee, *William Faulkner*, 76.

2. McHaney, *Faulkner's "The Wild Palms*," 49, 30, 52-54, 72, 99; François Pitavy, "Forgetting Jerusalem: An Ironical Chart for *The Wild Palms*," in Gresset and Polk, *Intertextuality in Faulkner*, 122; Harrington, *Faulkner's Fables of Creativity*, 69-71, 84.

3. Page, *Faulkner's Women*, 122, 128-29, 133; William Price Cushman, "Knowledge and Involvement in Faulkner's *The Wild Palms*," in Carey, *Faulkner*, 33-35; Bernhardt, " 'Being Worthy Enough,' " 351, 355; Levins, *Faulkner's Heroic Design*, 135-36; Anne Goodwyn Jones, " 'The Kotex Age': Women, Popular Culture, and *The Wild Palms*," in Fowler and Abadie, *Faulkner and Popular Culture*, 154-55; Millgate, *Achievement of William Faulkner*, 174; Wittenberg, *Faulkner*, 174-75; Broughton, *William Faulkner*, 142-44.

4. Broughton, "Interview with Meta Carpenter Wilde," 777, 797; Wilde and Borsten, *Loving Gentleman*, 48, 62-63, 279, 42, 18, 77-78.

5. Judith L. Sensibar, " 'Drowsing Maidenhead Symbol's Self': Faulkner and the Fictions of Love," in Fowler and Abadie, *Faulkner and the Craft of Fiction*, 137; Wilde and Borsten, *Loving Gentleman*, 52, 46. Some recent Faulkner biographers have failed to comprehend his complex relationship with Estelle, erroneously depicting the marriage as loveless and unredeemable. Fredrick R. Karl, for example, speaks of Faulkner as being "in actuality, divorced from his wife" while living in "a home almost disintegrating." See Karl, *Faulkner: American Writer*, 597, 607, and Oates, *William Faulkner*, 83-84.

6. Sensibar, " 'Drowsing Maidenhead Symbol's Self,' " 134-35, 143-44; Wilde and Borsten, *Loving Gentleman*, 181, 184-85, 311, 195; Wittenberg, *Faulkner*, 171; Grimwood, *Heart in Conflict*, 88.

7. Joseph Blotner, "William Faulkner: Life and Art," in Fowler and Abadie, *Faulkner and Women*, 16; Blotner, *Faulkner*, 1:419, 438, 509-10, 2:978, 981-82; Gray, *Life of William Faulkner*, 241-42; McHaney, *Faulkner's "The Wild Palms*," 21-22; Zender, "Unpublished Letters," 535-36, 538. McHaney suggests still another possible model for Charlotte in Sherwood Anderson's former wife, Tennessee Mitchell, a sexually active woman who liked to fashion satirical figures out of clay. However, since Faulkner probably never met Mitchell, it seems doubtful that she would exercise as powerful a hold on his imagination as Meta and Helen Baird clearly did. See McHaney, *Faulkner's "The Wild Palms*," 10-12.

8. Faulkner, *Wild Palms*, 102, 99-100, 47, 91, 89; Page, *Faulkner's Women*, 128; Eldred, "Faulkner's Still Life," 148-49. Andre Bleikasten has taken note of the affinity between Faulkner and Giacometti; see his *Ink of Melancholy*, 27.

9. Faulkner, *Wild Palms*, 141, 88, 109, 87.

10. McHaney, *Faulkner's "The Wild Palms*," xviii, 27; Faulkner, *Wild Palms*, 31-33, 279-80, 16.

11. Faulkner, *Wild Palms*, 34-35, 38-39; Brooks, *William Faulkner: Toward Yoknapatawpha*, 209.

12. Faulkner, *Wild Palms*, 45-48; Cushman, "Knowledge and Involvement," 32; Bernhardt, " 'Being Worthy Enough,' " 355.

13. Faulkner, *Wild Palms*, 89, 81-83, 4, 85.

14. Ibid., 40–41, 89, 38, 133, 96–97; Sergei Chakovsky, "Women in Faulkner's Novels: Author's Attitude and Artistic Function," in Fowler and Abadie, *Faulkner and Women*, 73–74, 78; Johnson, "Gender, Sexuality, and the Artist," 6.
15. Faulkner, *Wild Palms*, 99, 110–12, 105, 48; Cushman, "Knowledge and Involvement," 33–34.
16. McHaney, *Faulkner's "The Wild Palms*," 94; Faulkner, *Wild Palms*, 116–17, 125–27, 132. McHaney stresses how Harry and Charlotte "sleep separately and engage in separate activities" at the lake to demonstrate how they fail to "achieve true rapport between themselves." But the middle-aged doctor and his wife, Faulkner tells us, have "slept in the same bed for twenty-three years" and spend much of their time together, yet we are plainly meant to regard their relationship as a living hell. One suspects that Charlotte's willingness *not* to force Harry to be with her all the time is a measure of her respect for his integrity as a person. See McHaney, *Faulkner's "The Wild Palms*," 91; Faulkner, *Wild Palms*, 4.
17. Faulkner, *Wild Palms*, 132–41, 196; McHaney, *Faulkner's "The Wild Palms*," 101, 105.
18. Waggoner, *William Faulkner*, 146; McHaney, *Faulkner's "The Wild Palms*," 16; Hemingway, *Farewell to Arms*, 289–92, 296, 302–3; Faulkner, *Wild Palms*, 180, 191–92, 183–84.
19. Faulkner, *Wild Palms*, 54, 203, 83.
20. Eldred, "Faulkner's Still Life," 143, 145–46; Faulkner, *Wild Palms*, 86, 205.
21. Faulkner, *Wild Palms*, 59, 125, 227–28; Bernhardt, " 'Being Worthy Enough,' " 357–58; McHaney, *Faulkner's "The Wild Palms*," 137.
22. Eldred, "Faulkner's Still Life," 147.
23. Joseph J. Moldenhauer, "Unity of Theme and Structure in *The Wild Palms*," in Hoffman and Vickery, *William Faulkner*, 308, 313; Minter, *William Faulkner*, 176.
24. Moldenhauer, "Unity of Theme and Structure," 310; Faulkner, *Wild Palms*, 109, 306; Faulkner, *Light in August*, 407.
25. Bleikasten, *Ink of Melancholy*, 330; Faulkner, *Wild Palms*, 109, 136; Niebuhr, *Interpretation of Christian Ethics*, 111–12; "Interview with Jean Stein vanden Heuvel," in Meriwether and Millgate, *Lion in the Garden*, 246–47; Faulkner, *Wild Palms*, 136.
26. McHaney, *Faulkner's "The Wild Palms*," 167; Hemingway, *Farewell to Arms*, 332, 327; Cushman, "Knowledge and Involvement," 34; Faulkner, *Wild Palms*, 54, 324; Eldred, "Faulkner's Still Life," 155. This scene of Harry in jail would strike a special resonance with French existentialist writers, epitomizing as it did their philosophy. Albert Camus, for one, drew heavily on it in *The Stranger*. His hero, Meursault, experiences a sensory rebirth much like Harry's while engaging the world through his prison window: " 'The stars were shining down on my face. Sounds of the countryside came faintly in, and the cool night air, veined with smells of earth and salt, fanned my cheeks.' " See Camus, *Stranger*, 153.
27. McHaney, *Faulkner's "The Wild Palms*," 193; Faulkner, *Wild Palms*, 315–16, 324, 120; Lynn, *Hemingway*, 386, 390. I am grateful to my former teaching partner, Anne Boyle, now a member of the Department of English at Wake Forest University, for sharing with me her insights about the final scene of *The Wild Palms* and about Faulkner's use of feminist imagery in general.

That Thomas McHaney and Gary Harrington view Harry's transformation as a spiritual triumph stands sharply at odds with their hostile characterizations of

Charlotte Rittenmeyer, the agent most responsible for bringing about that transformation. According to McHaney, Harry in jail "discovers that there is a fierce joy to life" and experiences nothing less than transcendence. Harrington speaks of how Harry's "epiphanic insight" leads him "to achieve a mature and authentic perspective on his past and present." Yet these two authors both lambaste Charlotte for her supposed superficiality and dishonesty. One has to ask how, if Charlotte is so worthless, can Harry be saved by remembering her? It would seem a major contradiction in their readings of the novel. See McHaney, *Faulkner's "The Wild Palms,"* 188, 190, 52–54, 81, and Harrington, "Distant Mirrors," 42–43, and *Faulkner's Fables of Creativity,* 85–86, 69–71.

28. Gwynn and Blotner, *Faulkner in the University,* 171; McHaney, *Faulkner's "The Wild Palms,"* 39.

29. Faulkner, *Wild Palms,* 284, 277, 61–61; Gray, *Life of William Faulkner,* 243–44.

30. Faulkner, *Wild Palms,* 232, 299.

31. Ibid., 23–25, 248, 338–39, 153; Feaster, "Faulkner's *Old Man,*" 90, 93; Cumpiano, "Motif of Return," 190.

32. Faulkner, *Wild Palms,* 326, 144–47, 156–57, 258, 251, 162–63, 173 74; Broughton, *William Faulkner,* 42–44.

33. Faulkner, *Wild Palms,* 339; Broughton, *William Faulkner,* 48; Jones, "'Kotex Age,'" 142–43; Gallagher, "'To Love and to Honor,'" 214. For examples of writers who claim the Tall Convict reflects Faulkner's own misogyny, see, for example, Grimwood, *Heart in Conflict,* 99; Mortimer, "Ironies of Transcendent Love," 41–42; and Wittenberg, *Faulkner,* 179.

34. Faulkner, *Wild Palms,* 327, 277, 339; Faulkner to Bennett Cerf, n.d. [received January 19, 1939], in Faulkner, *Selected Letters,* 109.

35. Harrington, *Faulkner's Fables of Creativity,* 87; Faulkner to Robert N. Linscott, March 13 [1946], in Faulkner, *Selected Letters,* 228; Faulkner, remarks at Nagano Seminar, reprinted in Meriwether and Millgate, *Lion in the Garden,* 146–47; Harrington, "Distant Mirrors," 41–44.

36. Snell, *Phil Stone of Oxford,* 197–98; Hoffman, *Faulkner's Country Matters,* 74–75; Faulkner, *Father Abraham,* 20.

37. Minter, *William Faulkner,* 177–78; Faulkner to Robert K. Haas, n.d [received December 15, 1938], in Faulkner, *Selected Letters,* 107; Faulkner, *Father Abraham,* 19, 14; Faulkner, *Hamlet,* 22, 52.

38. Faulkner, *Father Abraham,* 20; Faulkner, *Hamlet,* 63–65, 67; Stineback, *Shifting World,* 145; Gray, *Life of William Faulkner,* 269. Some question exists as to the time when the events in *The Hamlet* are set. In a letter written while the novel was being composed, Faulkner told his editor that the concluding section "happens in 1890, approximately." Asked about this during a class session at the University of Virginia in 1957, he responded that the correct date should be either 1906 or 1907. That not only makes better sense, but it agrees almost exactly with John Pilkington's result when he cleverly works forward and backward from the dates on Eula Varner Snopes's tombstone in *The Mansion.* See Faulkner to Saxe Commins, n.d. [October 1939], in Faulkner, *Selected Letters,* 115; Gwynn and Blotner, *Faulkner in the University,* 29; Pilkington, *Heart of Yoknapatawpha,* 223.

39. Faulkner, *Town,* 283; Faulkner, *Hamlet,* 19, 66; Waggoner, *William Faulkner,* 185.

40. Faulkner, *Hamlet*, 24, 270, 28–29.
41. Ibid., 15–17, 50, 90; Faulkner, "Barn Burning," in Faulkner, *Collected Stories*, 7–8; Milum, "Faulkner and the Cavalier Tradition," 585.
42. Faulkner, *Hamlet*, 23, 30; Hoffman, *Faulkner's Country Matters*, 80, 85; Vickery, *Novels of William Faulkner*, 172; Kartiganer, *Fragile Thread*, 116.
43. Faulkner, *Hamlet*, 54–58, 90, 51, 275, 146, 7; Noel Polk, "Faulkner and Respectability," in Fowler and Abadie, *Fifty Years of Yoknapatawpha*, 120; Minter, *William Faulkner*, 181.
44. Wyatt-Brown, *Southern Honor*, 34–35, 45, 155–56, 172.
45. T. Y. Greet, "The Theme and Structure of Faulkner's *The Hamlet*," in Hoffman and Vickery, *William Faulkner*, 343; Meeter, "Male and Female," 413; Hoffman, *Faulkner's Country Matters*, 102; Faulkner, quoted in Creighton, *William Faulkner's Craft of Revision*, 26.
46. Faulkner, *Hamlet*, 32–36, 40–46, 27, 30; Hoffman, *Faulkner's Country Matters*, 83–84.
47. Faulkner, *Hamlet*, 103–5, 113, 119–22, 124, 127.
48. Ibid., 132–34, 139, 141.
49. Ibid., 63, 209, 214–15; Minter, *William Faulkner*, 6–7.
50. Faulkner, *Hamlet*, 217–20.
51. Ibid., 74–75, 223, 240, 243.
52. Ibid., 221–22, 224; Backman, *Faulkner*, 154.
53. Guerard, *Triumph of the Novel*, 217; Watson, *Snopes Dilemma*, 54, 56; Faulkner, *Hamlet*, 222, 227, 262; Beck, *Man in Motion*, 28; Kartiganer, *Fragile Thread*, 124.
54. Faulkner, *Hamlet*, 90–91, 13, 55–56, 367; Millgate, *Achievement of Faulkner*, 197; Creighton, *William Faulkner's Craft of Revision*, 27–28.
55. Brooks, *William Faulkner: The Yoknapatawpha Country*, 185; Elizabeth D. Rankin, "Chasing Spotted Horses: The Quest for Human Dignity in Faulkner's Snopes Trilogy," in Carey, *Faulkner*, 143; Watson, *Snopes Dilemma*, 59–60; Faulkner, *Hamlet*, 279, 283, 290.
56. Milton Rugoff, review of *The Hamlet* in the *New York Herald Tribune*, March 31, 1940, quoted in Blotner, *Faulkner*, 2:1040; Waggoner, *William Faulkner*, 184; Watson, *Snopes Dilemma*, 12; Grimwood, *Heart in Conflict*, 163–65; Faulkner, interview with Michel Mok, October 17, 1939, in Meriwether and Millgate, *Lion in the Garden*, 39; Lawson, "Grotesque-Comic in the Snopes Trilogy," 113.
57. Blotner, *Faulkner*, 1:258–60; Williamson, *Faulkner and Southern History*, 194, 60; Grimwood, *Heart in Conflict*, 164; Duclos, "Son of Sorrow," 320, 322.
58. Friedman, *William Faulkner*, 157; Woodrow Stroble, "Flem Snopes: A Crazed Mirror," in Carey, *Faulkner*, 201; Gwynn and Blotner, *Faulkner in the University*, 33.
59. Faulkner, *Hamlet*, 371–73, 23; Wittenberg, *Faulkner*, 189; Stineback, *Shifting World*, 145, 150.

CHAPTER TEN

1. Andre Bleikasten, "A Private Man's Public Voice," in Gresset and Ohashi, *Faulkner: After the Nobel Prize*, 47, 49.

2. Ibid., 48, 53; Faulkner quoted in Malcolm Cowley, *Faulkner-Cowley File*, 114; Gray, *Life of William Faulkner*, 274–75; Wittenberg, *Faulkner*, 191.

3. Richard H. King, "Lucas Beauchamp and William Faulkner: Blood Brothers," in Kinney, *Critical Essays: The McCaslin Family*, 234; Howe, *William Faulkner*, 122.

4. Dardis, *Thirsty Muse*, 33, 37, 43–44, 67, 26–29; Karl, *Faulkner: American Writer*, 445–46.

5. For the information in this and subsequent paragraphs regarding the effect of alcohol on the brain and Faulkner's neurological status, I am indebted to two specialists in neurology who were kind enough to share their expertise with me, Dr. Andrew Stern of Rochester General Hospital and Dr. David Goldblatt of the University of Rochester Medical Center, and to my colleague H. Wesley Perkins of the Department of Anthropology and Sociology at Hobart and William Smith Colleges. I am also grateful to Professor Charles W. Eagles of the University of Mississippi, who attempted to track down Faulkner's medical records within Oxford. It appears that those records, if they ever existed, were destroyed when the hospital at which he was treated went out of business.

See also the *Eighth Special Report to the U.S. Congress on Alcohol and Health*, 100, 182–83, which speaks, among other things, of a syndrome known as "intermediate duration organic mental disorder" that is frequently found in chronic alcoholics. Such patients "show no overt behavioral signs of profound cognitive dysfunction" but rather exhibit deficits that "are subtle in nature," including "impairments in abstraction ability and problem solving," as well as "mild learning and memory deficits." In fact, this decline in function is produced as much by poor nutrition (alcoholics are notorious for not eating while intoxicated) as by the direct chemical impact of alcohol on brain tissue. As a consequence, it can be partially reversed with extended abstinence and the return to a normal diet. It would seem likely that Faulkner suffered from a syndrome of this sort brought on by his long-term drinking *in addition* to any irreversible neurologic damage that might have been inflicted through acute injury.

6. Blotner, *Faulkner*, 2:1064; Grimwood, *Heart in Conflict*, 224, 254–55, 260–61; Faulkner to Bennett Cerf, n.d. [probably June 23, 1942], in Faulkner, *Selected Letters*, 154; Wilde and Borsten, *Loving Gentleman*, 323–24; Dardis, *Thirsty Muse*, 76.

7. Faulkner to Malcolm Cowley, n.d. [November 1, 1948], in Cowley, *Faulkner-Cowley File*, 115–16; Reed, *Faulkner's Narrative*, 203.

8. Faulkner to Professor Warren Beck, July 6, 1941, in Faulkner, *Selected Letters*, 142.

9. Gwynn and Blotner, *Faulkner in the University*, 77.

10. Faulkner to Robert K. Haas, n.d. [May 22, 1940], Faulkner to Haas, n.d. [October 5, 1940], in Faulkner, *Selected Letters*, 124, 136–37; Blotner, *Faulkner*, 2:1036, 1039, 1042; Grimwood, *Heart in Conflict*, 225, 228, 254–56.

11. Faulkner to Robert K. Haas, n.d., [May 1, 1941], in Faulkner, *Selected Letters*, 139–40; Grimwood, *Heart in Conflict*, 277–81; Gray, *Life of William Faulkner*, 274; Pilkington, *Heart of Yoknapatawpha*, 245. Mark R. Hochberg argues that Faulkner did succeed in integrating the novel thematically by structuring it around a sharp contrast between the races. The nonwhite characters, according to this reading, display a genuine reverence for their families, the land they farm, and the wilderness they hunt, while the whites "feel no ethical responsibility toward women, the

land, or its creatures." Though the thesis is intriguing, the text will not fully sustain it. Cass Edmunds, for instance, shows great "ethical responsibility" toward the land in section 4 of "The Bear," while the majority of the white hunters exhibit considerable reverence toward the "creatures" they kill, especially the totem bear Old Ben. See Hochberg, "Unity of *Go Down, Moses*," 58, 63.

12. Faulkner, *Go Down, Moses*, 135.
13. Ibid., 151, 136, 138–40; Stoneback, "Faulkner's Blues," 241–42, 244; Taylor, *Annotations*, 74; Jenkins, *Faulkner and Black-White Relations*, 250.
14. Faulkner, *Go Down, Moses*, 154–57; Walter Taylor, "'Pantaloon': The Negro Anomaly at the Heart of *Go Down, Moses*," in Budd and Cady, *On Faulkner*, 63–64.
15. Faulkner, *Go Down, Moses*, 149, 159.
16. Grimwood, *Heart in Conflict*, 227; Creighton, *William Faulkner's Craft of Revision*, 115.
17. Early, *Making of "Go Down, Moses,"* 7–9; Creighton, *William Faulkner's Craft of Revision*, 98–99, 102–3.
18. King, "Lucas Beauchamp and William Faulkner," 234; Faulkner, *Go Down, Moses*, 104, 66; Annette Bernert, "The Four Fathers of Isaac McCaslin," in Kinney, *Critical Essays: The McCaslin Family*, 186.
19. Jenkins, *Faulkner and Black-White Relations*, 252–53; Faulkner, *Go Down, Moses*, 118, 129; Bassett, *Visions and Revisions*, 156.
20. Faulkner, "On Fear: Deep South in Labor: Mississippi," in Faulkner, *Essays, Speeches, and Public Letters*, 94, 101; Noel Polk, "Man in the Middle: Faulkner and the Southern White Moderate," in Fowler and Abadie, *Faulkner and Race*, 145–46, 149; Blotner, *Faulkner*, 2:1582–85; Faulkner to Jean Stein, n.d. [November 28 or 29, 1955], Faulkner to Paul Pollard, February 24, 1960, in Faulkner, *Selected Letters*, 388, 444. On Faulkner's problematic public pronouncements on race relations during the 1950s, see Peavy, *Go Slow Now*; Brodsky, "Faulkner and the Racial Crisis"; and Petesch, "Faulkner on Negroes."
21. Faulkner, *Go Down, Moses*, 35, 42; Jenkins, *Faulkner and Black-White Relations*, 254; Hoffman, *Faulkner's Country Matters*, 171–72.
22. Faulkner, *Go Down, Moses*, 45, 104, 116, 128.
23. Ibid., 79, 38–41, 87; Vickery, *Novels of William Faulkner*, 127.
24. Faulkner, *Go Down, Moses*, 101–2, 122, 131; Elisabeth Muhlenfeld, "The Distaff Side: The Women of *Go Down, Moses*," in Kinney, *Critical Essays: The McCaslin Family*, 208–9. On Faulkner's depiction of black families in *Go Down, Moses* as having far stronger emotional ties than those of whites, see Albert J. Devlin, "History, Sexuality, and the Wilderness in the McCaslin Family Chronicle," in Kinney, *Critical Essays: The McCaslin Family*, 189–90, and Creighton, *William Faulkner's Craft of Revision*, 113. Gray is one of several authors who argues, in his words, that Lucas "functions purely within a white framework of reference," devoid of "all black memories and status." But surely that overlooks Lucas's deep commitment to the fire on the hearth, as well as his capacity to "read" objects and incidents from the standpoint of the primal religion that Faulkner identifies as the crux of black culture. Walking through the graveyard where Rider's wife, Mannie, is buried, Lucas, one feels sure, would instinctively grasp the meaning of those "shards of pottery and broken bottles and old brick" and know why they were "fatal to touch." It is, after all, his family cemetery. For the contrary point of view,

see Gray, *Life of William Faulkner*, 280, and Bernard W. Bell, "William Faulkner's 'Shining Star': Lucas Beauchamp as a Marginal Man," in Kinney, *Critical Essays: The McCaslin Family*, 228, 232–33.

25. Faulkner, *Go Down, Moses*, 55, 47.

26. Ibid., 53–54; Winn, "Lineage and the South," 455–56; Backman, *Faulkner*, 163.

27. Faulkner, *Go Down, Moses*, 57, 59; Dawson, "Fate and Freedom," 397; Hoffman, *Faulkner's Country Matters*, 132.

28. Faulkner, *Go Down, Moses*, 371, 376, 369–70; Kuyk, *Threads Cable-strong*, 169–70.

29. Selzer, "'Go Down, Moses,'" 91–93; Faulkner, *Go Down, Moses*, 380–81; Watson, *Forensic Fictions*, 103.

30. Faulkner, *Go Down, Moses*, 372–73; Thadious M. Davis, "Crying in the Wilderness: Legal, Racial, amd Moral Codes in *Go Down, Moses*," in Kinney, *Critical Essays: The McCaslin Family*, 150.

31. Faulkner, *Go Down, Moses*, 382, 378, 383.

32. Blotner, *Faulkner*, 2:1055–62; Faulkner to Robert K. Haas, n.d. [October 5, 1940], in Faulkner, *Selected Letters*, 136–37.

33. Bleikasten, "Private Man's Public Voice," 47, 53.

34. Faulkner, "Delta Autumn," in Faulkner, *Uncollected Stories*, 278–79; Davis, "Crying in the Wilderness," 152; Harter, "Winter of Isaac McCaslin," 220.

35. Faulkner, "Delta Autumn," 275, 279; Grimwood, *Heart in Conflict*, 258, 261–63.

36. Faulkner, "The Tall Men," in Faulkner, *Collected Stories*, 58, 60; Grimwood, *Heart in Conflict*, 259–60; Faulkner, *Pylon*, 228.

37. Turner, *Spirit of Place*, 222; Faulkner, *Flags in the Dust*, 400; Faulkner, *Light in August*, 4.

38. Faulkner, *Go Down, Moses*, 163, 175, 177; Hoffman, *Faulkner's Country Matters*, 137; Levins, *Faulkner's Heroic Design*, 75, 77.

39. Faulkner, *Go Down, Moses*, 165, 170–71, 167, 182, 184; Donaldson, "Isaac McCaslin," 38–39; Hoffman, *Faulkner's Country Matters*, 163.

40. Faulkner, *Go Down, Moses*, 193–94; Kuyk, *Threads Cable-strong*, 100; Donaldson, "Isaac McCaslin," 39.

41. Graham Clarke, "Marking Out and Digging In: Language as Ritual in *Go Down, Moses*," in Lee, *William Faulkner*, 154–56; Page, "Faulkner's Sense of the Sacred," in Wolfe, *Faulkner*, 118; Gray, *Life of William Faulkner*, 276; Harter, "Winter of Isaac McCaslin," 212.

42. Faulkner, *Go Down, Moses*, 193, 209, 226.

43. Friedman, *William Faulkner*, 129; Blotner, *Faulkner*, 2.1087; Faulkner to Robert K. Haas, December 2 [1941], in Faulkner, *Selected Letters*, 146.

44. Blotner, *Faulkner*, 2:1087–1090.

45. Faulkner, *Go Down, Moses*, 288, 256–57, 298; Reed, *Faulkner's Narrative*, 194.

46. "Interview with Cynthia Grenier," in Meriwether and Millgate, *Lion in the Garden*, 225; Gwynn and Blotner, *Faulkner in the University*, 54.

47. Clarke, "Marking Out and Digging In," 155; Faulkner, *Go Down, Moses*, 260; Bassett, *Visions and Revisions*, 157–58; Fowler, *Faulkner's Changing Vision*, 48; Rollyson, *Uses of the Past in Faulkner*, 139.

48. Faulkner, *Go Down, Moses*, 289–91; Pilkington, *Heart of Yoknapatawpha*, 275; Backman, *Faulkner*, 172. That Jews, or the descendants of Jews, would join the Klan seems quite incredible, yet that is what Faulkner's passage says if one parses it,

since they are included in what he calls the "third race." However, this may simply represent carelessness on his part—and further evidence of the haste with which he produced this section of "The Bear."

49. Zender, *Crossing of the Ways*, 67–70, 73; Grimwood, *Heart in Conflict*, 284–85; Faulkner, *Go Down, Moses*, 3.

50. Faulkner, *Go Down, Moses*, 192–93, 200, 210–11, 198.

CODA

1. Minter, *William Faulkner*, 192; Faulkner to Robert K. Haas, n.d. [October 3, 1947], Faulkner to Else Johnson, n.d., [February 22, 1953], and n.d. [March 31, 1953], in Faulkner, *Selected Letters*, 256, 346–47; Saxe Commins to Dorothy Commins, October 8, 1952, and Commins to Robert K. Haas and Bennett Cerf, October 8, 1952, in Brodsky and Hamblin, *Faulkner*, 2:89–91. Blotner reports that the "extensive testing" done by Dr. S. Bernard Wortis, the chairman of the department of psychiatry and neurology at New York University Medical Center, "indicated that [Faulkner] was neurologically and physiologically all right." But it is important to remember that the instruments employed to scan and test the brain at that time were exceedingly crude in comparison with the magnetic resonance imaging technology now available and would not have picked up the sort of damage that would account for a subtle change in artistic performance. See Blotner, *Faulkner*, 2:1453.

2. Blotner, *Faulkner*, 2:1701–3, 1705–9; 1831–32; Jill Faulkner, quoted in Gray, *Life of William Faulkner*, 347; Minter, *William Faulkner*, 241.

3. Faulkner to Joan Williams, n.d. [January 2, 1953], Faulkner to Saxe Commins, n.d. [January 5, 1953], in Faulkner, *Selected Letters*, 344–45; Faulkner to Saxe Commins, n.d. [January, 1956], in Brodsky and Hamblin, *Faulkner*, 189–90.

4. Faulkner, *Town*, 163, 202; Brooks, *William Faulkner: The Yoknapatawpha Country*, 216; Andrew Hook, "The Snopes Trilogy," in Lee, *William Faulkner*, 165, 168–69; Mark Leaf, "Faulkner's Snopes Trilogy," in French, *Fifties*, 51.

5. Brooks, *William Faulkner: The Yoknapatawpha Country*, 216; Wittenberg, *Faulkner*, 232; Reed, *Faulkner's Narrative*, 252; Gold, *William Faulkner*, 173.

On the prospects for reversing neurological damage through decreased drinking or abstinence, see *Eighth Special Report on Alcohol and Health*, 101, 183. The reversal, it should be noted, often comes about as much through improved nutrition as from the absence of liquor itself. Alcoholics, as Saxe Commins discovered during his emergency visit to Rowan Oak, virtually stop eating for prolonged periods of time, which can lead to a serious deficiency of thiamine (vitamin B), a substance vital to the functioning of the nervous system. The return to a normal diet can, in and of itself, boost cerebral performance and trigger the repair of diseased tissue, though "this reversal is likely to be due to generation of nonneuronal support cells or increased growth of surviving neuronal axons or dendrites" rather than an actual replacement of the neurons that have died.

To judge from Blotner's account of his life, Faulkner appears to have been eating more regularly at the time he was writing *The Mansion* than he had been five to ten years earlier, when he was frequently depressed and intoxicated. By coincidence, the restaurant he would visit night after night for a hearty meal while in Oxford was called "The Mansion." See Blotner, *Faulkner*, 2:1713.

6. Faulkner to Robert K. Haas, n.d. [received December 15, 1938], in Faulkner, *Selected Letters*, 108; Fulton, "Linda Snopes Kohl," 427, 425; Brooks, *William Faulkner: The Yoknapatawpha Country*, 224; Stonum, *Faulkner's Career*, 184; Millgate, *Achievement of William Faulkner*, 249; Blotner, *Faulkner*, 2:1714; Creighton, "Dilemma of the Human Heart," 39; Leaf, "Faulkner's Snopes Trilogy," 59.

It is worth noting that while Brooks does let his political bias get in the way of his understanding of Linda, he is such an honest, painstaking reader that he is also willing to report how Faulkner approaches her "with great dramatic sympathy." Her "lack of feminine softness" and strange voice "give her a manner that could make her grotesque, but Faulkner does not treat her so. She has force and dignity" and "never becomes the shrill and frenetic embodiment of a cause." One suspects that it is this commitment to accuracy as a reader, even when that puts him at odds with his own interpretive framework and prejudices, that explains why Brooks's work on Faulkner is still valuable nearly forty years after it was first written. See *William Faulkner: The Yoknapatawpha Country*, 225–26.

7. Faulkner, *Mansion*, 109, 218, 222, 238; Blotner, *Faulkner*, 2:1030.

8. Faulkner, *Mansion*, 174, 230, 203, 211, 216, 359, 199; Page, *Faulkner's Women*, 171; Sergei Chakovsky, "Women in Faulkner's Novels: Author's Attitude and Artistic Function," in Fowler and Abadie, *Faulkner and Women*, 78.

9. Faulkner, *Mansion*, 211, 401, 357, 217; "Interview with Jean Stein vanden Heuvel," in Meriwether and Millgate, *Lion in the Garden*, 247. For more on Faulkner's conception of the Christ story and his use of castration as a modern-day equivalent of crucifixion, see Chapter 9 above, page 238.

10. Faulkner, *Mansion*, 350–51.

11. Faulkner, *Mansion*, 353; Faith Pullin, "Faulkner, Women, and Yoknapatawpha: From Symbol to Autonomy," in Lee, *William Faulkner*, 64–66.

12. Faulkner, *Mansion*, 200, 353, 244–45, 350, 225–28.

13. Faulkner, *Mansion*, 222; Watson, *Forensic Fictions*, 217; Page, *Faulkner's Women*, 172.

14. Crabtree, "Plots of Punishment," 536–37; Faulkner, *Mansion*, 425–29.

15. "Interview with Russell Howe," in Meriwether and Millgate, *Lion in the Garden*, 261; "Interview with Jean Stein vanden Heuvel," in ibid., 255; Gray, *Life of William Faulkner*, 361–63.

BIBLIOGRAPHY

MANUSCRIPT COLLECTIONS

Charlottesville, Virginia
  Edwin A. Alderman Library
    William Faulkner Papers
New Haven, Connecticut
  Yale University Library
    William Faulkner Papers
Oxford, Mississippi
  University of Mississippi Library
    Rowan Oak Papers
    William Faulkner Papers
Princeton, New Jersey
  Princeton University Library
    William Faulkner Papers

PUBLISHED WORKS

Ackerman, R. D. "The Immolation of Isaac McCaslin." *Texas Studies in Literature and Language* 16 (Fall 1974): 557–65.

Adamowski, T. H. "Bayard Sartoris: Mourning and Melancholia." *Literature and Psychology* 23 (1973): 149–58.

———. "Isaac McCaslin and the Wilderness of the Imagination." *Centennial Review* 17 (Winter 1973): 92–112.

———. " 'Meet Mrs. Bundren': *As I Lay Dying*—Gentility, Tact, and Psychoanalysis." *University of Toronto Quarterly* 49 (Spring 1980): 205–27.

Adams, Richard P. *Faulkner: Myth and Motion*. Princeton, 1968.

Allister, Mark. "Faulkner's Aristocratic Families: The Grand Design and the Plantation House." *Midwest Quarterly* 25 (Autumn 1983): 90–101.

Anderson, Carl L. "Faulkner's 'Was': 'A Deadlier Purpose Than Simple Pleasure.' " *American Literature* 61 (October 1989): 414–28.

Anderson, George. "Toward a Reading of *The Town* as a Chronicle: Respectability and Race in Three Episodes." *Mississippi Quarterly* 43 (Summer 1990): 377–85.

Anderson, Sherwood. *Dark Laughter*. New York, 1925.

———. *Sherwood Anderson's Memoirs: A Critical Edition*. Edited by Ray Lewis White. Chapel Hill, 1969.

———. *Sherwood Anderson's Notebook*. New York, 1926.

Arnold, Matthew. *Culture and Anarchy*. Edited by J. Dover Wilson. Cambridge, England, 1971.

Backman, Melvin. *Faulkner: The Major Years: A Critical Study*. Bloomington, Ind., 1966.

Balakian, Anna. *The Symbolist Movement: A Critical Appraisal*. New York, 1977.

Banning, Margaret Culkin. "Changing Moral Standards in Fiction." *Saturday Review of Literature*, July 1, 1939, 1, 4, 14.

Barstad, Joel I. "Faulkner's Pantaloon in Black." *Explicator* 41 (Spring 1983): 51–53.

Barth, J. Robert, ed. *Religious Perspectives in Faulkner's Fiction*. Notre Dame, Ind., 1972.

Bassett, John E. *Visions and Revisions: Essays on Faulkner*. West Cornwall, Conn., 1989.

Baumeister, Roy F. *Identity: Cultural Change and the Struggle for Self*. New York, 1986.

Beck, Warren. *Faulkner*. Madison, Wisc., 1976.

———. *Man in Motion: Faulkner's Trilogy*. Madison, Wisc., 1963.

Behrens, Ralph. "Collapse of Dynasty: The Thematic Center of *Absalom, Absalom!*" *PMLA* 89 (January 1974): 24–32.

Bell, Daniel. *The Cultural Contradictions of Capitalism*. New York, 1976.

Bender, Thomas. *New York Intellect: A History of Intellectual Life in New York City from 1750 to the Beginnings of Our Own Time*. Baltimore, 1987.

Bernhardt, Laurie A. " 'Being Worthy Enough': The Tragedy of Charlotte Rittenmeyer." *Mississippi Quarterly* 39 (Summer 1986): 351–64.

Bezzerides, A. J. *William Faulkner: A Life on Paper*. Jackson, Miss., 1980.

Bleikasten, Andre. *Faulkner's "As I Lay Dying."* Bloomington, Ind., 1973.

———. *The Ink of Melancholy: Faulkner's Novels from "The Sound and the Fury" to "Light in August."* Bloomington, Ind., 1990.

———. *The Most Splendid Failure: Faulkner's "The Sound and the Fury."* Bloomington, Ind., 1976.

———, ed. *William Faulkner's "The Sound and the Fury": A Critical Casebook*. New York, 1982.

Blotner, Joseph L. "The Falkners and the Fictional Families." *Georgia Review* 30 (Fall 1976): 572–92.

———. *Faulkner: A Biography*. 2 vols. New York, 1974.

Bluestein, Gene. "Faulkner and Miscegenation." *Arizona Quarterly* 43 (Summer 1987): 151–64.

Bosha, Francis J. "A Source for the Names Charles and Wash in *Absalom, Absalom!*" *Notes on Modern American Literature* 4 (Spring 1980), no. 13.

Bradbury, Malcolm, and James McFarlane, eds. *Modernism, 1890–1930*. New York, 1976.

Brady, Ruth H. "Faulkner's *As I Lay Dying*." *Explicator* 33 (March 1975): 60–61.

Breit, Harvey. "A Sense of Faulkner." *Partisan Review* 18 (January–February 1951): 88–94.

Briggs, Asa. *Victorian People: A Reassessment of Persons and Themes, 1851–1867*. Chicago, 1955.

Brodhead, Richard H., ed. *Faulkner: New Perspectives*. Englewood Cliffs, N.J., 1983.

Brodsky, Louis Daniel. "Faulkner and the Racial Crisis, 1956." *Southern Review* 24 (Autumn 1988): 791–807.

———. *William Faulkner: Life Glimpses*. Austin, Tex., 1990.

Brodsky, Louis Daniel, and Robert W. Hamblin, eds., *Faulkner: A Comprehensive Guide to the Brodsky Collection*. Vol. 2, *The Letters*. Jackson, Miss., 1984.

Brooks, Cleanth. *William Faulkner: Toward Yoknapatawpha and Beyond*. New Haven, 1978.

———. *William Faulkner: The Yoknapatawpha Country*. New Haven, 1963.

Broughton, Panthea Reid. "An Interview with Meta Carpenter Wilde." *Southern Review* 18 (October 1982): 776–801.

———. "Masculinity and Menfolk in *The Hamlet*." *Mississippi Quarterly* 22 (Summer 1969): 181–89.

———. *William Faulkner: The Abstract and the Actual*. Baton Rouge, 1974.

Brown, May Cameron. "The Language of Chaos: Quentin Compson in *The Sound and the Fury*." *American Literature* 51 (January 1980): 544-53.

Browning, Robert. *Robert Browning: The Poems*. Edited by John Pettigrew. New Haven, 1981.

Brumm, Ursala. *American Religious Thought and Typology*. New Brunswick, N.J., 1970.

Bruner, Jerome S. *Acts of Meaning*. Cambridge, Mass., 1990.

———. *On Knowing: Essays for the Left Hand*. Cambridge, Mass., 1962.

Buck, Paul Herman. *The Road to Reunion, 1865–1890*. Boston, 1937.

Buckley, Jerome. *The Victorian Temper: A Study in Literary Culture*. Cambridge, Mass., 1951.

Budd, Louis J., and Edwin H. Cady, eds. *On Faulkner: The Best from "American Literature."* Durham, N.C., 1989.

Budick, Emily Miller. *Fiction and Historical Consciousness: The American Romance Tradition*. New Haven, 1989.

Burn, W. L. *The Age of Equipoise: A Study of the Mid-Victorian Generation*. New York, 1964.

Butler, Christopher *Early Modernism: Literature, Music, and Painting in Europe, 1900–1916*. Oxford, England, 1994.

Camus, Albert. *The Stranger*. Translated by Stuart Gilbert. New York, 1953.

Canfield, J. Douglas. "Faulkner's Grecian Urn and Ike McCaslin's Empty Legacies." *Arizona Quarterly* 36 (Winter 1980): 359-84.

———, ed. *Twentieth Century Interpretations of "Sanctuary": A Collection of Critical Essays*. Englewood Cliffs, N.J., 1982.

Cantor, Norman F. *Twentieth-Century Culture: Modernism to Deconstruction*. New York, 1988.

Carey, Glenn O., ed. *Faulkner: The Unappeased Imagination*. Troy, N.Y., 1980.

Cash, Wilbur J. *The Mind of the South*. New York, 1941.

Castille, Philip, and William Osborne, eds. *Southern Literature in Transition: Heritage and Promise*. Memphis, 1983.

Charbot, C. Barry. "Faulkner's Rescued Patrimony." *Review of Existential Psychology and Psychiatry* 13 (1974): 274–86.

Chefdor, Monique, Ricardo Quinones, and Albert Wachtel, eds. *Modernism: Challenges and Perspectives*. Urbana, Ill., 1986.

Claridge, Laura P. "Isaac McCaslin's Failed Bid for Adulthood." *American Literature* 55 (May 1983): 241-51.

Clark, G. Kitson. *The Making of Victorian England*. New York, 1974.

Clark, William Bedford. "The Serpent of Lust in the Southern Garden." *Southern Review* 10 (October 1974): 805-22.

Clayton, Bruce. *The Savage Ideal: Intolerance and Intellectual Leadership in the South, 1890–1914*. Baltimore, 1972.

Cohen, Philip, and Doreen Fowler. "Faulkner's Introduction to *The Sound and the Fury*." *American Literature* 62 (June 1990): 262–83.

Collins, R. G. "*Light in August*: Faulkner's Stained Glass Triptych." *Mosaic* 7 (Fall 1973): 97–157.

Cominos, Peter T. "Late-Victorian Sexual Respectability and the Social System." *International Review of Social History* 8 (1963): 18–48.

Connolly, Thomas E. "Joyce and Faulkner." *James Joyce Quarterly* 16 (Summer 1979): 513–15.

Cook, Sylvia Jenkins. *From Tobacco Road to Route 66: The Southern Poor White in Fiction*. Chapel Hill, 1976.

Cornell, Brenda G. "Faulkner's 'Evangeline': A Preliminary Stage." *Southern Quarterly* 22 (Summer 1984): 22–41.

Cott, Nancy F., and Elizabeth H. Pleck, eds. *A Heritage of Her Own: Toward a New Social History of American Women*. New York, 1979.

Cowan, James C. "Dream-Work in the Quentin Section of *The Sound and the Fury*." *Literature and Psychology* 24 (1974): 91–98.

Cowley, Malcolm. *Exile's Return: A Literary Odyssey of the 1920s*. 1951. Reprint, New York, 1976.

———. *The Faulkner-Cowley File: Letters and Memories, 1944–1962*. New York, 1966.

Cox, Leland H., ed. *William Faulkner: Critical Collection*. Detroit, 1982.

Coy, Javier, and Michel Gresset, eds. *Faulkner and History*. Salamanca, Spain, 1986.

Crabtree, Claire. "Plots of Punishment and Faulkner's Injured Women: Charlotte Rittenmeyer and Linda Snopes." *Michigan Academician* 24 (1992): 527–39.

Creighton, Joanne V. "The Dilemma of the Human Heart in *The Mansion*." *Renascence* 25 (Autumn 1972): 35–45.

———. "Self-Destructive Evil in *Sanctuary*." *Twentieth-Century Literature* 18 (October 1972): 259–70.

———. *William Faulkner's Craft of Revision: The Snopes Trilogy, "The Unvanquished," and "Go Down, Moses."* Detroit, 1977.

Cumpiano, Marion W. "The Motif of Return: Currents and Counter Currents in 'Old Man' by William Faulkner." *Southern Humanities Review* 12 (Summer 1978): 185–93.

Dahl, James. "A Faulkner Reminiscence: Conversations with Mrs. Maud Falkner." *Journal of Modern Literature* 3 (April 1974): 1026–30.

Dardis, Thomas A. *The Thirsty Muse: Alcohol and the American Writer*. New York, 1989.

Davis, Robert Con, ed. *The Fictional Father: Lacanian Readings of the Text*. Amherst, Mass., 1981.

Davis, Thadious M. *Faulkner's "Negro": Art and the Southern Context*. Baton Rouge, 1983.

Dawson, William P. "Fate and Freedom: The Classical Background of *Go Down, Moses*." *Mississippi Quarterly* 43 (Summer 1990): 387–412.

Denniston, Dorothy L. "Faulkner's Image of Blacks in *Go Down, Moses*." *Phylon* 44 (Spring 1983): 33–43.

Desmond, John F. "The Scriptual Tradition and Faulkner's Gnostic Style." *Southern Review* 25 (July 1989): 563–68.

Dewey, John. *The Child and the Curriculum/The School and Society*. 1902. Reprint, Chicago, 1956.

Donald, David Herbert. *Look Homeward: A Life of Thomas Wolfe*. New York, 1987.

Donaldson, Susan V. "Isaac McCaslin and the Possibilities of Vision." *Southern Review* 22 (January 1986): 37–50.

Douglas, Paul. *Bergson, Eliot, and American Literature*. Lexington, Ky., 1986.

Doyle, Don H. "The Mississippi Frontier in Faulkner's Fiction and in Fact." *Southern Quarterly* 29 (1991): 145–60.

Doyle, Esther M., and Virginia H. Floyd, eds. *Studies in Interpretation*. Amsterdam, 1972.

Duclos, Donald P. "Son of Sorrow: The Life, Works, and Influence of Colonel William C. Falkner, 1825–1889." Ph.D. diss., University of Michigan, 1962.

Duvall, John N. *Faulkner's Marginal Couple: Invisible, Outlaw, and Unspeakable Communities*. Austin, Tex., 1990.

Early, James. *The Making of "Go Down, Moses."* Dallas, 1972.

Edelman, Gerald M. *Bright Air, Brilliant Fire: On the Matter of Mind*. New York, 1992.

Edwards, Duane. "Flem Snopes and Thomas Sutpen: Two Versions of Respectability." *Dalhousie Review* 51 (Winter 1971–72): 559–70.

Eighth Special Report to the U.S. Congress on Alcohol and Health from the Secretary of Health and Human Services, 1993. Rockville, Md., 1994.

Eldred, Janet Carey. "Faulkner's Still Life: Art and Abortion in *The Wild Palms*." *Faulkner Journal* 4 (1988–89): 139–58.

Erikson, Erik H. *Childhood and Society*. Rev. ed. New York, 1963.

———. *Identity: Youth and Crisis*. New York, 1968.

———. *Identity and the Life Cycle*. New York, 1959.

Faber, M. D. "Faulkner's *The Sound and the Fury*: Object Relations and Narrative Structure." *American Imago* 34 (Winter 1977): 327–50.

Fadiman, Regina K. *Faulkner's "Light in August": A Description and Interpretation of the Revisions*. Charlottesville, 1975.

Falkner, Murry C. *The Falkners of Mississippi: A Memoir*. Baton Rouge, 1967.

Falkner, William C. *Rapid Ramblings in Europe*. Philadelphia, 1884.

———. *The White Rose of Memphis*. 1881. Reprint, New York, 1953.

Fass, Paula S. *The Damned and the Beautiful: American Youth in the 1920s*. New York, 1977.

Faulkner, Peter. *Modernism*. London, 1977.

Faulkner, William. *Absalom, Absalom!* 1936. Reprint, New York, 1990.

———. *As I Lay Dying*. 1930. Reprint, New York, 1964.

———. *Collected Stories of William Faulkner*. New York, 1976.

———. "Elmer." Edited by Dianne L. Cox. *Mississippi Quarterly* 36 (Summer 1983): 343–447.

———. *Essays, Speeches, and Public Letters*. Edited by James B. Meriwether. New York, 1965.

———. *Father Abraham*. New York, 1984.

———. *Flags in the Dust*. Edited by Douglas Day. New York, 1973.

———. *Go Down, Moses*. New York, 1942.

———. *The Hamlet*. 1940. Reprint, New York, 1960.

———. "Helen: A Courtship" and "Mississippi Poems." Edited by Carvel Collins and Joseph L. Blotner (respectively). Oxford, Miss., and New Orleans, 1981.

———. "An Introduction for *The Sound and the Fury*." Edited by James B. Meriwether. *Southern Review* 8 (October 1972): 705-10.

———. *Intruder in the Dust*. New York, 1948.

———. *Knight's Gambit*. 1949. Reprint, New York, 1978.

———. *Light in August*. 1932. Reprint, New York, 1959.

———. *The Mansion*. New York, 1959.

———. *The Marble Faun*. Boston, 1924.

———. *Marionettes: A Play in One Act*. Oxford, Miss., 1975.

———. *Mayday*. Notre Dame, Ind., 1977.

———. *Mosquitoes*. 1927. Reprint, New York, 1965.

———. *New Orleans Sketches*. New Brunswick, N.J., 1958.

———. *Pylon*. 1935. Reprint, New York, 1987.

———. *The Reivers*. New York, 1962.

———. "The Rejected Manuscript Opening of *Flags in the Dust*." Edited by George F. Hayhoe. *Mississippi Quarterly* 33 (Summer 1980): 371-83.

———. *Requiem for a Nun*. New York, 1951.

———. *Sanctuary*. 1931. Reprint, New York, 1954.

———. *Sartoris*. 1929. Reprint, New York, 1953.

———. *Selected Letters of William Faulkner*. Edited by Joseph L. Blotner. New York, 1977.

———. *Soldiers' Pay*. 1926. Reprint, New York, 1951.

———. *The Sound and the Fury*. 1929. Reprint, New York, 1946.

———. *The Sound and the Fury* (corrected edition). 1929. Reprint, New York, 1984.

———. *Thinking of Home: William Faulkner's Letters to His Mother and Father, 1918–1925*. Edited by James G. Watson. New York, 1992.

———. *The Town*. New York, 1957.

———. *Uncollected Stories of William Faulkner*. Edited by Joseph L. Blotner. New York, 1979.

———. *The Unvanquished*. 1938. Reprint, New York, 1959.

———. *Vision In Spring*. Edited by Judith L. Sensibar. Austin, Tex., 1984.

———. *The Wild Palms*. New York, 1939.

———. *William Faulkner: Early Prose and Poetry*. Edited by Carvel Collins. Boston, 1962.

———. "William Faulkner's Essay on the Composition of *Sartoris*." Edited by Joseph L. Blotner. *Yale University Library Gazette* 37 (January 1974): 121-24.

Faust, Drew Gilpin. *A Sacred Circle: The Dilemma of the Intellectual in the Old South, 1840–1860*. Baltimore, 1977.

Feaster, John. "Faulkner's *Old Man*: A Psychoanalytic Approach." *Modern Fiction Studies* 13 (Spring 1967): 89-93.

Fenichel, Otto. *The Psychoanalytic Theory of Neurosis*. New York, 1945.

Fiedler, Leslie A. *Love and Death in the American Novel*. New York, 1960.

Flynn, Peggy. "The Sister Figure and 'Little Sister Death' in the Fiction of William Faulkner." *University of Mississippi Studies in English* 14 (1976): 99-117.

Ford, Dan, ed. *Heir and Prototype: Original and Derived Characterizations in Faulkner*. Conway, Ark., 1987.

Foster, Thomas C. *Form and Society in Modern Literature.* De Kalb, Ill., 1988.

Fowler, Doreen. *Faulkner's Changing Vision: From Outrage to Affirmation.* Ann Arbor, 1983.

Fowler, Doreen, and Ann J. Abadie, eds. *"A Cosmos of My Own": Faulkner and Yoknapatawpha, 1980.* Jackson, Miss., 1981.

———. *Faulkner and Humor: Faulkner and Yoknapatawpha, 1984.* Jackson, Miss., 1985.

———. *Faulkner and Popular Culture: Faulkner and Yoknapatawpha, 1988.* Jackson, Miss., 1989.

———. *Faulkner and Race: Faulkner and Yoknapatawpha, 1986.* Jackson, Miss., 1987.

———. *Faulkner and Religion: Faulkner and Yoknapatawpha, 1989.* Jackson, Miss., 1990.

———. *Faulkner and the Craft of Fiction: Faulkner and Yoknapatawpha, 1987.* Jackson, Miss., 1989.

———. *Faulkner and the Southern Renaissance: Faulkner and Yoknapatawpha, 1981.* Jackson, Miss., 1982.

———. *Faulkner and Women: Faulkner and Yoknapatawpha, 1985.* Jackson, Miss., 1986.

———. *Fifty Years of Yoknapatawpha: Faulkner and Yoknapatawpha, 1979.* Jackson, Miss., 1980.

——— *New Directions in Faulkner Studies: Faulkner and Yoknapatawpha, 1983.* Jackson, Miss., 1984.

Frazer, James George. *The Golden Bough: A Study in Magic and Religion.* 1922. Reprint, New York, 1951.

French, Warren, ed. *The Fifties: Fiction, Poetry, Drama.* Deland, Fla., 1970.

Freud, Sigmund. *A General Introduction to Psychoanalysis.* 1924. Reprint, New York, 1952.

———. *General Psychological Theory.* Edited by Philip Rieff. New York, 1963.

——— *Sexuality and the Psychology of Love.* Edited by Philip Rieff. New York, 1963.

Friedman, Alan Warren. *William Faulkner.* New York, 1984.

Frontain, Raymond-Jean, and Jan Wojcik, eds. *The David Myth in Western Literature.* West Lafayette, Ind., 1980.

Fulton, Keith Louise. "Linda Snopes Kohl: Faulkner's Radical Woman." *Modern Fiction Studies* 34 (Autumn 1988): 425–36.

Gallagher, Susan "To Love and to Honor: Brothers and Sisters in Faulkner's Yoknapatawpha County." *Essays in Literature* 7 (Fall 1980): 213–24.

Gamache, Lawrence B., and Ian S. MacNiven, eds. *The Modernists: Studies in a Literary Phenomenon.* Rutherford, N.J., 1987.

Garzilli, Enrico. *Circles without Center: Paths to the Discovery and Creation of Self in Modern Literature.* Cambridge, Mass., 1972.

Gaston, Paul M. *The New South Creed: A Study in Southern Mythmaking.* New York, 1970.

Gay, Peter. *The Bourgeois Experience: Victoria to Freud.* Vol. 1, *The Education of the Senses.* New York, 1984.

———. *Freud, Jews, and Other Germans: Masters and Victims in Modernist Culture.* New York, 1978.

Gidley, Mick. "The Later Faulkner, Bergson, and God." *Mississippi Quarterly* 37 (Summer 1984): 377–83.

Gilmer, Walker. *Horace Liveright: Publisher of the Twenties.* New York, 1970.

Godden, Richard. "Call Me Nigger! Race and Speech in Faulkner's *Light in August*." *Journal of American Studies* 14 (August 1980): 235–48.

Gold, Joseph. *William Faulkner: A Study in Humanism from Metaphor to Discourse.* Norman, Okla., 1966.

Graham, Hugh Davis, and Ted Robert Gurr, eds. *Violence in America: Historical and Comparative Perspectives.* New York, 1969.

Gray, Richard. *The Life of William Faulkner: A Critical Biography.* Oxford, England, 1994.

Greenough, William T., James E. Black, and Christopher S. Wallace. "Experience and Brain Development." *Child Development* 58 (June 1987): 539–59.

Gresset, Michel. *Fascination: Faulkner's Fiction, 1919–1936.* Durham, N.C., 1989.

———. "Faulkner's Self-Portraits." *Faulkner Journal* 2 (Fall 1986): 2–13.

Gresset, Michel, and Kenzaburo Ohashi, eds. *Faulkner: After the Nobel Prize.* Kyoto, Japan, 1987.

Gresset, Michel, and Noel Polk, eds. *Intertextuality in Faulkner.* Jackson, Miss., 1985.

Gresset, Michel, and Patrick Samway, eds. *Faulkner and Idealism: Perspectives from Paris.* Jackson, Miss., 1983.

Grimwood, Michael. *Heart in Conflict: Faulkner's Struggles with Vocation.* Athens, Ga., 1987.

Guerard, Albert J. *The Triumph of the Novel: Dickens, Dostoevsky, Faulkner.* New York, 1976.

Gwynn, Frederick L., and Joseph L. Blotner, eds. *Faulkner in the University: Class Conferences at the University of Virginia, 1957–1958.* Charlottesville, 1959.

Hall, Constance H. *Incest in Faulkner: A Metaphor for the Fall.* Ann Arbor, 1986.

Hall, David D. "The Victorian Connection." *American Quarterly* 27, (December 1975): 561–74.

Haller, John S., and Robin M. Haller. *The Physician and Sexuality in Victorian America.* New York, 1977.

Halttunen, Karen. *Confidence Men and Painted Women: A Study of Middle-Class Culture in America, 1830–1870.* New Haven, 1982.

Hamblin, Robert W. " 'Carcassonne': Faulkner's Allegory of Art and the Artist." *Southern Review* 15 (April 1979): 355–65.

Hanna, Thomas, ed. *The Bergsonian Heritage.* New York, 1962.

Harley, Marta Powell. "Faulkner's Medievalism and *Sir Gawain and the Green Knight.*" *American Notes and Queries* 21 (March–April 1983): 111–14.

Harrington, Evans, and Ann J. Abadie, eds. *Faulkner, Modernism, and Film: Faulkner and Yoknapatawpha, 1978.* Jackson, Miss., 1979.

———. *The Maker and the Myth: Faulkner and Yoknapatawpha, 1977.* Jackson, Miss., 1978.

———. *The South and Faulkner's Yoknapatawpha: The Actual and the Apocryphal.* Jackson, Miss., 1976.

Harrington, Gary. "Distant Mirrors: The Intertextual Relationship of Quentin Compson and Harry Wilbourne." *Faulkner Journal* 1 (Fall 1985): 41–45.

———. *Faulkner's Fables of Creativity: The Non-Yoknapatawpha Novels.* Athens, Ga., 1990.

Harter, Carol Clancey. "The Winter of Isaac McCaslin: Revisions and Irony in Faulkner's 'Delta Autumn.' " *Journal of Modern Literature* 1 (1970–71): 209–25.

Hayes, Ann L., John A. Hart, Ralph A. Ciancio, Beekman W. Cottrell, and Neal Woodruff Jr. *Studies in Faulkner*. Pittsburgh, 1961.

Healy, Jane M. *Endangered Minds: Why Children Don't Think and What We Can Do about It*. New York, 1990.

Hemingway, Ernest. *A Farewell to Arms*. 1929. Reprint, New York, 1969.

Henderson, Harry B. *Versions of the Past: The Historical Imagination in American Fiction*. New York, 1974.

Himmelfarb, Gertrude. *Victorian Minds*. New York, 1968.

Hlavsa, Virginia V. James. *Faulkner and the Thoroughly Modern Novel*. Charlottesville, 1991.

———. "The Mirror, the Lamp, and the Bed: Faulkner and the Modernists." *American Literature* 57 (March 1985): 23–43.

Hochberg, Mark R. "The Unity of *Go Down, Moses*." *Tennessee Studies in Literature* 21 (1976): 58–65.

Hoffman, Daniel. *Faulkner's Country Matters: Folklore and Fable in Yoknapatawpha*. Baton Rouge, 1989.

———. "The Last of the Chickasaws." *Shenandoah* 39 (Spring 1989): 51–59.

Hoffman, Frederick J. *The Twenties: American Writing in the Postwar Decade*. New York, 1962.

Hoffman, Frederick J., and Olga W. Vickery, eds. *William Faulkner: Three Decades of Criticism*. New York, 1960.

Honnighausen, Lothar, ed. *Faulkner's Discourse: An International Symposium*. Tubingen, 1989.

Houghton, Walter E. *The Victorian Frame of Mind, 1830–1870*. New Haven, 1957.

Howe, Daniel Walker. "American Victorianism as a Culture." *American Quarterly* 27 (December 1975): 507–32.

Howe, Irving. *The Decline of the New*. New York, 1968.

———, ed. *The Idea of the Modern in Literature and the Arts*. New York, 1967.

———. *William Faulkner: A Critical Study*. New York, 1952.

Hunt, John W. "Keeping the Hoop Skirts Out: Historiography in Faulkner's *Absalom, Absalom!*" in *Faulkner Studies* 1 (1980): 38–47.

———. *William Faulkner: Art in Theological Tension*. Syracuse, N.Y., 1965.

Irwin, John T. *Doubling and Incest/Repetition and Revenge: A Speculative Reading of Faulkner*. Baltimore, 1975.

Jackson, Blyden. "Faulkner's Depiction of the Negro." *University of Mississippi Studies in English* 15 (1978): 33–47.

Jameson, Fredric. "Postmodernism, or the Cultural Logic of Late Capitalism." *New Left Review*, no. 146 (July–August 1984): 53–92.

Jehlen, Myra. *Class and Character in Faulkner's South*. New York, 1976.

Jenkins, Lee. *Faulkner and Black-White Relations: A Psychoanalytic Approach*. New York, 1981.

Johnson, Elaine D. "Faulkner's *The Hamlet*." *Explicator* 41 (Spring 1983): 48–51.

Johnson, Karen Ramsay. "Gender, Sexuality, and the Artist in Faulkner's Novels." *American Literature* 61 (March 1989): 1–15.

Jordan, Winthrop D. *White over Black: American Attitudes toward the Negro, 1550–1812*. Chapel Hill, 1968.

Justus, James H. "Hemingway and Faulkner: Vision and Repudiation." *Kenyon Review* 7 (Fall 1985): 1–14.

Kaplan, Justin. *Mr. Clemens and Mark Twain: A Biography.* New York, 1966.

Karl, Frederick R. *William Faulkner: American Writer.* New York, 1989.

Kartiganer, Donald M. *The Fragile Thread: The Meaning of Form in Faulkner's Novels.* Amherst, Mass., 1979.

Kartiganer, Donald M., and Ann J. Abadie, eds. *Faulkner and Psychology: Faulkner and Yoknapatawpha, 1991.* Jackson, Miss., 1994.

Kegan, Robert. *The Evolving Self: Problem and Process in Human Development.* Cambridge, Mass., 1982.

Kellner, R. Scott. "A Reconsideration of Character: Relationships in *Absalom, Absalom!*" *Notes on Mississippi Writers* 7 (Fall 1974): 39–43.

Kellogg, Stuart, ed. *Essays on Gay Literature.* New York, 1985.

Kenner, Hugh. *A Homemade World: The American Modernist Writers.* New York, 1975.

Kern, Stephen. *The Culture of Love: Victorians to Moderns.* Cambridge, Mass., 1992.

———. *The Culture of Time and Space, 1880–1918.* Cambridge, Mass., 1983.

Kerr, Elizabeth M. *William Faulkner's Gothic Domain.* Port Washington, N.Y., 1979.

———. *Yoknapatawpha: Faulkner's "Little Postage Stamp of Native Soil."* New York, 1976.

Kidd, Millie M. "The Dialogic Perspective in William Faulkner's *The Hamlet.*" *Mississippi Quarterly* 44 (Summer 1991): 309–20.

Kiely, Robert, ed. *Modernism Reconsidered.* Cambridge, Mass., 1983.

King, Richard H. "*A Fable*: Faulkner's Political Novel?" *Southern Literary Journal* 42 (Spring 1985): 3–17.

———. *A Southern Renaissance: The Cultural Awakening of the American South, 1930–1955.* New York, 1980.

Kinney, Arthur F., ed. *Critical Essays on William Faulkner: The Compson Family.* Boston, 1982.

———, ed. *Critical Essays on William Faulkner: The McCaslin Family.* Boston, 1990.

———, ed. *Critical Essays on William Faulkner: The Sartoris Family.* Boston, 1985.

———. The Family-Centered Nature of Faulkner's World." *College Literature* 16 (Winter 1989): 83–102.

———. "Faulkner and the Possibilities for Heroism." *Southern Review* 6 (October 1970): 1110–25.

———. "Form and Function in *Absalom, Absalom!*" *Southern Review* 14 (August 1978): 677–91.

Klivington, Kenneth, ed. *The Science of Mind.* Cambridge, Mass., 1989.

Kloss, Robert J. "Faulkner's *As I Lay Dying.*" *American Imago* 38 (Winter 1981): 429–44.

Kreiswirth, Martin. *William Faulkner: The Making of a Novelist.* Athens, Ga., 1983.

Kreyling, Michael. *Figures of the Hero in Southern Narrative.* Baton Rouge, 1987.

Krupnick, Mark. *Lionel Trilling and the Fate of Cultural Criticism.* Evanston, Ill., 1986.

Kumar, Shiv K. *Bergson and the Stream of Consciousness Novel.* New York, 1963.

Kuspit, Donald, and Lynn Gamwell. *Health and Happiness in Twentieth Century Avant-Garde Art.* Ithaca, N.Y., 1996.

Kuyk, Dirk, Jr. *Sutpen's Design: Interpreting Faulkner's "Absalom, Absalom!"* Charlottesville, 1990.

———. *Threads Cable-strong: William Faulkner's "Go Down, Moses."* Lewisburg, Pa., 1983.

Kuyk, Dirk, Jr., Betty M. Kuyk, and James A. Miller. "Black Culture in William Faulkner's 'That Evening Sun.'" *Journal of American Studies* 20 (April 1986): 33–50.

Laing, R. D. *The Divided Self.* New York, 1969.

Langbaum, Robert. *The Mysteries of Identity: A Theme in Modern Literature.* New York, 1977.

Langford, Gerald. *Faulkner's Revision of "Absalom, Absalom!": A Collation of the Manuscript and the Published Book.* Austin, Tex., 1971.

———. *Faulkner's Revision of "Sanctuary": A Collation of the Unrevised Galleys and the Published Book.* Austin, Tex., 1972.

Lawson, Lewis A. "The Grotesque-Comic in the Snopes Trilogy." *Literature and Psychology* 15 (1965): 107–19.

Leahy, Sharon L. "Poker and Semantics: Unravelling the Gordian Knot in Faulkner's 'Was.'" *American Literature* 57 (March 1958): 129–37.

Leaver, Florence. "The Structure of *The Hamlet.*" *Twentieth-Century Literature* 1 (July 1955): 77–84.

Lee, A. Robert, ed. *William Faulkner: The Yoknapatawpha Fiction.* New York, 1990.

Lensing, George S. "The Metaphor of Family in *Absalom, Absalom!*" *Southern Review* 11 (January 1975): 99–117.

Lester, Cheryl. "To Market, to Market: *The Portable Faulkner.*" *Criticism* 29 (Summer 1987): 371–92.

Levenson, Michael H. *A Genealogy of Modernism: A Study of English Literary Doctrine, 1908–1922.* Cambridge, England, 1984.

Levins, Lynn Gartrell. *Faulkner's Heroic Design: The Yoknapatawpha Novels.* Athens, Ga., 1976.

Lewis, R. W. B. *The Picaresque Saint: Representative Figures in Contemporary Fiction.* Philadelphia, 1961.

Link, Arthur S., and Rembert W. Patrick, eds. *Writing Southern History: Essays in Historiography in Honor of Fletcher M. Green.* Baton Rouge, 1965.

Little, Anne Colclough. "Reconsidering Maggie, Charles, and Gavin in *The Town.*" *Mississippi Quarterly* 46 (Summer 1992): 463–77.

Longley, John Lewis, Jr. *The Tragic Mask: A Study of Faulkner's Heroes.* Chapel Hill, 1963.

Lowe, John. "*The Unvanquished*: Faulkner's Nietzschean Skirmish with the Civil War." *Mississippi Quarterly* 46 (Summer 1992): 407–36.

Lunn, Eugene. *Marxism and Modernism: An Historical Study of Lukacs, Brecht, Benjamin, and Adorno.* Berkeley, Calif., 1982.

Lynd, Helen Merrell. *On Shame and the Search for Identity.* New York, 1958.

Lynn, Kenneth S. *Hemingway.* New York, 1987.

MacMillan, Duane. "*Pylon*: From Short Stories to Major Work." *Mosaic* 7 (Fall 1973): 185–212.

Magny, Claude-Edmonde. *The Age of the American Novel: The Film Aesthetic of Fiction between the Two Wars.* New York, 1972.

Martin, Jay. *Who Am I This Time? Uncovering the Fictive Personality.* New York, 1988.

———. "'The Whole Burden of Man's History of His Impossible Heart's Desire':

The Early Life of William Faulkner." *American Literature* 53 (January 1982): 607-29.

Matthews, John T. *The Play of Faulkner's Language*. Ithaca, N.Y., 1982.

McCormick, John. *Fiction as Knowledge: The Modern Post-Romantic Novel*. New Brunswick, N.J., 1975.

McGee, Patrick. "Gender and Generation in Faulkner's 'The Bear.' " *Faulkner Journal* 1 (Fall 1985): 46-54.

McHaney, Thomas L. "An Episode of War in *The Unvanquished*." *Faulkner Journal* 2 (Spring 1987): 35-44.

———. *William Faulkner's "The Wild Palms": A Study*. Jackson, Miss., 1975.

McKitrick, Eric L., ed. *Slavery Defended: The Views of the Old South*. Englewood Cliffs, N.J., 1963.

Meeter, Glenn. "Male and Female in *Light in August* and *The Hamlet*: Faulkner's 'Mythical Method.' " *Studies in the Novel* 20 (Winter 1988): 404-16.

Meriwether, James B., ed. *A Faulkner Miscellany*. Jackson, Miss., 1974.

———. "Sartoris and Snopes: An Early Notice." *Library Chronicle of the University of Texas* 7 (Summer 1962): 36-39.

Meriwether, James B., and Michael Millgate, eds. *Lion in the Garden: Interviews with William Faulkner, 1926-1962*. New York, 1968.

Meyer, Donald H. "American Intellectuals and the Victorian Crisis of Faith." *American Quarterly* 27 (December 1975): 585-603.

Mickelsen, David. "The Campfire and the Hearth in *Go Down, Moses*." *Mississippi Quarterly* 38 (Summer 1985): 311-27.

Millgate, Michael. *The Achievement of William Faulkner*. New York, 1966.

———, ed. *New Essays on "Light in August."* Cambridge, England, 1987.

Milum, Richard A. "Faulkner and the Cavalier Tradition: The French Bequest." *American Literature* 45 (January 1974): 580-89.

Minter, David. *William Faulkner: His Life and Work*. Baltimore, 1980.

Miyoshi, Masao. *The Divided Self: A Perspective on the Literature of the Victorians*. New York, 1969.

Monteiro, George. "The Limits of Professionalism: A Sociological Approach to Faulkner, Fitzgerald, and Hemingway." *Criticism* 15 (Spring 1973): 145-55.

Moreland, Richard C. *Faulkner and Modernism: Rereading and Rewriting*. Madison, Wisc., 1990.

Morris, Wesley. *Friday's Footprint: Structuralism and the Articulated Text*. Columbus, Ohio, 1979.

Morris, Wesley, with Barbara Alverson Morris. *Reading Faulkner*. Madison, Wisc., 1989.

Mortimer, Gail L. "The Ironies of Transcendent Love in Faulkner's *The Wild Palms*." *Faulkner Journal* 1 (Spring 1986): 30-42.

———. "The Smooth, Suave Shape of Desire: Paradox in Faulknerian Imagery of Women." *Women's Studies* 13 (December 1986): 149-61.

Muhlenfeld, Elisabeth, ed. *William Faulkner's "Absalom, Absalom!": A Critical Casebook*. New York, 1984.

Myers, Gerald E. *William James: His Life and Thought*. New Haven, 1986.

Nicholls, Peter. *Modernisms: A Literary Guide*. Berkeley, Calif., 1995.

Niebuhr, Reinhold. *An Interpretation of Christian Ethics*. 1935. Reprint, New York, 1956.

Nilon, Charles H. *Faulkner and the Negro*. 1962. Reprint, New York, 1965.

Norris, Nancy. "*The Hamlet*, *The Town*, and *The Mansion*: A Psychological Reading of the Snopes Trilogy." *Mosaic* 7 (Fall 1973): 213–35.

Oakes, James. *The Ruling Class: A History of American Slaveholders*. New York, 1982.

Oates, Stephen B. *William Faulkner: The Man and the Artist*. New York, 1987.

Orr, John. *The Making of the Twentieth-Century Novel: Lawrence, Joyce, Faulkner, and Beyond*. New York, 1987.

Page, Sally R. *Faulkner's Women: Characterization and Meaning*. Deland, Fla., 1972.

Palliser, Charles. "Fate and Madness: The Determinist Vision of Darl Bundren." *American Literature* 49 (January 1978): 619–33.

Panichas, George A., ed. *The Politics of Twentieth-Century Novelists*. New York, 1971.

Parker, Robert Dale. "*Absalom, Absalom!*": *The Questioning of Fictions*. Boston, 1991.

Peavy, Charles D. *Go Slow Now: Faulkner and the Race Question*. Eugene, Oreg., 1971.

———. "'If I'd Just Had a Mother': Faulkner's Quentin Compson." *Literature and Psychology* 23 (1973): 114–21.

Petesch, Donald A. "Faulkner on Negroes: The Conflict between the Public Man and the Private Art." *Southern Humanities Review* 10 (1976): 55–64.

Phillips, K. J. "Faulkner in the Garden of Eden." *Southern Humanities Review* 19 (Winter 1985): 1–19.

Pilkington, John. *The Heart of Yoknapatawpha*. Jackson, Miss., 1981.

Polk, Noel. "The Manuscript of *Absalom, Absalom!*" *Mississippi Quarterly* 25 (Summer 1972): 359–67.

Porter, Carolyn. *Seeing and Being: The Plight of the Participant Observer in Emerson, James, Adams, and Faulkner*. Middletown, Conn., 1981.

Price, Steve. "Shreve's Bon in *Absalom, Absalom!*" *Mississippi Quarterly* 39 (Summer 1986): 325–35.

Pryse, Marjorie. "Miniaturizing Yoknapatawpha: *The Unvanquished* as Faulkner's Theory of Realism." *Mississippi Quarterly* 33 (Summer 1980): 343–54.

Putzel, Max. *Genius of Place: William Faulkner's Triumphant Beginnings*. Baton Rouge, 1985.

Radloff, Bernhard. "Dialogue and Insight: The Priority of the Heritage in *Absalom, Absalom!*" *Mississippi Quarterly* 42 (Summer 1989): 261–72.

———. "The Fate of Demonism in William Faulkner." *Arizona Quarterly* 46 (Spring 1990): 27–50.

Ragan, David Paul. *Annotations to Faulkner's "Absalom, Absalom!"* New York, 1991.

———. "The Evolution of Roth Edmonds in *Go Down, Moses*." *Mississippi Quarterly* 38 (Summer 1985): 295–309.

———. *William Faulkner's "Absalom, Absalom!": A Critical Study*. Ann Arbor, 1987.

Reed, Joseph W., Jr. *Faulkner's Narrative*. New Haven, 1973.

Reesman, Jeanne Campbell. *American Designs: The Late Novels of James and Faulkner*. Philadelphia, 1991.

Reeves, Carolyn H. "*The Wild Palms*: Faulkner's Chaotic Cosmos." *Mississippi Quarterly* 20 (Summer 1967): 148–57.

Richards, Lewis A. "Sex under *The Wild Palms* and a Moral Question." *Arizona Quarterly* 28 (Winter 1972): 326–32.

Richardson, H. Edward. *William Faulkner: The Journey to Self-Discovery*. Columbia, Mo., 1969.

Ricks, Beatrice, ed. *William Faulkner: A Bibliography of Secondary Works*. Metuchen, N.J., 1981.

Rollyson, Carl E., Jr. "'Counterpull': Estelle and William Faulkner." *South Atlantic Quarterly* 85 (Summer 1986): 215–27.

———. *Uses of the Past in the Novels of William Faulkner*. Ann Arbor, 1984.

Rose, Maxine. "From Genesis to Revelation: The Grand Design of William Faulkner's *Absalom, Absalom!*" *Studies in American Fiction* 8 (Autumn 1980): 219–27.

Rosenberg, Rosalind. *Beyond Separate Spheres: Intellectual Roots of Modern Feminism*. New Haven, 1982.

Rosenzweig, Paul J. "Faulkner's Motif of Food in *Light in August*." *American Imago* 37 (Spring 1980): 93–112.

Ross, Dorothy, ed. *Modernist Impulses in the Human Sciences, 1870–1930*. Baltimore, 1994.

Rubin, Louis D., Jr., and Kilpatrick, James J., eds. *The Lasting South*. Chicago, 1957.

Ruotolo, Lucio P. *Six Existential Heroes: The Politics of Faith*. Cambridge, Mass., 1973.

Ruppersburg, Hugh M. *Voice and Eye in Faulkner's Fiction*. Athens, Ga., 1983.

Ryan, Judith. *The Vanishing Subject: Early Psychology and Literary Modernism*. Chicago, 1991.

Ryan, Steven T. "Faulkner and Quantum Mechanics." *Western Humanities Review* 33 (Autumn 1979): 329–39.

Sabiston, Elizabeth. "Women, Blacks, and Thomas Sutpen's Mythopoeic Drive in *Absalom, Absalom!*" *Modernist Studies* 1 (1974–75): 15–26.

Sams, Larry Marshall. "Isaac McCaslin and Keat's 'Ode on a Grecian Urn.'" *Southern Review* 12 (July 1976): 632–39.

Schmidtberger, Loren F. "*Absalom, Absalom!*: What Clytie Knew." *Mississippi Quarterly* 35 (Summer 1982): 255–63.

———. "Names in *Absalom, Absalom!*" *American Literature* 55 (March 1983): 83–88.

Schoenberg, Estella. *Old Tales and Talking: Quentin Compson in William Faulkner's "Absalom, Absalom!" and Related Works*. Jackson, Miss., 1977.

Schwartz, Lawrence H. *Creating Faulkner's Reputation: The Politics of Modern Literary Criticism*. Knoxville, Tenn., 1988.

Schwartz, Sanford. *The Matrix of Modernism: Pound, Eliot, and Early Twentieth-Century Thought*. Princeton, 1985.

Scott, Anne. *The Southern Lady: From Pedestal to Politics, 1830–1930*. Chicago, 1970.

Seidel, Kathryn Lee. *The Southern Belle in the American Novel*. Tampa, Fla., 1985.

Seigel, Jerrold. *Bohemian Paris: Culture, Politics, and the Boundaries of Bourgeois Life, 1830–1930*. New York, 1986.

Selzer, John L. "'Go Down, Moses' and *Go Down, Moses*." *Studies in American Fiction* 13 (Spring 1985): 89–96.

Sensibar, Judith L. *The Origins of Faulkner's Art*. Austin, Tex., 1984.

Seymour, Thom. "Faulkner's *The Sound and the Fury*." *Explicator* 39 (Fall 1980): 24–25.

Shafer, Ingrid H., ed. *The Incarnate Imagination: Essays in Theology, the Arts, and Social Sciences*. Bowling Green, Ohio, 1988.

Shattuck, Roger. *The Banquet Years: The Arts in France, 1885–1918*. New York, 1958.

Singal, Daniel Joseph. "Toward a Definition of American Modernism." *American Quarterly* 39 (Spring 1987): 7–26.

———. *The War Within: From Victorian to Modernist Thought in the South, 1919–1945*. Chapel Hill, 1982.

Skura, Meredith Anne. "Creativity: Transgressing the Limits of Consciousness." *Daedalus* 109 (1980): 127–46.

———. *The Literary Use of the Psychoanalytic Process*. New Haven, 1981.

Slater, Judith. "Quentin's Tunnel Vision: Modes of Perception and Their Stylistic Realization in *The Sound and the Fury*." *Literature and Psychology* 27 (1977): 4–15.

Slatoff, Walter J. *Quest for Failure: A Study of William Faulkner*. Ithaca, N.Y., 1960.

Snead, James A. *Figures of Division: William Faulkner's Major Novels*. New York, 1986.

Snell, Susan. *Phil Stone of Oxford: A Vicarious Life*. Athens, Ga., 1991.

Sontag, Susan. *The Susan Sontag Reader*. New York, 1982.

Sowder, William J. *Existential-Phenomenological Readings on Faulkner*. Conway, Ark., 1991.

Spratling, William. *File on Spratling: An Autobiography*. Boston, 1967.

Stineback, David C. *Shifting World: Social Change and Nostalgia in the American Novel*. Lewisburg, Pa., 1976.

Stoneback, H. R. "Faulkner's Blues: 'Pantaloon in Black.' " *Modern Fiction Studies* 21 (Summer 1975): 241–45.

Stonum, Gary Lee. *Faulkner's Career: An Internal Literary History*. Ithaca, N.Y., 1979.

———. "Modernism and Its Discontents: Faulkner Studies Enter the Nineties." *Mississippi Quarterly* 44 (Summer 1991): 355–64.

Strandberg, Victor. "Between Truth and Fact: Faulkner's Symbols of Identity." *Modern Fiction Studies* 21 (Autumn 1975): 445–57.

———. *A Faulkner Overview: Six Perspectives*. Port Washington, N.Y., 1981.

Sundquist, Eric J. *Faulkner: The House Divided*. Baltimore, 1983.

Susman, Warren I. *Culture as History: The Transformation of American Society in the Twentieth Century*. New York, 1984.

Swiggart, Peter. *The Art of Faulkner's Novels*. Austin, Tex., 1962.

Taylor, Charles. *The Ethics of Authenticity*. Cambridge, Mass., 1991.

Taylor, Nancy Dew. *Annotations to Faulkner's "Go Down, Moses."* New York, 1994.

———. " 'Moral Housecleaning' and Colonel Sartoris's Dream." *Mississippi Quarterly* 37 (Summer 1984): 353–63.

Taylor, Walter. *Faulkner's Search for a South*. Urbana, Ill., 1983.

Taylor, William R. *Cavalier and Yankee: The Old South and American National Character*. Garden City, N.Y., 1963.

Torsney, Cheryl B. "The Vampire Motif in *Absalom, Absalom!*" *Southern Review* 20 (July 1984): 562–69.

Towner, Theresa M. " 'It Aint Funny A-Tall': The Transfigured Tales of *The Town*." *Mississippi Quarterly* 44 (Summer 1991): 321–36.

Traschen, Isadore. "The Tragic Form of *The Sound and the Fury*." *Southern Review* 12 (October 1976): 798–813.

Trilling, Lionel. *Beyond Culture: Essays on Literature and Learning*. New York, 1968.

———. *Sincerity and Authenticity*. Cambridge, Mass., 1972.

Trouard, Dawn. "Making Labove Cast a Shadow: The Rhetoric of Neurosis." *Literature and Psychology* 31 (1981): 32–38.

Tully, Susan Hayes. "Joanna Burden: 'It's the Dead Folks That Do Him the Damage.'" *Mississippi Quarterly* 40 (Fall 1987): 355–71.

Turner, Frederick. *Spirit of Place: The Making of an American Literary Landscape*. San Francisco, 1989.

Twain, Mark. *The Innocents Abroad: or, The New Pilgrim's Progress*. New York, 1899.

Urgo, Joseph R. "*Absalom, Absalom!*: The Movie." *American Literature* 62 (March 1990): 56–73.

———. *Faulkner's Apocrypha: "A Fable," Snopes, and the Spirit of Human Rebellion*. Jackson, Miss., 1989.

Utley, Francis Lee, Lynn Z. Bloom, and Arthur F. Kinney, eds. *Bear, Man, and God: Eight Approaches to William Faulkner's "The Bear."* New York, 1971.

Vande Kieft, Ruth M. "Faulkner's Defeat of Time in *Absalom, Absalom!*" *Southern Review* 6 (October 1970): 1100–1109.

Vickery, Olga W. *The Novels of William Faulkner: A Critical Interpretation*. Baton Rouge, 1959.

Waggoner, Hyatt H. *William Faulkner: From Jefferson to the World*. Lexington, Ky., 1966.

Wagner, Linda W., ed. *William Faulkner: Four Decades of Criticism*. East Lansing, Mich., 1973.

Warren, Robert Penn, ed. *Faulkner: A Collection of Critical Essays*. Englewood Cliffs, N.J., 1966.

Wasson, Ben. *Count No 'Count: Flashbacks to Faulkner*. Jackson, Miss., 1983.

———. *A Memory of Marionettes*. Oxford, Miss., 1975.

Watson, James Gray. *The Snopes Dilemma: Faulkner's Trilogy*. Coral Gables, Fla., 1970.

———. *William Faulkner: Letters and Fictions*. Austin, Tex., 1987.

Watson, Jay. *Forensic Fictions: The Lawyer Figure in Faulkner*. Athens, Ga., 1993.

Watts, Steven. *The Magic Kingdom: Walt Disney and Modern American Culture*. New York, 1996.

Webb, James W., and A. Wigfall Green, eds. *William Faulkner of Oxford*. Baton Rouge, 1965.

Weinstein, Philip M. *Faulkner's Subject: A Cosmos No One Owns*. New York, 1992.

Werner, Craig. "Tell Old Pharoah: The Afro-American Response to Faulkner." *Southern Review* 19 (October 1983): 711–35.

Wilde, Alan. *Horizons of Assent: Modernism, Postmodernism, and the Ironic Imagination*. Philadelphia, 1987.

Wilde, Meta Carpenter, and Orin Borsten. *A Loving Gentleman: The Love Story of William Faulkner and Meta Carpenter*. New York, 1976.

Williams, David. *Faulkner's Women: The Myth and the Muse*. Montreal, 1977.

Williamson, Joel. *The Crucible of Race: Black-White Relations in the American South since Emancipation*. New York, 1984.

———. *William Faulkner and Southern History*. New York, 1993.

Winn, Harbour. "Lineage and the South: The Unity of Faulkner's *Go Down, Moses*." *Midwest Quarterly* 32 (Summer 1991): 453–73.

Wittenberg, Judith. *Faulkner: The Transfiguration of Biography*. Lincoln, Nebr., 1979.

Wolfe, George A., ed. *Faulkner: Fifty Years after the Marble Faun*. University, Ala., 1976.

Wolin, Richard. "Modernism vs. Postmodernism." *Telos* 62 (Winter 1984–85): 9–29.

Woolf, Virginia. *Mr. Bennett and Mrs. Brown*. London, 1924.

Wyatt, David. *Prodigal Sons: A Study in Authorship and Authority*. Baltimore, 1980.

Wyatt-Brown, Bertram. *Southern Honor: Ethics and Behavior in the Old South*. New York, 1982.

Yonce, Margaret J. "The Composition of *Soldiers' Pay*." *Mississippi Quarterly* 33 (Summer 1980): 291–326.

Zender, Karl F. *The Crossing of the Ways: William Faulkner, the South, and the Modern World*. New Brunswick, N.J., 1989.

———. "Faulkner at Forty: The Artist at Home." *Southern Review* 17 (April 1981): 288–302.

———. "A Hand of Poker: Game and Ritual in Faulkner's 'Was.'" *Studies in Short Fiction* 11 (Winter 1974): 53–60.

———. "Two Unpublished Letters from William Faulkner to Helen Baird." *American Literature* 63 (September 1991): 535–38.

INDEX

Fairchild, Dawson, 83–86, 88–89, 92

Falkner, John Wesley Thompson, 22, 39–42, 254, 258, 298 (n. 2), 300 (n. 2)

Falkner, Maud Butler, 42, 52–53, 59, 73, 88n, 163, 189, 305 (n. 12), 306 (n. 14); as Victorian, 2, 21, 40, 50, 118, 251; as character in son's writings, 77–79, 111, 125, 289, 319 (n. 54). *See also* "Dianalike girl"

Falkner, Murry Cuthbert, 39–40, 79, 118, 251, 258, 300 (n. 2)

Falkner, Colonel William Clark, 22, 45n, 77, 254–55, 258, 285, 298 (nn. 2, 3); monument of, 22, 98, 104, 214; life of, 24–28, 299 (n. 9); and black "shadow family," 27; as example of southern Victorian, 28–36, 38, 52; literary career of, 28–38, 48, 299 (n. 14), self-made identity as gentle-man, 32–34, 38; Faulkner's image of, 41, 55, 57, 67, 105, 162n, 224, 283; literary incarnations of in Faulkner, 69–70, 89, 92, 95–99, 103–4, 185–88, 194, 199, 266, 283, 290. See also *Little Brick Church; Rapid Ramblings in Europe; White Rose of Memphis*

A Farewell to Arms (Hemingway), 235, 239–40

"Father Abraham," 93, 244

Faulkner, Estelle Oldham, 42, 44–45, 53, 68n, 92, 115, 169, 189, 191, 313 (n. 24); marriage to William Faulkner, 153, 229, 243, 284–85, 321 (n. 5)

Faulkner, Jill, 158, 189, 229, 237, 284–85

Faulkner, William
—and alcohol, 16, 42, 46, 48, 53–54, 114, 258–60, 284, 286, 309 (n. 3), 325 (n. 5), 328 (n. 5)
—birth and childhood, 39–42
—conflict of cultures within, 2, 50, 54, 76–77, 99, 105, 114, 116, 188, 192
—decline in writing after 1940, 256–62, 275–78, 281–83, 284–86
—dual self structure, 15–20, 115, 149, 168–70, 222, 227, 261, 298 (n. 47);

process of formation, 53, 80, 94, 113–14
—"falcon" identity, 67, 89, 95, 100–101, 103, 230–31, 235, 245
—and First World War, 16, 44–46, 61–63
—flying, interest in, 44–46, 189, 275
—and Hollywood, 16–17, 154, 189–91, 202n, 222, 227, 257, 284
—and hunting, 259, 262, 285
—identities and public images: as untutored bumpkin, 1–2; as artist, 15, 82, 85–86, 88–89, 91; as southern aristocrat, 21–22, 41–42, 67, 89, 104, 189, 283, 285, 292; as wounded pilot, 45–46, 290–91, 301 (n. 10)
—identity crisis of, 46, 48, 54, 116; use of characters to form own identity, 82–86, 88–91, 116, 148–52, 169–70
—Modernist self, 35n, 50, 227, 258; description of, 16–17, 94, 114–15, 168; and Modernist perspective, 55, 99, 105, 184–85, 214–15, 243, 255; embodied in characters, 104, 138, 149–50, 217–19, 230, 290–91, 293; weakened after 1940, 261, 275, 277, 282–83, 287
—neurological problems, 259–60, 284, 286, 325 (n. 5), 328 (nn. 1, 5)
—as observer of his community, 40–42, 54, 94
—as poet, 48–53, 56, 61, 83, 86, 159, 189
—as post-Victorian, 48–53, 56, 57, 61, 64–67, 75–78, 80–81, 89–90, 114, 214
—reading during early years, 40, 44, 50, 53
—short story writing: for commercial magazines, 153, 167, 221, 262, 266, 275, 278
—and South: as subject, 69–70, 85, 93–94, 105, 112, 191, 307 (n. 5)
—Victorian self, 21, 50, 54, 77, 215–16, 243, 254, 291; description of, 16–17, 168; gains dominance after 1940, 18, 261, 275, 277, 282–83, 292; functions

Pound, Ezra, 8, 44, 56, 72
Putzel, Max, 83n, 96, 154
Pylon, 192–93, 209, 277, 289

Quinones, Ricardo, 8

Race, 6, 18, 58, 187, 201–2n; "nigger"
stereotype, 18, 127–28, 169, 172,
173–76, 178–80, 182, 184, 188,
206–7, 223–24, 264n, 265; portrait of
black culture, 65, 140–41, 180–81,
263–74, 278, 315 (n. 24), 326 (n. 24);
black southern identity, 126–28, 169–
70, 180–81, 268–70, 310 (n. 26), 315
(n. 12); and religion, 140–41, 180;
dual racial selves of Joe Christmas,
169–71, 175–85; Faulkner's position
on, 174–75, 220–21, 268–69, 273–74,
291–93, 303 (nn. 37, 38), 320 (n. 63);
white obsession with racial purity,
195, 201–2, 206–8, 220–21; difficulty
of interracial understanding, 263–66,
269–76, 317 (n. 20). *See also* Miscegenation
Radloff, Bernhard, 217
Random House, 243, 244, 262, 280, 284
Rapid Ramblings in Europe (William C.
Falkner), 38
Reconstruction: in the South, 96, 186,
188, 222–24, 282
Reed, Joseph W., Jr., 260, 281
The Reivers, 256, 292
Religion, critique of traditional, 63, 173,
179; African-American, 65, 140–41,
180, 326 (n. 26); Modernist style of,
138, 233, 239, 279. *See also* Christ fig-
ures, in Faulkner's work
Requiem for a Nun, 256
Richardson, H. Edward, 49, 69
Ripley, Miss., 22, 24, 27, 39
Rittenmeyer, Charlotte, 19–20, 225–27,
230–44 passim, 277, 289, 321 (n. 7),
322 (n. 16), 323 (n. 27)
Rodin, Auguste, 73, 88, 91
Rollyson, Carl E., Jr., 282
Rosenberg, Rosalind, 4

Rostand, Edmond, 90
Rowan Oak, 16, 167–68, 189, 229, 328
(n. 5)
Royal Air Force (RAF), 45, 61, 301
(n. 10)
Rubin, Louis D., Jr., 89, 298 (n. 47)
Ruppersburg, Hugo M., 216
Ryan, Judith, 14

Sanctuary, 17, 111, 154–65 passim, 167,
185
Sandburg, Carl, 54–55
Sartoris, 153, 307–8 (n. 6)
Sartoris, Bayard, 95, 99–107, 109–11,
125, 166, 192, 290, 315 (n. 24)
Sartoris, Bayard ("Old Bayard"), 95, 98,
222–23
Sartoris, Colonel John, 28, 89, 95–99,
125, 130, 186, 188, 221–24, 293
Sartoris, John, 95, 99–105, 192, 194, 231
Saturday Evening Post, 192, 280
Scribner's, 192, 245
Second World War, 258, 280, 290
Sensibar, Judith L., 51–53, 80, 229, 300
(n. 2)
Sexuality, 249–50; Victorian attitude
toward, 3–4, 84; and southern lady, 7,
110–11; and Faulkner's personal life,
17, 227; in early works, 49–53, 65–68;
association with creativity, 75–79,
82–83, 89–90; attack on Victorian
suppression of, 108–11, 121–23,
131–33, 154–56, 160–62, 177; and
black identity, 173–75; Modernist
approach to, 226–27, 231, 233
Shakespeare, William, 1, 40, 110
Slatoff, Walter J., 1
Snead, James A., 221
Snopes, Flem, 244–49, 251–55, 285,
287, 291
Snopes, Mink, 250–53, 291
Snopesism, 93, 244–45, 254, 285–88;
Modernist view of, 245–46, 255
Soldiers' Pay, 45, 61, 70, 74–75, 79–80,
83, 95, 140, 180, 263
Sontag, Susan, 11

Warren, Robert Penn, 181, 184

Wasson, Ben, 51, 109, 154, 157

Watson, James G., 216, 254

Watson, Jay, 291

Weinstein, Philip M., 206, 212n

The White Rose of Memphis (William C. Falkner), 28–37

Wilbourne, Harry, 226, 229–44, 277, 322–23 (nn. 16, 26, 27)

Wilde, Alan, 296 (n. 19)

Wilde, Oscar, 49, 51

Wilderness: as theme in Faulkner's works, 262, 276–82, 325–26 (n. 11)

The Wild Palms, 19, 191, 225–27, 230–45 passim, 277, 283, 289

Williams, David, 155

Williamson, Joel, 7, 27, 286n

Wittenberg, Judith Bryant, 79, 151, 257, 305–6 (n. 14), 313 (n. 24)

Wolfe, Thomas, 302 (n. 24)

Women, Faulkner's attitudes toward: misogyny, 20, 157–58, 212–13, 243, 313 (n. 26); incipient feminism, 20, 243, 313 (n. 26); desire for virginal purity, 77–79, 111; critique of Victorian ideal, 107–11, 131–33, 158, 163; Modernist view, 212–13, 226, 233, 242–43, 288–93. *See also* Abortion: Faulkner on; "Dianalike girl"; Gender; Southern lady

Woolf, Virginia, 7

Wyatt, David, 298 (n. 2)

Wyatt-Brown, Bertram, 248

Yale University, 42, 45

Yeats, William Butler, 15, 44, 144

Zeitlin, Michael, 78

Zender, Karl F., 283

Read: Bergson, The _munovion_,

Assign: Intro — excellent intro to terms & concepts. (To p. 15 l. 6 only)

Find: Pound's "Victorian slither"

little magazines: 44,

W, Faulkner novel, use Fitzthugh from Heath.